Discourse/Counter-Discourse

Discourse/ Counter-Discourse

The Theory and Practice of Symbolic Resistance in Nineteenth-Century France

RICHARD TERDIMAN

CORNELL UNIVERSITY PRESS

ITHACA AND LONDON

CORNELL UNIVERSITY PRESS GRATEFULLY ACKNOWLEDGES
A GRANT FROM THE ANDREW W. MELLON FOUNDATION
THAT AIDED IN BRINGING THIS BOOK TO PUBLICATION.

First published 1985 by Cornell University Press.
Published in the United Kingdom by Cornell University Press Ltd., London.

International Standard Book Number 0-8014-1750-3
Library of Congress Catalog Card Number 84-17666

Printed in the United States of America

*Librarians: Library of Congress cataloging information appears
on the last page of the book.*

*The paper in this book is acid-free and meets the guidelines for
permanence and durability of the Committee on Production Guidelines
for Book Longevity of the Council on Library Resources.*

This book is for my family, here and gone.

Contents

7

CONTENTS

PART THREE
Absolute Counter-Discourse

8

List of Illustrations

Preface

The point of departure for this book might have been an ironic little phrase of Flaubert's. In two words it depicts a characteristic behavior of the nineteenth-century middle class, whose bluster and sententiousness provide the matter of his *Dictionnaire des idées reçues*: "Tonner contre"—"Thunder against" (Denounce, as we might translate it, vituperate, condemn). This sardonic motto stigmatizes the intolerance of an increasingly dominant bourgeoisie, whose opinions the *Dictionnaire* seeks to represent in all their smug vulgarity.

Flaubert's phrase is double-edged. It describes an attitude of the middle class, one of intense discursive combat. And it brings this attitude under judgment. The writer thus engages himself in the combat which is his subject. Such a complex engagement—reproduced in many major writers and artists in the nineteenth century—will concern me in this study.

"Tonner contre" then punctuates Flaubert's rehearsal of the views of his middle-class antagonists like a stinging refrain (in "Baccalauréat," "Député," "Encyclopédie," and numerous other *Dictionnaire* entries). It translates his fury at what seemed to him the degradation of his period. The tactic appeared a simple one. In order to satirize this degradation he had to give it voice. His hope was that its absurdity (the mock-Jovian grandiloquence of "tonner contre," for example) would become patent, that the overdrawn rhetoric of middle-class denunciation would in effect denounce itself.

But once deployed, Flaubert's tactic unexpectedly became labyrinthine. Citing the bourgeoisie turned out to implicate the citing voice as well, and suddenly Flaubert's intention of castigating them began to escape beyond his control (I will consider this slippage in detail in Chapter 4). For in denouncing their denunciation of anything that unsettled their class's self-congratulatory complacency, Flaubert found himself thrown back within the limits of the rhetoric from which he had sought to distinguish his own. How then could he mark his difference?

This effort to assert the constantly elusive separation which permits critique, this always-frustrated impulse to contradict the discourse of one's antagonist and make the contradiction stick, is at the heart of my study. I want to examine a series of techniques and practices by which nineteenth-century intellectuals and artists contested the dominant habits of mind and expression of their contemporaries. Indeed no effort was more characteristic of them, no dynamic motivated their production more intensely, than this project of subverting the middle-class world which was being constructed before their eyes. But at the same time, no experience was more constant than their discovery of the contradictions inherent in the modes of combat which they brought to bear.

Flaubert's perception of this combat is as clear as any. But all of the figures I will examine in this book—principally Balzac, Daumier, Baudelaire, Mallarmé, and Marx—share it with him. Their work is driven by a *negative* passion, to displace and annihilate a dominant depiction of the world. At times all the energy of nineteenth-century social existence seems to have been bent to fighting the intricate and paradoxical struggle this project engendered. Such struggle and such intricacy are what I want to explore in this book.

In this generalized contestation at the heart of the culture, the functioning of its languages and images began to measure itself. The power of discourses—of a culture's determined and determining structures of representation and practice—came into focus. No effort to understand the influence of such structuring structures, those which provide a culture with its understanding of itself and define its encounter with

the world confronting it, can ignore the nineteenth century's reflections on the enigma they pose at the center of social life.

In the face of the frustrations experienced in struggling to change it,
the writers of Flaubert's period conceptualized the apparent seamlessness of social domination, the seeming capacity of established discourses to ignore or absorb would-be subversion. Yet such frustrations
were not unmitigated defeats. For the effort to think through the
mechanisms by which the culture's discourses sustained its stability
opened a deeper perception of those discourses' contingence and permeability. I will try to recount here how consciousness of the confrontation between constituted reality and its subversion grew and was
theorized. I will argue that nineteenth-century intellectuals experienced their struggle almost as if they were living the dialectic of history
itself, an intricate and continuous interplay of stability and destabiliza-
tion which produces the social world for all of its actors. The very locus
at which cultural and historical change occurred began to reveal itself
in such an investigation. And so the combat continued with all the
ingeniousness which could be generated by a group of discursive innovators whose originality can have had few equals in other periods of
our cultural history.

I want, then, to trace a variety of strains of opposition to the modes
of perception and assertion which writers and artists in the nineteenth
century experienced as the dominant discourse. Of course they could
"thunder against" ("tonner contre") the bourgeoisie all they wanted—
the bourgeoisie didn't appear to notice. Intellectuals thereby discovered that the blustering intolerance Flaubert had satirized in his
Dictionnaire was an inalienable attribute of *power*. Such power, they
found, *they* did not possess. They realized that their own opposition
required more subtle modulations, and these will occupy me in this
study.

Consequently this book will examine both the constitution of certain dominant strains of nineteenth-century discourse and a number of
the principal discursive systems by which writers and artists sought to
project an alternative, liberating *newness* against the absorptive capacity
of those established discourses. I call these alternative systems "counter-discourses." But necessarily each encounters in its own way the
paradox I alluded to earlier: the problem of sustaining the crucial claim

of "difference" against reinfection by the constituted *sameness,* the apparent stability and inertia, of the dominant. Such reinfection can take multiple forms, but its result is constant. It is to subvert subversion itself.

The process by which this frustrating reversal occurs and recurs can best be understood if we situate ourselves (provisionally at least) on the terrain of dominant discourse. Then the paradox of projecting alternatives to it emerges clearly. Such a perspective to some degree is that of all the members of any culture, submerged as we inevitably are in the functioning semiotic and practical systems which sustain our social existence. From within dominant discourse, "difference" nearly eludes us. We struggle for a language which might express it. But the very fact of its difference makes such a language hard to seize. Our efforts to produce difference—the new, the subversive, the *other*—inevitably meet the resistance that sustains the stability of all cultural systems.

Such stability is always totalitarian by implication. However innocent its intentions, it functions to exclude the heterogeneous from the domain of utterance. It defines the social field as an ideological preserve. Only thus can a cultural system be stable to begin with. Its exclusions thus seem asserted for the best of reasons. But its antagonists can claim a justification equally compelling. The problem is that these two logics—of the stabilization of the "same" and of the production of "difference"—are fundamentally incompatible.

To the extent that they dominate in real social situations, the discourses of stability are limited by the internal necessity that defines them: not only are they unable to admit difference, in a sense they are incapable of imagining it. This is so for a simple reason. Once imagined, even so that it might be proscribed, difference acquires a phantom but fundamental existence. If it is countenanced at all, its legitimation, its inclusion within the canons of the orthodox, has to that extent begun. Thus even the work of proscribing it must be proscribed. For this reason the discourses that ensure cultural stability never conceive their action as "repression." From within such discourses it is hard to think that there is anything to repress.

Dominant languages are thus constrained to project a world defined by the equilibrium and homogeneity of language itself—very much in the image of Saussure's notion of *langue,* to which I will return in my Introduction. Such a projection of unity naturalizes our blindness concerning the alternative discourses which would contest the stability of its stabilizing norms. The operation of a dominant discourse is thus in essence political. Foucault explained this dynamic in *L'ordre du discours.* "Discourses," he wrote, "must be conceived as a violence which we perform against things, or in any case as a practice which we impose on them" (p. 55). But such practices impose their violence not only upon things, but upon us too.

Yet in this very fact dominant discourses disclose the paradox which sustains them. For though they function only when their dominance is perceived as "natural" and hence as eternal, their disguised contingency emerges in the police operation by which they seek to exclude their antagonists. But such exclusions require the expenditure of considerable energy (we might think in the burlesque mode of the thundering in "tonner contre"). The traces of this expenditure subsist and are detectable. They undercut the assumption of self-evidence which is intrinsic to established discourses.

Indeed such assumptions paradoxically undo themselves on an even more fundamental level. For if we accept them, it becomes hard to imagine what language's utility might be at all. Why have language if there is theoretically nothing *different* to say? Why say anything if the linguistic—and by implication the social—field is harmonized in some crystalline oneness? The discourse we might be able to imagine in such a concordant world would at best be an endless, unchanging interior monologue. It could be nothing like the dynamic exchange of heterogeneous signs and intentions—still less their struggle for predominance—which we conceive as necessitating social communication to begin with. *Language presupposes difference.* It exists only within a "differential" world, a world of conflicts and oppositions.

Otherness, difference, the heterological, are thus essential attributes of the realm of words, signs, and discourses. Indeed their theoretical potentiality is everywhere presupposed by the ideological police which seek to exclude them while never admitting that they might already exist. But in turn this conflicted relation with dominant language defines a crucial privilege of any language of difference, of any counter-discourse. Situated as other, counter-discourses have the capacity to *situate:* to relativize the authority and stability of a dominant system of utterances which cannot even countenance their existence. They read that which cannot read them at all.

In examining a series of powerful attempts to contest the period's dominant discursive structures, I seek in this book to describe dynamics which contributed to forming nineteenth-century culture in France. In this history the *mode* of contestation which ties these counter-discourses to their dominant antagonist is of the greatest moment. I will outline this relation in my Introduction. I argue that the discourses of a society are structured in a shifting, multiform network of linked assertions and subversions, of normalized and heterodox speech. The linkage is essential, and its character is complex. Fredric Jameson expresses the *active* notion of "difference" which underlies this dialectic: "a relational concept, rather than the mere inert inventory of unrelated diversity" (*The Political Unconscious*, p. 41). Thus counter-discourses are always interlocked with the domination they contest. It is this conflicted intimacy which is signified by the slash in this book's title.

Mainstream thinking about culture has privileged the activity of thought by tending to bracket the complex of determinations which condition cultural production. Of course the reality of dominant discourses—of concrete social life, of established practice, of habit, of naturalized expectation—has had to be attended to. Typically they have been admitted as a "context" that somehow encloses the privileged realm of art, but without exercising more than a kind of diffuse and unwelcome influence upon what happens within the enclosure.

Art is then conceived as something like a principality tolerated by surrounding states to avoid upsetting some delicate political balance or because its affairs are too negligible to bother with. This is as close to idealism as contemporary thinking on culture can get without crossing over into a complete denial of the reality of human activity outside the esthetic realm. So the "context" is allowed to surround the privileged text, but such enclosure is experienced in the mode of *resentment*: not as an enabling condition of any cultural expression, but as a regrettable limitation upon it.

Context is thus marginalized. Treated as something like a background, it is refused status as a ground at all. Once seemingly acknowledged, it becomes increasingly diffuse, transparent, until—like the Cheshire cat in *Alice*—it simply disappears. The way it is managed makes it function as what Jameson calls a "strategy of containment": a mechanism to disguise the existence of a conflict unresolved.

So the relationship which context sustains with text is handled not as an intertextuality but as something (in the invidious sense) like a *sub*-textuality. It is assimilated to the text: that is, absorbed. But this perpetrates a metalepsis—the caused becomes causal; the determining determined. The text's environment is treated like an inconvenience, like an unfortunate entanglement which, on the whole, one would rather have been able to ignore or forget.

But (to reinstate for a moment my geopolitical metaphor) the relations between culture (even elite culture) and social existence are not foreign relations. The forms of society's work, family structure, gender roles, property distribution, educational and political organization all live within the signs of which every text is made. The sources of many of its determinations lie there. Frequently, to project a space for its existence, the counter-discourse will seek to deny this determination. Such work of the negative is crucial. But it cannot be thought to exhaust the significance of the cultural object, still less to fully explain its production.

In any text, what we term the "context"—nominally a liminal reality at the edge of consciousness—inhabits and decenters the text itself. The text is marginalized by what we had taken to frame it; the frame comes unexpectedly to determine the center. This exchange of positions and prerogatives reverses our sense of the relations between literary subjectivity and what we often think of as the dumb objectivity of the "climate" or "atmosphere" within—or against—which the text seeks to stake its claims. The result is that it almost comes to seem that *there is only context*. The difficulty of generating and sustaining a counter-discourse becomes perceptible in this unaccustomed vision of a world turned inside-out.

By comparison with frequent projections of the art object as self-determined, my attention to its "contextual" grounds—the dominant system which it implicitly or explicitly contests—might almost seem to marginalize the art object itself. And it is true that my insistence upon the determinations exercised by dominant discourse has meant a certain modesty about the claims which might be made for the counter-discursive. Counter-discourses work as opposition to their dominant antagonists. But to think that they *efface* them would be to allow a focus on contestation to bracket the very conditions which frame and engender the struggle to begin with.

So in tracing the relation between the text "proper" and the trans-textual, I have sought to avoid the latter's domestication. Any attempt to bring the "outside" flatfootedly into the text would invalidate the quality which defined its difference and made its determinant force possible. On the other hand, as I will argue in detail in my Introduction, some mediation connecting the two realms, not as matter and antimatter, but endowed with some mode of commonality, is indispensable. If we take the image of topographic division between "inside" and "outside" literally, we render our problem opaque. Only a dialectic for which the outside is always already inside can open the problem to a solution. Then there is no disjunction between the realms at all, but rather complex modes of translation and transformation between them which must be carefully specified. Then the "making" of the text *as text* begins to be thinkable as a process connected to the world beyond the text itself and inevitably intimate with it.

The crucial question is not one of some abstract alterity but of concrete conditions of *power*. Counter-discourses inhabit and struggle with the dominant which inhabits them. But their footing is never equal. If, as Foucault claims, all discourses are impositions, still the range and penetration of their hegemonies vary greatly. By their nature, as Flaubert and his contemporaries discovered, counter-discourses are never sovereign. And they are least so when sovereignty is the claim they most insistently assert. I will make this argument in detail in Part 3.

In my representation of the dominant I have tried to grasp the way its adversaries perceived it during the period I will examine. Only a subjective conception of the dominant as unanswerable might account for the despair of those who in the nineteenth century struggled against its influence. For them it was the discourse of "le bourgeois"; but only a vision of its influence as absolute could explain their blanket designation. Of course there was not just *one* bourgeois, not just *one* bourgeoisie. And the "dominant" itself, like any social discourse, was internally fragmented. All languages, even the discourses of dominant power, are always what Bakhtin calls "heteroglot," representing "the co-existence of socio-ideological contradictions between the present and the past, between differing epochs of the past, between different socio-groups in the present, between tendencies, schools, circles and so forth" (*Dialogic Imagination*, p. 291).

But in the nineteenth century, middle-class intellectuals were unable to take heart in the perception of such inherent diversity. They simply felt crushed. Their tactics were marshaled on the assumption of an overmastering unity on the part of their adversaries. Only on the basis of such perceived hegemony could the *power* of the dominant be explained or even contemplated. It seemed to organize the weight of majorities so great as to leave our poor accursed poets experiencing their difference from the mass as a grotesque and impotent exile. Whence the antinomic structure pitting *us* against *them* by which nineteenth-century intellectuals conceived their combat.

But having inflated the power of their antagonist, they then set out systematically to repudiate it. Much of our criticism since that time has been an effort to situate, *and to accept our situation by,* the social forces which the texts of the nineteenth century could manage only by such deformations. Here I seek a balance between the pessimism about cultural production which, like Bataille, sees in poetry only a "minor attitude" in the face of established order (*La littérature et le mal*, pp. 38–39), and the contrary idealization of the mental realm on the faith of which (as I will discuss in Part 3) Mallarmé was moved to claim that there was *nothing but* poetry in language. Such symmetrical reductions dematerialize us altogether. They are really structures of denial. They denote a cultural and social stress which it is the task of historically conscious criticism to identify and elucidate.

Both of these discouraging exaggerations proceed from a reality which it would be more responsible and more productive for us to contest than to repress. Criticism, as its name suggests, is one mode of such contestation. So though the dominant surrounds us, we need not be lamed by it. Though counter-discourses are not sovereign and do not exhaust reality, reality can neither exist nor change without them. My celebration of their power in this study remains measured. But it is nonetheless a celebration.

Note on Translations

The length of this book has made it necessary to omit the original French texts of much of the quoted material. Inevitably translations involve compromises, but I have provided the original text whenever the translation could not capture necessary nuances. Unless otherwise noted, all translations are my own, and reference is given to the French original to facilitate checking when desired.

Acknowledgments

At the moment of thanking those who helped this project toward completion, it seems possible to believe that the ideal of collective work which has alternately attracted and resisted us might be realizable even under contemporary conditions of production. Surely the generosities I want to remember here belong to the kind of world we work for, rather than to the one against which we struggle.

Let me thank first of all three of my former students whose work helped me to think through problems which arose in the process of writing this book: Marie-Hélène Chabut, Karin Dillman, and Eugene Holland.

I am grateful to the colleagues who read my manuscript—some of them more than once—at various stages. In the process of reflection and revision which their reading and criticism sustained, something like the dialectic seemed patiently at work. I thank them here: Jeanne Bem, Pierre Bourdieu, Michel de Certeau, Priscilla Clark, Walter Cohen, Jaime Concha, Robert Elliott, Françoise Gaillard, Philippe Hamon, Fredric Jameson, Barbara Johnson, Dominick LaCapra, Richard Ohmann, Edward Said, Michael Schudson, André Stoll, Don Wayne, and Donald Wesling.

Other colleagues gave help in other ways—help not less material nor less gratefully acknowledged. I thank them here: Stephen Arkin, Howard Bloch, Joseph Duggan, Luce Giard, Jean-François Lyotard, Scott McLean, Roy Harvey Pearce, Gayatri Spivak, and Andrew Wright.

For generous assistance in the preparation of the manuscript, I thank Rick Accurso, Christa Beran, Mary Ann Buckles, Marren Kingsford, Carol McCartney, Jesusa Melad, Michael O'Hagan, Coe Senour, and Geoff Walton. I am grateful for the help offered by the Committee on Research, University of California, San Diego.

For the kind and intelligent assistance they gave me in the course of my research, I thank the staffs of the Bibliothèque Nationale, Paris, and the main libraries of the University of California, Berkeley and San Diego.

I thank the Armand Hammer Foundation and the Armand Hammer Daumier Collection for their assistance in securing the photographs of plates from *Le Charivari* and allied publications which are reproduced in this book. Lisa Tremper has my gratitude for her help in arranging for these reproductions.

My thanks to those who helped the manuscript through the stages of its production: particularly, to Cynthia Gration, Bernhard Kendler, Brian Keeling, Marilyn Sale, and Terry Vatter of Cornell University Press; to Joanne Ainsworth, whose copy editing was meticulous and intelligent; and to Julia Ingram, who assisted me greatly with the proofreading.

Chapters 1 and 4 are revised versions of portions of two articles that appeared in *Yale French Studies*, No. 63 (1982) (copyright © *Yale French Studies*, 1982) and *Diacritics*, vol. 9 (September 1979), respectively. I am grateful to the editors and publishers of these journals for permission to use this material here.

RICHARD TERDIMAN

La Jolla, California

Discourse/Counter-Discourse

Introduction:
On Symbolic Resistance

The Practices of Difference:
From Structuralism to Social Semiotics

Culture as a *field of struggle:* the notion drives important strains of thinking on the problem of social discourse. Such a characterization of the network within which our meanings are made meaningful has a strategic advantage: it draws attention to the intensity of social contradiction within the linguistic and the symbolic realms. It conceives these as the loci within which, the mediums by which, such contradictions receive expression and determine representation. Much of the bearing of recent materialist criticism has been to show how deeply the struggle for control of meaning inscribes itself in the languages of culture.

What has been at stake in this effort to theorize the ways in which the conflicts of our history find their inscription within the texts of our imagination is the socialization of signs and discourses. The developments in this realm of theorization have passed through several phases.

At an early stage in the process, structuralism foregrounded the tendency within imaginative production to organize meaning through oppositions: relationally. As a result it became difficult to conceive of individual signs or elements of discourse in isolation. In the structuralist perspective, signs always come *linked together*. Barthes put this clearly: "We must doubtless resort to pairings . . . in order to approach what distinguishes structuralism from other modes of thought."[1]

This concept of an intrinsic binarism can be taken as the first moment in the process of de-absolutizing the sign. It begins to project a theoretical basis for understanding the networks within which cultures *organize* their signs. If every semiotic element exists in some complex differential resonance with another, if the sign cannot stand alone, then the relations which bind it can be mapped and read. At the limit, it becomes possible to comprehend it as *determined*. This dynamic can fruitfully be forced beyond the relative abstraction of the structuralist pairing.

To be sure, Saussure had never thought to proceed so far. His conception of language in terms of omnipresent, proliferating, theoretically limitless doublets seems to have been an effort to think his way beyond the airless closure of singularity. The isolated term, the *one* with no connection to an *other,* is accessible to no discourse. It is hard to imagine how it might even be spoken about at all: authentic unities are silent. So the master perception of the structuralist model of relation is to found the *dyad* as irreducible element within sign systems. The dyad establishes the necessity of conceiving the sign in terms of others. The nature of the network within which it is fixed then becomes an object of intense investigation and, indeed, of intense controversy.

Saussure wished to limit, to cloture, the semiotic paradigm at this point. Having demonstrated the necessity of duality, he sought to insulate the figure of *two* from any slippage toward higher cardinalities or more complex orders of relation—particularly, we might surmise, toward the more supple differential triads of the dialectic in its various forms. Denying the pertinence of any scalar element in his pairings was thus strategic: they *were,* but they were *dimensionless, directionless.* Thus in a familiar passage: "*In language there are only differences.* What's more: a difference in general presupposes positive terms between which it is established; but in language there are only differences *with-*

---

1. Barthes, *Critical Essays,* p. 213. On structuralism in general, the most synthetic accounts are no doubt those of Fredric Jameson, *Prison-House of Language,* and Jonathan Culler, *Structuralist Poetics.* More recently, Frank Lentricchia has given an account of the advent of structuralism in American critical consciousness and of the attendant conflicts; see *After the New Criticism,* esp. chap. 4.

out positive terms."[2] The elements in Saussure's model thus exhibited the simplicity and the clarity which characterize any binary system: presence or absence, one or zero. But they refused the possibility of any grid or scale beyond the twin elements of the dyad, against which attributes like *dimension* or *quality* might be figured. The *tertium quid* was thus excluded; there could be no entry into the system for any heterogeneous element, nor any hierarchical relation between its terms.

The result was to deadlock the dyad. A prototype of relation was posited, but it proved unavailable for relation with *anything else*. No dynamism could be posited within the Saussurian structure which might drive it beyond itself. Ever since, such a structure has dominated structuralism, despite Saussure's explicit statement that language was theoretically unlike any other social institution (see *Cours de linguistique,* p. 110). Like a clone, the dyad and its abstract internal relation can reproduce, indeed endlessly—but only at the price of remaining forever unchanged.

Time thus reveals itself as the third dimension exluded from Saussure's dyadic structure. This should come as no surprise, given that his synchronism was quite conscious and explicit in declining it. Saussure enables us to conceive relation, but at the price of refusing *this* fundamental relation. We might have thought time essential in any model which sought to conceptualize an element of social existence as fundamental as the use of signs. But from within binarism it is theoretically unimaginable.

My effort will be to conceive of the semiotic and the discursive fields in *directional* terms. Much of the work which lies behind it depends on transcending the residual abstraction, the consequent relative sterility, of Saussure's exclusive bipolar structure. I want to model difference not simply as diversity or abstract variation but as inscribing authentic conflict and projecting authentic change. Only on such grounds, it seems to me, can we conceive a truly *social* semiotics.

A third term within its paradigm is thus indispensable if the semiotic is to become capable of figuring its own mutability, its relation to other systems and orders of social discourse—in a word, its own *determination.* Of course the advent of such a supplementary element within

2. *Cours de linguistique générale,* p. 166; Saussure's italics.

27

the model of the sign by no means necessitates canceling Saussure's insights concerning the dyad itself. They may persist as long as we remain on the grounds, and within the range, which he himself specified as those of the dyad's pertinence: the radical arbitrariness of *langue* conceived as an abstract system, presupposing its indeterminacy in relation to any system or series outside itself. As long, in other words, as we *define* the system as closed, we need not concern ourselves with any disruption from outside it, and the satisfying purity of the dyadic relation can be sustained.[3]

But the decline in structuralism's prominence as a methodology for literary analysis would appear to reflect a growing (if at first grudging) recognition that, however defensible on its own grounds, such systemic abstraction becomes disabling when its own object of analysis draws the paradigm toward violating just these rigorous conditions. Such would seem to be the case whenever the system is called upon to master elements which are unassimilable to its reductions: mutations in systemic elements *over time;* nondiscrete (or "continuous," or "analogue") modifications which are irreducible to the digital differentiations of binarism (see Culler, *Structuralist Poetics,* p. 14); interventions of determinants which have the power to disrupt the arbitrariness of the signifier-signified relation and thereby to force disruptions of the crystalline symmetries of *langue.*

These elements unassimilable for binarism are invariably attributes of the temporal or social. And I will argue that a model with the capacity to accommodate a third term—*not* as some incomprehensible disruption from without, but as an integral element of the analytical paradigm and of the identity of the sign—is a minimal condition for their adequate theorization.

To say so is to register a modification in the grounds of the problem as it was conceived in Saussure's period and for a long time thereafter by the major tradition of semiotic analysis. The implication of Saussure's tactic of excluding the diachronic and what we might call (provisionally adopting his perspective) the "extralinguistic" was to achieve a clear field to operate in. Within it, all elements could be seen as *intrin-*

---

3. See Paul Ricoeur, *Le conflit des interprétations,* pp. 80–97, esp. pp. 82–83, resuming Hjelmslev's analysis in *Prolegomena to a Theory of Language* (1943) of the presuppositions of the Saussurian paradigm.

sically related. It was a system where the external held no sway. Saussure's object was to define his analytical series *purely,* to exclude from its logic all heterogeneous series, however significant they might appear on other grounds. Causation was to be exclusively *intrasystemic* (see Jameson, *Prison-House of Language,* pp. 8–10), and the theoretical problem of its motivation was comfortably solved in advance.

What has changed is the status posited for elements which seemed extrinsic to the sign. Triadic models of semiotic or discursive elements by no means oblige us to tolerate some irrational or alien element within the paradigm. Rather, such theoretical initiatives seek to register dynamics intrinsic to, constitutive of, the individual sign. They drive it beyond itself—or at least beyond any momentary impression of its stability. The insistent energy of such dynamics has emerged in conceptualization in the period since Saussure's original model.

Still, from the side of the linguistic it was Saussure's reconception of relation and difference which, in however incipient a form, placed these notions on our critical agenda. And though within his system they may seem underdeveloped when compared with those necessary for an authentically *social* semiotics, they bear within themselves the potential for movement beyond directionless variation or disparity to authentic difference. I will argue that such a development arising in Saussure's problematic is essential to the foundation of the subversive "counter-discourse" which will be the concern of the chapters to follow.

In order to detect the force of such a dynamic within semiotic model building, I want to suggest several theoretical systems in which some form of third term has been brought to bear in a manner which might be seen to resolve or to ventilate the closure of the semiotic dyad. Such a rehearsal is not meant to be exhaustive, merely exemplary of a widely perceived impulse to conceive language *in relation* to the multiform attributes which it bears within itself, or which constitutively bear upon it.

Consider Charles Sanders Peirce's notion of the sign's fundamental incompleteness, requiring for its comprehension an additional linguistic element in the form of what he called the "explanation" or "interpretant." Such an element cannot be figured from within the duplex sign itself, but together with it constitutes a fully formed, now triplex, sign.[4] Peirce's model projects the endless reproduction of such reconceived signs, each reenveloped at the next higher level of comprehension by another like it supplying *its* interpretant and intrinsically requiring further reinscription one stage beyond itself.

For such a limitless slippage from sign to higher sign we may legitimately project a horizon at which what seems like repetition and pure qualitative change passes beyond itself into something like a new *category* of interpretant. The Peircian paradigm seems to be striving toward the inclusion *within* the sign of the vast stores of *social knowledge*— relative, historicized, accessible to interpretation now by disciplines resembling a sociology of knowledge, an anthropology of culture, a dialectical history of social formations—which surely seemed very distant, if not theoretically invisible, at the moment we began our rising movement up the chain of signs.

As a second system in which three-part structures function to open up the hermeticism of the dyad, we might consider the work of Louis Hjelmslev. Hjelmslev problematized Saussure's distinction between *langue* and *parole* by introducing a positive, concrete term—"usage"— between them. The notion seeks to understand the *functioning* of language (as opposed to Hjelmslev's "schema," which seeks to seize its abstract systematicity) in terms both of those features imposed by social convention (pointing in the direction of *langue*) and those improvised by an individual (cf. *parole*).

"Usage" is thus more than a compromise or an attempt to strike an average. It upsets the idea that language structures can usefully be split into a system, on the one hand, and nonsystemic, somehow degraded or irrational manifestations on the other. "Usage" is neither a purely abstract, idealist hypothesis like *langue* not an idiosyncratic, accidental utterance like *parole*. It projects not a private, unique *act* but a pattern *active* in a community, a preestablished set of determinate possibilities and limits. Hjelmslev's "usage" thus designates a social *practice*. And it refers us inevitably to the social system within which it functions.[5]

4. Peirce, *Elements of Logic,* p. 156; see also Culler, *Structuralist Poetics,* pp. 19–20, and Ducrot and Todorov, *Encyclopedic Dictionary,* pp. 85–86. The prominence of the triad in Peirce, as opposed to the dyad in Saussure, has been widely commented upon.

5. See Hjelmslev, "Langue et parole," p. 88. See also Holland, "Toward a Redefinition of Masochism," pp. 121–22. A notion like usage is easily historicizable; compare Barthes's "mode of writing," *Writing Degree Zero,* p. 13. Curiously, a similar structure

The case of Greimas further clarifies the implications of any movement beyond the occlusions intrinsic to the dyad. This becomes evident in Fredric Jameson's analysis of Greimas's celebrated semantic rectangle. Jameson suggests how what appears in it as nothing more than a reduplicated binarism, a dyad to the second power, in fact reaches beyond the logic of antinomy toward the figuration of social struggle itself.[6] I quote from Jameson's analysis:

> The operational validity . . . of the Greimassian semiotic rectangle derives . . . from its vocation specifically to model ideological closure and to articulate the workings of binary oppositions, here the privileged form of what we have called the antinomy. A dialectical reevaluation of the findings of semiotics intervenes, however, at this point in which the entire system of ideological closure is taken as the symptomatic projection of something quite different, namely of social contradiction.[7]

Greimas's rectangle can function in the way Jameson has asserted because it is more than just a double dyad. For the second vector, which permits construction of the rectangle to begin with, provides that *scalar dimension*—situating directionality between the terms in relation—upon whose denial in Saussure I commented. Within what we might call Greimas's ideological horizon, this element becomes the third term, whose effect is to open the model both to its own previously suppressed developmental dynamic and to orders of phenomena—beyond the semantic narrowly conceived—in which it almost seems to project its own reinscription.[8]

---

appears in Herbert Marcuse's triplex account of "expressed meaning" in language; see *One-Dimensional Man*, pp. 196–97, where Marcuse proposes a hierarchy of "individual project," "established supra-individual system of ideas, values and objectives," and a "particular society integrating conflicting individual and supra-individual projects."

6. Jameson, *Political Unconscious*, pp. 47–48, 83.

7. Ibid., p. 83.

8. On the rectangle, see also Jameson, *Prison-House of Language*, pp. 162–68. Greimas's pertinence to the analysis of the internal limitations of classical semiotics is considerable. On another front, that of temporality, and in the height of an often uncritical model-building euphoria during the structuralist period in France, Greimas provided a strikingly honest account of the inability of the semiotic paradigm to model development—in other words, to conceive the temporal. See his "Structure et histoire."

As Jameson's earlier analysis in *Prison-House of Language* had demonstrated, in constructing Greimas's rectangle there is no way for a specific complex of terms, in a specific textual situation, to avoid interrogation of the structured *social* relations which are its mystified referent. In the repertoire of connections, exclusions, and contradictions within such a larger structure, we inevitably find the terms which appropriately fill the rectangle's semantic blanks. Greimas's semantics *presupposes* the social knowledge, the total social network which his rectangle appears to map almost as if they were intrinsic properties of abstract language. It then becomes clear that the rectangle's ultimate referent is ideology and, particularly, the most painful points of unresolved social contradiction. With Greimas the rectangle thus opens up to figure something like the social space its geometry seems to mime. And such a space is always occupied by the kind of conjunctural stress which thereby comes to inhabit the semiotic *from within* and for the first time begins to link the orders of meaning and materiality.

This is a small sampling of efforts to seize as integral to the sign, as part of its form and its definition, the social contents to which it would seem we must appeal if we are to understand the centrality of the semiotic in human phenomena at all. To them respond certain formulations emerging within a more consciously materialist and dialectical tradition, which I will consider below. I would not suggest that these varying solutions are automatically or even easily transcodable one to another. Their common ground is the impulse to transcend the closure of the dyad, and the perception that a model built upon it is cut off both from any authentic internal development and from any effective reckoning with other orders of phenomena. In the shared perception of these diverse models, the sign and the discourse are conceived as legitimately more complex and constitutively more socialized than Saussure's binary paradigm had allowed. Such complication and socialization are seen as intrinsic to the human operation of semiosis.

In an unexpected way Derrida stands as a mediatory term between these two tendencies. With Derrida two points are essential. By now both are familiar in the American context. But their tactical significance for the argument I am making here may be less obvious. With regard to the theoretical structure and conceptual coherence of the dyad, Derrida upsets its closure in the notion of *différance,* and its nondirectionality in his detection, through the protocols of deconstruction, of hierarchies which inevitably inscribe themselves within what appeared the neutral oppositions of Saussure's binary form. *Différance* thus provides a perspective on the sign which enables—and indeed necessitates—its disengagement from the conceptual impasse of directionless difference and abstract variation.[9]

In the Derridean conception *time* always inserts itself into the substance of the semiotic. The truth about the sign then becomes its *story*: a narration of the unfolding of its meaning which can no longer be conceived *sub specie aeternitatis*, as a preexisting substance. It must be comprehended as *production*, as determined by its relation to other social series beyond itself. To these series questions of its full meaning must inevitably be referred.[10] Citing Derrida's *Positions*, Gayatri Spivak thus asserts in her preface to his *Grammatology* that our criticism needs to accommodate "the irruptive emergence of a new 'concept'" of the sign, which can no longer be contained within the atemporal binarism, the abstract system of oppositions, which the tradition has derived from Saussure (p. lxxvii). In the context of my argument here, Spivak is referring to the emergence of the third term that disrupts the hermeticism of the dyadic model and opens it, in and through time, to something like a social world of reference which forces it beyond itself.

If *différance* introduces the notion of an inevitable displacement within binary opposition and projects the temporal priority of one of the terms in relation, Derrida's notion of "deconstruction" socializes this directionality more radically still. It detects within binary oppositions a *hierarchy*, socially determined and determining. Within poststructuralism this notion begins to give conceptual substance and coherence to that image of culture as "field of struggle" with which I began. It thus emerges that in its temporal dynamism and its inscription of social power, the sign begins to figure something like an elemental *machine for domination*.[11]

---

9. On the notion of *différance* see Derrida's essay by the same title, pp. 1–29; Culler, *On Deconstruction*; Lentricchia, *After the New Criticism*, pp. 170ff.; Jameson, *Prison-House of Language*, p. 174; and Christopher Norris, *Deconstruction*. Gayatri Spivak's preface to her translation of Derrida's *Of Grammatology* is indispensable to an understanding of these problems.

10. See my "Deconstruction/Mediation."

11. See Spivak's preface to Derrida's *Of Grammatology*, p. lxxvii, and Derrida, *Positions*, p. 57.

The perspective on language projected in these theoretical impulses would seem to have received its most suggestive materialist expression in the work of Mikhail Bakhtin and his circle. The cogency of his critiques of formalism and structuralism is becoming clear as our own thinking grapples with the methodological closures of these models of signs and discourses. Very early, Bakhtin argued that in human language binary oppositions are never simply logical, never simply describable in terms of a purely internal relationality. They cannot be value neutral. For Bakhtin the oppositions stressing higher units of cultural meaning were unlike those within language's phonemic structure. They resembled much more closely the contradictions of social struggle than the differences of logical antinomy.

In Bakhtin's conceptualization, such internally stressed cultural units were burdened with—or rather, constituted by—an intentionality, ultimately a *politics,* whose socially determined adversative energies were inevitable. Signs did not exist without such energies inscribed within them; in a sense, they *were* nothing but the inscription of such energies. For Bakhtin the meaning of the sign generated itself in an apparently familiar bipolar structure. But social life was never constituted by an abstract mathematical oscillation between possible poles. In Bakhtin's conception the networks of distinction within which social meaning occurs are always sites of intense and multileveled struggle. So a sign always inscribes interests and is inscribed within mechanisms of control which can be specified only by reference to the conjuncture in which such signs and the articulated discourses that are built upon them operate.

One might think Saussure's notion of the "referent" might have opened up his own model of the sign to a parallel theoretical development, to broader modes of social relationality—to a degree. The problem lies in the referent's almost completely untheorized relation to its sign. Saussure can conceive of such relation only as purely accidental or conventional—what later theorists have called "unmotivated"— connection. Such a paradigm of relation, while better than none at all, hardly offers a fertile field for deeper analysis. The contrast with Bakhtin's solution is instructive.

For Saussure the second relation, between sign and referent, involves a radical (and perhaps ultimately incomprehensible) change in *order*—from conceptual to concrete, from idealist to materialist. In contrast the modes of relation of the sign posited by Bakhtin, both internal and outward looking, bear the *same* character and imply no alteration of mode. Both are governed by binary *contradiction;* in other words, both are always available for passage beyond the stage of blind opposition to one in which the adversative energies which oppose them can in some manner be resolved. In turn such conciliation could be understood as a direct response to the tension inscribed within the semiotic realm by the originary conceptual or social conflict. By thus soliciting the social and the conjunctural *within* the notion of the sign itself, Bakhtin projects a solution to the conceptual impasse.[12]

In the light of the foregoing, even the starting point of semiotic analysis to which Saussure has accustomed the entire tradition might usefully undergo a decisive modification. Rather than bleaching out the content of contradiction which is inscribed in, and provides the meaning of, difference—as happens when the linguistic model is projected upon more intensely conflicted social contents—we might re-open the question of the phonemic itself. We could then conceive its contrastive systematization as a form of difference not yet fully mature, as yet incompletely invested with its social content. The apparently abstract and directionless antithesis of the phonemic realm would then be reinscribed in structures more adequate to conceptualize the social nature of language in terms of sociality itself, according to Walter Banjamin's suggestion that forms in a circuit of constant but meaningless oscillation can best be comprehended as "the figurative appearance of the dialectic, the law of the dialectic at a standstill."[13]

The work of Bakhtin available in Western languages has almost all appeared in the past decade or so (the earliest translation into English, *Rabelais and His World,* was published in 1968).[14] It is now widely

---

12. There have been other attempts to seek solution in something like homologous forms. At the conclusion of his *Eléments de Sémiologie,* Barthes asserts that "the future surely will belong to a linguistics of connotation" (in *Degré zéro*). He thereby acknowledges the need for conceptualization of the sign to achieve a dynamism beyond the sign element itself and toward the social usage which organizes its concrete and situational functionality. Another solution is Umberto's Eco's in his *Theory of Semiotics.* The pertinence of Eco's theoretical system to these questions is expressed in an article by Tom Lewis, "Notes toward a Theory of the Referent," *PMLA* 94, no. 3 (May 1979): 459–75.

13. Benjamin, *Baudelaire,* p. 171. See also Jameson, *Political Unconscious,* pp. 82–83, on the relation between contradiction and antimony.

14. The principal works by or attributable to Bakhtin available in French or English are as follows: *Rabelais and His World; Problems of Dostoevskii's Poetics;* [V. N. Vol-

agreed that several books largely written by Bakhtin appeared in the Soviet Union under the names of members of his circle: *Marxism and the Philosophy of Language* and *Freudianism*, attributed to Vološinov; *The Formal Method in Literary Scholarship*, to Medvedev. Some of the important notions developed in Bakhtin's texts will be discussed in the chapters to follow. In the context of my argument concerning the semiotic realm as the site of social conflict, it may suffice at this point to note two of them. The first is the notion of *value accent* (or "evaluative accentuation"). I quote from *Marxism and the Philosophy of Language*:

> Every stage in the development of a society has its own special and restricted circle of items which alone have access to that society's attention, and which are endowed with evaluative accentuation by that attention. Only items within that circle will achieve sign formation and become objects in semiotic communication. . . . Various different classes will use one and the same language. As a result, differently oriented accents intersect in every ideological sign. Sign becomes an arena of the class struggle. This social *multiaccentuality* of the ideological sign is a very crucial aspect. [Pp. 21–23]

Something like Saussure's binarism thus reappears in Bakhtin's dialectical and materialist critique of the Saussurian system. But it takes the form of prototypical social opposition, of fundamental paradigmatic struggle for the control of a sign's use, range of reference, and ultimate meaning. A sign is invested with the competing meanings of social groups and refuses to remain static as an immediate consequence of such conflict inscribed in its use. Conflict is thus as characteristic of the semiotic realm as of the social. Bakhtin is quite clear: "There is no such thing as a word without evaluative accent" (p. 103).

It follows from the sign's inherent multiaccentuality that no discourse is ever a monologue, nor could it ever be adequately analyzed "intrinsically." Its assertions, its tone, its rhetoric—everything that constitutes it—always presuppose a horizon of competing, contrary utterances against which it asserts its own energies. These configura-

---

ošinov], *Marxism and the Philosophy of Language;* [Vološinov], *Freudianism; [P. N. Medvedev and Bahktin], Formal Method in Literary Scholarship; Dialogic Imagination; Esthétique et théorie du roman.*

tions are specific, conjunctural. But the phenomenon, which Bakhtin terms *dialogism* or *the dialogic,* is transhistorical for all human communities, at least pending the resolution of the conflicts which inscribe themselves as multiaccentuality in the signs available to all users of language.[15] This inherently adversative character of all discourse is the foundation for the forms of counter-discursive expression and conflict which I will analyze in the pages which follow.[16] The discourses I will consider will be conceived as mapping the multivocality of any semiotic structure bathed in cultural stress.

What then unfolds is a world in which language intrinsically carries the traces of struggle, and in which such traces can be read. The contradictions of the social world configure themselves as oriented networks of semantic and discursive clashes and campaigns for predominance in such a way that the inscription of conflict is no longer conceived as a contamination of the linguistic but as its properly defining function.

From the direction of the sign's binarism, of its constitutive internal difference, we thus come unexpectedly upon what looks very much like a resolution of the problem of materialism in language, of what it might mean to attribute material weight and resistance to something as impalpable and seemingly mobile as the world of signs. Against the play of certain structuralist and poststructuralist projections of symbolic exchange and semiotic transformation freed of the dross of context and of conflict, the vision of language emerging here roots any linguistic production or performance in a network of constraints and linkages—ultimately of *determinations*—which bind individual speak-

---

15. For more on this question, see below, Chapter 1, n. 37.

16. On dialogism, see *Dialogic Imagination,* glossary, p. 426, with reference to Bakhtin's own text. There are convergences between these inherently dialectical notions and those developed by Jan Mukařovsky; see the translators' preface to his *Structure, Sign, and Function,* trans. John Burbank and Peter Steiner (New Haven: Yale University Press, 1977), and Steiner's introduction to the same volume. The following quotation from Mukařovsky's "Art as a Semiotic Fact" will be suggestive: "It has become increasingly clear that the framework of individual consciousness is constituted, even in its innermost layers, of contents belonging to the social consciousness. As a result the problems of sign and meaning become more and more urgent" (*Structure, Sign, and Function,* p. 82). The collection of essays edited by Peter V. Zima entitled *Semiotics and Dialectics: Ideology and the Text* is of considerable interest in relation to the problems at issue here.

ers and producers of texts. But at the same time—and perhaps for the first time—such a conception offers the possibility of comprehending their production systematically.

In such a context we can begin to understand Sartre's assertion in *Saint-Genet* of "a causality of imaginary" and comprehend what Foucault has termed the "the materialism of the incorporeal."[17] The deeply socialized and contextualized semiotics emerging from my argument insists upon the weight of meanings laden, just beyond the immediate field of vision which perceives them, with the conflicted interests they sustain or contest. They carry all the ideological and structural weight of the already-constituted paradigms and patterns which involuntarily occupy our memories and appropriate our creativities. Such structures determine the realms of our freedom with the weight of constituted practice, which would seem to be an irreducible element of our existence in society.

Thus whether posited on very different assumptions by Derrida or by Bakhtin, a fundamental asymmetry is a primary fact in the world of discourse. Engaged with the realities of power, human communities use words not in contemplation but in *competition*. Such struggles are never equal ones. The facts of domination, of control, are inscribed in the signs avaible for use by all members of a social formation. The weight of tradition, the promise held out by reputation, the fear of repression, all contrive to establish what we call an "establishment" and an established language. In this sense, Marx's celebrated assertion that the ruling ideas are the ideas of the ruling class,[18] however provocative in tone, translates a universal phenomenon in societies in which the arrangement for dividing labor and distributing surplus is unequal.

A certain discourse is always normalized within speech communities and social formations. Certain linguistic and conceptual elements, from pronunciation and vocabulary to the large and methodologically diffuse question of "world view," are valorized by and infused with the implicit acceptance by and of the norm. This is what gives theoretical substance to the widely articulated notion of "domination by the code"

17. Sartre, *Saint-Genet*, p. 368; Foucault, *L'ordre du discours*, p. 60.
18. Marx and Engels, *German Ideology*, p. 67; the passage in the more easily available International Publishers abridgment (New York, 1970) is on p. 64.

and to the submission of the subject to what Vincent Descombes, resuming an influential tradition, terms the "law of the signifier."[19] The overarching regulation of the cultural field by codes, specifically linguistic and languagelike, transcends the generative and critical capacities of any individual speaker or speech act. And when it is adequately historicized, this systematicity turns into the structure of ideological *power* which organizes a social formation.

Such forms of speech and of thought would remain transparent and radically ahistorical for all speakers if they were all that speakers had at their disposal, if they translated the full experience of existence for the members of a community. And it has often been argued that periods in which signs are taken to have unproblematic relations to those who utter them and to their extralinguistic referents correspond to epochs in which the domination of a particular ideological structure is so pervasive that the presence of alternatives appears negligible. If today, on the other hand, the crisis of the referent, the problematization of the sign, has become acute, surely this phenomenon—itself historicizing language and theories about language in such a way as to divide our own period from the others about which we know—must be connected to the lack of social consensus, to an atmosphere of conflict, not only about how signs communicate meaning but about every element within a worldwide cultural and political discourse.

In our period, dominant forms of discourse have achieved unprecedented degrees of penetration and an astonishingly sophisticated capacity to enforce their control of the forms of social communication and social practice which provide the configurations of modern existence. But at the same time, in intimate connection with the power of such an apparatus, discourses of resistance ceaselessly interrupt what would otherwise be the seamless serenity of the dominant, its obliviousness to any contestation. For every level at which the discourse of power determines dominant forms of speech and thinking, counter-dominant strains challenge and subvert the appearance of inevitability

19. *Modern French Philosophy*, p. 97. Compare Vološinov/Bakhtin, *Marxism and the Philosophy of Language*, p. 22: "Individual choice under these circumstances . . . can have no meaning at all." The recent study of Foucault by Dreyfus and Rabinow, *Michel Foucault*, is of considerable interest on these issues, particularly chaps. 7 and 8, on the genealogy of the modern individual as *object* and as *subject*, respectively.

which is ideology's primary mechanism for sustaining its own self-reproduction.

It thus becomes apparent that the world of discourse is structured very much like materialist models of the dialectic which seek to capture not only the multivocality of any social or historical process but, crucially, the hierarchized struggle in which it plays itself out. As I have already suggested, the dialectic does not lay out synchronic states because its terms insist that synchrony is nothing more than a convenient shorthand way of looking at the dynamic elements which motivate the dialectical course itself.

What is at stake in language, then, is *power*.[20] In this sense the "will to domination" which characterizes the "symbolic power and art and culture" (upon which Fredric Jameson reflects at the conclusion of *The Political Unconscious* [p. 299]) inevitably forms the object—and no doubt the means—of any cultural criticism.[21] For more than a decade the assumptions of structuralism tended to render such considerations inaccessible. In that sense the movement of thought in France since that time has reacted against such closure in a salutary way. Foucault's corrective to the abstractly antinomic structuralist paradigm provides a striking example of these tendencies, whatever their internal diversity. He put it thus: "The history which bears and determines us has the form of a war rather than that of a language: relations of power, not relations of meaning."[22] In such a formulation the struggle within the elements of the semiotic reasserts a centrality which structuralism was unable to figure. Yet a further step in this evolution begins to be conceivable at this point. On the basis of the investigation of the sign whose itinerary I have sought to trace, it would be possible to radicalize even Foucault's striking formulation. For against his own antinomic posing of the linguistic and military alternatives themselves, and in our own counter-discursive formulation of a fundamental model for cultural analysis, we would need to assert that *the form of language itself is contradiction*.

20. Cf. Foucault, *L'ordre du discours*, p. 22: "What then is at stake, unless it be desire and power."

21. For a parallel formulation in Derrida, see Lentricchia, *After the New Criticism*, p. 175.

22. *Power/Knowledge*, p. 114.

This would seem to be the conception of the semiotic toward which these diverse strains of cultural and linguistic theory have been reaching.[23] In it the sign's self-identity fractures; its synchronous, timeless present opens from within into nonsimultaneity; its independence, even its arbitrariness, reveal themselves as temporary limitations in our perception of language itself. Behind such notions the operations of a history conceal themselves. Its recovery within semiosis then begins to seem possible. The sign and the social discourse it composes acquire an intrinsic depth and an internal richness which defy the reassuring simplicity of the dyad.

One theoretical problem deserves particular notice in this connection, for the transformations of semiotic theory renew it strikingly. On the microscopic as on the macroscopic levels, language, I have argued, rearticulates itself in terms of competing interests within the linguistic, cultural, and social space. As the traditional preoccupation of ideological criticism, consideration of such culturally competitive structures has been distinctly out of fashion. But the realm of the ideological now reacquires its pertinance.[24] Its story turns out to be that of language

23. Compare Bakhtin's notions of "heteroglossia" ("*within* a language . . . the problem of internal differentiation, the stratification characteristic of any national language" [*Dialogic Imagination*, p. 67]) and "polyglossia" (the co-presence within a culture of multiple languages; see the glossary in *Dialogic Imagination*, p. 430, s.v. "social language"; and Holquist's introduction, p. xix). In *Marxism and Literature*, pp. 121–27, Raymond Williams, inspired by Gramsci, argues for the coexistence, in any cultural conjuncture, of what he terms "residual," "dominant," and "emergent" discourses and processes which place any synchronic depiction of the cultural situation under stress. We have already seen how in the notion of "différance" Derrida theorizes a parallel desynchronization of the present. His conception, however abstract its detail, promises development into a theory able to grasp the inner complexity of diverse practices and temporalities in social formations; cf. Lentricchia, *After the New Criticism*, p. 175, and particularly Michael Ryan, *Marxism and Deconstruction*. In *Political Unconscious*, p. 97, Fredric Jameson recalls Ernst Bloch's notion of nonsynchronous development ("Ungleichzeitigkeit"), which could easily serve a parallel function. In *Révolution du langage poétique*, p. 364, Julia Kristeva emphasizes the temporal displacement by which any text relates to its own period through the particular mode of negativity it brings to bear against the dominant it contests. And Hayden White, echoing Jameson in *Political Unconscious,* has employed the image of something like a palimpsest to figure the same phenomenon: "Historical epochs are not monolithically integrated social formations but, on the contrary, complex *overlays* of different modes of production" ("Getting Out of History," p. 13).

24. For a partial bibliography and summary discussion, see below, Chapter 1, notes 44 and 49.

itself and of the patterns of socialization and conflict which language determines.

In a familiar formulation, ideology produces us as subjects. As Raymond Williams puts it in terms which resonate clearly with those of my discussion above, ideology figures

> a conscious system of ideas and beliefs, but [in addition] the whole lived social process as practically organized by specific and dominant meanings and values. . . . [It is] a saturation of the whole process of living . . . , of the whole substance of lived identities and relationships . . . , a whole body of practices and expectations . . . , our senses and assignments of energy, our shaping perceptions of ourselves and our world. It is a living system of meanings and values—constitutive and constituting—which . . . appear as reciprocally confirming . . . a sense of absolute reality beyond which it is very difficult . . . to move.[25]

The work of Antonio Gramsci is at the origin of this renewal of concern with the ideological, and it has permitted important advances in an account of its social and cultural functioning. Gramsci distinguished between the familiar modes of control characteristic of the traditional authoritarian state, and those of the more modern formations which (following Vico and Hegel) he termed "civil society." Such a distinction brought to consciousness an epochal inflection in the manners and mechanisms by which, under the conditions of existence since the political and economic revolutions of the nineteenth century, languages and discourses themselves have organized those subjected to their systematicity and their domination. From the concretely coercive use of police or judicial authority, the modes of social control have inflected to more immanent means of organizing behavior, to the establishment of atmospheric assumptions about what attitudes and activities are permissible to the citizen in liberal societies.

Gramsci conceptualized the dominant form of this ideological determination under the notion of "hegemony." He saw modern social and political existence as an ongoing and multifaceted struggle between the hegemony by which a class is able to articulate its interests in terms

25. *Marxism and Literature*, pp. 109–10.

which other social groups accept as their own, and the contestatory, "counter-hegemonic" initiatives of competing social fragments.

What is of particular importance here is that this image of competing discursive systems strikingly reproduces at the macroscopic level the conjunctural stress within the sign which Bakhtin described.[26] In Gramsci's notion of hegemony the whole question of the rule or domination of one group over another is radically transformed. The multilayered, palimpsest discourses which we saw critics in diverse traditions striving to conceptualize begin to be comprehensible as the traces of the competitive process of domination and contestation by which society is constituted in the modern period. This formulation is essential to the notion of the counter-discourse which, I will argue, occupied a crucial place in nineteenth-century cultural production.

Contested Terrain: On the Situation of Discourse in Nineteenth-Century France

In a world saturated by discourse, language itself becomes contested terrain. I will argue that such saturation is the cultural *differentia specifica* distinguishing the modern period from earlier formations. And surely the theoretical effort since the nineteenth century to understand the phenomenon of language and the complexities of the discursive responds to that saturation. It is as if toward the end of the century the dry science of linguistics suddenly found itself at the center of efforts to manage an unprecedented cultural crisis. We have been battling with it ever since. Julia Kristeva evokes this continuity in *La révolution du langage poétique:* "Our century is still living on the nineteenth century's momentum" (p. 618).

Of course the privilege of a period is always relative. But Kristeva's remark suggests that the discursive combats of the nineteenth century can fruitfully be studied not only from the perspective of their explicit thematic conflicts, which are well known, but in the often subterranean struggles of their forms. The effort to achieve predominance in the social formation which emerged from the twin revolution of the nine-

---

26. On these questions, see Williams, *Marxism and Literature,* pp. 108–14; Gramsci, *Prison Notebooks;* and Chantal Mouffe's collection *Gramsci and Marxist Theory.*

teenth century did not play itself out at the level of politics and programs alone. The paradigms of the entire complex of social discourses
by which the emerging formation organized and understood its existence were at stake. It seems clear today that in the nineteenth century
the techniques for assuring discursive penetration solidified themselves
astonishingly. Such innovation sustained liberal capitalism and all its
associated institutions—indeed, it might be taken as their condition of
possibility. From our vantage today these techniques often appear to
have achieved an uncontested sovereignty in the period. But my claim
will be that as the techniques for assuring discursive control underwent
a radical development, so too did those of symbolic subversion.

This assertion might not seem immediately apparent. For many of
the figures of high cultural importance to us today, the nineteenth
century was a period of seemingly impotent lamentation. Flaubert's
plaint, in a letter written to his uncle Parrain after his departure from
Egypt, is characteristic:

> Dear old friend, have you ever reflected upon the utter serenity of
> imbeciles? Stupidity [*la bêtise*] is something unshakeable; nothing
> comes up against it without being destroyed. It's like granite, hard and
> resistant. In Alexandria, a certain Thompson, from Sunderland, has
> inscribed his name on Pompey's column in letters six feet high. You
> can read it from a quarter-league away. You can't even see the column
> without seeing Thompson's name, therefore without thinking of
> Thompson. This cretin has incorporated himself into the monument
> and perpetuated himself with it. It's even worse than that: he has
> outdone the column by the splendor of his gigantic inscription. All
> imbeciles are more or less like Thompson of Sunderland. And they
> always defeat us [*ils nous enfoncent toujours*]; they are so numerous,
> there's no way to stamp them out [*ils reviennent si souvent*], they are
> simply too healthy. You meet a lot of them while traveling. In everyday
> life they end up driving you crazy.[27]

Flaubert's protest is characteristic. It opposes the lone voice of a
cultural Jeremiah against the voice of an age. And it practices a typical
counter-discursive tactic (no doubt one of the simplest): a resigned
sarcasm. J.-K. Huysmans was even more desperately direct in damning

---

27. 6 Oct. 1850; *Correspondance,* ed. Jean Bruneau, vol. 1 (Paris: Gallimard-Pléiade,
1973), p. 689.

the period in which he felt condemned to live: "Good God, what a mess! And to think that this century is enthusiastic and full of praise about itself! It has only one thing on its mind—progress. Whose progress? the progress of what? for this miserable century has not invented much."[28] But from my perspective, Huysmans was wrong. In the realm that interests me here, the inventions of his period are intensely important.

Our own critical discourse can metonymically evoke the whole but can never display it. What Flaubert called the "immense Nouveau qui déborde de partout" ("the immense innovation which submerges us from all sides")[29] proves ungraspable in its very pervasiveness. Nonetheless it may be useful to mention a few of the loci within the social field which were touched and transformed by the nineteenth century's unprecedented resituation of discourse. Politics is probably the most obvious of these. In this realm the multiple revolutions of the nineteenth century had profound discursive consequences.

Consider the dismaying figure of Louis-Napoléon. Eric Hobsbawm evokes him as follows: "[He] was . . . the first of the modern chiefs of state who ruled not by simple armed force, but by the sort of demagogy and public relations which are so much more easily operated from the top of the state than from anywhere else."[30] Twenty years earlier, Louis-Philippe had already adumbrated certain parallel techniques. Thus Theodore Zeldin characterizes the Orléanist king as a *fake* bourgeois seeking through consciously planned self-misrepresentation to create an *image* of rule, of a conjuncturally appropriate form of legitimacy responding to the realities of a transformed politics: "He cultivated his image as a bourgeois king in order to win popularity. . . . His umbrella, his famous wig, were publicity stunts."[31] Of course it would be naive to imagine that monarchs had been unconcerned with the opinion of their subjects prior to the nineteenth cen-

28. Huysmans, *Là-bas* (Paris: Plon, 1912), p. 172.
29. Letter to Bouilhet, 19 Dec. 1850; *Correspondance*, vol. 1, p. 730.
30. *Age of Capital*, pp. 22–23. Hobsbawm further observes (p. 109) that Louis-Napoléon was the "first ruler of a large state outside the United States to come to power by means of universal (masculine) suffrage, and never forgot it." The interaction of the two political practices—discursive manipulation; required electoral feedback—is clear. It maps much of the social landscape of the period.
31. *France*, vol. 1, p. 415.

tury. Yet the altered intensity—and the cynical, instrumental ingeniousness—of preoccupation with such considerations in the period of
concern to me here begins to frame the *problem of the discursive* around
which my discussion will turn.

In this regard Umberto Eco's definition of the realm of the sign is
crucial: "Semiotics is in principle the discipline studying everything
which can be used *in order to lie.*"[32] Some measure of the saturation of
the social field by what I am calling the discursive begins to be visible
against the background of an increasing pervasion of semiotic material,
and the increasingly broadcast intention to use it to mystify and to
manipulate.

Fredric Jameson has put this idea clearly: "Unfortunately, no society
has ever been quite so mystified in quite so many ways as our own,
saturated as it is with messages and information, the very vehicle of
mystification (language, as Talleyrand put it, having been given us in
order to conceal our thoughts)."[33] Under the transformed conditions
of social existence in the nineteenth century, signs and discourses increasingly become exchange values. They are offered, desired, and
acquired; they circulate and are consumed. Yet they remain mysti-
fyingly impalpable. In their protean fluidity and commutability they
thus mirror that sense of being adrift which is a characteristic, if de-
spairing, complaint in the period of concern to us.

In this perspective, the fears of intellectuals that they might be slipping into the undifferentiated mass of common people, ideas, and
values may acquire some theoretical depth. For it was the increasingly
rootless exchangeability of signs which provided the material basis for
such fears. Flaubert's reaction is characteristic:

> A truth seems to me to emerge from all this. It is that we have no real
> need of the common people [*le vulgaire*], of the populous elements, of
> majorities, of approval, of ratification [*la consécration*]. 1789 demolished
> the monarchy and the aristocracy, 1848 the bourgeoisie, and 1851 the
> *people*. There's *nothing* left except an imbecilic and vulgar mass [*une
> tourbe canaille et imbécile*].—We are all driven down [*enfoncés*] to the
> same level in a common mediocrity. Social equality has spread to the
> Mind. We produce books for everyone, art for everyone, science for
> everyone, like we build railroads and public waiting rooms. Humanity

32. *Theory of Semiotics*, p. 7; my italics.
33. *Political Unconscious*, pp. 60–61.

46

is rabid with moral degradation [*abaissement moral*].—And I'm furious with humanity, because I belong to it.[34]

The developments in the realm of social meaning at the heart of Flaubert's lament in fact define an entire problematic, for the decline of certain signifiers which bore *distinction* as an essential signified left those needing to distinguish themselves baffled. Thus, for example, Zeldin observes that in the early part of the nineteenth century, a cashmere shawl cost about 450 francs, the equivalent of the annual wages of a laborer. By midcentury, however, Scottish tartan shawls made in Reims sold for a *fiftieth* of this price, and what Zeldin calls "cheap parodies of luxury" became the pride of every working woman.[35] On another front, and in what is only an apparent paradox, the distinction of family name itself was radically diluted after 1789, not only because of the temporary abolition of the aristocracy, but because, beginning with the Restoration, the number of people falsely claiming titles increased dramatically.[36]

At the same time, the nation, indeed the world, was rapidly becoming a continuous market for discourses. In Chapter 2 below I will discuss the rise and proliferation of the daily newspaper. The rates of its expansion and penetration of the social field can have had few parallels in social history: newspaper circulation in France increased by *4,000 percent* in the half century after 1830. In turn the pervasive circulation of the news evokes other sorts of circulation whose rates and facility were strikingly modified. Thus Hobsbawm comments on the fact that the celebrated eighty-day journey of Phileas Fogg around the world in 1872 would have taken fully four times as long only twenty-five years earlier.[37] And he observes that the advent of the telegraph transformed the circulation of all information in the 1860s and after (in 1860 the automatic telegraph was patended by Wheatstone; in 1865 the first transatlantic cable was completed), with a corresponding leap in the defensive sense of those concerned about the perfusion of the entire world by such discourses.[38] The sorts of developments which

34. Letter to Louise Colet, 22 Sept. 1853, *Correspondance*, vol. 2, p. 437.
35. *France*, vol. 2, p. 615.
36. See ibid., vol. 1, p. 16.
37. *Age of Capital*, p. 53.
38. Compare Flaubert's letter to Bouilhet (19 Dec. 1850; *Correspondance*, vol. 1, p. 730), a portion of which (on the "immense Nouveau") I quoted above. The letter's

these rapid soundings suggest penetrated even to the level of practices as intimate as the use of familiar nicknames. Hobsbawm comments on the decline of microcultures evidenced in their diminishing frequency in Normandy villages. At the same time the literacy rate in the countryside—and thus the availability of subjects for the more standardized and centralized discourses of the print medium—increased dramatically (for men it attained 80 percent in 1876; see *Age of Capital*, pp. 210–11).

Under these circumstances, the bourgeoisie, or at least those fragments whose self-perception and social status were put at risk by the increasing penetration of the mechanisms of production and exchange which gave the class as a whole its power, entered something like a crisis of self-conception. Sartre in his study of Mallarmé seizes this danger: after 1848 "la bourgeoisie se dissout elle-même. Elle deviendra peuple ou aristocratie; elle se perdra dans l'universelle équivalence, à moins qu'elle ne rétablisse à son profit l'esprit de synthèse" ("the bourgeoisie is itself in the process of dissolution. It risked absorption into the common people or into the aristocracy, dissolution through universal equivalence, unless it could succeed in reestablishing to its own advantage the ability to conceive the whole [of society] and dominate it.")[39]

A crucial condition of the problem was that the ideology of liberalism could not make any distinctions between citizens. Coordinately, increasing social and geographic mobility made group boundary lines much more uncertain. Under such circumstances, the use of cultural signs to indicate status becomes a much more subtle, less enforceable, yet at the same time more necessary calculus than previously.

Consequently the centrality of those citizens specially qualified to manipulate the signs and discourses through which social exchanges of all sorts were transacted greatly increased. The intelligentsia was acquiring its social function and its self-conception. And in a paradox that underlies its drama to the present day, it was discovering that its

occasion—the specific innovation which stimulated Flaubert's cry of despair—was precisely the Law of 1850 which made communication by telegraph (previously reserved for official state purposes) available to individuals.

39. "L'engagement de Mallarmé," p. 173.

own interests increasingly parted company from those of the class of which it was an uncomfortable and unwilling fragment. Pierre Bourdieu has seized the pertinence of the struggle thus founded:

> But the locus par excellence of symbolic struggles is the dominant class itself: struggles for the definition of legitimized culture which confront intellectuals and artists are only an aspect of the continuing struggles in which the different fractions of the dominant class confront each other, battling for the imposition of their own definition of the stakes and the legitimate means in social struggle or, if one prefers, for the principle of legitimate domination.[40]

Quite early the bourgeoisie began to develop tactics to keep its dissident members in line. The defensive rhetoric which articulated the interests of the dominant fractions of the middle-class was constant. This rhetoric argued for the subordination of the intellectuals to the larger interests of their own class, of which they were inevitably to some degree clients. The dominant position asserted that, at a time when such conduct appeared quite consequential, when the interclass struggle was still quite open, those tending toward any other social identification were simply class traitors. Thus, characteristically, this self-serving extract from an article by L. de Carné in the *Revue des Deux Mondes*, 1 August 1853: "We take it as evident that government in France must have the intellectuals [*les intelligences*] as instrument, and financial power [*les intérêts*] as ballast, and that access to domination of the men who represent the double power of thought and of capital is a normal and legitimate fact."[41] Such a nakedly manipulative assertion in one of the most influential of the establishment media we may take as evidence of a struggle which had already been going on for some time. It was to reach unprecedented intensity in the remaining part of the century.

The result of this complex of conditions and the coordinate discursive constraints is well known. It has become a commonplace that intellectuals in the period which concerns me tended to experience the world as unendurable. Many of their most significant productions

40. *Distinction*, p. 284.
41. Quoted in Duchet, *Manuel d'histoire littéraire*, p. 253.

resulted from the impulse to contest it. The fact of such opposition to the power of their own class has become so internalized for us as to be virtually transparent. But the *modes* of such opposition might usefully be reconsidered in light of the transformed notion of the semiotic realm, and the intimate mechanisms of conflict that play themselves out within it, which I sketched above. I will argue that the varieties of discursive contestation in this formative period of liberal society are more internally diverse, and considerably more complex and ingenious, than we have sometimes tended to think.

Again it was Gramsci who, in connection with his effort to understand the mechanisms by which social organizations reproduce themselves under the more fluid conditions of the modern polity and socioeconomy, brought to critical consciousness the conflicted concept of the "intellectual." Particularly, Gramsci helps us to see the intellectuals' transformed role as originators and propagators of the discourse and practices which both assure hegemony and, conversely, contest it.[42]

In Gramsci's speculations, intellectuals were divided into two categories: the "organic intellectuals," whose function was to articulate the interests and perspectives of a rising or dominant class; and the "traditional intellectuals," which such a class found already installed in positions of social and structural influence (for example, clergy, teachers, men of letters of various kinds). Between the two categories, the conflict of hegemonic and counter-hegemonic impulses was systemically inevitable.[43]

Placing dissident intellectuals at the "traditional" pole of the opposition may seem to depreciate their significance and ignore their own sense of themselves (particularly later in the century) as an "avant-garde." Gramsci had in mind the fact that the values of the members of this increasingly influential social fraction, according to which they defined that which they were struggling for or against, essentially appealed—through whatever formations or deformations of memo-

42. We should note that the formation of the notion of "intellectual" itself dates from our period. Under the term, Saint-Simon combined the skills of the man of letters and imagination of the artist with the knowledge and prestige of the scientist to produce what is essentially the modern conception; see Zeldin, *France*, vol. 1, p. 430.

43. See Gramsci, "The Intellectuals," *Prison Notebooks*, pp. 5–23, and passim; and Chantal Mouffe, "Hegemony and Ideology in Gramsci," p. 187.

ry—to a notion of status or prestige whose model clearly derived from an earlier historical period.[44]

In his study of Baudelaire, Walter Benjamin characterized their consciousness well: each "was in a more or less obscure state of revolt against society, and faced a more or less precarious future" (p. 20). But these members of what in 1874 Gambetta called the "couches nouvelles," these "new layers" of society, had *voices*.[45] Indeed, their possession of the culture's languages *defined* them as a social group. And though (in the now familiar self-characterization emerging from Lautréamont, Rimbaud, and Verlaine) they felt themselves to be *maudits*, "damned,"[46] or no doubt *because* they felt themselves to be damned, they turned their voices against the dominant discourse which sought either to enlist or to marginalize them. With the discursive capacity which distinguished them, they strove to desaturate and disestablish its ideological predominance.

In this regard it is essential to note the *strategic* location of writers, and of the practice of writing, in this early period of struggle to subvert the dominant. The intimate connection of writers with the processes producing and reproducing discourses first focalized discourses themselves *as objects,* and hence as subject to subversion. Knowing how discourses were made served as ideal preparation for those who were seeking increasingly in this period to unmake them.

Under earlier, more absolutist social and sign systems, any cultural expression of resistance issued immediately into the political realm, if only because a social formation based upon formal notions of status (the *états* or *Stände*) and of differential allocations of legal privilege ("liberties") automatically perceived any challenge or competition as a *threat*. Such formations lack more supple mechanisms for dealing with dissidence. They tend thus to process it through mechanisms which to us seem draconian.

---

44. On such derivation of the intellectuals' self-conception, see Horkheimer, "Feudal Lord," pp. 124–35. On the number of intellectuals and their increase in nineteenth-century France, see Zeldin, *France*, vol. 1, p. 480, and vol. 2, p. 376, and Hobsbawm, *Age of Capital*, p. 330.

45. Duchet, *Manuel d'histoire littéraire*, p. 15.

46. See Bernard, *Poème en prose*, p. 217; Duchet, *Manuel d'histoire littéraire*, p. 369, and part 2, chap. 4; Rimbaud, "L'homme juste," l. 23; *Oeuvres*, ed. Suzanne Bernard and André Guyaux (Paris: Garnier, 1981), p. 113. I will return to the problem of the poet's malediction in Part 3.

We may then historicize Gramsci's distinction between *rule* and *hegemony*—or parallel to it, Althusser's contrast between *repressive* and *ideological* apparatuses.[47] The characteristic means of controlling counter-discourses in social formations before nineteenth-century liberal capitalism was simply to choke them off. But in the nineteenth century both the production and the management of such cultures of resistance, from the nascent to the most fully formed and systematic, entered a period of considerable transition, uncertainty, and innovation. A space was opened up within which discourse could explore multivalent (and, I will argue, immensely creative) strategies of dissidence and dissent. These developments are what makes the problematic I intend to examine here pertinent and rich.

This study celebrates the power and the inventiveness of a certain mode of cultural resistance in the nineteenth century; but simultaneously, it must mark the limits of such resistance. For at every turn, counter-discourses registered the difficulty of any authentic victory over the domination against which they discovered they were struggling.

Of course it would be naive to think that explicitly repressive mechanisms ceased altogether to be employed. About the nineteenth century's history of counterrevolutionary violence nothing we might say could take the measure of the brutality exercised against opposition to established power. And the history of censorship in the period—intimately tied to that of active revolutionary efforts but also to that of more subtle battles over class self-conception, reputation, morality, and the like—demonstrates an equal, if more subtle, violence. The trials of Daumier and Philipon, of Baudelaire and Flaubert, testify sufficiently to this.[48] Such efforts by the state modified the possibilities for certain strategies of counter-discourse and opened the way to energizing others, in ways which will prove illuminating.

Nonetheless, all sides of the dispute took the market phenomenon to be the most characteristic modality of social interaction in nineteenth-century society—whether they praised the profusion of goods which it placed in circulation or condemned its debasing function, its adultera-

47. On the Althusserian parallel to Gramsci, see "Ideology and Ideological State Apparatuses," pp. 127–86.

48. For a striking reading of Flaubert's trial and its ideological-historical meaning, see LaCapra, *"Madame Bovary" on Trial.*

tion of the community remembered (falsely or not) from earlier formations. The phenomenon of the market operated in the world of discursive production as well. Of course this was so first because the writer had to sell his product—a fact which has long been studied, and of which the essay on Balzac's *Lost Illusions* in Lukács's *Studies in European Realism* is no doubt the major expression. But in a more subtle sense the market operated because the relative depoliticization of liberal society loosened the relation between counter-discursive production and any direct political threat. It was constitutive of the system, a figure of its distinctness, that "opposition" was legitimized. Parties, factions, were no longer viewed as incipient conspiracies whose existence must be decisively expunged (though this habit of mind lingered on as a residual element of consciousness, particularly among the reactionary politicians of the period) but as normal expressions and analogues of the competitive process at the heart of the social formation.

This conception of the market mediated the birth of an entirely new discursive system. Within it, modes of resistance and subversion could exhibit a variety of strategies for marking their adversative position which probably had no parallel in any earlier period. The suppleness of the system increased substantially in proportion to its internal complication and differentiation. And the sensitivity of modulations marking the affirmative or negative bearing of any discursive expression led progressively to a more delicate and more minute social calculus than any which had previously been seen. I will argue in the chapters which follow that as the modes of living or of writing one's opposition to the dominant forms of social existence or to its characteristic discourse became more varied and more subtle, the entire phenomenon of opposition itself was fundamentally transformed.

What made such a resituation of discursive contestation possible was the same process by which power in this period diffused through the social formation, by which it simultaneously increased the range and the subtlety of its exercise. These inflections situate Gramsci's notion of the hegemonic. The concept attempts to take account of the increasingly intricate means by which the social force of dominant interests in society could be exerted over larger and more diverse populations than could ever have been coerced by the older mechanisms of the traditional oppressive state.

The rise and progressive definition of a materialist concept of "determination" in this period is isomorphic with these developments, co-determinate with them. From this perspective, older forms of mechanical materialism—directly imposed action of a sovereign subject upon a dependent object—seem homologous with superseded forms of the state and with the immediate exertion of its power. Of course control still needed to be exercised and was exercised, but typically with less of the overt violence which had characterized previous regimes of power. New notions of more complex and more covert determination attempted to grasp the new conditions under which social power was deployed. Both in its practice and in its theory liberal society was discovering *mediation*—ideologically necessary for preserving its new structures of legitimation, practically indispensable for organizing its affairs.

But under the transformed conditions of liberal capitalism, the quintessential mediations by which society ceaselessly and almost imperceptibly produces and reproduces its forms are its proliferating and omnipresent discourses. The problem of discourse thus turns out to be the problem of the modern seized from the inside. And the struggles in this realm become the most characteristic locus of the contestation by which resistance to dominant tendencies has never ceased to be exercised by significant forces within the social whole.

Cultures of Resistance:
On the Conflict of Discourse

Against a background like the one figured by these sociohistorical traces, the problem of ideology, and the attendant notion of the discourse, emerged into pertinence in the nineteenth century in Europe. Put simply, discourses are the complexes of signs and practices which organize social existence and social reproduction. In their structured, material persistence, discourses are what give differential substance to membership in a social group or class or formation, which mediate an internal sense of belonging, an outward sense of otherness.

But we need to be careful about *defining* a concept like the discourse. Such a notion must be referred to the problematic from which it emerges, for this determines its operational sense. This is particularly true for concepts within the theoretical field of historical materialism.

Raymond Williams makes the point clearly in discussion of the Gramscian notion of "hegemony," which, as I have argued, is the point in theoretical development at which the concept of the discourse emerges as a crucial formation: "Like any . . . Marxist concept, [hegemony] is particularly susceptible to epochal as distinct from historical definition, and to categorical as distinct from substantial description. Any isolation of its 'organizing principles,' or of its 'determining features,' which have indeed to be grasped in experience and by analysis, can lead very quickly to a totalizing abstraction."[49] This methodological caveat needs to be kept in mind as we consider the problem of dominant- and counter-discourses and their conflict in the nineteenth century.

Influential strains from outside the Marxist tradition seem in agreement with its thinking about these questions. The most systematic contemporary development of the concept of the discourse is that of Michel Foucault. Foucault seems to be echoing Gramsci and, beyond him, Marx himself, in one of his most striking statements concerning the question: "Discourse is not simply that which expresses struggles or systems of domination, but that for which, and by which, one struggles; it is the power which one is striving to seize."[50] The reminiscence of Marx's description of ideology in the 1859 preface to *A Contribution to the Critique of Political Economy* is clear. Marx's passage runs as follows: "In studying such [revolutionary] transformations, it is always necessary to distinguish between the material transformation of the economic conditions of production, which can be determined with the precision of natural science, and the legal, political, religious, artistic or philosophic—in short, ideological forms in which men become conscious of this conflict and fight it out" (p. 21). In turn, Gramsci's image of two hegemonic principles tensely confronting each other in the paradigmatic situation of social conflict seems just over the horizon of Foucault's description, if not already present within it.[51]

One can detect an evolution in Foucault's work which draws his notion of discourses steadily *toward* the conceptualization which has long been central to the Marxist tradition. Essentially he moves from an early conception of discourse as static object to a notion of *discursive*

49. *Marxism and Literature*, p. 112.
50. *L'ordre du discours*, p. 12.
51. See the *Quaderni del Carcere*, ed. V. Gerratana (Turin: Einaudi, 1975), vol. 2, p. 1236; and Mouffe, "Hegemony and Ideology in Gramsci," p. 186.

practice or production. (See Cavallari, "*Savoir* and *Pouvoir*," p. 57 and n. 5.) Foucault himself clarifies the bearing of such a distinction: "Discursive practices are not purely and simply ways of producing discourse, they are embodied in technical processes, in institutions, in patterns for general behavior, in forms for transmission and diffusion, and in pedagogical forms which, at once, impose and maintain them."[52]

In *L'ordre du discours*, Foucault systematizes his notion of the constraints which are the other side of the dialectic of free individual discourse production. Such constraints produce the "order of discourse" and maintain intelligibility and sociocultural significance in the face of the contingency of individual impulse. Foucault distinguishes three modes of such ordering: the coercive taboo upon the forbidden, the irrational, the mad, and the false; the internalization by individuals of such outward authority in the form of "naturalized" habits and practices; finally, material control over access to or production of discourse through barriers to appropriation, circulation, and so on.

Yet it is essential that none of these principles of constraint can ever operate with totalitarian consistency. In modern societies the loci of individual discourses are simply too diffuse (as indeed are those of the authority which might sanction or suppress them), the social interests in play are too divergent, for any policy of discursive policing ever fully to expunge the subversive. The space for the counter-discourses which will occupy me below is opened in that structural limitation of social control.

So no dominant discourse is ever fully protected from contestation. Of course the counter-discourses which exploit such vulnerability implicitly evoke a principle of order just as systematic as that which sustains the discourses they seek to subvert. Ultimately, in the image of the counterhegemonic—conceived now as the emergent principle of history's dynamism, as the force which ensures the flow of social time

---

52. *Language, Counter-Memory, Practice*, p. 200. The pedagogical aspect of such practices will be considered in some detail in Chapter 1 below. On the extension of the notion of discourse to institutions and practices which we do not ordinarily think of as lying within the category of speech or text, see Jameson, *Political Unconscious*, pp. 296–97. For example, in Chapter 2 below I will make the argument that the unprecedented practices of shopping and consumer behavior which developed in response to nineteenth-century innovations in merchandising, and particularly to the advent of the department store, represent a discourse, and are analyzable as such.

itself—the counter-discourse always projects, just over its own horizon, the dream of victoriously replacing its antagonist.

Yet for all this the dominant dominates. And it is the means by which it does so that makes its analysis so baffling. How can we locate, and how characterize, the ubiquitous? This is the problem which faces the analyst of a dominant discourse—and it is no different in its configuration from the one confronting its contesters. Essentially the problem is to achieve the necessary distance, to project the metalanguage on the basis of which a hegemonic discourse can be reconfigured as relative, as contingent, and thus as potentially transcendable.

It is in the nature of the problem that no empirical "proof" of the existence of a dominant discourse is possible. Transparency is one of its conditions of existence. Conversely, demonstrations of its incompleteness, its partiality, its internal ruptures cannot invalidate the conviction that such hegemonic discourses are operative and determinant. But I will argue that the very work of contestation which detects such ruptures makes us most directly aware of the dominant's massive, seemingly ineradicable power.

If a notion like "dominant discourse" is to be useful at all, it must be made so in light of the definitional caveat I alluded to earlier. We must not be taken in by the rhetorical abbreviation in the phrase "dominant discourse." The moving and flowing network of practices and assumptions by which, at any of a series of endlessly divisible given moments, social life is structured ought not be abstractly reified. Such a hypostatization would ignore that dominant discourse is not a "thing" but a complex and shifting formation. It is as diffuse as a way of feeling, of experiencing the body, of perceiving sensorially, of living work and leisure, of assimilating information, of communicating with others within the social world, of comprehending the organization of conflict, of experiencing the inevitable hierarchizations of social existence.

In the chapters that follow, however, it will be possible to offer only instantiations of a dominant discourse which, nowhere and everywhere at once, must never be taken to represent some higher structure, some more authentic reality, lying beyond or behind the examples and practices in which it is bodied forth. Dominant discourse is an unlimited series of instances of which only a few of the more pervasive can be evidenced here. At most the articulations between such instances point up the coherent social interests which they further, and those which they tend, most often quietly and subtly, to subordinate.

As already suggested in Foucault's delimitation of the field of the discursive, it is in institutions, particularly those embodying innovative responses to the changing context in which discursive formations become operative, that such functioning itself can be most readily detected. Perhaps the most totalizing of these for our period is the "nation" itself. It was of course not a spontaneous growth but a constructed artifact. And the institutions—primarily the state in its role as administrator of civil society, as national employer, as national educator and defender—capable of *imposing* uniformity around practices harmonious with dominant interests will preoccupy me at several points in the chapters to follow.

Such institutions and such practices are mutually legitimating. Pierre Bourdieu has put this relation well: "Because any language that can command attention is an 'authorized language,' invested with the authority of a group, the things it designates are not simply expressed, but also authorized and legitimated."[53] Bourdieu goes on to point out that this is true not only of what he calls "establishment language" but also of "heretical discourses" much like those which will concern me throughout. But it is evident that, if all such discourses draw their authority from the groups over which they exercise their power and whose definition they reciprocally establish, the authority and the power exercised by the nation will generally play a predominating role.

As such structures tend toward internalization in the subjects practicing them according to Foucault's tripartite conceptualization of the mechanism by which discursive reproduction and stability are sustained, they form themselves into something which looks very much like what Bourdieu understands in the notion of the "habitus":

> The structures constitutive of a particular type of environment (e.g. the material conditions of existence characteristic of a class condition) produce *habitus,* systems of durable, transposable *dispositions,* structured structures predisposed to function as structuring structures, that is, as principles of the generation and structuring of practices and

53. *Theory of Practice,* p. 170.

representations which can be objectively "regulated" and "regular" without in any way being the product of obedience to rules.[54]

But just as, according to Bourdieu, we can read in the habitus the inscription of "history turned into nature" (p. 78), we can equally well see in it registrations of all the other shaping disciplines which configure our existence: the politics, the economics, the sociology, and so on.

Their inscriptions in the practices of everyday existence, more or less determined from without, more or less internalized and rendered habitual, lead to an important realization concerning the character of habitus, of ideology, of dominant discourse, in the nineteenth century in Europe. For during periods of rapid change, the penetration of the habitus, the internalization of dominant discourse, will necessarily be less complete than in periods of relative social stability. And this differential perfusion of the social field can become an important analytical tool.

Thus, for example, the extraordinary virulence of the critique directed against the nineteenth-century bourgeoisie, the clear angry sense of oppression felt by the antagonists of that class in its growing domination, appear to us as an effect of the relatively *early* stage of its consolidation of (discursive) power. Later on, it will become harder to feel this clarity, precisely as middle-class power increases and its struggle to become orthodoxy succeeds (see *Theory of Practice*, p. 190).

A fully functional habitus, a system of dominant discourse which has passed from the stage of coercion to that of hegemony in Gramsci's terms, would ensure the continuity of the established order in an automatic way. Those dominating the system could be confident that, left on its own, it would reproduce the conditions by which such domination is made possible. But such automatism was far from the case in the nineteenth century. The structures of hegemony were simply too new, and the energy of those contesting them too great. The interests such energy sustained proved too cantankerously resistant for the critiques and the subversions they directed against dominant discourse ever to cease or to be completely neutralized. A relative fluidity, in which the outcome of the battle might almost seem still to have been

---

54. *Theory of Practice*, p. 72.

in doubt, thus characterizes the period and the counter-discourses active within it, which never quite abandoned the dream of disrupting the habitus so fully that it would simply collapse.

One case, to be analyzed in detail in Chapter 4, deserves particular mention here. Though not all of the counter-discourses which sought to subvert the transparence of the dominant were primarily literary, the one which most systematically attempted to expunge the "way people thought and talked" under the new conditions of nineteenth-century existence—the technique I will term "re/citation"—specifically marshaled the resources of the literary to engage the everyday. Yet as Flaubert discovered, the dominant discourse which he sought to destroy by displaying it was impossible to *produce*, since it was inexhaustible.

A quintessential difference between the literary realm of discourse and the more diffuse world of social existence was disastrously figured thereby. For the apparatus of dominant discourse, unlike the text, has no final sentence and never concludes. The clichés run along endlessly under their own power. Under such conditions of combat, the literary inevitably appears outflanked, *dépassé*. The perception of such a constitutive inadequacy will haunt a number of the figures whose combats will be examined below. But the fact of such discursive sedimentation is crucial. It mirrors the division of labor, which was greatly increasing in complexity in our period. And as such it inevitably inscribes a hierarchy. Such a situation clearly implies a tactic for deflecting contestation. If, as Mary Louise Pratt argues, the notion of "literature" is itself normative, its assertion as such must be counted as a defensive reaction against the tactics of marginalization within the broader field of social discourse.[55] This dialectic of exclusion and approbation will become particularly crucial in the discussion of *avant-garde* prose in Part 3 below.

55. *Speech Act Theory*, p. 123. The model for such marginalization forms the substance of Herbert Marcuse's concern in *One-Dimensional Man*. See also Kristeva, *Révolution du langage poétique*, p. 440. There is an evident relation between the phenomenon in question here and what Fredric Jameson has called the "strategy of containment" (*Political Unconscious*, p. 10). Dominant discourse, when it is fully functional, projects the most airtight strategy of containment of any discourse. Through it a censorship is imposed which brackets any questioning of the very content and form of the dominant; counter-discourses are simply rendered invisible.

The inherent tendency of a dominant discourse is to "go without saying." The dominant is the discourse whose presence is defined by *the social impossibility of its absence*. Because of that implicit potential toward automatism, the dominant is the discourse which, being everywhere, comes from nowhere: to it is granted the structural privilege of appearing to be unaware of the very question of its own legitimacy. Bourdieu calls this self-assured divorce from consciousness of its own contingency "genesis amnesia."[56] And it is one of the conditions of possibility of that assumption of (false) totalization by which the dominant tends to efface anything which does not fall within its own orbit or appear consonant with its own interests.

Such false totalization is an immanent law in capitalist socioeconomies. It was recognized as such at least as early as Marx's assertion in the first volume of *Capital* that an essential characteristic of capitalist production requires that the total amount of capital, and hence the fraction of a socioeconomy subsumed within the capitalist mode of production, must always increase (p. 480). This implicit dynamic helps us to understand the frequency and diversity of the ideological impulse toward seeing dominant social practices and perceptions as "universal." Such a dynamic particularly explains the constant imputation of ubiquity to the dominant commercial, ideological, and political mechanisms of the nineteenth century. An entire social form was commandeered and transformed to organize their celebration: the traditional fair. The "universal" expositions of the nineteenth century were one of its striking innovations. Their deepest function, from my perspective here, was to consecrate the triumphs of the dominant mechanism. Such celebrations of universality powerfully focused nineteenth-century imaginations.[57]

56. *Theory of Practice*, p. 79.

57. This illusion finds its most sophisticated theoretical expression in Hegel's projection of the administrative bourgeoisie as "universal class"—an illusion which Marx deflated. See Kristeva, *Révolution du langage poétique*, pp. 379–80. On the extraordinary popularity of the "universal" expositions, see Zeldin, *France*, vol. 2, p. 613, and particularly Benjamin, *Baudelaire*, p. 165: "World exhibitions were places of pilgrimage to the fetish commodity." The relation between these imputations of totality to the technical-commercial perspective of the dominant middle class will return as a concern in Chapter 2 below, in my discussion of the transformed field of social exchange in the daily newspaper and the department store.

The claim of universality was sustainable because, as even its opponents in the period conceived it, "there was no alternative to capitalism as a method of economic development."[58] But acceptance of such an unanswerable premise entailed acceptance of an entire network of ideological and rhetorical consequences. The dominant discourses thus came to appear as the naturalized expression of the social formation itself, as the self-evident form of utterance, the system of sense-making which, precisely, "went without saying."

In modern societies it is by this transparency that the "ruling ideas" rule. And in the nineteenth century on the basis of such transparency it became possible to imagine something like a coherent interpretive community whose expectations and reactions could be projected in advance and assumed as stable and consistent. The function of such a community, from my perspective, would seem to be to close off the play of signs and discourses around a sense determined according to its own rules for closure. The dominant discourse thus projects what Gerald Prince has called a *narrataire*—politics would term him or her a citizen—who figures as the internalized conscience of the conventional, and simultaneously as resistance to any deviation from its norms.[59] The narrataires of a culture—in some sense, all of us—know the dominant discourse by heart. For these members of the group the dominant becomes the discourse within which the consecrated phrase "and so forth" represents a usable discursive move. For we know the next line of the social script, even without knowing *that* we know it or how we learned it. The dominant is the discourse whose content is always already performable by the general member of the population.

So dominant discourse is a *necessary language,* unreflectively present to itself but—what may be more significant—also present for any *other* discourse, even in denial or absence. It is thus the creator of problems for any alternative representation of the world: "A dominant discourse is the imposition, not so much of certain truths . . . as of a certain language . . . , which the opposition itself is obliged to employ to make its objections known."[60] We may call it an "establishment lan-

58. Hobsbawm, *Age of Capital,* p. 275.

59. See Gerald Prince, "Introduction à l'étude du narrataire." On the notion of convention, see David K. Lewis, *Convention,* and Becker, *Art Worlds,* pp. 55–56, and passim.

60. Descombes, *Modern French Philosophy,* p. 108.

guage" (Bourdieu); a "langue obligatoire" (an "obligatory language"; Michel de Certeau); "langage normalisé" ("normalized language"; Kristeva)—among numerous alternative designations. But whatever its name, the dominant discourse appears within the social formation like the unmarked case in linguistics—noticed only in its violation, effective precisely because it seems to require no special assertion to achieve such effectivity.[61]

I need to acknowledge that there is something suspect in speaking about a dominant discourse in the context of a period so alive with contradictions and diversity as the nineteenth century. The complex succession of nineteenth-century governments in France imposes a periodization of political history which might lead one to suppose that no coherent dominant discourse could be defined for the sweep of the entire epoch. But as against such a notion, the infrastructural arguments of the Marxist tradition, based upon the longer-term hypothesis of a progressively developing "mode of production," would suggest that such a dominant discourse underlay the volatility of the period's diverse political discourses, and, indeed, even of its literary styles.

There were surely changes over the long span of time, some of which I will consider below. Notably, in the earlier part of the century, when one might say that the game was still up for grabs, counter-discourse tended to take the form of direct *thematic* contestation. Conversely, as the period wore on, the increasing hegemony of an infrastructural discourse became the first condition under which any other discourse could be produced and socially circulated. It is in such a situation, I will argue, that the more subtly subversive *formal and functional* strategies which I will examine here become pertinent.

Having asserted as an operational hypothesis the power of a reigning sociosymbolic and discursive system in the form of what Marcuse

---

61. Bourdieu, *Theory of Practice*, p. 170; de Certeau, *L'invention du quotidien*, vol. 1, p. 18; Kristeva, *Révolution du langage poétique*, p. 13. On the "unmarked case," see Pratt, *Speech Act Theory*, p. 55, n. 3, and p. 205. Derrida remarks on the essentially negative valence of "neutral" cases ("De l'économie restreinte à l'économie générale," p. 402). Concerning the apparently effortless power of dominant ideologies, Bourdieu remarks that what identifies such formations is their capacity to cause even ideological analysis itself to be accused of the sin of ideology ("faire tomber la science de l'idéologie sous l'accusation d'idéologie"). See *Ce que parler veut dire*, p. 196.

called a "status quo which defies all transcendence,"[62] it would seem essential to begin to map the dialectic which opens a space for attempts at its subversion. Two points seem essential. The first is implicit in Bourdieu's distinction between what he calls "doxa"—"quasi-perfect correspondence between the objective order and the subjective principles of organization (as in ancient societies), [in which] the natural and social world appears as self-evident"—and "orthodoxy"—"straight, or rather *straightened* opinion, which aims, without ever entirely succeeding, at restoring the primal state of innocence of doxa."[63]

We may leave aside the question of whether anything like "doxa" has ever existed as other than a theoretical construct. It follows from Bourdieu's distinction that in historical societies dominant discourses always have a guilty conscience. Because "genesis amnesia" can never be total, at some level the dominant knows itself to be a usurpation. Such an act of force, of what Bourdieu and Passeron call "symbolic violence,"[64] presents its own ideological dangers within liberal society, predicated as it is on the fiction of consent. And, as I will argue, the consciousness (however vague) of such usurpations is exploitable by those who would seek to dethrone the discourses which they sustain.

Secondly, a dominant discourse necessarily suffers the drawbacks of its own virtues. When a particular social practice emerges as hegemonic, its relation to other competing and contesting practices is subtly altered. By virtue of its status as dominant, it becomes the target for "vampirization," for colonization, for subversion by its rivals. It begins to be the inevitable referent of their counter-assertions. And, as in the parable about the jailer and the jailed, those seeking to undo it necessarily spend more time and energy toward this end than the dominant can spend countering such efforts.

In any case, the process of such a dialectic rigidifies the forms of the dominant itself, precisely because its proponents and its antagonists together hypostatize it as the dominant practice. Yet because it is not constituted once for all as a static object but as a complex of functions the most crucial of which is its capacity to *signify* the dominant, to be recognized and exploited as such, dominant discourse is immediately

62. *One-Dimensional Man*, p. 17.
63. *Theory of Practice*, pp. 164, 169.
64. *Reproduction*, p. xi and passim.

opened to microinterventionist contestation, to functional disruptions of the sorts which Michel de Certeau has so effectively focalized within a theory of everyday life in *L'invention du quotidien*.

It is this hypostatization of the dominant discourse as the target for all dissident marksmen that lends certain discursive battles their apparently contentless quality, as if the combat were purely formal. In the formalization of such struggles, certain practices and signs take on an emblematic class character which could in no sense have been predicted or posited for them. They are *positioned* as such, caught up in the struggle defined by the sorts of dyadic oppositions I began by examining, articulated as ideological elements in a struggle between two would-be hegemonic formations. Yet behind the abstract opposition, the diacritical, semiotic contradiction figured by such competitions is a complex of real, competing interests which struggle, under their own forms, to realize themselves as Marx suggested, to "become aware of the battle and fight it out."[65]

We might thus posit something like a Newton's Third Law in the discursive realm: for every dominant discourse, a contrary and transgressive counter-discourse. The fundamental paradox of such linkage is well expressed in a remark by Fredric Jameson concerning desire: "It is a commonplace that transgressions presupposing the laws or norms or taboos against which they function, thereby end up precisely reconfirming such laws."[66]

I will argue that the consciousness of such systemic reversals feeds back into the counter-discourse itself as the most profound antagonist against which it seeks its own assertion. The contesters discover that the authority they sought to undermine is reinforced by the very fact of its having been chosen, as dominant discourse, for opposition.

The conditions of possibility of counter-discursive assertion need to be further theorized. What is the space, what are the modalities, for discursive contestation? What is the place of discursive engagement? The counter-discourse situates its struggle somehow and somewhere

---

65. Bourdieu discusses the movement of *diacrisis* in *Ce que parler veut dire*, Part 2, chaps. 2 and 3. On the almost arbitrary attribution of discursive signification, see particularly Mouffe, "Hegemony and Ideology in Gramsci," pp. 193–94, and her discussion with Ernesto Laclau, "Recasting Marxism," p. 101.

66. *Political Unconscious*, p. 68.

within the conflicted cultural field with whose projection I began my discussion. And it functions by a kind of violence (see Kristeva, *Révolution du langage poétique,* p. 14) whose specific economy we will need to comprehend. It will be necessary to demonstrate the critical functionality of the counter-discourse, its tactics of opposition, its point of leverage against—and thereby, of contact with—the discourses which it contests, whose hegemony it seeks to subvert.

The nineteenth century is no doubt the counter-discourse's classic moment. The open and virulent anger felt by the antibourgeois for the bourgeois can rarely have been more evident or more focused. Indeed, as my Preface suggested, it was all the more corrosive because typically it was driven by the personal guilt of a conflicted class identity, by personal implication in the detested formation itself. Alienated middle-class writers may have cherished alienation, but they *hated* an irretrievably middle-class identity. The anger generated out of such a crux provides the subjective dynamism of the counter-discourse; its virulence becomes the principle of the counter-discourse's social importance. It constituted what Kristeva termed an "assault of negativity" against the social and discursive real.[67]

Immense energy was released by the bourgeois revolution, liberated by the new mode of production. But in cultural terms it required reinvestment, recontainment. This necessity is at the heart of counter-discursive combat. For in an early version of capitalism's fundamental contradictions, in a kind of structural unemployment of the discursive workforce, it turned out that a significant proportion of such new energy simply could not be reabsorbed. It could find no adequate accommodation within the society's dominant economic and sociosymbolic structures. So the energy of negation which alienated artists and their counter-discourses directed against the dominant might almost seem the massive production of discursive surplus values unable to find any authorized or acceptable mode for reentering the system. They were thereby obliged to an uncomfortable and unstable existence on its margins. Such marginalization will concern me repeatedly in the chapters to follow, particularly in consideration of the prose poem in Chapters 6 and 7.

But here, parallel to a description of the social need which deter-

---

67. *Révolution du langage poétique,* p. 612.

mined counter-discursive strategies in the nineteenth century, it would seem necessary to explain how the attempt to conceptualize the counter-discursive function itself becomes imaginable. One clue toward such an accounting (depending upon the modes of reinvestment available for the discursive surplus values to which I have alluded) would be to suppose that a particularly privileged form of counter-discourse in our period—that of mass anticapitalist and antibourgeois popular social movements—increasingly appeared to have failed. Such mass political movements for a time had plausibly asserted themselves as alternatives to envelopment by the dominant here-and-now. But after 1848, after 1871 particularly, such assertion came to seem hollow. The force of the more formal counter-discursive tactics which grew up as the century wore on would seem to depend on such a decline.

In other words the totality of the nineteenth-century discursive system can be conceived by us as such *because* the revolutionary social force which at times seemed so close to overturning the internal hierarchy of the dominant has, since its failure, become radically displaced in consciousness. The imaginative locus of the *alternative* has shifted in response to inflections in the course of social history itself. But from our perspective the memory of *real* revolutions has made it possible to analyze and to situate the naively hopeful metaphoricity of those *poetic* revolutions of which the nineteenth century made so much. We can conceive the systemic character of the discursive system precisely insofar as in nineteenth-century social experience it manifested itself, intermittently but crucially, as contingent, threatened, potentially unbalanceable: it *might* have been overturned, and it *did* severely shake from time to time. It is such experiences which make analysis of the more mediated, more subterranean subversions of the dominant modes of social life both pertinent and intellectually possible. So these counter-discourses inscribe within themselves a failure of social struggle to achieve infrastructural resolution of the stresses within the new formation. To invert the classic Marxian formulation, in our period the criticism of weapons had of necessity to be replaced by the weapons of criticism.[68]

This fact frames the discursive field and clarifies the internal tensions which stress it. Like all subversive thought, the counter-discourse is

---

68. See "Toward the Critique of Hegel's Philosophy of Law," p. 257.

intensely—if surreptitiously—parasitic upon its antagonist. The dialogical theory of signs and discourses which emerges from Bakhtin argues persuasively that the realm of social discourse is always the locus of such tension. But it was particularly strong, and bore particularly complex disguises, in nineteenth-century France.

It is therefore critical to provide as precise an account as can be derived from the conjuncture in which each counter-discourse appeared of its individual *mode* of relation, its specific tactic of opposition, to the adversary which it projected for itself. Such accounts constitute a map. For in their opposition to the dominant, counter-discourses function to survey its limits and its internal weaknesses. From this dialectic of discursive struggle, truths about the social formation—its characteristic modes of reproduction and its previously hidden vulnerabilities—inevitably emerge.[69]

Once one posits consciousness of a dominant discourse, then a series of diverse and unpredictable openings toward strategies of counter-discourse will successively be detected and exploited. The varieties of counter-discourse are related only in that they contest the dominant. There will be no necessary homology among them. Still, the existence of such counter-discourses retroactively demonstrates on both theoretical and empirical levels that at a given moment the possibility of some *échappée*, some opening to undermine or to problematize the dominant, presented itself to imagination under the given ideological, linguistic, and practical conditions. Under such conditions the tactics for exploiting the opening took form. Their angle of contestation can only be discovered empirically; we cannot "deduce" from any set of possible strategies the one imagination devised to pursue the combat. But however distant such a strategy may be from the protocols of the discourse which it contests, we should never lose sight of the fact that they are its inevitable referent. We might argue that counter-discourses tend, in their relation to the dominant, to homology with the body's reaction to disease: either they seek to surround their antagonist and neutralize or explode it (the technique which in Chapter 4 I will term re/citation); or they strive to exclude it totally, to expunge it (what I will call de/citation in the discussion of the prose poem in Chapters 6 and 7). Between these theoretical extremes, like an unpredictable series

---

69. Concerning such mapping, see de Certeau, *La fable mystique*, Introduction.

of guerrilla skirmishes, the multiform violations of the norms of the dominant constitute the realm of functionality of the counter-discourse.

It is important to realize that although norms can be violated in a number of ways, this number is not infinite. Such violation is not random. We might compare the general problem with the more specific one of syntax and its violation in Mallarmé which I will discuss in my final chapter. Mallarmé's writing places syntax under stress almost to the point of rupture. But the actual *suspension* of syntax would interrupt intelligibility altogether. Such a text could achieve no socially effective intervention at all. No one would understand it. So in relation to the norm, its violation strives for the greatest possible distance, but *without* disconnection.

In thus acting upon dominant discourse in the mode almost of a Hegelian dialectical opposition, the counter-discourse produces a "reading" of the discursive system as a whole in its possibilities and in its operations—a kind of *état présent* of the residual and emergent tendencies within it which force any synchronic or unitary account of the cultural situation toward the movement of the diachronic and drive it beyond itself. Through such implicit tracing by the counter-discursive, an energetics or thermodynamics within the system emerges into critical consciousness.

This profoundly conflicted relationship with the dominant might be resumed in the image of Mallarmé's activity as editor of the fashion magazine which he called *La Dernière Mode:* "After picking up several articles from here and there, I attempted to compose on my own [the articles on] women's clothing, jewelry, furniture, and even the theater column and the recipes, in a periodical, *La Dernière Mode,* whose eight or ten published numbers, when I brush off the dust upon them, still send me into long reveries."[70] In our terms, the discourses of *la mode,* of fashion, are the very sign of what comes to appear, socially, as *unanswerable:* the sign of the dominant. An ambivalent consciousness of it, an ambiguous *attraction to it,* thus becomes a crucial focus of the counter-discursive. The reverie which Mallarmé describes himself falling into is itself an attitude whose relation to the phenomenon in

70. *Oeuvres complètes,* ed. Henri Mondor and G. Jean-Aubry (Paris: Gallimard-Pléiade, 1945), pp. 664, 1624–25. Baudelaire's *dandysme* would have to be discussed in relation to the profound and paradoxical *attraction* exercised by the fashionable, by the *mode,* on these most radically nonconformist and pattern-breaking imaginations.

question here is worth some thought. Like the dreams of escape—to the Americas, to the Orient—which haunted the romantics and their successors (and which I will consider in Chapter 5), it represents a preverbal avatar of the fantasy projection of total withdrawal from the orbit of the dominant which, just above, I termed "de/citation." I will return to it at the end of this study.

It may well be, as Georges Bataille argued, that the "individualist insurrection" against the middle-class is only "an anti-bourgeois style [*allure*] of bourgeois individualism."[71] But even if this were so, it would only represent a more pernicious and persistent presence within the logic of the counter-discourse of the perverse and subterranean fascination which the dominant exercises over its antagonist. What we seem to encounter is an endless play of discursive subversion and reenvelopment, for which no effective *verbal* conclusion would seem ever to be possible.

Such a configuration evokes the problem of a metalanguage on the basis of which any criticism of a discursive system might be produced. The image of the hierarchy implies by the etymology of "*meta*-language" reveals that we are dealing here with the phenomenon of differential power in yet another of its disguises. Thus a technique like re/citation, when I come to it in discussion of Flaubert's invention of the *sottisier* in Chapter 4, will appear as a doomed attempt to frame or contain that which (as Flaubert himself will discover) ends up seeming rather to contain us in our turn. In another example of the process, Kristeva points out that the most striking of the thematic (as opposed to the formal) contestations of dominant discourse—socialist and anarchist writing—remained despite itself "determined by the same internal economy as that against which it struggles."[72] In a similar way, Benjamin noted that Fourier's elaborate anticapitalist scheme of the Phalanstery surreptitiously expressed a social mechanism in the image of the machine which, usually wielded rather by Fourier's middle-class antagonists, might have seemed the very symbol of their power.[73]

In connection with this unexpected reinscription of the dominant discourse at the center of the discourses which seek its transgression, it would be possible to augment the specificity of my observation con-

71. *La littérature et le mal,* p. 60.
72. *Révolution du langage poétique,* p. 334.
73. *Baudelaire,* pp. 159–60.

cerning the relationship between revolutionary political movements and the more general category of counter-discursive formations. The major utopian and socialist doctrines all developed before 1848: Saint-Simon and Enfantin; Fourier and Considérant; Louis Blanc; Etienne Cabet; Buchez; Proudhon; Pierre Leroux.[74] The change of climate after 1848 was decisive. Direct thematic, programmatic contestation produced counter-discourse only as long as the fluidity of the social formation sustained the belief that the daily history of the society was one of *authentic* competition for control of the structure of events. It was necessary to imagine at least a potential openness to the political struggle, an absence of invisible mechanisms of control restricting the exercise of popular desire to alter the system.

I would thus argue that prior to 1848, perception of the emerging mechanisms of modern hegemony and the infrastructurally regulative function of social discourses was relatively shallow. June 1848 and the aftermath of the counterrevolution shattered this idealized image of a "free market" of ideas. The midcentury reaction decisively brought the *domination* of the dominant organization of society, its hierarchy and its mediations—in addition to the full panoply of its bloody repressive mechanisms—into consciousness. Consequently the locus of combat was displaced. Henceforth counter-discourse proceeded in more subterranean and more subtle ways. But we can speculate that something like the dynamic which had previously sustained explicitly political counter-discourses in their negation of the degraded here-and-now and their projection of a more optimistic alternative were reinvested in these more subtle forms of contestation.[75]

Thus in reflecting on the possibility of a critical or cultural metalanguage, it is important to recall that among the major subversive theoretical positions of the nineteenth century, the only one which developed substantially *after* 1848 was Marx's. This suggests the pertinence of an investigation of the intersection between Marx's own discourse and Flaubert's, which, however unexpected, I will seek to develop in Chapter 4. But already at this point it is reasonable to suggest

74. Zeldin, *France,* vol. 1, p. 453, and chap. 16.

75. On this point see Marcuse, *One-Dimensional Man,* pp. 67–68, quoting Valéry on the commitment of poetic language to negation; and Jameson's argument that all class consciousness, whether hegemonic or oppositional, by its nature projects a utopian moment or impulse (*Political Unconscious,* p. 289).

that in the second half of the century Marx stands as a crucial Other of all of these oppositional doctrines and subversive counter-discourses— if only because after 1848 his system alone projected persuasive super-session of the forms of the here-and-now, a demonstrably alternative structure of social organization. The materialistic dialectic might then figure *the* privileged metalanguage which could situate and contest the fundamental principles by which the existing social formation pro-duced, reproduced, persisted.[76] But of course such a metalanguage— as the cultural and political history of the West over more than a century has demonstrated—has operated under a crucial taboo pre-cisely *because* of its "strategic difference."

The sequence of counter-discourses which will concern me can thus be viewed as a series of attempts *short* of the "revolutionary" to gener-ate what Foucault called "cette parole qui pourtant faisait la différence" ("that language which, despite everything, has made a difference/sus-tained difference").[77] As an example of such a differential language— belonging very much to the nineteenth century but linking it with intense concerns from our own period—we might consider the dis-course of feminism.

It was Fourier who invested the word "feminism" in the first place.[78] The *tactical* significance of the notion, at least, is clear. In the intensely phallocentric universe of the nineteenth-century middle class, the complex of signifiers signifying "female" became available—in-deed, in the constitutive oppositions of social life, it more or less imposed itself—as a crucial figure of social difference.

Of course in the nineteenth century the social group and the cultural values designated by feminist discourse represented a mode of chal-lenge to the dominant formation quite different from that of the hos-tile underclass which never ceased to obsess middle-class imagination.

---

76. A reflection on the possibility of a metalanguage and on the frustrating resistance of the social world to permit its generation is illuminated by the distinction between "strategy" and "tactics" which de Certeau develops early in *L'invention du quotidien,* vol. 1, pp. 20–21. Put simply, a strategy is elaborated from within a discursive space charac-terized by an authentic and sustainable *différence* from the space of its object. The tactic, on the other hand, must live and move within the space of its adversary. Clearly, the counter-discourse situates itself in general in the latter realm. On metalanguages, see Barthes, *Eléments de sémiologie,* pp. 166ff., and Henri Lefebvre, *Everyday Life,* pp. 127–29.

77. *L'ordre du discours,* p. 14.

78. See Zeldin, *France,* vol. 1, p. 345.

However significant the respective claims of the programs which artic-ulated these two subversive perspectives, in the concrete combat of social discourses they differed according to the degree of their practical threat to established values. For the dominant, feminism was a dissi-dent discourse; but the working-class movement was an immediate and chilling *danger*. Consequently, the early discourse of feminism might well seem the archetype of a *specifically* counter-discursive forma-tion in the conjuncture. It had at that point at least still to disengage the full potential of its claims to overturn fundamental elements of the dominant social system. These claims of course have emerged more and more persuasively since that time. But in the nineteenth century, feminism largely remained a still-assimilable, recuperable form of dissi-dence. This then is how we might understand Kristeva's unexpected claim that *women* were the audience projected for the avant-garde texts of the late nineteenth century, or even Derrida's much more recent assertion that "I want to write like a woman."[79] In the context of the problematic under investigation, these ventures are strivings for *dif-ference,* toward the discursive subversion of conjunctural dominance. By overturning precisely the mechanisms which such dominance estab-lishes, they contest a determinate structure of power.

Yet in the case of feminist discourse the constitutive limitations of such counter-discursive undertakings emerge clearly—particularly be-cause the discourse of feminism has grown continuously in social depth and theoretical power since the period which most immediately concerns me here. In the perspective provided by a century of its development, its involuntary implication in the discourse which it contests unveils itself. In this, of course, it is no different from any counter-hegemonic movement. We cannot repeat it often enough: the dominant *remains dominant;* its antagonists are ceaselessly obliged to internalize this fact which defines *all* social reality up to the horizon of the revolutionary. Feminist criticism has itself reflected upon the para-dox: that in feminists' deconstruction of the ideological blindness at the heart of patriarchal practice and theory, their own discourse, how-ever uncomfortably, inevitably locates itself *within* the margins of the dominant. This is no product of some imaginary subservience of the

79. Kristeva, *Révolution du langage poétique,* p. 614; Derrida, "La question du style," p. 228.

feminist perspective to dominant patriarchy: such a situation haunts *all* counter-discursive vision, however hostile, however subversive.[80] And sometimes the absorption of the dissident by its seemingly sovereign antagonist seems all but total.

In "L'engagement de Mallarmé," Sartre was constrained to acknowledge that, while literature was systematically giving society "the silent treatment" (its "grève du silence," p. 172) for almost the entire second half of the nineteenth century, the public hardly noticed. It is this sort of perception which, at their most pessimistic moments, led the figures who sustained such a "strike" against middle-class hegemony to imagine an ironclad, seamless capacity on the part of the structures of power which confronted them simply to ignore any possible subversion, no matter how profoundly felt, no matter how ingeniously crafted.

Yet at the same time that transformations in the socioeconomic realm had profoundly altered the context in which the counter-discursive functioned, in one crucial sense such change modified the vulnerability of its dominant object. Social discourses became the locus of an increasingly conscious struggle. And we might then say that the most fundamental innovation of counter-discourse in the nineteenth century was to have permitted a "reading" of a new economy of power under the transformed conditions of liberal middle-class society. For as I suggested earlier, the system of discourse was deeply sensitive to the new influence of the intelligentsia. Their allegiance was more materially significant than it had ever been before. New disciplines and bodies of knowledge were developing in response to the challenges and opportunities of the new formation: statistics, management and organization, educational pedagogies on all levels of the socialization process, but above all, opinion formation and manipulation of the sort upon which I have already touched, and which I will explore in considerable detail in the discussion of nineteenth-century journalism to fol-

---

80. In the case of feminism the configuration of this complex intertwining emerges in Coppélia Kahn's persuasive discussion in "Excavating Literature." The entire issue of *Diacritics* 12, no. 2, entitled "Feminist Critique/Feminine Text," is of great interest. On the problem of sex roles in the nineteenth century, see my *Dialectics of Isolation*, pp. 53–54. Jonathan Culler discusses the significance of feminism for contemporary critical paradigms in *On Deconstruction*, pp. 172–73.

low in Chapters 2 and 3. These new, or newly central, discourses brought into existence a newly influential category of citizens able to utilize, to administer, the new mechanisms.

Thus as the modality of social organization inflected (in Gramsci's terms) from the mode of "rule" to that of hegemony, the discursive realm, and thus the realm of social power, became subject to perturbation and contestation in unprecedented ways. Ernest Renan was sarcastically clear about this phenomenon at the time:

> In order for free thinking to be possible, it is necessary to be sure that what one publishes will have no consequences. In a state governed by a sovereign master of military power, one is more secure, because one knows that society is protected against its own errors. One becomes timid when society rests only upon itself, and, if one breathes too vigorously, one fears shaking the frail edifice which shelters one.[81]

The analyses of the Frankfurt School, and those of Marcuse and Habermas particularly,[82] have clarified to what degree the stability of social power in the modern period depends upon the manufactured self-evidence of dominant structures. The counter-discourses developing in the nineteenth century seemed to sense such fragility under the surface of seamless bourgeois self-confidence. And they sought to disturb the easy reproduction and reception of dominant discourse. They wanted to breach its self-evidence, to make it appear curious, puzzling. Eventually through such denaturalization they aimed to cast it as positively suspect, as groundless, for the dominant discourse within a liberal formation functions smoothly only as long as its means of functioning go unnoticed. The most deeply critical implications of our century-long tradition of investigation into the phenomena of language and social reproduction emerge from the project to render such mechanisms conscious.

Essentially, then, the object of the counter-discourses under the transformed conditions of the later nineteenth century was to unmask the *fetish character* of modern forms of social domination. Gerald A. Cohen has analyzed this phenomenon and the theory which attempts

---

81. "Dialogues et fragments philosophiques," in *Oeuvres complètes* (Paris: Calmann-Lévy, 1947), vol. 1, p. 553; cited by Kristeva, *Révolution du langage poétique*, p. 480, n. 17.
82. See Marcuse, *One-Dimensional Man,* and Habermas, *Legitimation Crisis.*

to account for it: "To make a fetish of something, or fetishize it, is to invest it with powers it does not in itself have."[83] This foregrounding of the discursive mechanisms mediating the flow of social power suggests the pertinence of Balzac's early investigation of the increasingly semiotized character of social reality in his period, which I will consider in detail in the next chapter. The new status of the sign and the coincident production of its concept and its analysis represent crucial moments in the emergence of any possibility of understanding the transformed mechanisms of social control and of altering them.

The most characteristic tone of the counter-discourse, though it may range through astonishing diversities of tactics, was a corrosive irony concerning the here-and-now. Of course, straight parody is only one mode of marshaling such irony. Bakhtin suggests the key point which opens the space for the investigation which follows here: "The nature and methods available for ridiculing something are highly varied, and not exhausted by parodying and travestying in a strict sense."[84] On the contrary, I will argue that rejection of the here-and-now in nineteenth-century discourses at times took highly unpredictable forms and produced deeply influential modes of writing.

In the course of suggestive discussion of the functioning of the ironic, Rainer Warning cites Hegel's definition of irony: "infinite absolute negativity."[85] But a distinction needs to be made between irony as a totalizing antithesis of some positive reality and irony as it functions in sociocultural contexts. There, for the reasons I have already examined, its negation can never be so absolute. As deployed in the counter-discourses of the nineteenth century, irony can be understood as the rhetorical figure of the *dialogic*. It materializes the counter-term which any dominant usage seeks to suppress. Its function is to project an alternative through which any element of the here-and-now may be shown as contingent, and thereby to subject the whole configuration of power within which it took its adversative meaning to the erosive, dialectical power of alterity. Particularly with the passing of the utopian impulse after midcentury, irony became the linguistic repository

---

83. See Cohen, *Karl Marx's Theory of History*, p. 115 and chap. 5 generally.
84. *Dialogic Imagination*, p. 52.
85. "Irony and the 'Order of Discourse,'" p. 263.

of difference. In itself, as trope, it represents something like a minimalist subversion, a zero-degree counter-discourse.

The nineteenth-century work of counter-discourse constitutes a mapping of the internal incoherence of the seemingly univocal and monumental institution of dominant discourse. My tactic will seek to chart its margins. A certain fragmentation is the inevitable result, for the counter-discourse cannot be conceived as an essentialist genre or institution which could be framed a priori. It forms its diverse varieties over time, in response to an impulse which may bear familiar names— revolt, nonconformity, alienation, resistance, rebellion—but whose disparate manifestations can be analyzed only in an investigation of their production as specific discursive practices.

Gramsci makes a point which frames my own: "The history of subaltern social groups is necessarily fragmented and episodic."[86] For analogous reasons I am obliged to take soundings in the sedimentary layers of counter-discursive production and reproduction: core samples which seek to read the tensions of color, texture, density, and apparent value which distinguish their contiguous and superposed layers. Such samples permit the mapping of the diverse moments at which these strata were laid down, and of the specific, conjunctural functionality attributable to each.

Yet in another sense, though less than a logic or an exhaustive typology, my counter-discursive examples constitute more than a haphazard sampling, for the distribution of counter-discourses is not random. They are more than simple antinomic formations dependent upon their antagonist in the manner of some perverse mirror image. We cannot deduce their tactics or their contents by mechanically negating elements of the dominant discourse. On the other hand, neither is the process that produces them simply an election of chance. Counter-discourses are the product of a theoretically unpredictable form of discursive labor and real transformation. No catalogue of them can ever be exhaustive.

Moreover, to be faithful to its cultural reality, each successive entry in the registry of such contestatory formations will have to be de-

86. *Prison Notebooks*, pp. 54–55.

scribed in considerable detail. Only in empirical precision can the *specific* character of the labor done upon the social materials be related to the *specific* pattern of resistances and vulnerabilities in the strain of dominant discourse against which it counterposes itself. Because by its nature each investigation is extensive, I cannot propose here to cover anything like the field of nineteenth century counter-discourses but only to examine a few of what I hope are exemplary loci within it. I pay the price of fragmentation in order to achieve something like material depth.

In the dialectical tradition, any conjuncture is comprehensible as a vast network of multileveled and multidirectional mediations and determinations. But by a paradox in the method—or in the material—itself, in practice only a meagre sampling of these can be produced. The discourse of the cultural history I want to provide thus seems condemned to the limitations of the metonymic. The parts, the sampling, try to take the measure of the dynamics by which an entire culture tried to undermine itself. In our economy of finite time, and even in a long book, there seems no way out of this methodological dilemma.

Yet given the cultural context and our disciplinary assumptions, description of such a fragmented and seemingly discontinuous space may well appear a deficiency. We are disposed to appreciate neater symmetries, and it would be satisfying if our typologies could seem integrally to embrace the discursive field of the period which they take as their object. They will not do so here. But in defense of such a failure of totalization, we need to consider the sources of such impulses to systematicity and plenitude. They reflect a privileging of the unified in the face of persuasive theoretical arguments that such unification is itself ideologically misleading, that it has been enlisted in support of certain—by no means innocent—interests. Such assumptions function very actively as "strategies of containment" to *suppress* the sorts of struggle which I have been attempting to understand in their most intimate insertion within language. The fragmented mapping of the counter-discursive realm which is all that can be offered here is a reflection of this mode's guerilla struggle against a dominant antagonist which *alone* has the privilege of apparent coherence and unity.

Such a privilege depends upon the impression of social *effectiveness* that is the distinctive sign of dominant discourse. The dominant seems to *work*, and thereby to cover the field of the socially functional. On the other hand, to their nineteenth-century practitioners particularly, counter-discourses at times appeared to occupy hardly any space at all. This, as I have suggested, is one of the consequences of the supersession of programmatic revolutionary discourse around midcentury. The magisterial spirit of these earlier utopian and socialist counter-discourses remains foreign to the atmosphere of their more subtly contestatory successors.

Such a difference reflects an even more radical distance from the protocols of the dominant than the utopians or socialists ever achieved in the first half of the century, precisely because the creators of the earlier forms of dissidence persisted in imagining that they might eventually *succeed*. Any programmatic discourse is in essence performative. But for the dissident intelligentsia after midcentury, recommending action in a period so suspicious of the active—a period in which the realm of the practical seemed totally to have been colonized by the "practical" men of the dominant middle class—must have appeared the absolute contrary of what one sought to do. Such a logic is implicit, for example, in Baudelaire's celebrated prose poem satirizing Proudhon and the other French socialists, "Assommons les pauvres!" (see below, Chapter 7). Later nineteenth-century counter-discourses will therefore insist upon appearing *resolutely nonperformative*. It is this fact which liberates their protean multiformity. In the absence of a "program," they gained the enormous privilege of what we might term "discursive fantasy."

Such abdication of thematic or programmatic contestation around midcentury had the advantage of opening up, for the first time, the depths of mechanisms of cultural and ideological constitution and reproduction which were previously invisible. The result was the discovery that the realm of social discourse itself was accessible both to analysis and to subversion. Much of what we know now about the ideological—the infrastructural, constitutive, transparently lived and previously unarticulated basis of social existence in a given conjuncture and within a given social formation—we have learned because the counter-discursive impulse was driven *out* of the realm of the programmatic and the performative after midcentury.

So it becomes apparent in what sense we can say that the blockage of energy directed to structural change of the social formation is an important condition of possibility for the *textual* revolution in which the intelligentsia reinvested some of the dynamism of that sociohistorical revolution which never occurred. In this sense, literary "revolution" is not simply an analogical formation, still less a trendy metaphor. It is the prolongation of a social process which was blocked off in more material arenas of productive activity and human struggle. Literary revolution is not revolution by homology, but by *intended function*. However distant from any project of immediate realization, from any material mutation of the social structures which sustain the here-and-now, it is part of the culture of resistance which plays a role in any oppositional movement.

Through the exploration of these strategies of resistance, through the elaboration of counter-discourses working on the discursive system sustaining nineteenth-century society, the mechanisms of textual constitution, the enigma of the sign, the process of socialization, were all determined as necessary areas of research, analysis, practice. And this is the most important sense in which the notion of the counter-discourse seeks to seize the bound relation between these areas of discursive production and the overall structure which binds them. The case for such determination needs again to be asserted in the face of a tendency within contemporary criticism to mystify the bases upon which such criticism itself is so ingeniously practiced—that is to say, the historical lags between those aspirations for liberation, and their blockage, that still represent the major social problem in our contemporary existence.

In the confused stasis of our present, one question haunts us: how can resistance happen? The question has two resonances. First, how might it be possible to resist at all? This interrogation is more poignant in our own time than it has ever been before. And second, if one does or can resist, through what modalities could such resistance ever become expressed and socially effective? It is this situation which makes investigation of certain modes of intraclass resistance within nineteenth-century liberal society interesting for our purposes and pertinent to our own situation. It turns out that the analysis of the stresses within written discourse since the twin revolutions of the nineteenth century is not so much a story written in the perfect tense and comfortably concluded by its distance from us, but rather a continuing serial which implicates us even as we seek our analytical distance from it. The forms of its complication turn out to be precisely the diverse and conflicted content of its own narration. It relates the discovery that such a story was central for our culture. Our criticism reproduces these counter-discursive configurations; we are writing the later chapters now.

PART ONE
DISCOURSES OF
DOMINATION

Discourses of Initiation: On Some Contradictions in Balzac's Encounter with the Sign

On ne secoue pas le joug de la langue. [We can't shake off the yoke of language.]

—BALZAC

A man must educate or re-educate himself for life in a world that is, from his point of view, enormous and foreign. . . . In Hegel's definition, the novel must educate man for life in bourgeois society.

—BAKHTIN, *Dialogic Imagination*

The *roman d'éducation* may not yet have taught us all it can. The genre arose with the new practices and discourses of emerging urban society. And it registered their power in the urgency with which its own discourse sought to master them. In the novels of education, the intensity of the effort to gain control of these broader social discourses, to encompass or recuperate them, stands as a measure of their developing domination. My object will be to reread this conflict of discourses.

The project of the roman d'éducation appears simple. The genre investigated how individuals approached and entered what their culture designated as adulthood. It examined their formation as subjects under the new conditions of liberal capitalism. But the conjuncture rendered such analysis problematic. For members of the middle class, the patterns of subjectification central to the new social formation wore a particularly difficult disguise, because the dominant discourses emerging in postrevolutionary society carried a message of their own invisibility. At the center of their mechanism of control these discourses signified that there *were* no mechanisms of control—at least none beyond those which an individual had voluntarily invented or chosen. They thus resisted precisely the understanding of determined social process—of *how* adults came into the specific form of their postrevolutionary adulthood—which the roman d'éducation aimed to achieve. The notion of control was veiled in such a way that in seeking to understand the power which subjectified individuals, the novels of their "education" were obliged to reinvent certain categories of the social. What emerged was an epochal discovery: the roman d'éducation functioned to detect and to theorize the regulative power of discourses.

Assuredly this was not the genre's intention, and the discovery undermined its conscious project gravely. I will need to trace the logic by which the initial project undid itself. This did not happen because the analytical tools deployed by the new genre were insufficient for the task set for them. In fact the contrary proved true. It was impossible for the analyst to *contain* the power of the tools she or he had thought to bring to bear. Their power rebounded upon the analyst because, though ideology had made the fact obscure, these tools of analysis turned out to be not only the means *but the mystified object* of the entire investigation. Thus without clearly realizing it, the roman d'éducation sought to perform a bootstrap operation: implicitly it asked central elements of the emerging dominant discourse to comprehend and explain themselves, to serve as their own metalanguage. It solicited of an ideology that it acknowledge its ideological character, that it openly proclaim this in a nonmystified way. In effect it required dominant discourse to deconstruct itself.

The notion of the counter-discursive permits resituating such a contradiction. In this perspective it becomes clear how the project of the roman d'éducation contested the structures of control which determined early capitalist subjectification. To the extent that any dominant discourse can be understood as an imposition upon individuals from outside, the effort by them to gain control of its power, to turn it to their own uses, serves the function that I have identified as "counter-discursive."

Subversion is the characteristic project of nineteenth-century counter-discourses. They attempted to disrupt the circuit in which the dominant construction of the world asserted its self-evidence, its naturalized currency. For the most part counter-discourses sought to imagine alternatives to such a mechanism. But the case of the roman d'éducation is significantly different, and its difference helps to situate the problem of symbolic resistance in general. One might think of the novel of education as a kind of transitional form in relation to the evolving discursive struggle. For the genre's tactic was not to *subvert* the dominant but rather to seek to *recontain* it. Instead of contesting the mechanism of domination, the genre contested its beneficiary. It aimed not to overturn domination but to domesticate or annex the power by which domination functioned.

The discursive constraints which are essential to any mechanism of domination seek to ensure that *all* are brought within the dominant's field of force so that its naturalized pervasiveness comes to define the limits of subjectivity and of autonomy. On the other hand, to turn the other's power to one's own account, to use the mechanism which sustained the other's predominance in order to evade it, indeed, even to predominate oneself—such was the adversative tactic of the roman d'éducation. But inevitably the attempt carried its contradiction with it.

Such a contradictory relationship continues into our period. It defines our critical stance. For we will find our investigation vexed by a difficulty which does not so much have a source as it does a structure which parallels the problematic of the roman d'éducation itself. The novel of education may look at first like a dead genre, a subset of the no-longer viable paradigms of nineteenth-century realism comfortably distanced from our contemporary critical concerns. Nonetheless it resists our penetration at successive levels of the discourse with which we attempt to surround and invest it. Our entanglement in the roman d'éducation then takes an unexpected Archimedian twist: it seems that outside of it we have nowhere to stand. To reread the form and themes, the whole mythic shape, of the nineteenth-century novel of education is to involve ourselves, but this time from the *inside,* in the very practices of discursive analysis and interpretation which the roman d'éducation itself functioned to conceptualize.

So our position as readers of the genre is paradoxical in the same way as that of its initiators. And the text of our reading, while it strives to achieve the status of critique, tends constantly to slip back toward recuperation within the protocols of what had appeared an obsolete form. The fascination of any attempt to reread a body of texts which at first seemed distant from us lies in this complex and embarrassing implication of our understanding in its own object. Our attempt to analyze the paradigms of representation which functioned within the roman d'éducation thus unexpectedly reenacts these same paradigms. We find that we are writing another novel of education.

Yet this perplexing mutual involution of the subject and object of our critical discourse is not quite the same thing as the incarceration in circularity—"Thinking about language is impossible without language itself"—which founds certain contemporary critiques of representation (I will return to this problem in Chapter 7). The forms of thought which begin as the object of analysis of the roman d'éducation seem to end up becoming our means for attaining it. But these forms are irreducibly historicized, and such historical specificity is the place where they may be seized. We need to examine their production within definite circumstances and in the patterns determined by these circumstances. As I have suggested, these forms coincide with certain of our own contemporary protocols of thinking. But no transhistorical impossibility of other paradigms of analysis, or theoretical disability of our own, is implied by such coincidence, only the persistence of certain operations of thought, and of the processes of social constitution which have determined them, from the postrevolutionary period to our own time. The formation within which our investigation moves is historical. And thereby the possibility of authentic differential, *dialectical* grasp of these structures begins to be thinkable within what might otherwise have appeared a constant frustrating reenactment of the same.

The fundamental mechanisms of such dialectical understanding of postrevolutionary social process were being systematized at the moment when the roman d'éducation and realism in general themselves arose.[1] The paradox alluded to at the outset of my discussion is already

1. A number of novels of the realist period in France exemplify what we might imagine as the ideal form of the roman d'éducation: in the *Comédie humaine, Le Père*

visible in the structure of such representation. It is a commonplace now to note that the writers who composed these texts, the consciousness out of which they emerged, were deeply implicated in the process whose production was depicted. As middle-class representation, realism was threatened by absorption in the structures of middle-class existence and domination. Authentic contradiction of postrevolutionary social reality was beyond its range. What it could establish was a situation of distance, of dissidence, which blocked the saturation of the world of discourse by the dominant ideology and situated a crucial fragment of the bourgeoisie in a characteristic attitude of internal emigration within the bourgeois world. This stance of negativity founded the imaginative production of these middle-class dissidents as the varied strains of a counter-discourse whose contents and structures subjected the dominant real to a generalized critique.

The roman d'éducation exhibits the dissonance which arises from its ambivalent existence within realist practice. The genre is suspended awkwardly somewhere on a continuum running from the approbation of the real to its denunciation, from complicity to contradiction. But for us its interest arises because within the genre such an intermediate situation preserves the traces of two master discourses which have defined the self-understanding of postrevolutionary society, which have constituted its dominant imaginative protocols and its underlying ideological system. In the roman d'éducation their conflict is brilliantly foregrounded.

Goriot, the Rubempré cycle, *Louis Lambert*, and *Un début dans la vie;* for Stendhal, *Le rouge et le noir* and *Lucien Leuwen* would probably serve as the clearest examples. On the other hand a certain number of texts, from Constant's *Adolphe* to Musset's *Confession*, would probably not be usefully included within the category, since they concentrate much more upon the subjective inner modulations of a love story than upon the exteriorized interchange between a hero and an objective world of social meaning which characterizes the roman d'éducation. In my discussion here, the use of the term designates a tendency to represent as determinant certain personal and social interactions (present to some degree in nearly every text of this period), rather than a specific genre or subgenre which might be clearly distinguished from others produced during the same period. The tendency toward depicting the interchange between individual experience and the cultural sphere in which individuality discovers, defines, and realizes itself—what the French call *formation*, the Germans *Bildung*—of course is fundamental to the whole project of realist fiction. It is thus a set of paradigms, of protocols for textualization, rather than a specific and exclusively defined body of texts, which I want to designate by the term "roman d'éducation" here.

The first of these master discourses is an extraordinary supple and constantly developing capacity for the analysis of generative process. Such a discourse is the basis of bourgeois production in all realms and establishes its norms of rationality. In turn the second of these dominant discursive paradigms is responsible for founding the conceptual form of the middle-class subject, represented (through however paradoxical a contradiction) as socially mobile but at the same time as radically independent of any social determination. In a world conceived as a generative process, the middle-class subject alone is somehow bracketed from the overall dynamic of production which middle-class thought conceives as determining all phenomena in the socioeconomic realm.

By applying the protocols which sustain the analysis of production in general to the formation of the self, by demonstrating the mechanism of cultural reproduction as it forms individuals in concrete historical situation, the roman d'éducation held two contradictory elements of its culture within the same discursive space. And it represented them there under maximum tension. Given the dissonant structure out of which the text itself was generated, this contradiction was not one which the roman d'éducation itself could explicitly confront or theorize. But even in the absence of such overt analysis, the form of the genre comes as close as any representation in the postrevolutionary period to exploding certain ideological exclusions which otherwise sustain the stability of middle-class consciousness.[2] The stresses, though not named, are recorded in the form's development; the contradictions propagate through the roman d'éducation which can neither identify nor ignore them. They generate a complex process of ideological formation, undermining, and reformulating.

The function of a text, as Lotman and Piatigorsky usefully define it, "is . . . its social role, its capacity to serve certain demands of the

---

2. Hegel was more cynical concerning the subversive potential of the corresponding German novels with which he was familiar. He underlined the eventual recuperation of the hero in such texts: "Still, as a rule he eventually finds his girl and some job or other, marries and becomes as much of a philistine as anybody else [*ein Philister so gut wie die anderen auch*]" (*Vorlesungen über die Aesthetik*, vol. 2, p. 220). The French examples are less reassuring to the dominant ideology, as we shall see.

community which creates the text."[3] Rarely in cultural history has there been a circuit of text production more satisfyingly exemplary than the one in which the novels of the realist period in France were generated. It is generally agreed that realism responded to a broadly experienced cultural crisis, in which change in virtually every aspect of social relations outdistanced imaginative expression and ideological mastery of social developments. This was particularly true for the new bourgeois strata whose emergence within a social context still dominated by the cultural forms of ancien régime France represented an unprecedented and perplexing social fact.[4]

What one might call the conceptual shortfall characterizing such situations determines the production of imaginative discourse. Balzac put it with succinct irony in his preface to the *Livre mystique* (1835): "If the society which the author has taken as his subject were perfect, no depiction of it would be possible; one would simply sing a magnificent social hallelujah and sit down at the feast to consume one's appropriate portion."[5] But in the absence of perfection, to understand one *writes*.

The phenomenon which Marx called the "uneven development of material production relative to . . . artistic development"[6] thus identifies the sociohistorical basis underlying a pressing imaginative need: a systemic demand for the development of structures and vocabularies—socially available discourses—which might explain the tense conjuncture and the contradictory situation of middle-class experience within it.[7]

---

3. "Text and Function," p. 233.

4. On the production of nineteenth-century realism and its relation to contemporary cultural crisis, the bibliography is large. See particularly the work of Pierre Barbéris, "Mal du siècle;" *Balzac et le mal du siècle,* esp. vol. 1, chaps. 1 and 6, and vol. 2, chaps. 7 and 8; and *Le monde de Balzac,* esp. part 3. The origin of the perception for Western criticism is probably to be found coordinately in Erich Auerbach (see *Mimesis,* chap. 18) and in Georg Lukács (see the 1948 preface to *Studies in European Realism*). In turn the concept that literature functions to make sense of periods of profound social transition probably came to Lukács from Lenin (see his articles on Tolstoy in *Lenin on Literature and Art*).

5. *Comédie humaine,* ed. Marcel Bouteron, vol. 11 (Paris: Gallimard-Pléiade, 1954), p. 266.

6. *Grundrisse,* p. 109.

7. On this development and the relation of mimetic fictions to it, see my "Materialist Imagination."

The emotional lexicon of the strains of French romanticism associated with the dispossessed aristocracy could serve the expressive needs of the nascent bourgeoisie only provisionally. At first middle-class writers tried them out. But though in the face of the new social world the two groups shared a sense of disorientation, inevitably its expression diverged in tone and quality. Unlike the aristocratic romantics, the bourgeoisie faced not exile but an uncomfortable installation; not solitude and powerlessness but an awkward and chilling intuition of their own class's *effectiveness*.

The romantic *mal du siècle* thus momentarily furnished bourgeois liberals in the late 1820s and early 1830s with a language to express their own apparently deteriorating situation. But as time went on such a language increasingly failed to correspond to the particular character of their experience. As the conjuncture evolved, the imaginative tonality whose expression middle-class intellectuals sought to sharpen inflected away from the tone of the romantic elegiac toward a global sense of mistrust, apprehension, and insecurity: Stendhal's "suspicion," Balzac's "doubt."[8] Coordinately, the sense of dislocation experienced by the members of the middle-class under the early July Monarchy (unlike that of the aristocratic romantics) came to be felt not as tragically and transcendently metaphysical but as concretely *situational*. In this context the functionality of the roman d'éducation, as the application of middle-class logic of process to the production of contemporary social existence itself, comes into clearest focus.

The social stress of this process of dislocation is figured in the familiar yet still astonishing statistics which characterize the first fifty years of the nineteenth century in France and attempt (however inadequately) to take the measure of its changes. During this half century, for example, the Paris population increased by a factor of 2.6; the proportion of the population of France living in the capital doubled.[9] From 1820 to 1848 the French national income rose by 50 to 60 percent;

8. Stendhal: "Poetic genuis is dead, but the genius of *suspicion* has come into the world" (*Souvenirs d'égotisme* [1832], ed. Henri Martineau [Paris: Divan, 1950], p. 7). Balzac: "The nineteenth century, whose immense portrait the author seeks to trace . . . is currently stressed by doubt [*travaillé par le doute*]" (preface to *Le livre mystique* [1835], p. 266).

9. Barbéris and Duchet, *Manuel d'histoire littéraire*, vol. 1, p. 314. During the same period, the greatest proportional population gain was on the Left Bank, whose resonances for the newly arrived provincial projecting a career in the professions or in

the stock of financial and industrial capital doubled; coal consumption went up by a factor of 5. By 1840, Paris, though not the largest city, had already become the greatest manufacturing center in the world, with more than 400,000 workers employed in industry. By comparison, the entire population of the city just forty years previously had been only 547,000.[10] And in a register somewhat different but relevant to my area of concern here, in the nineteenth century, while only a quarter to a third of French writers were born in Paris, fully one-half of the members of the literary profession died there.[11]

What is evoked by this rapid sampling of demographic evidence (whose overall pattern was as familiar to Balzac himself as it has become to twentieth-century specialists)[12] is an immense internal migration which brought to Paris men and women of all classes having no previous roots in the capital. To a degree previously unexperienced, such a movement determined alterations in social status. These changes in the scale and the character of the urban environment changed nearly everything.

Within the complex evoked by such statistics, the roman d'éducation both inscribes and attempts to achieve mastery of an unprecedented crisis of socialization. The theme and the dominant social experience of this period is a massive displacement of individuals and of whole social structures within which their existences are determined. In response an entire corpus of texts depicting the signs and status signals, the employments and amusements, the dangers and the blunders—the mapping of a cultural system as intricate and mobile as that of nineteenth-century Paris—arose to initiate successive cohorts of new arrivals. Department stores and display windows, popular newspapers and mass advertising (all Parisian inventions in the 1820s and 1830s), sought to codify the world of dominant and desirable values for a population unprepared for the complex hierarchizations of the capital (I will consider these phenomena in more detail in the next two chapters).

---

literature are well known (see ibid., p. 315). It was about half way through this period that the growth rate of the urban population in France began to exceed that of the rural. See E. J. Hobsbawm, *Age of Revolution*, p. 207.

10. Cameron, *France and the Economic Development of Europe*, pp. 52–53.

11. Barbéris and Duchet, *Manuel d'histoire littéraire*, vol. 1, p. 305.

12. Louis Chevalier speaks admiringly of the accuracy and breadth of Balzac's demographic knowledge (*Classes laborieuses*, p. 12).

Whence arose those curious subgenres providing orientation within this mysterious world of social signs—the *Codes, Tableaux, Dictionnaires, Traités, Monographies, Physiologies,* and so on which flourished in the 1820s and early 1830s.

These novel subgenres of the social text educated those not born to them to an increasingly complex world of hierarchized objects and behaviors. The roman d'éducation itself can be understood both as the furthest development of such tendencies and as their cognitive metatext. The genre represents an early phase of what was to prove a long reflection within the culture upon the existence and the functionality of its new institutions and processes.

The roman d'éducation arose in part because the education required in the context of new social realities under early capitalism was unavailable through any other mechanism. The texts themselves reflect this absence. It is significant how many of their protagonists are launched upon their fictional courses at just the moment when their formal schooling terminates or even aborts. In the fictions, such schooling is presented as vacuous or as irrelevant to the later itineraries of those subjected to it. One thinks of Lucien Leuwen expelled from the Ecole Polytechnique in the first line of his novel; of David Séchard's futile apprenticeship with the Didots in Paris before he returns to Angoulême as the story opens; of the cavalier elision of Rastignac's law studies, passed over in Balzac's consideration of his hero's "successive initiations" into the complex "human stratifications which make up society."[13] Along the same lines we might recall Raphaël de Valentin's autobiography which launches the second part (and situates the entire action) of *La peau de chagrin.* He begins it by stating that he will skip over his schooling because it had no bearing whatever on his experience.

The tendency is significant. It reflects the perceived failure of France's notoriously deficient system of primary education,[14] of her twenty-two universities, even of the numerous institutions of higher education, like Polytechnique, which had been founded during the revolutionary period to respond to the realities of a world in conscious process of transformation. These institutions simply failed to offer

13. See *Le Père Goriot,* ed. P. G. Castex (Paris: Garnier, 1963), p. 40.
14. Hobsbawm, *Age of Revolution,* p. 227.

initiation into the structure of experience which young people newly in the cities, newly confronting transformed relations of social production and reproduction, encountered as a mystery for which they were radically unprepared and within which they needed to learn to move.

So it becomes important to inquire what elements in the roman d'éducation established its functionality. Generally speaking, the stress within a structure experiencing the kind of tension we have observed produces itself under conditions of the sort of historical hysteresis, the *déphasage* between material production and cultural or imaginative development which Marx sketched in the *Grundrisse*. An uneven development of this type, problematizing the self-representation of postrevolutionary society, lies at the heart of the crisis experienced by the middle-class intelligentsia during the late Restoration and July Monarchy.

Their case was increasingly distinct from that of more traditional social fragments. For the formerly dominant aristocratic groups with whose interests ancien régime values had developed harmoniously over time, the institutions inculcating such values were already well established and had long functioned more or less transparently. But members of the new social strata experienced a more conflicted situation. On one hand, as a rising class, they were subjected to the assimilation and reproduction of the same traditional systems of value.[15] But they were simultaneously excluded from the corresponding initiatory mechanisms: the one thing they were *not* free to become was old nobility. Practically speaking, their need was thus to catalogue, master, and institutionalize the knowledge that would enable them to move within a cultural system in which meaning was signified by counters which were alien to their experience and their understanding.

But in epochal transitions of this sort, the project of historicocultural innovation rarely operates on the level of such immediate instrumen-

---

15. Hobsbawm puts the constraint clearly: "Rising classes naturally tend to see the symbols of their wealth and power in terms of what their former superior groups have established as . . . standards. . . . A culture as profoundly formed by court and aristocracy as the French would not [suddenly] lose the imprint" (ibid., pp. 218–19). See also the essay by Max Horkheimer, "Feudal Lord." On the general problem of new social status patterns and their limitations, see Ranum, *Paris in the Age of Absolutism*, p. 27. The structure of social "distinction" upon which such instituted hierarchies depend will be examined in greater detail in Chapter 6.

tality alone. In this regard, Barthes's celebrated denegration of bourgeois writing in the period before 1848 represses something crucial.[16]
For him such writing was an unself-reflexive and unproblematized
practice of representation. It is true that in the period which concerns
us, the profusion of *Physiologies, Traités* and the like seems indeed to
have been a response to the instrumental exigency which characterized
the historical moment and the situation of the middle class.[17] And on a
second level, the itinerary dramatized in the roman d'éducation surely
did serve to provide the cognitive basis for a perfectly practical paradigm of socialization which the genre made available to members of
the newer strata seeking their way in what still remained confusing
social territory.

Such considerations appear harmonious with the patterns of middle-class rationality and instrumentality which Barthes deplored. Yet
the process of production of these texts simultaneously generated another text—more tentative and diffuse, perhaps, but deeply innovative
and subversive in its implications. This parallel text represents an early
but powerful theorization concerning crucial ideological structures of
postrevolutionary life. Its importance for our cultural history is great,
for beyond any immediately practical objective, it instituted a process
that was to lead, at the beginning of our own century, to systematic
disengagement of the notion of the sign.[18]

So we need to look again at what was at stake in the roman d'éducation. The education which it represented turns out to be *education into
signs:* into an experience of the semiotic which now we see to be crucial
in modern relations of economic production and social reproduction.
Today such experience seems so well internalized that one might almost suppose it had always been there. But in the early postrevolutionary period its formation constituted a crisis. It is in this sense that the

16. Barthes's judgment has become a founding assessment in structuralist and poststructuralist revaluations of our literary history. "Instrumentality" is his misprizing term
for bourgeois writing in the period prior to Flaubert (*Degré zéro*, p. 52). I will return to
this problem in my final chapter. On Barthes's own evolution beyond this influential
position, see Jameson, *Political Unconscious*, p. 18.

17. Hobsbawm, *Age of Revolution*, p. 219, comments on the wide diffusion of such
pedagogical texts, along with manuals of etiquette and gracious living, in the period.

18. No argument concerning the "origin" of the sign is in question here. No more
than Saussure, the realists did not "invent" it. What concerns me is the process by
which its concept entered the broad discourse of cultural reflection.

roman d'éducation registered the initiation not only of a young hero but of a new and conflicted process of socialization. The genre staged the penetration into cultural consciousness of a new paradigm for social life. Its domination has only increased in the intervening 150 years.

The roman d'éducation must therefore not be seen only in the ungrateful role of forerunner within some now obsolescent prehistory of contemporary scientific knowledge. These texts *practiced the sign*. They foregrounded the process by which it became problematized within discourse. Simultaneously they initiated the bases for a critique of its functioning, and indeed a reflection upon the conditions under which the notion of sign itself became pertinent, under which it rose into consciousness. These aspects of the roman d'éducation provide the relevant response to my question concerning the genre's functionality and influence in its own moment. In a society in which the discourses of social life were losing their transparency and their self-evidence, the roman d'éducation offered not only a systematic mapping of the new terrain of meaning, but a powerful reflection on the phenomenon of signification itself.

There is no process of institution in social life without preceding, and determining, destitution. As the transparency characterizing areas of social existence not previously experienced as problematical is progressively lost, the effort to master such areas in their transformed state attempts, paradoxically, to reproduce a dying innocence through the concerted mobilization of knowledge. By their nature, of course, such strained efforts to recover a time when no special effort was required can never succeed cleanly. The institution of forms of consciousness as epochal as the complex I have been examining reflects this double movement in particularly interesting ways.

For our purposes, it can be said that the process which determined both the thematics and the narrative structure of the roman d'éducation proceeded on a double front. Lotman and Uspensky observe that periods of social change generally are characterized by an intensification in what they term "semiotic behavior."[19] An increasingly acute consciousness of the coded nature of social life tends to arise in such

19. "On the Semiotic Mechanism," pp. 211–12.

transitional periods. Consequently the diverse practices of the sign (naming and designating, classifying, distinguishing, and hierarchizing), as well as the forms of its theorization, force themselves into social representation and into conceptual discourse.

Such developments are never uncontroversial. Critiques were mounted against the penetration of the sign into social consciousness and against the unanticipated structure of constraints on the forms and performances of social life which the emergence of the semiotic phenomenon seemed to determine. Of course it may seem quixotic to have thought that one might somehow abolish or dispense with the sign. But in the moment when an emerging culture becomes conscious, creates a model, of itself,[20] the distinctive elements of the model become the critical area for any contestation of the new configuration of the world.

For Balzac, signs were everywhere: "Notre civilisation est . . . immense de détails" ("Our civilization is pregnant with details").[21] And the codes which such signs composed presented themselves to understanding as determined historical products. For example: "In France, parties only become possible from the time when contrary interests confronted each other; the revolutions began in material things and in interests before they occurred in ideas."[22] The consciousness of such historicized realities necessarily gave rise to a science of decoding the social signs we call objects and characters: to a hermeneutics.[23] Bernard Vannier (who has counted) writes that Balzac interrupts the course of narration in the *Comédie humaine* more than five hundred times so that he can provide the description of a character.[24] Such appearances then become the text for the exigesis so familiar in Balzac:

> Who has not noticed that at the Opera, as in every part of Paris, there is a mode of being which reveals what you are, what you do, where you come from, and what you want?[25]

20. See ibid., p. 227.
21. Preface to *Une fille d'Eve*, cited by Barbéris, *Monde de Balzac*, p. 104.
22. "Sur la situation du parti royaliste" (1831), cited by Barbéris, *Monde de Balzac*, p. 163. Balzac here curiously anticipates Foucault's analysis in *Les mots et les choses*. See Foucault, *The Order of Things*, p. 368.
23. See Foucault, *The Order of Things*, pp. 297–98.
24. *L'inscription du corps*, p. 15.
25. *Splendeurs et misères des courtisanes*, ed. Antoine Adam (Paris: Garnier, 1964), p. 6.

These judges, who had matured in the knowledge of Parisian depravities, were carefully examining a woman who could be deciphered by them alone.[26]

Have you sufficiently grasped the thousand details of that hovel sitting five hundred paces from the attractive gateway to Les Aigues? Well, its roof covered with velvety moss, its cackling chickens, the pig browsing: all its pastoral poetry carried a horrible meaning.[27]

Barthes's claim had been that the discourse of the early realist period failed to grasp language *itself* as problematized. In his image, realist writing never experienced that "solitude of language" which marks the crisis of representation that has occupied us since.[28] Foucault was less categorical in *The Order of Things*. For him the transition had occurred earlier. The passage from the classical to the modern episteme, which he localizes between 1775 and 1825, had already altered consciousness of the linguistic phenomenon profoundly: "From the nineteenth century, language began to fold in upon itself, to acquire its own particular density, to deploy a history, an objectivity, and laws of its own." (p. 296; cf. p. 221).

Balzac's perceptions concerning the historical and interpretive contingency of language would seem to pose the basis for such an objectification of the semiotic. Once one begins to look for them, the characteristic traces of such a reflection turn up frequently in his text. For example we find him acutely conscious of the phenomenon of polysemy in linguistic systems, and of the sociohistorical process by which such multiplication of sense occurs: "Words can take on several meanings, and giving them new ones is what I call creating. The process enriches a language. A language is impoverished by taking on new words, but enriched by having few of them but giving them many meanings."[29] On another front, in a reflection relevant to what is still a controversial area of semiotic thinking, we find Balzac musing on the vexed problem of the relationship between sound and sense in the divagation on language at the beginning of *Louis Lambert:* "Doesn't

26. Ibid., p. 24.

27. *Les paysans,* ed. J. H. Donnard (Paris: Garnier, 1964), p. 51.

28. *Degré zéro,* p. 52.

29. Letter to Louis Aimé, April 1844; *Correspondance,* ed. Roger Pierrot (Paris: Garnier, 1966), vol. 4, p. 690.

the word *vrai* (true) exhibit a kind of extraordinary honesty [*rectitude fantastique*]?"[30] Yet the traditional myth of some natural relationship between signifier and signified ("cratylism") to which Balzac longingly refers here seems invoked precisely because its central assumption was coming under increasing pressure within social and historical experience.[31] Contingency and factitiousness, rather than transparent naturalness, increasingly appeared to characterize such relations. The inflated rhetoric of the passage from *Louis Lambert* seems to transmit a disguised defensiveness, to denote the uncertainty of its own assertion.

The issue of arbitrary connection raised by its denial in Balzac's text has been put in a useful perspective in two recent theoretical reflections. In *Pour une critique de l'économie politique du signe*, Jean Baudrillard argued that any "arbitrary" relation between discrete signifiers and signifieds is nonetheless founded by an act of social choice. A specific system of sociality, a specific historical conjuncture, are thus inscribed in the institution of any sign. And the notion that the parameters of such choices are recoverable in analysis—thereby distinguishing them from purely random or gratuitous connections—furnishes a key methodological basis for Pierre Bourdieu and Jean-Claude Passeron in their work on the functioning of educational systems.[32] It will become evident that such a perception is crucial to the paradigms of socialization, and to the initiation to the social sign, which Balzac conceptualizes in the roman d'éducation.

But we need to pursue a bit further the investigation into Balzac's problematization of language and his objectification of the sign. Among the profusion of details which struck Balzac as characterizing postrevolutionary culture, and which he sought to catalogue and classify, certain linguistic phenomena have a central place. Consider the attempt to seize and imitate the variety of dialects and accents which one finds in his texts: for example, Nucingen ("*Le tiaple n'egssisde*

30. *Comédie humaine*, vol. 10, p. 356.
31. See de Certeau, Julia, and Revel, *Une politique de la langue*, p. 87. The most systematic examination of Balzac's reflections on language, though from a perspective quite different from that taken here, is Martin Kanes's *Balzac's Comedy of Words;* see particularly chap. 4.
32. Baudrillard, *Pour une critique*, p. 180; Bourdieu and Passeron, *Reproduction*, pp. 8–9. The problem of arbitrary relation has been raised again by Jonathan Culler. See his *Ferdinand de Saussure* and the review article by Marie-Laure Ryan, "Is there Life for Saussure after Structuralism?"

boinde, dit le baron,")[33] or Père Fourchon in the celebrated description of the otter-hunt ("Elle ne vous coûtera pas cher, si elle a du blanc sur le dos, car *eul Souparfait m'disait éque nout Muséon* n'en a qu'une de ce genre-là").[34]

Such divergences from normalized, transparent speech help Balzac to objectify the complex social-significatory process of language, to figure the contingency of semiotic behavior (in terms of historical period, region, class, work activity, and individual mentality) which constituted the world for him as a vast coded network awaiting adequate decipherment. Balzac's texts record intent consciousness of the most diverse linguistic phenomena (argots, specialized and obsolete usages persisting despite historical change, verbal tics, word games such as those played by the *pensionnaires* at Madame Vauquer's, and so on). And they register a broad range of "nonstandard" communicative situations (overhearing, misunderstanding, ambiguity, deliberate deception). The variety and frequency of such manifestations in his novels reflect the dual character of any social semiotics: both the material complexity and the ultimate systematicity which render semiotic interpretation at once empirically arduous and theoretically possible.

The ultimate testing ground for such a notion of semiotic objectification in Balzac would seem to be those cases, like Père Fourchon's otter, in which disguise, secrecy, concealment, or falsification are present. (Let us recall that Eco designates the possibility of lying as distinguishing the semiotic field.)[35] Such situations, where interpretation of evidence proves difficult or impossible, provide Balzac with a representation both of the structure and of the difficulty of the semiotic phenomenon. Configurations of this kind (one thinks of their centrality in *L'histoire des Treize* or in *Splendeurs et misères,* among many other texts) create theoretical models of the interpretive situation which he was striving to conceptualize. And in turn the disguises by which characters overlay their truth with a false representation create opportunities for the hermeneutic activity which provides much of the

---

33. *Splendeurs,* p. 89.

34. *Les paysans,* p. 42. Of course the otter itself is a fiction, a sign invoked to trick Blondet. No one is more surprised than Père Fourchon when his semiotic invention, his imaginary exchange value, transforms itself into a real, material otter. Again, the conceptual distance between sign and referent is clearly marked.

35. Eco, *Theory of Semiotics,* p. 6.

energy in the Balzac text—an activity ranging from the stolid explanatory "voici pourquoi," which Proust pastiched so cuttingly, to the brilliant apparition of Vautrin in his guise as ultimate decipherer of the social text.

The Vautrin novels are tales full of mystery—which means they are the paradigmatic romans d'éducation in the Balzac canon. The initiator needs someone to initiate; the uninitiated need to learn. Whence Rastignac or Rubempré. Vautrin's power within these texts is signified in part through the staging of interpretive competitions between him and the other figures in the text whose rival claims to such capacity are explicit.

In *Splendeurs et misères* a sequence of such incidents provides the critical bite in the confrontation between a series of extraordinary interpreters. The first moment of the process pits the Banker Nucingen against the detective-spy Corentin. Their encounter is a combat of readings, and for once—surprisingly—Nucingen loses: "Corentin remained for Nucingen what an inscription lacking three-quarters of its characters would be for an archeologist" (p. 164). In turn Corentin, valorized by his triumph over Nucingen, encounters but fails to comprehend the traces of Vautrin: "'For whose profit was Nucingen's passion being held to ransom?' For the first time, the two brilliant spies [Corentin and his associate Contenson] had met an indecipherable text" (p. 267).

Such suspenseful failures to understand, though they are integral to the social and financial intrigue of this story, really typify a much more universal situation. In the Vautrin novels, in the roman d'éducation in general, the uncertainty which stresses an individual with the consciousness that she or he cannot achieve understanding within a code of signs is a repeated and intense experience. And one is constrained to wonder whether it does not constitute a significant anticipation of that "solitude of language"—that secretion of language itself as an *anxiety* inseparable from the human condition—which for Barthes valorized the textual practice of a later period.

Barthes might have argued that in Balzac the theoretical interpretability of such codes is in no way abolished by the interpretive difficulties which particular individuals may encounter in concrete circumstances. The crises of interpretation in Balzac would thus seem situational, not systemic. But we need to go on to consider the paradigm of initiation which lies at the heart of the roman d'éducation and of its counter-discursive intent. I will argue that such initiation, far from confirming the unproblematic relation between sign and referent which has been taken as the constitutive protocol of realism, in fact rather opens up an experience of personal and social alienation *through the operation of the semiotic system itself.* It is an experience of imprisonment in language whose implications are as profound as those explored later in the century by figures like Flaubert, Mallarmé, and Nietzsche.

The textual mechanism for exploring these complexities is at the heart of the roman d'éducation. Its project is really to gain an understanding of the manner by which codes and signs in the social world are constituted, transmitted, and manipulated. For it is in the structure of initiation—in the process by which significations for the first time objectify and make themselves explicit—that the sign as a constitutive form and as a comprehensible content of the social world is most clearly perceived and most adequately conceptualized. Bakhtin lays a basis for understanding the mechanism we are examining when he writes that "every sign . . . is a construct between socially organized persons in the process of their interaction."[36] Initiation is the moment when such *construction* becomes visible. Initiation objectifies the sign, denaturalizes it, forces it to reveal itself for what it is.

The interpenetration of *knowledge* and *power* in the social functioning of any semiotic element then emerges with great clarity.[37] For there is

36. See Vološinov/Bakhtin, *Marxism and the Philosophy of Language*, p. 21.

37. Vološinov/Bakhtin puts this point in a nearly formulaic way: "sign becomes an arena of the class struggle" (*Marxism and the Philosophy of Language*, p. 23). But the insight is less doctrinaire than the blunt language of this proposition suggests. For the Marxist tradition the basis of conflict over meaning can be traced to the unequal arrangement within any social formation for dividing labor and for distributing surplus. The anthropological basis for such a notion seems if anything more strongly founded now than it was in Marx's time (see *Capital*, vol. 1, pp. 470ff). This basis is convincingly argued by Marshall Sahlins in *Stone Age Economics*. Necessarily such structures include institutionalized systems of ideological-semiological control and regulation (see Ivanov, "Science of Semiotics," p. 200), which are at once assumed as natural by those in power, imitated and internalized by those seeking power, and contested and denaturalized by those dissatisfied with the structure of power which they sustain. Such a complex of differential relations to the dominant sign system describes the sort of struggle over meaning, or over the meaningful, to which Bakhtin refers. Moreover, the existence of such a struggle provides the basis for the directionality of change in the meaning of signs. The play of forces striving for hegemony over such structures of meaning does not simply form an abstract *combinatoire*, a neutral and potentially revers-

no abstract content which a sign might inscribe while somehow remaining isolated from the constitutive conflicts of the social process. In that sense, Barthes's strictures against the instrumentality of meaning in the early bourgeois period really need to be extended to *all* signification. For signification *never* exists "just for itself." From this perspective Barthes's valorization of the *scriptible* (writable) text begins to seem a curious holdover of an idealist, romantic ideology.[38]

In consequence we observe initiation as a profoundly self-centered process in the texts which concern me here. No character within them wants to learn simply in order to know. In this educational system— reflecting the struggle over the interests of the real social world—there are no disinterested scholars. The bipolar structure formed by the initiator and the pupil thus figures more than a structure of epistemology: it represents a nexus of social power and a trajectory of projected social movement.

One of the simplest cases in Balzac is that of Oscar Husson in *Un début dans la vie*. Instructed by a sequence of initiators, in the end Oscar "arrives," as Balzac puts it in one of his most sardonic conclusions: "Oscar is an ordinary man, mild, without pretension, modest, and, like his government, constantly in the [political] center. He attracts neither jealousy nor scorn. He is, in sum, the modern bourgeois."[39] What is depicted here is a recuperation by dominant ideology which suggests that there is nothing more to the initiation paradigm than Hegel's cynical dismissal had suggested: uncritical capitulation to the enveloping structure of dominant discourse as long as one gets one's share of the rewards (see above, n. 2).

---

ible "communications system." Bourdieu and Passeron make this clear when they write, concerning the sort of education paradigm which occupies me here, "P[edagogic] A[ction] can produce its own specifically symbolic effect only when provided with the social conditions for imposition and inculcation, i.e., the power relations that are not implied in a formal definition of communication" (*Reproduction*, p. 7, cf. pp. 19 and 23). A social and historical materiality resisting any imagined free play of signs is thus inscribed in the very nature of the semiotic process—as indeed in the process of initiation by which meanings are taught and learned. And these can (at least after the fact) become objects of analysis and understanding. See also Gould, *Marx's Social Ontology*, pp. 29 and 56–58, and Fowler, *Language and Control*.

38. See Barthes, *S/Z*, p. 10, and Culler, *Structuralist Poetics*, pp. 190–91. I return to the problem in my final chapter.

39. *Un début dans la vie* (1842), ed. Guy Robert and Georges Matoré (Geneva: Droz-Textes Littéraires Français, 1950), p. 217.

On the level of plot, then, *Un début dans la vie* does seem to inscribe consciousness of an unproblematized world, a structure perhaps complex but nonetheless manipulable. Yet while Oscar "arrives," Balzac sneers. The existence of a contradiction begins to be detectable in the realm of tone, if not of plot; one almost thinks of the sardonic apotheosis of Homais.

The situation in the most powerful of the romans d'éducation deeply complicates this perception of dissonance. At the conclusion of *Le Père Goriot* Rastignac fantasizes the possibility of social "arrival"—at a level far beyond what Oscar Husson attains—which has been sketched for him in the enticements of Madame de Beauséant and of Vautrin himself. But his subsequent story in the *Comédie humaine* resonates much more ambiguously.[40] More disturbing still is the case of Lucien de Rubempré. After receiving sophisticated instruction from Madame de Bargeton, from Lousteau, from the members of the Cénacle, and from his continuing, daily tutorial with Vautrin, Lucien graduates by killing himself in the Conciergerie. Something has entered the circuit to perturb this structure of projected accomplishment, of "arrival," even on the level of imagined plot itself.

What becomes visible in these more complex representations of the initiation paradigm in Balzac's later texts is the degree to which the practice of the sign binds rather than frees. And this happens *systematically*. Two distinct species of ignorance are implied in the process of initiation plotted in these texts. One of these is remediable, but it turns out that the other is not. All of the heroes in these fictions receive instruction concerning the hidden cultural significance of a large number of signs. With practice they learn to understand the code, and even to read that hermetic text which Vautrin maintains is inscribed like a palimpsest below the apparent surface of the social real: "There are two Histories: official History—illusory [*menteuse*], the one they teach; and secret History."[41]

But despite his extraordinary acumen in the reading of codes, Vautrin is no more capable than his pupils of understanding something essential about *the determining mechanism of codes themselves*. The techniques of semiotic exegesis which Vautrin controls more than any

---

40. See Barbéris, *Balzac et le mal du siècle*, vol. 1, p. 130, and Terdiman, *Dialectics of Isolation*, p. 42.

41. *Illusions perdues*, ed. Antoine Adam (Paris: Garnier, 1961), p. 709.

other character in these fictions carry social analysis to an astonishingly sophisticated level. They enable him to understand signs which no one else can read. *But they cannot penetrate the regulative structure of the semiotic phenomenon itself.* It remains opaque for him and for all the characters within these texts. Balzac has thus begun to seize what Vautrin cannot perceive as a constitutive failure in his understanding of the structure of the world. The demonstration is in the structure of the Rubempré story itself—specifically in Vautrin's loss of Lucien. Balzac conceives the *logic* of this failure of control, and with it he locates a contradiction at the heart of the initiatory paradigm whose representation the roman d'éducation was striving to achieve.

The initiation sought by the characters in these texts really figures the distance between two modes of understanding within the middle class's experience, and at a crucial moment in its historical development. Initiation traces a myth which carried both the fundamental content of an unrealized need and the emerging contradiction at its center. The initiation paradigm which Balzac elaborates represents the ambition to penetrate the dominant sign system, to inhabit it as known territory and manipulate it freely from a secure position at its heart. But simultaneously it communicates a confused projection of the system's transcendence of such control. Despite its intentions, it represents the dominant discourse's resistance to such counter-discursive recuperation.

Within a social structure in which any authority is mediated by the endless process of competing individualisms, no individual can achieve stable domination of the sort which Vautrin promises to Lucien. The society's own paradigms of exchange render this ungovernable quality irreducible. In the early nineteenth century the sign system inscribes this irrationality in the form of an ideology of the arbitrary: of some impenetrable and unmanageable randomness within the system itself. This is how it figures its own transcendence of control by any individual, how it understands that even figures as powerful as Vautrin cannot impose their will upon the system whose code they have so exhaustively mastered. What lies at the center of the dilemma of initiation in the early postrevolutionary period is thus the perception of a new social configuration, and of the contradictory situation of any individual will within it.

Within these texts, the initiation process has as its referent a concrete

structure of interests and power relations: "'These days, there's nothing left but self-interest,' replied des Lupeaulx."[42] The process tests the
possibility of domination over such a structure of interests. But once
initiated, the would-be subjects are immersed in the structure of relations which they sought to dominate. They discover that they are
involuntarily speaking the referent *as its own object*. The social system
over which the initiatory process had sought control thus controls the
process even in the form of its seeking; the power over which control
was sought turns out to be *power over those who seek power*. Within the
hermetic configuration of such a dominant discourse, there is no exit
from the ironic circle which recuperates desire by having itself engendered it.

The significance of ambition as it functions in Balzac's texts lies here.
We could understand ambition as the socialized form of desire specific
to early capitalism. Through the plots it generates, ambition becomes a
primary means of investigating structures of determination in social
existence which had not yet been adequately conceptualized for bourgeois consciousness. Middle-class individuals in the postrevolutionary
period found themselves neither as bound as they had been nor as free
as they had hoped. The limits of their autonomy, and the mechanisms—no longer primarily legal and political—which mediated such
constraints, needed to be more adequately understood.

André Wurmser studied the manifestations of "ambition" in texts
from our period. He concluded with a pessimistic political judgment
of its significance: "ambition is reactionary."[43] And it is a fact that
ambition may seem to us the name of the reactionary tendency to
accept the structures of domination (however oppressive) with which
we previously struggled, once they appear to have been maneuvered
into working in our favor. But however accurately perceived in its own
terms, this formula fails to seize the overdetermination of such political
consequences by the contradicted functioning of the sign in
postrevolutionary existence. Such overdetermination—the formation
of the structures of domination themselves—is what the roman d'éducation strove to textualize.

Complex systems of determination are inherently mystificatory:

42. Balzac, *Splendeurs*, p. 11.
43. *La comédie inhumaine*, pp. 167–92, esp. p. 182.

their social functionality and their representation within culture necessarily diverge.[44] But mystification is a process, not a state. For this
reason its structures can be more clearly seized in their incipient phase,
when memory of an alternative social consciousness is still active and
before the colonization of imagination by the new discursive patterns
proceeds too far. This is the dialectical moment at which penetration
by the new structures can be fleetingly thematized in imaginative representation. It is a moment analogous to that of an individual's early
initiation to the postrevolutionary semiotic phenomenon, when the
material quality of the sign and the historical contingency of its operation could be objectified, before its internalization in the middle-class
adult (like Oscar Husson for example) rendered the structure frus-
tratingly opaque. This dialectical moment defines the privilege of early
nineteenth-century realism, and the determining element in its representational force.

In our own time, beyond this transition point in the constitution of
middle-class paradigms of meaning (for example, in the work of theorists like Althusser, Lacan, Baudrillard, among others), the system
itself has tended to be conceived as autonomous, the structure of signs
as *self*-generating.[45] Such notions represent the overall regulative
structure of sign and discourse which the roman d'éducation strove to

44. The question of such mystification, which founds the problematic of ideology,
has constantly preoccupied the Marxist tradition, from Marx's Fourth Thesis on Feuerbach and *The German Ideology* to Althusser and his followers. Fredric Jameson discusses
a number of the influential positions on the issue in *Marxism and Form*. The canonical
case of a demystificatory critique, which provides a model for all such ideological
analyses within the tradition, is Marx's penetration of the illusions inherent to the
commodity under capitalism (*Capital*, vol. 1, part 1, chap. 1, sec. 4). The structure and
assumptions of this analysis and its implications for social knowledge are given a full
discussion in Cohen, *Marx's Theory of History*, chap. 9 and app. 1. The general problematic and its history within post-Marxist sociology of knowledge is clearly outlined in
Berger and Luckman, *Social Construction of Reality*. A collection of articles bearing on
the problem of ideology can be found in Mepham and Rubin, *Issues in Marxist Philosophy*, vol. 3. Another useful collection is Michèle Barrett et al., *Ideology and Cultural
Production*. Most recently, Philippe Hamon has provided a valuable review of previous
arguments, and a retheorization of the problem on a semiotic basis. See his *Texte et
idéologie*, esp. chap. 1.

45. This is the bearing of Althusser's "theoretical antihumanism"; see his *For Marx*,
p. 229. As a characteristic example of the tendency, consider the lapidary assertion of
Baudrillard: "Il n'y a de besoins que parce que le système en a besoin" ("Needs only
exist because the system needs them"; *Pour une critique*, p. 87).

seize, but they risk rigidifying it out of history altogether. In a sense, these reifications capitulate to the structures of postindustrial capitalism—as if they had succeeded finally in penetrating even to the deepest levels of social and individual consciousness.

Nonetheless, the force and centrality of these structures (if not their absorption and domination of the entire field of social existence in certain modern theorizations of them) are clearly perceived in our early nineteenth-century texts, and the perception continues to our own time. This continuity is what makes our own relation to the roman d'éducation in some sense a playing out of its own analytical procedures.

It was the process of envelopment in the structures of dominant discourse which first secreted the sign *as a problem* for a definable social population. What then emerged in the roman d'éducation was conception of a *network* linking the initiator, his pupil, and the semiotic content which is the substance of their transaction. This construct reconceived the abstract individualism of the character which we (and the texts of the period in question) have known as the "hero." Indeed, it is in this period that the concept of the hero itself became absorbed in the structure of initiation which dominates him as irrefutably as he attempts to dominate it. One need only try to imagine Fabrice del Dongo without Gina, or Lucien de Rubempré without Carlos Herrera, to see how profoundly derivative such individualities are rendered in these fictions.

This framing of individuals within the initiatory situation, and their ultimate domination by the form of the relationship itself, are conveyed in Vautrin's initial conversation with Lucien. It is central among the conditions which are to govern any future collaboration between them: "I don't know what name you would give to this rapid lesson . . . ; but it is the code of ambition. . . . You have no choice. . . . You have to accept the code."[46] The irony of such domination by the code is involuntary for Vautrin, but Balzac penetrates its logic. This is why the tie between Lucien and Carlos, as it develops, vacillates wildly from the most selfless dedication to the most egotistical possessiveness. It is neither their wills to create their relationship as they want nor the language controlled by either of them in

46. *Illusions perdues*, pp. 719–20.

defining it that determines its character. It is the structure of the link itself.

Constant slippage—for example, between dedication and domination—evidences the stress that the initiatory relation exercises upon those it links. Thus Vautrin to Lucien: "Enfin je me ferai vous!" ("In sum, I will become you!");[47] but only a few moments before: "Vous m'appartenez comme la créature est au créateur!"). Such vacillation, of course, harmonizes with the dependent personality of Lucien. But it is paradoxical in the case of a figure like Vautrin, who embodies so much of the dialectical tension of early bourgeois consciousness, particularly the contradiction between an ideology of rationality and control and a critique of the individual and social results of its practice.

Vautrin's evolution, even his celebrated defection to the side of "Order" at the end, uncovers these contraries, but without hinting at any possibility of their harmonization within middle-class society. What emerges is a suspicion that there may be *no* adequate conclusion for the initiatory structure. Its plot, which for a moment appeared resolvable in a story like Oscar Husson's, reveals its own unanticipated undoing, its own inexorable miscarriage. It is a particularly painful paradox for cultural theorization to discover that its paradigms of initiation issue unexpectedly into a *negative* consciousness. The paradigms themselves produce the realization of an inability to master the reality to which the sign system refers. Initiation appears to undergo a disorienting dialectical flip and is rewritten as *expulsion*.

The logic of Lucien's suicide lies in this fact, not in some depth-psychological "weakness," still less in the stereotypical "femininity" of character which Vautrin repeatedly attributes to him. Lucien's suicide means the failure of initiation to transform him, to develop within him the power which had been promised, to inscribe itself as historically *productive*. Lucien says precisely this to Herrera-Vautrin in his last letter: "You wanted to make me powerful and admired, you have dropped me into the abyss of suicide, that's the whole story [*voilà tout*]."[48] The contradiction at the center of the relationship concentrates itself in the final lines of Lucien's letter: "Don't mourn me: my contempt for you was as great as my admiration."

47. Ibid., p. 719.
48. *Splendeurs*, p. 473.

The trajectory of initiation thus conceived as overturning its own process provides a reading of the representations of *disillusionment* which are so characteristic of nineteenth-century consciousness. They appear as the most forceful manifestations of the paradox which determines the roman d'éducation from the beginning. What seems to happen is that in these representations *fate* takes on a new, more specifically material substructure. The configuration of sociality in the early capitalist world, objectified in the paradigm of initiation to the semiotic which intimately determines and sustains that world, for the first time is plotted as a grave destiny. For the first time the discourses regulating socialization are figured as an impasse.

Bourdieu and Passeron have attempted to theorize this cultural structure with their notions of "pedagogic authority" and "symbolic violence." If we read *Reproduction in Education, Society, and Culture* with these nineteenth-century texts in mind, we will begin to see how the concepts developed in the first part of that work unlock essential dynamics in the roman d'éducation. Bourdieu and Passeron sought to clarify the relations of compulsion and constraint which ideology has necessarily obscured within the pedagogical structure. They demystify the "gift" of education and place it firmly within a social setting which recognizes both the systemic need for semiotic initiation and the mechanisms of hierarchy and domination by which individuals are rendered subject to this need without necessarily having chosen to serve it.

Bourdieu and Passeron's work (along with Renée Balibar's *Les français fictifs* and her joint study with Dominique Laporte of *Le français national*) might thus be seen as a prolongation of Althusser's reflections on ideological apparatuses. Althusser is very clear about the centrality of the institution which has concerned me here: "I believe I have good reason for thinking that behind the scenes of its political Ideological State Apparatuses . . . , what the bourgeoisie has installed as its . . . dominant ideological State apparatus, is the educational apparatus."[49] The roman d'éducation perceived this centrality at an early

___

49. Althusser, "Ideology and Ideological State Apparatuses," p. 153. Let us recall that central to Althusser's concept of the ISA is that all such apparatuses "contribute . . . to the reproduction of the relations of production" (p. 154), even impose this—but *without* invoking the threat of explicit state repression, of overt violence (pp. 144–45). This perception of the education function (what Bourdieu and Passeron call "ped-

point in the implantation of capitalism's structures. Its paradigm, the initiatory relation, already embodied the mystified mechanism of social regulation which still seems essential to capitalist reproduction today. And by objectifying this relation, the genre establishes the conditions of possibility for its critique.

For my purposes, then, the theoretical perception of Bourdieu and Passeron is essential. They argue that any practice of inculcating the meanings which attach to social signifiers and discourses—any teaching—tends both to legitimize the social system within which such meanings function and to be legitimized (even imposed) by the power relations which underlie the system itself.[50] While we attend to the content of our instruction, we are modeled by its form; the ideological representation of the world is involuntarily naturalized even through critique of its specific detail.[51]

The contradictions which define the significance of Lucien de Rubempré's suicide in the most important of the romans d'éducation are clarified within such a framework. For it enables us to see that the mystification of the original pedagogical transaction between Lucien and Vautrin is *inevitable*. Lucien is promised the transcendence of social law. But he discovers that the very process of initiation which pledges such liberation itself inscribes the structure of power relations which was to be transcended. So Lucien learns that he has exchanged a more diffuse form of domination (in *Illusions perdues*) for one which in *Splendeurs et misères* proves immediate, continuous, and intolerably oppressive. In entering into an initiatory relation with Vautrin, he finds he has only tightened what we might see as the quintessential modern form of a master-slave dialectic that binds both of the actors within it. And the structure is all the more perplexing because the violence which its configuration determines is radically mystified for

---

agogic action") has a long history within the Marxist tradition. It begins as far back as Marx's Third Thesis on Feuerbach (on "educating the educator"). Prior to Althusser, as I discussed in my Introduction, it receives its most powerful development in Gramsci's notion of class hegemony as a mode of domination which not only determines explicitly political behavior but saturates the entire process of living without overtly exercising violence or coercion—a perception in turn akin to Marcuse's notion of "forms of control" in *One-Dimensional Man*.

50. *Reproduction*, pp. 4–7.
51. See Althusser, "Ideology," p. 157.

each of them. This is why Vautrin cannot liberate his pupil. Both are imprisoned in the relation which was to have freed them. The double-bind is hermetic.[52] Lucien exits from it in the only way he can.

The novels comprising Lucien's story still take individual destinies seriously, whence the emotional charge of his suicide and of Vautrin's eulogy. Whence also the shock of recognition Vautrin's final apostasy causes in us as we recognize, in the text's last demystification, the underlying *continuity* of his role throughout. Not only as *chef de la Police* but *all along,* and particularly as Lucien's instructor-protector, Vautrin has systematically enacted the structural authority, the mode of control, which sustains our modern form of domination: the power to determine meaning and to order the exchange of signs.

These problems sound much like some which still preoccupy us today, and clear relations tie the problematic central in the roman d'éducation to more contemporary concerns. Our institutions of criticism and of initiation still honor the mythic—the ideological—shape of a certain form of initiation, indissolubly associated with the dream of social mobility by the middle class and in the image of its own rise to power. It is true that the imaginative sources of this still-dominant discourse lie in part in the texts which have concerned me here. But its narratives functioned simultaneously to impeach the myth itself.

To some degree our contemporary critical discourses may tend to ignore the counter-discursive implications of this discovery of their dominant frame. They suppose a sovereignty (of the imaginative text, of the critical act, of the signifier itself) which in the context of my discussion may seem uncomfortably similar to the supposition, in the novel of education, that one could crack the code of signs without somehow being mastered by it in the process. There is something unsettling in this reproduction of a pattern which our own investiga-

---

52. Bourdieu and Passeron put the bind in the form of a classical paradox which illuminates the lock-up holding Vautrin and Lucien: "The idea of a P[edagogic] A[ction] exercised without P[edagogic] Au[thority] is a logical contradiction and a sociological impossibility; a PA which aimed to reveal, in its very exercise, its objective reality of violence and thereby to destroy the basis of the agent's PAu, would be self-destructive. The paradox of Epimenides the liar would then appear in a new form: either you believe I'm not lying when I tell you education is violence and my teaching isn't legitimate, so you can't believe me; or you believe I'm lying and my teaching is legitimate, so you still can't believe what I say when I tell you it is violence" (*Reproduction*, p. 12).

tion instructs us bears crucial contradictions within it. The very fact of positing such imaginative or semiotic independence may turn out, in practice, to have sources, and serve interests, other than those we thought.

We might recall in this regard Baudrillard's insistence that the arbitrary relation of signifier and signified that constitutes the sign already implies within itself a regulated sociality which stands both as institutional guarantor and as a kind of subterranean referent of the semiotic relation. Initiation offers instruction not only in the discrete content of signs but in the structure of regulatedness which sustains them. It thereby reinforces the systematicity of the social whole. Yet this systematicity, like the sign itself, is never abstract but (as the French say) "oriented": partisan, exploitative, consonant with certain specific social interests, structures, positions. As such, it constitutes the constraints of a *régime de sens,* of a system governing meaning, whose operation is the more binding on account of its transparency.

An economy like ours, founded on exchange, functions on the assumption that everyone emerges happy from trading. Exchange values pass through the system, in the subject's exercise of rational choice, and to the end of general contentment—or so the system believes on our behalf. And signs, in their position as quintessential exchange values under advanced capitalism, seem to circulate freely through the universe of social meaning.[53] Their transmission seems to carry no responsibility, to implicate no one.

A certain liberal ideology of freedom is inscribed in this very insouciance. The projection some have made of this free play—whether in a fantasy of language's self-reflexive autonomy and of the liberation of the text or in the homologous fantasy of a corporate economy of such profusion and productivity that no needs need go unsatisfied—seems a vision of the commodity's own utopia, the dream that exchange value itself might have of its radical domination of all social and imaginative existence.[54] As such, these representations remain enveloped within

---

53. This relation has been studied in detail, particularly by Baudrillard in *Pour une critique,* by Jean-Joseph Goux in *Economie et symbolique,* and by Ferruccio Rossi-Landi in *Linguistics and Economics.*

54. My formula imitates certain of Marx's concerning an imputed or imagined language of commodities. See *Capital,* vol. 1, p. 176: "If commodities could speak, they would say. . ."

the hegemonic régime de sens which they believed themselves to have transcended.

The contradictory structure of Balzacian initiation might then stand as a model of more complex figurations of the same operation in contemporary experience. The structure represents a paradigm of investigation of the semiotic and the socioeconomic transactions which link the discourses of social existence to their authentic productivity, to their real structures of transformation and control. The model argues for our criticism to seek its own status of *critique:* to foreground its sometimes mystified situation as counter-discourse and to begin to locate the dominant discourse which ceaselessly threatens to reenvelop it.

Dialectical thought is always dialectical against something and toward something else. Even to provide a sense of the directionality of the movement which has produced our current impressions of non-movement controverts the stasis in which we seem to find ourselves, the flattened imaginative range of our own period, and that contemporary reification of social relations whose production under capitalism Marx was the first to theorize.

In this regard it is fundamental that the interrogation of the sign which still preoccupies us—of the process of its transmission and its exchange and of the social structures which such processes seem to determine—emerged in the early nineteenth century in a period of the middle class's conquest and definition of its power. The inscription, even the complicity, of the social sign within a determinate structure of power became mystified as the process of conquest which had first motivated the interrogation moved toward later stages of historical and ideological consolidation. The critical bite, the virulence, of the early postrevolutionary analysis and practice of the sign has thus slowly diminished. Today these analyses and practices may strike us as easily assimilable within the apparently seamless ideological protocols of advanced capitalism.

But uncovering contradictions within the sign inscribed in a complex set of power relations in the period of the roman d'éducation may to some degree permit us to overcome more contemporary repression of the problematic which was thus laid bare. The history of these developments remains recoverable. This is why our investigation of these phenomena reproduces analytical protocols from the genre which has occupied us, why we still find ourselves writing a form of roman d'éducation a century and a half after the original examples revealed the necessity of understanding how initiation into signs and discourses functioned within a modern exchange economy. The key is still to uncover the mystified *inequality* of these exchanges, the secret productivity which is inscribed in any transfer of the sign.

Such an inequality—irreversible in the realm of thought alone and rooted in the materiality of a social formation and its institutions— defines the differential status of the counter-discourse and its dominant antagonist. These differentials are the mark of history. Thus, understanding the variety of the counter-discourses which arose within such a formation means investigating the discourses of domination by which they were framed. Their institution in the nineteenth century was driven by a dynamic of social transformation more powerful and more pervasive, perhaps, than any which had previously been seen. And, no less than their counter-discursive rivals, the ingeniousness of their forms was exemplary. One in particular, an innovation in our period, resumes the mode of their pervasiveness and their unprecedented power. It has become the most banal of our objects: the daily paper. We need to consider the development of this strain of dominant discourse, whose function was to regulate the exchange by which an entire social formation organized its affairs.

CHAPTER 2

Newspaper Culture: Institutions of Discourse; Discourse of Institutions

Les journaux . . . nous coûteront douze mille francs. [The newspapers will cost us twelve thousand francs.]
——BALZAC, *César Birotteau* (1837)

Je ne comprends pas qu'une main pure puisse toucher un journal sans une convulsion de dégoût. [I don't understand how an uncorrupted hand could touch a newspaper without a convulsion of disgust.]
——BAUDELAIRE, "Mon coeur mis à nu"

Newspapers: their ubiquity, their very banality, stand as signs of dominant discourse self-confidently bodied forth. Such hegemonic discourse daunts the analyst. We cannot display the content of such a diffuse formation. But to comprehend it at all, we need to consider some important strains and subsystems—here, the early mass dailies and some allied elements of commercial practices and discourses—which have come to make it up.

In the nineteenth century, much of "literature" defines its condition of existence as counter-discursive. Its status as "literary" *marks* it as oppositional. For this reason, any attempt to seize dominant discourse leads one *outside* the high cultural realm and into areas which might almost seem drearily down to earth. If we are conscious of it at all, in a sense the dominant is something we would prefer to forget about. But methodologically speaking we ought not to. In this chapter I will examine two networks of words and practices, subsystems of the nineteenth century's emerging dominant discourse: the early mass daily newspapers; the nascent department stores and the consuming practices they introduced. They were closely interrelated. In our period they and their analogues were slowly constituting the shape and texture of what we have come to know as modern life. But they motivated powerful tactics of resistance to such hegemonic penetration. In the case of the newspapers, such interplay of dominant discourse and counter-discourse is particularly instructive. In the chapter following this one such an interrelation will help to situate a characteristic and brilliant form of subversion: the antibourgeois critique embodied in the practice of the satirical newspaper and particularly in its extraordinary caricatures.

Since the early nineteenth century, newspapers have seemed to *go without saying*. What they speak has become so deeply internalized within us that the origins of their utterance, and of the practices of reading and perception they have taught us, appear diffused through the social formation—without any specific locus, transhistorical, attributable to no one. Whatever our attitude toward them as products of our culture, they and their discursive patterns have become essential to our modern construction of the world. Indeed, at times the "world" and the "news" might almost seem to have merged for us.

Newspaper proliferated extraordinarily in the period I am considering here, both in the number and variety of individual publications and in their overall circulation. At the end of the Restoration in 1830, the total circulation of Parisian dailies was approximately 50,000 copies. Fifteen years later this figure had tripled. It increased by a further factor of nearly 7 by 1870, then doubled again by 1880. Overall this was a multiplication of forty times—4,000 percent—in fifty years.[1] This sudden perfusion of the social field by the journalistic has become a familiar theme of nineteenth-century history.[2] But the modes of the newspaper's early penetration into structures of cultural and individual consciousness deserve parallel consideration.

---

1. Claude Bellanger et al., eds., *Histoire générale de la presse française*, vol. 2 (hereafter cited as *HGPF*), pp. 18, 24, 120, 259; Zeldin, *France*, vol. 2, p. 540.

2. See for example Crubellier, *Histoire culturelle*, chap. 8.

The persistence and the power of dominant forms of discourse—most centrally, their capacity to recontain the counter-discourses which seek to undermine or to displace them—were already clear in the novel of education. Through its protocols, Balzac had sought to turn the dominant discourse of the nascent middle-class inside out, to mobilize its instrumental power against itself. But the effort to overturn the autonomy of the social sign had ended disastrously by reconfirming it. Against the strategies for limiting its power, however ingeniously deployed, dominant discourse had survived and prospered, all the while solidifying its structures.

These structures epitomize themselves, and can fruitfully be read, in the daily paper. It became the most characteristic informational and commercial institution of the nineteenth century. So clearly does the newspaper epitomize the period that we could almost claim the century *invented* it.[3] Newspapers have formed so central a part of the discourse which has organized our social life since the 1830s that their very name—"daily," "quotidien"—has reappeared in that of the notion by which, since Henri Lefebvre, cultural theory has tried to seize the complex of practices which surround and frame us: "le quotidien," "daily (or everyday) life."[4]

Daily life and the daily paper grew up together, in response to the same determinants: "Until the nineteenth century, until the advent of competitive capitalism and the expansion of the world of trade, the

3. Invented or rediscovered: of course the newspaper existed prior to the nineteenth century, but it was in this period that its functionality in daily existence was devised, defined, and continuously refined. The standard history of the French press in our period is *HGPF*, which contains extensive bibliography. Also extremely valuable is the "Kiosque" collection published by Armand Colin, particularly Bellet, *Presse et journalisme*; Lethève, *La caricature*; and Henriette Vannier, *La mode et ses métiers*. (The range of the latter volume is considerably broader than its title suggests.) The most penetrating recent reflection on the institution (focused, however, on American examples) is Schudson's *Discovering the News*. Schudson's claim (pp. 22–31) that the penny papers "invented" news roughly parallels my own assertion here.

4. See Lefebvre, *Everyday Life in the Modern World*. Most recently, de Certeau, Giard, and Mayol, in *L'invention du quotidien*, have advanced theorization of *le quotidien* by investigating the interplay of individual resistance and acceptance—what in our terminology we might call the competition between counter- and dominant-discursive modes of representing and practicing the social—which structures all activity in the modern world. The "invention" of the daily paper—*le quotidien*—and of everyday life—*le quotidien*—coincides in the title of their study. But though they do not explicitly comment upon it, this semantic superposition is more than fortuitous. Through

quotidian as such did not exist."5 Lefebvre's assertion could as well describe the transformations by which the newspaper became an indispensable element of emerging everyday life. Significant elements of such a parallelism are clear. In its routinized, quotidian recurrence, in its quintessential prosaicism, in its unrepentant commercialism, the newspaper almost seems to have been devised to represent the pattern of variation without change, the repetitiveness, autonomization, and commodification which, since the twin revolutions of the nineteenth century, have marked fundamental patterns of our social existence. As such the newspaper becomes a characteristic metonym for modern life itself.

Indeed, the daily paper was arguably the *first* consumer commodity: made to be perishable, purchased to be thrown away. It became the most ubiquitous example of the habits of consciousness and of socioeconomic practice which in more explicit, thematic forms it sought to impart to its audience—or, as we might say, within its market. In selling a transformed perception of its culture, it sold itself first of all. The disenchanted intelligentsia, the alienated writers, reacted predictably. For them the newspaper became the quintessential figure for the discourse of their middle-class enemy, the *name* for the writing against which they sought to counterpose their own—as the epigraph from Baudelaire's "Mon coeur mis à nu" at the head of this chapter already sufficiently suggests.

But in the nineteenth century the daily had not yet retreated into the transparency of dailiness. This was the period in which newspapers with significant circulation, and thereby perceptible diffusion within the more general cultural discourse, were just beginning. For the analyst this period of incipience offers considerable advantages. They lie in two closely related areas. First, in the period of its early institutionalization a sociocultural form leaves traces of its operation which later, as it solidifies its domination, become considerably harder to detect. Only with time do specific practices integrate themselves into

---

it their title turns out to enfold a double meaning which inscribes the manner in which the daily paper itself takes a privileged place as figure for the constant, recurring practices by which daily life is produced and reproduced, for the complex of modes of attention which the nineteenth century organized in response to the needs of a transforming socioeconomy.

5. Lefebvre, *Everyday Life*, p. 38.

the network of the culturally normalized, the self-evident, the socially transparent. Early on, their "fit" is rougher, their functioning more strained. This makes it possible to detect, in their transitional period, a configuration which has since become organized as invisibility for us.

Second, such early penetration of a new cultural form or practice typically produces explicit—indeed, sometimes violent—movements of resistance: counter-hegemonic dynamics, counter-discursive practices, whose angles of attack can assist us in perceiving an emerging dominant form before it becomes fully absorbed into the network of the ideological. In the early phases of its constitution as a social practice, we can read its configuration in part through the disruptions and reactions it is perceived to cause. With great conjunctural sensitivity, counter-discourses thus map the points of stress within the social system which accompany the slow institutionalization of the new.

The isolation of the sign from its embedding in the sociocultural flux, which I argued was a response to the rapidity of transformation in the socioeconomy of early nineteenth-century France, and its foregrounding as an object of discursive and practical *concern* in the activities of daily living within urban culture—these phenomena provide a perspective on the institution of the newspaper in the same period. And as with the roman d'éducation, the dialectic of resistance to these new forms of attention and consciousness develops not only outside of them but *internally*, within the emerging discourse itself. In the case of the roman d'éducation, this resistance became perceptible in the ambition to annex or recontain the instrumentalism of middle-class discourse, to dominate the dominant social sign. In the case of the newspaper, as I will argue in the next chapter, it occurs in the form of a wild satirical impulse *within* the medium to sap its own protocols of domination, to undermine the institution in whose service these protocols were being so brilliantly and so influentially developed.

The logic and techniques of such subversion arise (by a paradox which is only apparent) in the discursive practices into whose forms the newspaper necessarily educated its clientele. If what I called "education into signs" in Chapter 1 is an indispensable part of the construction of a modern economic formation, then for nineteenth-century culture the newspaper becomes something like an *empire des signes*, a realm of signifiers perceived and valued in isolation from one another, precisely *because* of such abstraction. Newspapers trained their readers in the apprehension of detached, independent, reified, decontextualized "articles"—and the ambiguity of the term (which might mean either an element of newspaper format, a "news item," or an element of commercial transaction, a "commodity") is itself significant. It will prove impossible to disengage these two elements of the newspaper's functionality—imparting information, selling goods—from each other.

Seen in this way, the newspaper can be understood as the first culturally influential *anti-organicist* mode of modern discursive construction. Its form *denies form*, overturns the consecrated canons of text structure and coherence which had operated in the period preceding its inception. Organicism, as it arose in the late eighteenth century, registered the necessity, first, of representing the world as conflicted, and second, of mastering the contradictions within it which were thereby foregrounded. Organicist writing sought the forms which might accommodate within imaginative representation growing experiences of dissonance in social and political existence. The theory behind such writing sanctioned expression of those experiences of conflict but simultaneously prescribed their containment and reharmonization.

As against such structures of reharmonization, the newspaper is built by addition of discrete, theoretically disconnected elements which juxtapose themselves only in response to the abstract requirements of "layout"—thus of a disposition of space whose logic, ultimately, is commercial. Nominally the daily is comprised of two differentiable kinds of space: it has room for articles (news, opinion) and for "articles" (advertising). But the relation between the two rapidly became mystified. In principle they were segregated by their position in each issue: the front page, for example, devoted to the "news," the back page to what we would call the "classifieds," and so on.

But in France this code for laying out the printed space broke down very early. Its ostensible purpose had been to serve as a metalanguage orienting readers concerning the *kind* of utterance confronting them, distinguishing between the presumably factual discourse of the "news" on the one hand, and the paid puffery of advertisements on the other. This mode was presumed to establish, for such an utterance, the quotient of "objectivity" attributable to it, and thereby the attitude with which it might be taken up by the reader. Of course such distinctions had become necessary only under the conditions of modern commercial journalism to begin with—under a system which presumed that the sale of space for advertising provided the income which made the collection and propagation of the news on a mass scale feasible; under a system which conversely purveyed the advertisements "for free" along with the news the purchaser nominally paid for.

In practice the liberal fiction that the discourses coexisting within the newspaper's pages might be segregated as to type and presumed truth-value fractured under the same pressures of quantification which had determined its institution in the first place. Once it had become clear that space could be *sold*, then *all* the space in the paper became potentially salable, potentially purchasable.

The papers' "zoning" restrictions were thus quickly and systematically transgressed. Beginning in the period after 1836 when Girardin (with *La Presse*) and Dutacq (with *Le Siècle*) created the archetypes of modern mass-circulation dailies (of which more shortly), a commercial code governing the *sale of space* annulled in secret the public code which ostensibly determined the position within the paper of the different modes of discourse which composed it. This system, known "to the trade," differentiated between four kinds of salable space, carefully apportioned them, and determined their value. It has been little noticed, but it stands as one of the most ingenious and influential early examples of what Max Weber termed "rationalization"—worked out in this particular case with a geometer's (or a business manager's) logic and precision.[6] The concrete experience of such an abstracting logic and rationalization was served up to readers with their daily paper.

The cheapest variety of salable space within the paper was the so-called English advertisement or *annonce*, undisguisedly commercial in intent and in presentation. Virtually all French dailies of the period published in a four-page format; such ads appeared on page 4, in

6. On Weberian rationalization, see his *Economy and Society*, esp. pp. 809ff. There is wide agreement that such rationalizations increasingly dominate our sense of "everyday life" since the nineteenth century: "Everything . . . is calculated because everything is numbered: money, minutes, metres, kilometres, calories" (Lefebvre, *Everyday Life*, p. 21). A quaint analogue to the calculus of value which invisibly underlay the disposition of space in the pages of the daily paper can be found in the proto-commodification of *time* in the nineteenth century *cabinets de lecture*, where one could rent books "by the month, by the year, by the sitting, by the volume, or by the day" (Allen, *Popular French Romanticism*, p. 139).

columns much like our modern "classifieds." This locus within the paper thus comprised the space most frankly and most single-mindedly dedicated to the business of business. Consequently it became a symbol of the crass instrumentalism for which intellectuals excoriated the middle class; it served as archetype of a dominant discourse, unredeemably *prosaic*, against which their counter-discourses increasingly were to be deployed. Thus Mallarmé's intense attack upon the discourse of the annonce: "Verse [poetry] is everywhere in language, except on page 4 of the newspapers."[7]

The second form of salable space was the *réclame*, which appeared on page 3 and which cost two-thirds more than the page 4 annonce. The réclames were more like modern display ads, with a somewhat greater typographical variety possible than in the annonce. But like the page 4 ads the réclames were perfectly frank in their commercial intent.

To this point, the topographical segregation of discourse types within the daily paper's format maintained itself. But it collapsed immediately in the third category of advertisement, the paid "fait divers" item, which appeared on page 2, and which cost an additional 30 percent over the space rate for the *réclame*. Here, the disguised colonization of "objective" informational discourse by the commercial began. It culminated in the opening of the papers' first pages to surreptitious paid publicity, the most frankly deceptive presentation of text in the arsenal of modes available to the editors and commercial directors of the nineteenth-century daily.

"Editorial publicity" on page 1 completely disguised its status as advertisement. It could consist of a recommendation, within a nominally factual *chronique*, of a stock share, or of a particular recent book within a literary *compte-rendu*. From within the world of journalism, this system induced a generalized cynicism concerning the interchangeability of facts, opinions, and money. Villemessant, the notorious editor of *Le Figaro* during the Second Empire, declared that he

---

7. "Sur l'évolution littéraire," *Oeuvres complètes*, ed. Henri Mondor and G. Jean-Aubry (Paris: Gallimard-Pléiade, 1945), p. 867; cf. "l'annonce, en quatrième page, entre une incohérence de cris inarticulés" ("the *annonce*, on page 4, amidst an incoherence of inarticulate [or unarticulated] cries"; "Le livre, instrument spirituel," *Oeuvres complètes*, p. 379). The specific referent of these attacks on "page 4" has not always been identified in discussions of these important texts.

was satisfied with an issue of his paper only when *every single line* within it had been bought and paid for in some way.[8]

It was this overtly venal sale of the newspaper which Balzac had chronicled in the second part of *Illusions perdues*. His objections were largely moral, and of course they had their weight. But in the context of my discussion of the newspaper's disposition of space, of the topology of its interpenetrating discourses, what is of greatest moment is the manner in which their juxtaposition schooled readers to the neutralization of any active perception of contradiction.

In consequence we could understand the institution, the specific social *practice* of the newspaper, as the earliest significant, broadly circulated and recognized representation of the sorts of pervasive dissonances and contradictions in modern existence about which it appears *nothing can or will be done*. Such at least would seem to be the discursive subtext emerging from the form itself. Randomly juxtaposed in the orderly columns of pages 1 through 4, items of news, publicity, comment, and information (which in these nineteenth-century dailies all appeared in pretty much the same typographical monotony) simultaneously confronted and studiously ignored each other. The form of the newspaper projects no thought or expectation of their harmonization or resolution, no notion that *collectively* they might make sense. It instructs us in the apparently irreducible fragmentation of daily experience, and by its normalization prepares us to live it.[9]

The newspaper thus bears its contradictions on its face, in a clashing,

8. The four-part page-rate system is outlined in Zeldin, *France*, vol. 2, pp. 513–14.

9. The typographical uniformity of nineteenth-century newspapers is discussed by Raymond Williams, "Advertising," pp. 175–76. See also Walter Benjamin, "The Paris of the Second Empire in Baudelaire," in *Baudelaire*, p. 28. The ideological effectiveness of modern informational media in imparting new habits of perception functional under the transformed conditions of modern capitalism was a preoccupation, particularly, of the members of the Frankfurt School. Benjamin, in his well-known essay "Some Motifs in Baudelaire," says this: "Man's inner concerns do not have their issueless private character by nature. They do so only when he is increasingly unable to assimilate the data of the world around him by way of experience. Newspapers contribute one of many evidences of such an inability. If it were the intention of the press to have the reader assimilate the information it supplies as part of his own experience, it would not achieve its purpose. But its intention is just the opposite, and it is achieved: to isolate what happens from the realm in which it could affect the experience of the reader. . . . Lack of connection between individual news items . . . contribute[s] as much to this as does the make-up of the pages and the paper's style" (*Baudelaire*, p. 112). Max

conflicted disposition of its discursive surface. But it devalues their adversative energy, and it projects this flattening into the experiential time of our reading, into the phenomenology of our practice of it, in a way no previous social text had done. This homogenization of the discourse represented more than a brilliant strategy for coining money. The perspective of the balance sheet of course is interesting. But we need to attend as well to that of the overall discursive system, slowly transforming itself within economic conditions and a general social formation which were both unprecedented. Within such a frame, the effect of commercializing information was to reduce the influence of *other* social and ideological determinants upon the formation of newspaper discourse. Particularly, such developments devalued certain traditional constraints upon structure, content, and potential audience.

The result of these changes was to augment the exchangeability of the discursive sign—at the price of a coordinate decline in its commitment to any network of social or political choice. Thus transformed, its availability for recombination substantially increased, moving the sign toward emulation of the status of universal equivalent enjoyed, as Marx argued in the first volume of *Capital*, by money itself. But then, like money, it began to seem *colorless*. This asymptotic approach of the semiotic and the economic has become an important notion in modern cultural theory. It is, however, worthwhile to keep in mind the material base and practical developments upon which such an epochal mutation began to be founded in our period.

In connection with this phenomenon of juxtaposition of the irreconcilable within newspaper space one might be tempted to think of cinematic montage.[10] Yet the sequence of film shots whose relations are unreadable without considerable analytical work differs crucially from the discontinuity and fragmentation which is our experience of newspaper form. Since the logic presiding over the disposition of its

---

Horkheimer addresses the more general situation of the consumer in his argument that the advance of corporate industrialism required that the "objects of organization"—the citizens of a modern liberal socioeconomy—"be disorganized as subjects" ("The End of Reason," p. 384). More recently, the work of Hans Magnus Enzensberger has focused on the area of concern to me here; see *The Consciousness Industry*.

10. Specifically, of Eisenstein's "montage of collision." See Gerald Mast, *A Short History of the Movies*, pp. 198ff.

content is nowhere expressible in the content itself, nothing in the daily paper recuperates the sense of radical dispersal which its layout induces in us. It thus stands as testimony to important modifications in our experience of time and space, and in our expectations concerning their organization, in the period since the rise of urban and capitalist structures in the nineteenth century.[11]

The commodity form would seem to be the underlying principle of such organization: as with the daily, each "article" is conceived as autonomous and detachable. It is related to the social whole only through the abstract principle of its availability, at any moment, to be marketed and consumed. But if *every* element of the social totality, through the operation of the market, may at any moment be randomly connected with any other element, then the notions of connection and (coordinately) of contradiction are drained of much of their explanatory and much of their critical force. So there is a real sense in which the principle of organization of these structures—of the market, of the daily paper—is a systematic emptying of any logic of connection. They rationalize disjunction; they are organized *as disorganization*.

The epochal alterations in space and time implied in these developments did not occur in a moment. They resulted from a process of inflection, refinement, and change in the material and ideological conditions determining newspaper production and consumption which form the profound history of nineteenth-century journalism in France. My intention here is not to examine in detail the successive stages of these developments or of the technical and commercial innovations which made them possible. For the purposes of a discussion of the competing modes of social discourse which arose on the one hand in the newspaper, and on the other in the struggle against the social forces whose discourse it was taken to represent, it may be sufficient to indicate a few cardinal points in this protracted and complex evolution.

---

11. Important analogues to our consideration of the phenomenology and social practice of space and discursive relation induced by the modern daily newspaper would be Jacques Le Goff, "Au Moyen-Age: Temps de l'église et temps du marchand," and E. P. Thompson, "Time, Work-Discipline, and Industrial Capitalism." The recent book by Donald M. Lowe, *History of Bourgeois Perception*, esp. chaps. 3 and 4, though not treating the newspaper in any detail, is of considerable interest in connection with the present discussion.

In the early part of the century, French newspapers most frequently positioned themselves as organs of a political party or faction.[12] This meant that as commercial undertakings they were not primarily oriented toward building their circulation. Rather, they profited from increases in the influence of their political or parliamentary tendency. Once a paper's political position was established, its circulation was relatively insensitive to variations in the paper's specific daily or weekly content and depended much more upon changes in the fortunes of the party behind it. Simply put, individual copies of these newspapers did not have to sell themselves. Under such conditions, a paper's circulation was relatively stable—and relatively static. In turn, advertising within the papers was largely informational, and its presentation was in general extremely conservative.

Overall, these publications made virtually no concessions to the seduction of the reader: "One needs to recall the look of the nineteenth-century daily, with its discreet headlines and the gray blur [*grisaille*] of its typography."[13] Such enterprises were often extremely profitable to their owners. We might recall the power of Finot in *Illusions perdues*, or one of the concluding remarks in Monsieur Prud'homme's (Henri Monnier's) autobiography, in which he blesses Providence for having at last made him, a good bourgeois, director of a newspaper.[14] Yet it would be hard to think of the newspapers of the Restoration or the early July Monarchy as commodities fully integrated into the circuit of a modern consumer economy.

Individual copies of newspapers in this period were not sold at all. One either subscribed—the normal price of a subscription to a major Paris daily in the period was 80 francs a year, or about a tenth of an average worker's wages—or one could rent a paper by the hour at a *cabinet de lecture*.[15] As a commercial product, the newspaper still re-

12. A rapid outline of these tendencies and the newspapers corresponding to them can be found in Duchet, *Manuel d'histoire littéraire*, pp. 453–54.

13. Lethève, *La caricature*, p. 64.

14. Cited in Melcher, *Monnier*, p. 192. There is, however, an ironic postscript in which we learn that Prudhomme's newspaper collapsed and he was completely ruined: money, the basis of his entire existence, at last simply evaporates.

15. On subscription costs, see Zeldin, *France*, vol. 2, pp. 494–95, and Duchet, *Manuel d'histoire littéraire*, p. 286. On the *cabinets de lecture*, see Barbéris and Duchet, *Manuel d'histoire littéraire*, vol. 1, 440–45; and Allen, *Popular French Romanticism*, pp. 139–45. See also Walter Benjamin, *Baudelaire*, p. 27.

sembled to some degree the "custom" item purveyed by early nineteenth-century artisans or tradespeople. The scale of its market—and the range of its commercial mentality—were coordinately restricted. It had yet to integrate within its structures the dynamism of nascent capitalist modes of production and circulation.

These were the conditions under which, in 1830, Parisian newspapers overall sold no more than a total of 50,000 copies a day—at a time when the population of the capital already exceeded one million (moreover, a significant proportion of these copies were mailed to subscribers in the provinces; Paris in this period comprised only 3 percent of the total population of France).[16]

Within fifty years, this circulation increased forty-fold. Even relative to the growing population of the capital, the newspaper's saturation of the Paris market half a century after the July 1830 revolution was fully *sixteen times* as great. Whatever its cultural influence around 1830, in the subsequent period which forms the heart of my investigation the newspaper as an institutionalized discourse would experience an extraordinary multiplication in its pervasiveness, in its penetration and domination of the world of words and social representations. For the first time, in these vertiginous changes, it begins to be possible to imagine an authentic *mass* medium.

The altered climate in which such increases were produced led to changes throughout the culture, particularly in forms of individual experience and individual practice. In the case of the daily paper these changes are strikingly readable. In most histories of the newspaper's growth during our period, two names are associated with these developments: Emile de Girardin and Moïse (known as Polydore) Millaud.

The innovations they brought about radically reconceived the cultural range and the internal space of the daily paper. They transformed its audience—its market—and the structure of its commercial and informational economy. They turned the daily into a commodity in terms of both its means of circulation and its content. As they recast and reorganized it, the newspaper was adapted to the implicit needs of commerce. It *became* the institutional incarnation of the dominant discourse for which I argued it could be taken—and indeed was taken—as a characteristic figure.

16. Barbéris and Duchet, *Manuel d'histoire littéraire*, vol. 1, p. 315.

Girardin's and Millaud's innovations are well known. In July 1836, Girardin brought out a new paper, *La Presse*, and undercut the going subscription rates for the other Paris dailies by 50 percent. His notion was simple: to make up in increased circulation what he lost on the individual subscription price.[17] But while the cost for subscribers was lower, his advertising rates remained just what the traditional dailies charged (in 1836, 1 franc 50 per line for an annonce and coordinately up the four-part scale I have already described).[18] The commercial promise was wider distribution of advertisements at no increase in the cost to the businessman.

But the reconceived market implied by Girardin's reduced subscription price entailed changes in the content of the daily which are less often discussed. In effect, his innovation reversed the economic importance of its informational and commercial space. By selling the whole paper for less but charging the same amount as the competition for advertisements, in effect Girardin skewed the value of the page space at his disposal *toward the commercial*. In the new economy his price structure established, an ad was worth relatively more than a news item. The influence of the advertiser tended to increase in proportion.

Simultaneously his scheme altered the newspaper's traditional content. The general tendency of the press under the July Monarchy (as under the Restoration) had been to map the political spectrum with a number of competing "journaux d'opinion." But Girardin's innovation rendered political definition of a paper's circulation base obsolete. For the first time, he produced a daily whose concept was *commercial* rather than political. Consequently he needed to appeal not just to the restricted audience of one or another parliamentary faction but to what we can already begin to project as a mass audience transcending any

17. Simultaneously, Girardin's former collaborator, Dutacq, began *Le Siècle*, to be sold at the same subscription price of 40 francs (provincial subscriptions were 48 francs). Soon, the other Paris dailies were forced to lower their rates in order to compete. Detailed accounts of these developments can be found in *HGPF*, pp. 114–20; and Barbéris and Duchet, *Manuel d'histoire littéraire*, vol. 1, pp. 450–53. On Girardin see also Barbéris, *Balzac et le mal du siècle*, vol. 2, pp. 942ff., and Josette Pare Young, "Emile de Girardin, le 'journal à deux sous' et la littérature romanesque à l'époque romantique," *French Review*, 56, no. 6 (May 1983): 869–75. We might note that the price-cut Girardin initiated in journalism was reproduced two years later, through the same logic, in book publishing: Charpentier halved the per volume price of his novels to 3 francs 50. See Allen, *Popular French Romanticism*, p. 140 and n. 41.

18. See Passeron, *Daumier*, pp. 136–37.

programmatic factionalism. Thus depoliticized, the *citizen* was evolving into the *consumer*.

The result was that the discourse of political *opinion* which had been a primary content of the traditional paper tended to be replaced by a flattened, "objective" discourse of *information*. For the first time, a newspaper began to conceive its audience not exclusively but *inclusively*, to project its mode of intervention in the broader social text not as confrontation and challenge but as *co-optation*. With *La Presse*, the valuation of conscious social and political difference was radically inverted.

Given its ideology of inclusiveness and of "objectivity," a cultural object conceived in this way tends to represent in its form the neutralization of contradiction which the newspaper was simultaneously realizing in the organization of its individual text elements. It produces itself as a false totalization of the social realm whose internal differentiation and conflict it mystifies. The explicitly political papers openly expressed their partisanship, their *partiality* (in both senses of the term). But the sort of daily Girardin projected implicitly claimed, for the first time, objectively and exhaustively to represent *the world*. The development of such a tendency can be read, at the other end of its evolution, in an 1893 editorial in *Le Petit Parisien*, which by that time had become one of the mass-circulation leaders in France: "To read one's newspaper is to live the universal life, the life of the whole capital, of the entire city, of all France, of all nations. . . . It is thus that in a great country like France, the same thought, at one and the same time, animates the whole population. . . . It is the newspaper which establishes this sublime communion of souls across distances."[19]

An innovation of this magnitude was bound to elicit resistance from elements of the traditional culture which it sought to devalue, co-opt, or replace. In the case of Girardin's *La Presse*, such resistance almost immediately took a naked and personal form. Three weeks after the first issue appeared, Armand Carrel, the politically courageous editor of the opposition republican paper *Le National*, publicly accused Girardin of having "reduced the noble mission of the journalist to that of a vulgar news-merchant." It was decided to settle the matter through that most traditionalist of institutions for resolving conflict: the pistol

19. Cited from Zeldin, *France*, vol. 2, p. 529; translation modified.

duel. Girardin dispatched Carrel with a single shot. The passing of a cultural order has rarely been symbolized so punctually or so instructively.[20]

Moïse Millaud realized in practice what had been potential in Girardin's rearticulation of the social space and the content of the daily. In February 1863 he launched *Le Petit Journal*, published in tabloid format and—for the first time—sold "au numéro," by the individual copy, at 5 centimes (1 sou) apiece. *Le Petit Journal* declared itself a nonpolitical daily ("quotidien non politique"), and was therefore exempted from payment of the *caution*, a deposit required of other newspapers by the government, to be set against possible fines in case their contents were found offensive by Napoléon III's censors.

Girardin's redefinition of the identity principle of *La Presse* a quarter century earlier, his depoliticization of the paper, was thus juridically recognized and institutionalized. Millaud's *Petit Journal* renounced expression of partisan political opinion and organized its space around the binary categories which still divide the ideological space of the daily: objective, nonpartisan "news" and paid advertising. And though

20. See Barbéris and Duchet, *Manuel d'histoire littéraire*, vol. 1, p. 453; Crubellier, *Histoire culturelle*, p. 172. Carrel's was not the only voice of protest (though he may have been the only fatality in the struggle). The most frequent comparison made was between Girardin and the famous swindler Robert Macaire, whose exploits had recently been revived on the stage by Frédéric Lemaître. (Soon, of course, as we will see in the next chapter, Macaire would become one of Daumier's stock characters for excoriating the middle class whose mentality Girardin's innovations so strikingly incarnated.) See Bellet, *Presse et journalisme*, p. 192. On Macaire and his ideological importance, see Wechsler, *Human Comedy*, pp. 82–84. For the sake of historical accuracy, it should be added that *La Presse* and *Le Siècle* never attained the commercial success which we might have imagined their innovations produced for them. That they did not do so in part reflects the response of the competition to which I have already alluded. But the fact also helps us to measure how profound these discursive innovations seemed in the period in which they occurred, or rather, how much social and cultural readjustment was still required to integrate them so that a true mass-circulation paper could succeed. Their circulation languished, attaining only 22,000 (*La Presse*) and 34,000 (*Le Siècle*) ten years after they began to appear (see *HGPF*, pp. 114–15). Finally, we should note developments in the areas of news gathering and distribution, and of distribution of published papers and books, which paralleled those in journalism. Between 1832 and 1852, Charles Havas (for the former activity) and Louis Hachette (for the latter) achieved monopolies in their respective areas. See Crubellier, *Histoire culturelle*, p. 171. The familiar patterns of capitalist concentration and market domination were emerging rapidly.

the *caution* was later abolished, the formula persisted, since its real logic was that of the market, not that of the law.

This time the journalistic/commercial revolution worked. By July 1863, daily circulation of *Le Petit Journal* had attained 38,000; by October, 83,000. By the end of 1865, it stood at 259,000 (by itself the equivalent of five times the total circulation of all Paris papers in 1830). It was to exceed 300,000 in 1869 and reach nearly 600,000 in 1880. By that point its circulation was four times that of its nearest rival.[21]

An examination of the prospectus Millaud published in 1863 for his new daily is instructive: "*Le Petit Journal* will regularly present official announcements, summaries of the general news of Paris, the *départements*, and foreign countries, accounts of major events, stock and bond summaries, programs and reviews of theatrical productions, accounts of court and trial proceedings, bibliographical notices, a substantial and varied literary section."[22] Within the omnium-gatherum rhetoric of the prospectus, what is striking is the exaggeration of the absence of organic logic, of precisely the same indiscriminate accumulative structure, which I asserted were characteristic of newspaper form and layout in general. The prospectus reads like the textual representation of the fundamental *disparity* constituting the newspaper's construction of social existence. In such a perspective the laconic juxtaposition of "accounts of major events [*faits saillants*]" and "stock and bond summaries" may seem to us particularly (if unwittingly) comic.

This logic of accumulation responds to the new conditions under which *Le Petit Journal* was distributed. The *vente au numéro*—single-copy sale—meant that every day each copy of the paper had to sell itself. By offering numerous categories of information, however disparate, the chances that one or another of them might correspond to a particular consumer's desire tended to increase—and in any case the price of the paper was so low that one could afford to buy it just to get

21. On *Le Petit Journal*, see particularly *HGPF*, pp. 327–28, Crubellier, *Histoire culturelle*, pp. 177–78, Duchet, *Manuel d'histoire littéraire*, pp. 186–87, Zeldin, *France*, vol. 2, pp. 526–27.

22. Cited in *HGPF*, p. 327. Compare the 1843 program of the weekly *L'Illustration*: "immense almanac which will narrate and illustrate . . . the facts: political events, public ceremonies, great national celebrations, important disasters, gossip of the capital, the deceases of the famous, contemporary biographies" etc. (cited by Crubellier, *Histoire culturelle*, p. 189). The topical breadth—or dispersion—of Millaud's prospectus is perceptibly greater.

the stock report. So *Le Petit Journal* was a daily not only by its frequency of publication, but also, for the first time, in its conception of the content by which it sought each day to present itself as uniquely desirable.

Even under the earlier conditions of distribution to subscribers and through the *cabinets de lecture*, editors had discovered that the presence of certain features—particularly the *roman-feuilleton* developed as a sales strategy by *La Presse* and *Le Siècle* in 1836—could considerably increase circulation. The classic case was the 1843 publication of Sue's *Le juif errant* in *Le Constitutionnel*: the paper's circulation quadrupled to 80,000 during its run there. But the less-literary consumer whom Moïse Millaud had targeted for *Le Petit Journal* was more susceptible to the attraction of a bloody *fait-divers* than of a *feuilleton*. Consequently the literary serials in *Le Petit Journal* never increased circulation by more than 50,000, whereas detailed accounts of the scandalous Affaire Troppman in 1869 easily doubled that figure.[23] Under such conditions, the antiliterary vulgarity for which alienated writers were already condemning the newspapers took on an even more explicit quality. In any case, from this time on, *l'information*, conceived as appealing to the desire for excitement and stimulation experienced by the average petit-bourgeois reader, increasingly dominated the increasingly dominant discourse of the mass-circulation dailies.

The absorption of information-gathering and distribution into the capitalist circuit was perfectly clear to the contemporaries of *La Presse* and *Le Petit Journal*. In 1839, Sainte-Beuve entitled an article on newspapers in *La Revue des Deux Mondes* "De la littérature industrielle" ("On Industrial Literature"), and pointed out how deeply the interpenetration of informational and commercial discourse in the pages of the daily rendered the former discourse suspect: "How could they

---

23. See Duchet, *Manuel d'histoire littéraire*, pp. 286–87; and Crubellier, *Histoire culturelle*, p. 177. Crubellier (pp. 184–86) has studied the techniques adopted to increase sales by mass-circulation papers after 1863. He divides these into five principal (and, in our own time, painfully familiar) categories: (1) "Du sang à la une": if possible, a bloody crime as lead story; (2) "Human interest": personalized stories of famous or curious individuals; (3) the use of headline typography to attract attention; (4) standardization of language and thought to make access automatic; (5) the attempt (through games, polls, etc.) to associate the reader with the contents of the paper, and personalize his or her relation to it.

damn a product about which it was said two inches below that it was a miracle of the epoch?" And the phrase "les industriels du journalisme" appeared regularly and critically through the century.[24]

With this increasingly successful conversion of the organization of newspaper space and the practice of newspaper reading to the needs of commerce and the commodity came modifications in the mechanisms of a closely coordinate area: shopping, the place of truth of consumer capitalism itself. Before going on in the next chapter to an examination of the counter-discourses of the newspaper, I want to consider the innovations which transformed the "downstream" end of the consumer circuit of which newspaper advertising provided an earlier crucial moment. In our period these innovations produced the unprecedented social practice of the department store, which, perhaps as much as the dailies themselves, played a crucial role in propagating the habits of what I am calling newspaper culture.

A phrase of Horkheimer's lucidly puts the relevance of an examination of nineteenth-century shopping practices: "The ideal place for observing bourgeois manners is the market place."[25] Here in the emporium, as with the experience of reading the newspaper, the practice of a culture was profoundly modified, and a new articulation of social space and of individual needs, desires, and expectations was produced for nineteenth-century French people.

At the beginning of her study of mass consumption in France in our period, Rosalind Williams recalls an extraordinary moment in Zola's *Au bonheur des dames*. Denise Baudu has newly arrived in Paris from her provincial village. She walks in astonishment through the first department store she has ever seen (it gives its name, almost like a proprietary trademark, to the novel itself) and contemplates a seductive

24. Sainte-Beuve is cited by Benjamin, *Baudelaire*, p. 27. On "les industriels," see *HGPF*, p. 123.

25. "Feudal Lord," p. 125. Investigation of the social practices of the marketplace in nineteenth-century France has recently advanced materially in the work of two American analysts: Michael B. Miller, *The Bon Marché*, and Rosalind H. Williams, *Dream Worlds*. Their work provides significant models for the study of crucial elements of everyday life since the Industrial Revolution. For parallel developments in England, despite differences in period and perspective, see also McKendrick, Brewer, and Plumb, *Birth of a Consumer Society*.

display of clothing. But there is a disquieting element: the manne-
quins' heads have been replaced by price tags.[26]

Reification is capitalism's master trope. Here, in a grotesquely comic
and revealing figure, reification takes the form of a radical reduction of
being to *exchange value*. The price tag substituting for the mannequin's
head (the anatomical part which most signifies representation of the
human) becomes the metonym of the whole display; simultaneously
the arrangement metaphorizes *desire* as *money*. This is the archetype of
the figural reduction and displacement, the modification of perceptual
structures, which the discourses of emerging capitalism sought to naturalize for the new populations of the city, and which the latter had to
learn to "read" in order to function in a world increasingly saturated by
the commercial.

In such a reduction we might perceive the whole story of commodification and the mystification of the human being's place in the
production process which commodity fetishism entails. The representational displacement Denise Baudu is exposed to—prices for manne-
quins for people—mediates the sort of astonishing and disorienting
transformation of the older, more organic forms of everyday experience which her identity as a woman fresh from the provinces is meant
to signify.

Zola made a striking discovery in the course of researching the
world of the department store for *Au bonheur des dames*. The Bon
Marché store has generally been thought of as, if not the first *grand
magasin*, then at least the most consistently innovative. Zola learned
that Boucicaut, its founder and presiding genius, had contrived *pur-
posefully* to orchestrate the confusion of the store's layout. He did this
in order to oblige shoppers to travel the length and breadth of the Bon
Marché to find the items they had come to purchase. In the meantime,
they were exposed to the display, to the seduction, of other items they
had not initially thought to acquire. These too, the merchandisers
learned, could profitably become imprinted with customers' desire. It
was a neat trick: turnover and sales volume increased substantially.
Viewed more structurally, however, the impression was of a constructed disorder that eliminated organic connections between the dif-

26. *Dream Worlds*, p. 2.

ferent *rayons* (departments), and perversely divorced them one from another.[27]

This ordered disorganization of the shopping space, and thereby of the time and the practice of shopping, recalls the newspaper's random disposition of unrelated articles which, I argued, induced in the reader a tolerance for unorganic confusion which served much more the needs of the layout editor than it did the reader's own. In both cases, the manipulations of space and time oblige the person who would navigate within them to submit to a logic which is incomprehensible in terms of anything the subject can know or feel. The discourses and practices determining such submission manufacture the sorts of behavior we know as consumer behavior.

To have come to that point itself represented a revolution in the commercial practices of domination. Just as the tolerance, then later the positive assertion of dispersion slowly increased in the world of the newspaper layout, so too it required some time before the attitude exemplified by Boucicaut—a positive and manipulative intervention in the moment-to-moment experience of the clientele—would take form. In the 1830s and 1840s, with the introduction of the *magasins de nouveautés*, the first steps in this direction had been taken.[28] Whereas up to this point the object of merchandising had been simply to foster establishment of contact between potential purchaser and potential seller—the meaning of the newspaper term "annonce" suggests as much—it now began to be thought that *one could intervene to increase the market*, to induce purchases which, without the practices of merchandising and advertising, would not have been made at all.

This anti-Malthusianism was an epochal departure, since it conceived the relationship between buyer and seller in *fundamentally* unequal terms. It was not simply a question now of which contending party, buyer or seller, got the better of a transaction (a theme which had occupied cultural imagination for a long time, as farces like *Pathelin* already suggest). The problem was rather to know which party contrived and more or less subtly controlled the notion of a transaction to begin with.

27. See Miller, *Bon Marché*, p. 168.
28. Ibid., pp. 21–26.

In the movement between the social structures figured by these two models of consumption, a notion like "dominant discourse" seems essential for making sense of what distinguishes them. We experience such domination when the very field we move in, the very language we speak, have invisibly been predetermined for us. And any continuation of the contract under such terms involuntarily reinforces the domination which frames the entire experience. These are the conditions which Boucicaut, Millaud, and others like them were beginning to organize for their contemporaries. They required the profound reconceptions of social space which these innovators and entrepreneurs were systematically devising.

Boucicaut's revolution in the experience of shopping amounted to replacing the principle of *supply* with that of *seduction*.[29] A world organized around the practice of use values was giving way to one in which exchange value dominated. This was the period of the arcades, the *passages*, which Walter Benjamin illuminated in his *Passagenarbeit*.[30] The arcade shops introduced an epochal innovation: the display window. *Things* were publicly offered to contemplation for the first time. People on their way through the center of the busy city, generously protected by the arcades' roofs from inclement weather, could in passing through the *passages* be tempted to consume. Commodities were being organized to create desire.

The arcades declined with Haussmann's reconstruction of the city. But almost simultaneously, the Boucicauts and others were conceiving a new type of emporium dedicated to the new social form, the new phenomenology, of the commodity. The elements of the new formulas for the practice of shopping were multiple and have been studied extensively.[31] A number of them resemble those which we have already examined in the transformation of the daily.

The most obvious was the theoretical revolution by which the entrepreneur shifted focus from maximizing profit on an individual item,

---

29. See Buck-Morss, "Walter Benjamin," pp. 71–73; and Raymond Williams, "Advertising," p. 177.

30. The portions of this work which have survived are published in his *Baudelaire*. The definitive study of the arcades will be found in Geist, *Arcades*. See also Artley, *Golden Age of Shop Design*, p. 175.

31. Most recently by Miller, *Bon Marché*, and Rosalind Williams, *Dream Worlds*; before them by Crubellier, *Histoire culturelle*, chap. 9.

an individual sale, to maximizing *volume*. For this reason if for no other, advertising was crucial in both the newspaper and the department store strategies. And there is a resemblance between the invisible advertising in the four-tier system of selling journalistic page space and the use by the department stores of mechanisms for attracting customers while those who organized them pretended to be thinking of something else entirely.

Consider the concerts which the Boucicauts organized in the park just outside their store (itself today renamed the Square Boucicaut). These concerts were intended to endow the store with an aura of "culture" in the perception of potential clients and, more cynically, to attract to the periphery of the selling area a large and happily disposed population of shoppers.[32]

Entry into what we might term the "shopping mode" was thus made increasingly easy—cheaper, we might say. No longer was there an assumption that if you entered a store, you were intending to buy. Begun by the *magasins de nouveautés*, the policy of "entrée libre" became a key element in the sales strategy of the *grands magasins* when they began to arise in the 1850s and 1860s. "Entrée libre" meant the freedom to browse without being committed to make a purchase or having to incur the embarrassment of declining one.

Other elements of the shopping process were becoming coordinately modified. In the traditional emporia, prices were not marked and could not have been said to be fixed at all. One engaged a salesperson to find out what things cost; the establishment of the price was a matter for negotiation between the two parties to the transaction. But the posting of prices on articles for sale which made the policy of "entrée libre" functional also meant that the consumer gave up the right to participate in such a negotiation: "Active verbal interchange between customer and retailer was replaced by the passive, mute response of consumer to things."[33] The basis of the shopping transaction thus quietly came under control of the merchandiser.

One final innovation completes the tableau of elements which transformed shopping practice. This was the department store's guarantee of the right of the consumer to return anything which did not satisfy.

---

32. Miller, *Bon Marché*, pp. 169ff.
33. Rosalind Williams, *Dream Worlds*, p. 67.

Again, the psychological—and the financial—costs of transactions in the new mode were being reduced, the threshold of resistance to entry into the commercial circuit lowered significantly. This was particularly true for shoppers who, because of their social origins or class status (one recalls Denise Baudu), might have felt reluctant to enter into the more delicate face-to-face negotiations required by traditional tradespeople.

From one perspective these innovations might seem to have increased the consumer's power and autonomy. Surely the stores advertised them as doing so. But the new code of social behavior and social discourses which they entailed for the shopper simultaneously organized a network of constraints and manipulations which bound her or him: nineteenth-century equivalents, microconstituents, of Althusser's "ideological apparatuses." To the extent that one could be led comfortably along and induced to accept profoundly transformed behaviors in the marketplace, more explicit mechanisms of social control could remain benignly in the background.[34]

The ideological and discursive mechanisms I am considering operate by representing the world *in their own terms* and simultaneously by making alternative representations difficult. It is well known how quickly the new mode of department store shopping threatened the traditional practices of the small tradesperson with enforced extinction. Practically speaking, one did not so much *choose* to patronize the department stores as one was driven to them by the overt pressures of price competition and the more subtle inducements of advertising. In fact the battle for domination of the market between small and large sellers was a furious one.

Yet significantly, in the construction of the social whole provided by these apparatuses, no trace of conflict is ever readable. On the contrary, the mood of this revolution of social practice was a carefully studied blitheness: all of these new structures, the newspaper like the department store, functioned by suppressing the traces of any adversarial relation between the parties to any social transaction—by flattening all expression of contradiction.

The effect of such rewriting of the social text was to render increasingly less accessible the consciousness of social difference, the

34. See Althusser, "Ideology," pp. 127–86. See also my Introduction.

experience of cultural choice. We saw how the newspaper, in order to achieve mass penetration, needed to repress the divisiveness of the political and factional. Not surprisingly, the department store followed the same tactic:

> House [store] solidarity brought one thing further, "a new conception," as the Bon Marché put it, "of the relations between capital and labor." In the Bon Marché vision there was no place for class discord or conflict, no place for that nagging bourgeois nightmare that its century of change, with all its conglomerations of money and men, might be carrying within it the seeds of its collapse. The Bon Marché world was a harmonious blend of order, authority, cooperation, and social unity.[35]

The alteration in the texture of social existence produced by these innovations have become transparent by now. Yet however tenuous these new structures of manipulation seem to us, however diaphanous their grip upon our experience and the usages which make up our lives, in the transitional period in which they were being implanted, consciousness of their power was intense and constant. And this was clearest among the dissident intelligentsia who devised the counter-discourses which will occupy me here. These new practices of the everyday, and the social perspective which sustained them, were resisted with ingeniousness and intensity.

There are characteristic outbursts: "Immense nausée des affiches" ("Enormous nausea of/from advertising posters").[36] In the fragment in "Mon coeur mis à nu" which thus recorded Baudelaire's reaction to the poster (one of the primary tools of commercial publicity which flourished beginning in his period), particularly in the overdrawn violence of his response, we get a sense of the passionate antipathy which these new structures and practices induced. It was as if the increasingly dominant discourses of the newspaper, the department store, and their allies had disarticulated the world of the everyday, the entire space of quotidian existence, in order to recombine them in an alien form serving only the needs of their own business.

35. Miller, *Bon Marché*, p. 227. Bourdieu discusses the suppression of signs of social conflict as a tactic of dominant forces in liberal societies. See *Ce que parler veut dire*, p. 155.

36. Baudelaire, *Oeuvres complètes*, ed. Y.-G. Le Dantec and Claude Pichois (Paris: Gallimard-Pléiade, 1961), p. 1279.

In the face of the anger of the alienated, those in control were complacently undistressed. In a telling characterization, Victor Hugo felt it sufficient to define the bourgeoisie simply as "the contented part of the population."[37] And along the same lines we might recall Flaubert's outburst concerning the ubiquity, the profusion, and the insufferable good health of middle-class *bêtise* (I will discuss Flaubert's relation to these questions in Chapters 4 and 5).

In the face of this infuriating and seemingly irresistible reconstruction of the world in favor of the middle class, what response was possible? In this first period perhaps the most constant figure deployed by capitalism's antagonists was a sardonic irony, the major genre of its expression a bitter satire. Particularly, as we shall see shortly, the satirical newspapers which arose at this time became a principal locus of counter-discursive resistance to increasingly pervasive domination by commercial discourse.

Under the July Monarchy, with the increasing social and cultural domination of its antagonist, antibourgeois satire *institutionalized* itself. Zeldin refers to this phenomenon, but he draws back from accrediting his own speculation concerning its significance:

> The manufacturing of humour by professional entertainers increased enormously in this period, and nowhere was the increase more pronounced than in humourous journalism. The growth of printed humour was on a hitherto unprecedented scale. It could perhaps be argued that this humour was an answer to the greater stresses and complexities of life . . . but, in the present state of knowledge, such a view could not be easily substantiated.[38]

But an examination of this humor can put us in a stronger position to confirm speculations concerning the upsurge and the insistence of the satirical in the nineteenth century.

37. Cited in Graña, *Bohemian versus Bourgeois.* p. 64; cf. p. 17.
38. *France*, vol. 2, p. 710. Zeldin himself provides significant evidence for the sorts of conclusions he nonetheless finds it uncongenial to draw. He recounts, for example, the satirical reviews of the Coignard brothers during the July Monarchy at the Théâtre de la Porte Saint-Martin. One of these, *1841 et 1941*, made fun of all new inventions and of railways in particular. A second, the *Iles marquises*, concerned a machine into which live sheep were inserted, to emerge at the other end transformed into ready-made overcoats and lamb chops (ibid.).

The logic of such a development can be illuminated by reference to a principle—a version, really, of Bakhtin's dialogic—articulated by Michael Riffaterre: "You need two texts to make a parody."[39] But the clarity of the satirical target is a precondition for any effectiveness on the part of the attack. After 1830 the dominant discourses of middle-class capitalism—the butts of such ridicule in our period (two of whose avatars or institutional subdialects I have sought to depict in the foregoing)—were becoming intensely focused. In the face of such a growing focus, the second, or parodic, texts—the counter-discourses—found it possible to respond. Of course they could not erase the dominance of the discourses against which they reacted. They were obliged to battle the dominant on its own terrain, and nowhere did they do so more poignantly than in the satirical daily. The attempt to use the mechanism of the newspaper, which functioned to establish the very set of social practices the satirists desired to contest, thus takes on a particularly ironic resonance. It resembles Balzac's thwarted attempt to mobilize control of the sign in a campaign to overturn its own power.

This relation in turn clarifies how fundamentally historicized such parodic or ironic texts must be understood to have been. Rainer Warning has put this well: "It can be presumed that, of all types of discourse, ironic discourse surely has flourished in the most clearly marked historical periods."[40] And Warning goes on to touch upon an indispensable condition for the sorts of adversary discourses we are considering: "[Ironic discourse] presupposes a public that is prepared to exclude itself from dominant value systems." Such discourse is thus dependent upon a structural potentiality in the culture which produces it. Without the counter-institution of a dissident intelligentsia in our period, the counter-discourses which concern me would not have been able to exist or to circulate at all.

Such an audience formed the core public for the satirical papers which began to flourish at the end of the Restoration. They proliferated with the July Revolution. The symptoms of dissident intellectuals' alienation from the dominant discourse have been so widely

39. *Semiotics of Poetry*, p. 108. See also Fineman, "The Parodic and Production," p. 70.

40. "Irony and the 'Order of Discourse,'" p. 264. This historical contingency of satire, particularly of caricature, was already clear to Henry James in his little study, *Daumier, Caricaturist*, pp. 1–2.

studied as to require no extended commentary here. They tried everything possible to dissociate themselves from what was going on all
around them; they sought to refuse virtually all of the elements of the
new system which was transforming the world. The manifestations of
their disaffection were particularly intricate and generalized:

> Many of the younger . . . set out deliberately to oppose all accepted
> notions, all conventions in conduct, clothes and morals. . . . With the
> common aim of providing amusement for themselves and an outlet for
> their scorn of the "grocer," they united into various groups or so-
> cieties. . . . They were named *Frileux, Bousingots, Purs-Sang, Infatiga-
> bles, Badouillards*, or *Jeune-France*. . . . The artist was young, hand-
> some, melancholy. He cultivated a noble brow by pushing back his
> long ringlets, and let his beard grow to give him a medieval appearance
> and to distinguish him from the clean-shaven bourgeois. . . . He
> smoked a pipe, or preferably a cigar, a new fashion so revolutionary
> that Balzac devoted an article to it in *La Caricature*.[41]

In their refusal of the world which their class was producing for them
they even organized suicide societies, though few cases of the constitu-
tional purpose of such organizations being carried out seem to have
been recorded.

So as the dominant discursive formations I have been chronicling
developed through the reign of Louis-Philippe, through the abortive
Second Republic and into Napoleon III's Empire; as the newspaper,
the department store, and the allied discourses of consumer capitalism
progressively naturalized themselves as elements of an everyday which
had never before been imagined, these new commercial institutions
were particularly taken as the objects of intense criticism and raillery by
disaffected writers and intellectuals.

In the case of the newspaper, the distinction typically drawn was
between the mode of reading which it induced and the mode appropriate to "serious" literary texts. For practitioners of the latter, it was all
too clear that the former seemed to be swamping them. Roger Bellet
resumes the perception at the time: "People read newspapers in the
street and along the boulevards. They read standing up, and Barbey
d'Aurevilly called the newspaper 'standing-up' reading [*la lecture de-*

---

41. Melcher, *Monnier*, pp. 122–23; See the notes on p. 123 for more on the social
valences of beard and cigar.

bout] as opposed to the 'sitting-down reading' [*la lecture assise*] of books. People read in all sorts of meeting places. They even read in Notre-Dame."[42]

The traditionalists were not slow to draw the most pessimistic conclusions. Thus, despairingly, the Goncourts: "Our age marks the beginning of the destruction of the book by the newspaper, of the man of letters by the journalism of the literati."[43] Thus—in the same vein but violently—Baudelaire in the "Salon de 1859," ridiculing Dutacq's *Le Siècle* in a transparently parodic quotation from *Le misanthrope* followed by its dead-serious sarcastic explication:

> "*The bad taste of the times [of "Le Siècle"] here alarms me.*" ["*Le mauvais goût du siècle en cela me fait peur.*"]
> There is a fine newspaper in which everyone knows everything and talks about everything, where every writer, as universal and encyclopedic as the citizens of ancient Rome, in turn teaches us about politics, religion, economics, fine arts, philosophy, literature, in this vast monument to stupidity.[44]

Thus—with his very different tone of serene sarcasm—Mallarmé, in response to accusations of poetic obscurity brought against him: "I prefer, in the face of this aggression, to respond that some contemporaries do not know how to read—Except newspapers; of course these provide the advantage of not interrupting the chorus of [daily] distractions [*le choeur des préoccupations*]."[45] In "Un spectacle interrompu," Mallarmé even went so far as to fantasize a newspaper published exclusively for dreamers—like himself—dissatisfied with the ordinary fare served up to them with their dailies.

---

42. *Presse et journalisme*, p. 195. The situation was humorously illustrated in one of Daumier's lithographs (*Le Charivari*, 8 May 1848) which depicts two respectable bourgeois walking in the street, so completely engrossed in reading their newspapers that they are about to collide violently with each other.

43. *Journal*, 22 July 1867; cited in Duchet, *Manuel d'histoire littéraire*, p. 42; see also Chapter 7 below.

44. *Oeuvres complètes*, pp. 1069–70; cf. pp. 1264 or 1309, where our acquaintance Girardin comes in for his dose of criticism. Or consider the "liste de canailles" in which Baudelaire names nearly a dozen of the most prominent newspaper directors and editors of his period, Buloz, Houssaye, Girardin, and so on ("Mon coeur mis à nu," ibid., p. 1288).

45. "Le mystère dans les lettres," *Oeuvres complètes*, p. 386; cf. also pp. 376, 381.

The mentality and practices of the *commerçant*, like those of the journalist, were subjected to violent critique. Baudelaire: "The mind of all shopkeepers is entirely corrupted";[46] Flaubert: "Let us launch ourselves into the Ideal, since we no longer have the means of dwelling in marble halls draped with imperial purple. . . . Let us cry out [*Gueulons*] against imitation silk gloves, desk chairs, raincoats, economy kitchen ranges, fake materials, fake luxury, fake pride. Industrialism has developed the ugly to gigantic proportions. . . . The Department store (or 'the cheap article') [*Le bon marché*] has rendered true luxury unimaginable."[47] And indeed, this rejection of the *commerçant* by dissident intellectuals was solidly based on fact. In a study of book ownership by members of middle-class occupational groups between 1815 and 1848, "boutiquiers"—shopkeepers—came in as the lowest category sampled by far: only 6.3 percent of them owned a single book.[48]

So from the perspective of the intelligentsia, the hated *épicier* was authentically different and dangerously degraded; the world which he and his mentality increasingly dominated did threaten *their* values very directly. And while the divergent strains of the intellectual opposition to the commercial middle class might have recommended profoundly different antidotes to their antagonists' increasing penetration of the social landscape, it would be possible to say about them what Heine said about the opposition parties (Carlist, republican, and so on) under the July Monarchy: "If they had not the same paradise, they had at least the same Hell."[49] For the intellectuals, Hell was the bourgeoisie. The satirical newspapers to which I now turn would seek to fix and to portray in unforgettable terms the infernal quality of middle-class discourses and practices.

46. *Oeuvres complètes*, p. 1297; cf. pp. 1274, 1278.
47. Letter to Louise Colet, 18 Jan. 1854; *Correspondance*, ed. Soc. des Etudes littéraires françaises (Paris: Club de l'honnête homme, 1972) vol. 13., pp. 462–63.
48. Allen, *Popular French Romanticism*, p. 137.
49. Cited by Vincent, *Daumier*, p. 32.

PART TWO
CORROSIVE
INTERTEXTUALITIES

CHAPTER 3

Counter-Images:
Daumier and *Le Charivari*

"... Comment pensent-ils ici?" "De fichus républicains,
des idéologues, quoi! ... Ils sont abonnés ... au
Charivari, à tous les mauvais journaux." ["What are their
politics here?" "They're damned republicans,
ideologues! ... They subscribe to *Le Charivari*, all those
damned papers."]

      —STENDHAL, *Lucien Leuwen* (1834–35)

Etudions le laid, messieurs, étudions le laid! [Let us
depict ugliness, gentlemen, let us depict ugliness!]

      —HENRY MONNIER, *Mémoires de
      Monsieur Joseph Prudhomme*

Counter-discourses function in their form. Their object is to represent
the world *differently*. But their projection of difference goes beyond
simply contradicting the dominant, beyond simply negating its assertions. The power of a dominant discourse lies in the codes by which it
regulates understanding of the social world. Counter-discourses seek
to detect and map such naturalized protocols and to project their
subversion. At stake in this discursive struggle are the paradigms of
social representation themselves.

In the crossfire of hegemony and counter-hegemony by which the
meaning and the control of all social symbols are contested, certain
signs and representations seem to take on secondary meanings. Such
meanings become detectable in the struggles fought over them. Typ-

ically they lie at some distance from the denotative ones which these representations normally express. Perhaps the most influential of these secondary, quasi-involuntary resonances which invested social representation in the nineteenth century was a pervasive association between writing and the commercial. As an institution, *prose itself* seemed to refer beyond the horizon of its varied specific meanings to the practices of commerce in whose service it seemed increasingly to be employed. Such a perceived relation is what makes the discourses of "newspaper culture" so characteristic of dominant nineteenth-century culture in general.

Like a phantom aura, a subterranean but persistent invocation of the marketplace thus seemed to adhere to written discourse in all its forms. In the final chapters of this study, I will argue that in the later part of the century such a resonance determined the forms of avant-garde, or "poetic," prose—what I will term "absolute counter-discourse." Here, I want to examine the role of this secondary or connotative association of prose writing in producing the effects of another counter-discursive institution whose period of cultural influence lay earlier in the century: the satirical newspaper.

I want to examine the counter-discourse of the satirical dailies from a particular point of view, not principally that of the individual text articles, which (however brilliantly executed) modeled themselves as a more or less systematic negation of those which occupied the pages of the traditional papers. Rather, I want to center consideration upon an element of the newspaper space which was unique to the satirical strain and to the practice of its reading: the caricatural *image*. In the image, distinction itself receives an authentically differential signifier.[1]

In a flow of words which in our period often appeared overwhelming to those subjected to its ever-increasing pervasiveness,[2] the images in the satirical newspapers must have appeared under the sign of fundamental heterogeneity. Not that the *specific* cultural or political valence of their distinction was a priori defined or immediately readable. The effect of each image, of course, was overdetermined by every

---

1. Such a perspective on them hardly provides a general history of the satirical dailies. But this history has been fairly well traced—most recently in Wechsler's intelligent study *A Human Comedy*. From the "Kiosque" collection see also Bellet, *Presse et journalisme*, and Lethève, *La caricature*.
2. Allen, *Popular French Romanticism*, p. 127.

aspect of its content, layout, and context. But images were *new*. As a form immediately distinguishable from the dense flux of printed text, *as image*, visual representation in the satirical daily could serve distinctively as a representation of the Other: as an alternative to the dominant real, to its discourse, to its characteristic system of expression. Particularly, the image possessed the potential to figure an alternative fully aware, and deeply critical, of the practice of words— and of their commercial resonances—which surrounded it.

It was the invention of lithography by Aloys Senefelder in 1798 which made illustration in the daily press possible. In principle, the medium could have been employed to any illustrative purpose whatever. But in practice the "serious" papers considered images to be frivolous and excluded them from their pages. In the previous chapter I suggested how strenuously the "informational" dailies resisted any interruption of the "gray blur" which their regular columns and orderly layout maintained. Such an appearance must have seemed the guarantor of their journalistic dignity (we might recall that until fairly recently the *London Times* maintained just this outward aspect, complete with its first page "English advertisements"). So it fell to the group of young artists brought together in the late 1820s by Charles Philipon to discover and define the cultural tone through which this new technical means of publishing images in mass-circulation periodicals could insert itself into concrete social discourse.[3]

Crucial elements of the satirical newspaper's counter-discourse thus began to come together: the differential use of the image; the consequent disruption of the newspaper text's *grisaille*, of what Mallarmé called its "insupportable colonne" [its "intolerable (or unsupportable) column"];[4] and more broadly, a fundamentally mocking tone of at first political, then later deeply social, satire.

So it was that *Le Charivari*, the most famous of these satirical papers, which Philipon founded in 1832 and which sustained uninter-

3. The history of lithography is resumed in Passeron, *Daumier*, pp. 40–41. Cf. also Wechsler, *Human Comedy*, chap. 3, n. 19. Vincent, *Daumier*, p. 8, notes that by 1828, twenty-three lithography establishments were licensed in the Seine Département, with 180 presses, 500 workmen, and an annual production value of 3 million francs. (Of course, not all such images were destined for the daily papers I am considering here.)

4. "Le livre, instrument spirituel," *Oeuvres complètes*, ed. Henri Mondor and G. Aubry (Paris: Gallimard-Pléiade, 1945), p. 381.

rupted daily publication (even including Sundays) for sixty years, took as the subtitle on its masthead a distinctive self-characterization: "Journal publiant chaque jour *un nouveau dessin*" ["Newspaper publishing *a new illustration* in every issue"] (my italics). Later on, fundamentally "straight" papers like *L'Illustration* (founded in 1843) would begin to utilize the resources of the image (we should note, however, that as a weekly it corresponded more closely to our contemporary newsmagazines than to the daily paper). But these more serious competitors of *Le Charivari* in the journalistic use of images nonetheless maintained their seriousness, and their distinction from Philipon's daily, by employing the engraving process, considered substantially more dignified than *Le Charivari*'s lithograph.[5] Lithography thus remained for some time under the sign of its difference as the medium of *specifically oppositional, counter-discursive illustration*. The medium itself was, in this early period, a distinctive *sign* of protest and critique.

We can best understand the satirical papers as the systematic ridicule of the bourgeois, as their first *institutionalized* counter-discourse. Appropriately, then, these publications arose punctually with the coming to power of the class which they would take as their butt. Thus Philipon's *La Caricature*, the immediate ancestor of *Le Charivari*, appeared on 4 November 1830, just a few months after the July Revolution had consecrated middle-class triumph. The paper's immediate predecessor, *La Silhouette* (in which Emile de Girardin had played an editorial and promotional role along with Philipon), had been a weekly variety magazine. In each issue it featured a lithograph whose character varied between pure illustration and parodic accompaniment to one of the paper's satirical text articles. Balzac had been an important contributor, beginning an association with Philipon which was to continue when the latter folded *La Silhouette* and founded *La Caricature* upon a principle of much more explicit and (after the July Revolution) much less restrained political and social raillery.[6]

At the outset of the new regime, of course, the objective conditions

5. Vincent, *Daumier*, p. 8, points out that it was about half a century between the advent of lithography for rapid illustrations in daily papers and the perfecting of halftone photographic reproduction. Of all of these forms, the engraving had the greatest *cachet*.

6. See ibid., p. 16, and Wechsler, *Human Comedy*, pp. 66–69.

of such satirical freedom were present. Indeed they legitimized the new regime itself. Louis-Philippe's *Charte* guaranteed an end, in perpetuity, to political censorship: "The French may publish and have printed their opinions in conformity with the laws. Censorship will never be established."[7] This liberal promise was not to last long; and in the meantime there still remained the *loi de cautionnement*, whose restrictive effects I have already mentioned. It applied to the satirical papers fully as much as to their more solemn competitors.

This potential threat to their independence notwithstanding, in the early years of the new government the satirical papers prosecuted against it a remarkably intense critique. And it seems clear that their combat on the battleground which we have come to call "public opinion" went a significant distance toward puncturing the July Monarchy's self-proclaimed liberalism. For the representation of the Orléanist regime which the satirical papers institutionalized has quietly but decisively become our own common wisdom. From the response of *La Caricature*, *Le Charivari*, and their imitators in the early period of Louis Philippe's monarchy, we have learned to conceive his politics and the entire atmosphere of his regime under the sign of ridiculous vulgarity and burlesque exaggeration.

The content of the representation thereby concorded precisely with the form which the satirical papers had developed to convey it, the caricature. As is well known, the word derives from the Italian *caricare*, "to load" or "overload." From it came the French *charger* and *la charge*, with their resonances of exaggeration or burlesque.[8] It was as if the regime—beginning with its pear-shaped monarch and including the whole grotesque swarm of figures subordinated to him—had been devised to serve as the objects of Daumier's parodic talent.

The farcical supplement of *la charge*, the *excess* it loads upon its object in order to bring it down, comprises an essential counter-discursive move. It signifies an assertion of *difference* in the strongest sense, a quantitative modification which translates qualitative rejection of the satirized original. Such signification of difference can be read even in the layout of the original *La Caricature*. Though it was a weekly it

7. Quoted by Vincent, *Daumier*, p. 13.

8. *La Caricature* itself commented on the term: "The depictions, carefully worked out, had to possess the energetic character, the burlesque element known as the *charge*" (26 April 1832; cited in Passeron, *Daumier*, p. 59).

appeared, like the dailies, in the standard four-page format discussed in the preceding chapter. *La Caricature* consisted of a first page of text, itself already heightened with decorative vignettes and typographical fantasies (the editor—and frequently the author—of this text page was none other than Balzac). Yet on opening the paper one found, not a continuation of the familiar "gray blur" of words, but a new and distinctly heightened, powerfully *exaggerated*, world of images: *two* full-page lithographs (one, moreover, printed in full color). Given the drab journalistic norms and the attendant cultural expectations of the period, the effect must have been startling. In it, we can read the express intention to utilize the resources of exaggeration to perform a complex and corrosive reconception of the objects of the satire.

From the outset, *La Caricature* achieved considerable notoriety. Philipon—the paper's organizational genius—and his team of artists and writers threw themselves into a battle against the regime, not least against its censors, who, though they could restrain publication of particular drawings or articles only under extraordinary circumstances, could and did use judicial process after the fact to fine and to imprison the authors and publishers of items deemed prejudicial to the dignity of the government.[9] The consequences of this repressive skirmishing were to be considerable.

The paper's success assisted Philipon in attracting Daumier to join his network. Philipon had discovered him and had associated him marginally with the earlier *La Silhouette*.[10] Daumier's first lithograph in *La Caricature* appeared on 9 February 1832, but he had already drawn a number which were deemed too controversial to be published in the paper itself (as a circulated periodical it was subjected to stricter legal regulation than were isolated images). Philipon had arranged for his publisher, Aubert, to sell these individual plates from their soon-to-be famous shop in the Galérie Véro-Dodat.[11]

9. Probably the best account of this period of political and judicial combat can be found in Edwin de T. Bechtel, *Freedom of the Press and "L'Association mensuelle"*. This volume also reproduces the 24 plates (including the celebrated "Rue Transnonain") distributed by the *Association mensuelle*, which Philipon founded as a private subscription society to evade the control of the censors, and to raise money to pay fines incurred by his papers. See also Passeron, *Daumier*, chs. 3 and 4. The principal studies of Daumier which may be consulted, in addition, are those of Jean Adhémar, *Daumier*; Vincent, *Daumier*; and Cherpin, *Daumier*.

10. See Passeron, *Daumier*, p. 49.

11. On this period, see ibid., pp. 49ff.

Before long, Philipon and Daumier were in more serious trouble than they had previously experienced. Daumier had drawn, and Aubert had sold, a now-celebrated lithograph entitled "Gargantua" (see illustration 1). It depicted a grotesque, gluttonous Louis-Philippe triumphantly enthroned on a *chaise-percée*. By mouth the king is ingesting the tribute offered by a horde of Orleanist sycophants; at the other end of his allegorical alimentary canal he dispenses dubious honors to another group, crouching underneath the throne.[12] On 23 February 1832 the lithograph and those involved in its production were tried on the very plausible charge of "excitation à la haine et au mépris du gouvernement du Roi."[13] Daumier, Aubert, and their printer, Delaporte, were condemned to six-month prison terms—initially suspended in the hope that a pending threat of incarceration might induce them to cease their violent attacks upon the person of the king and the conduct of his government. But the tactic failed, and Daumier entered Sainte-Pélagie prison in September 1832. He found Philipon already languishing there by virtue of an earlier condemnation.

The regime was to suffer more from this cohabitation in Sainte-Pélagie than did its nominal victims. For the product of their enforced sabbatical was the invention of the world's first satirical *daily* newspaper, *Le Charivari*. In this prison which so manifestly gave the lie to the regime's pretensions of liberalism and reform, it was as if Daumier and Philipon had determined that the social world had become sufficiently counterfeit, sufficiently contemptible, and sufficiently perceived as such, to justify *quotidian* castigation.

Le Charivari began publishing on 1 December 1832; Daumier's first appearance in the paper was less than two months later, on 24 January 1833. Thus began one of the most extraordinary collaborations in what it would seem justifiable to call "media history." For *Le Charivari* was not just an individualist gesture of disaffection, of which the nineteenth century saw many. On the contrary, in a recognizably modern form, it founded and nurtured a dissident cultural *apparatus*. Its relation to its audience, its whole social and economic base, were new. By the inevitably *collective* character of its counter-discursive codes and

---

12. *Dépôt légal*, 15 Dec. 1831. The standard catalogue of Daumier's lithographs, in 10 volumes plus index, is Loys Delteil, *Daumier*. Daumier's lithographs are identified here according to their number in Delteil's catalogue. "Gargantua" is thus L.D. 34.

13. See Cherpin, *Daumier*, pp. 68, 87.

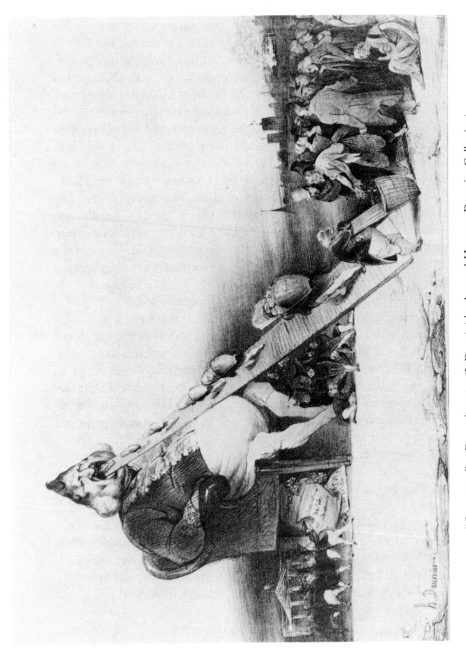

1. "Gargantua," 15 December 1831 (L.D. 34) (the Armand Hammer Daumier Collection)

156

languages, of its production and social circulation, *Le Charivari* power-fully developed new modes of cultural functionality, which in this period were emerging in what we have since come to call the "public sphere."

Throughout its sixty years of uninterrupted appearance—over twenty thousand successive issues—*Le Charivari* averaged between two and three thousand subscribers.[14] Though their sociology has not been studied in detail, one fact is clear. We know from the broad consciousness of the periodical over its life (and from more or less uninterrupted efforts by successive governments to contain its influence) that *Le Charivari*'s readers were well placed in the emerging structures of opinion formation. We need to consider the character of the paper's social base and of its cultural power.

First of all, it is necessary to distinguish between two modes of relation between the satirical paper and its subscribers. The first and more traditional of these was programmatically political. The staff of *Le Charivari* were resolutely republican in sentiment; the critique they directed in the paper's early years against Louis-Philippe was uncompromisingly oriented from that perspective. A readership of a kind with which we are already familiar, attaching itself to the organ expressing its own shade of political belief, thus guaranteed a base of republican subscribers. They formed what we might call the political Left of the *Charivari* spectrum.

It was in response to considerations of this clearly political order that Louis-Philippe's government surreptitiously began sponsorship of a competitor to *Le Charivari*. They called it *La Charge* and launched it in 1833.[15] It attempted to defend the political line of the regime while maintaining a tone and even a layout which closely imitated its rival's. Not surprisingly, it never achieved much success. But this early example of the tactic of reenvelopment by which, since the rise to power of the middle class, dominant discourse has attempted to neutralize its counter-discursive opponents by *adopting* their language and ex-

14. The "run" of a particular lithograph averaged 3,000, although certain popular series (like Daumier's Robert Macaire) were typically printed in editions of 5,500 (see Passeron, *Daumier*, pp. 96, 117; *HGPF*, p. 146). On the other hand, the announcement of *Le Charivari*'s inception in 1832 was printed as a broadside and poster in an edition of 200,000 copies (see Cherpin, *Daumier*, p. 71).

15. See Vincent, *Daumier*, p. 51.

pressive protocols, is worth noting. In its title to begin with, and in the whole panoply of techniques of exaggeration and deformation which it deployed in the service of those against whom they had originally been developed, *La Charge* amounted to a now-familiar tactic of co-optation which sought to devalue the social base and polemical bearing of *Le Charivari*'s new satirical mode.

This sort of development—the state-sponsored creation of a captive medium for influencing public opinion—denotes a stage of political and social development on the edge of epochal discoveries. Though still conceiving itself as a fundamentally political entity, and still functioning largely through traditional political mechanisms, the state was nonetheless becoming conscious that the modern polity (what Vico and Hegel already termed "civil society") could exercise its hegemony most effectively through more atmospheric, nonpolitical modes of manipulation. This is the point—indeed, the invention of *La Charge* might almost be said to localize the moment—at which the state seemed to discover the regulative force of administered culture.

This inflection illuminates a second mode of relation between *Le Charivari* and its audience. It uncovers the increasing influence of the cultural sphere, of opinion formation and the delicate mechanisms of liberal consensus, which the sponsorship of *La Charge* by Louis-Philippe's government acknowledged by surreptitiously seeking to manipulate them. From this perspective, this alternative logic of connection, and the consequent second body of readers we can posit for *Le Charivari*, are substantially more interesting. The cast of the second group was less "engagé," more conservative when judged in traditional political terms. They were not the staunch republicans of the first group. But as time went on, particularly with the paper's enforced shift from political to more atmospheric social satire, the significance of this newer manner of conceiving relationship to *Le Charivari*'s polemical targets certainly increased.

This second group of subscribers and readers was composed of people who were, we might say, disinclined to celebrate the triumph of the middle class and of its modes of social practice which all chroniclers of the period agree was visible to those living through its transformations. Their resistance to the new social dominant in liberal society was thus more traditionalist than in the case of their republican co-subscribers. Explicitly *political* mechanisms to express their sense of disenchantment were generally lacking.[16] *Le Charivari* was able to focus these diffuse social perceptions and resistances which, for most of the more or less explicitly disenchanted under consideration here, had no more immediate or "practical" outlet.

This would seem to be the situation of the subscribers to *Le Charivari* whom Stendhal depicted in the Nancy of *Lucien Leuwen* (the staunch republican Gauthier would be an exception, and one would rather expect to find him in our first group of subscribers). Stendhal captured the atmosphere of diffuse disaffection from the regime in the comical affliction to which the commander of Lucien's division, Général de Thérance, was regularly exposed as he passed among the citizenry. Their lack of respect he rightly reads as symbolic, not personal. The constant mocking presence of the seditious *poire* which he encountered everywhere orients him and us concerning the political and social bearing of this disaffection. (The role of *Le Charivari* in organizing it is humorously conveyed in the epigraph from the novel at the head of this chapter.)[17] And there is other significant testimony to the popularity of *Le Charivari* among groups which could hardly be imagined to have figured as part of that republican "Left" political faction to which I have referred.[18]

With this second strain of its clientele, then, *Le Charivari* was beginning to organize a readership along lines which could not be described in traditional factional terms. The principle of its coherence was a diffuse opposition to the sorts of developments which *Le Charivari* daily ridiculed—in other words, more or less, to what was going on in society in general. The paper was mediating formation of that crucial group of internal emigrés whose political affiliations might have been very diverse but whose *social* perspective increasingly alienated them from the dominant manners, attitudes, and practices which *Le Chari-*

16. The term "désenchantement" is Balzac's and appeared in the important "Lettres sur Paris," which he published after the July Revolution in Girardin's *Le voleur* (10 Jan. 1831). See Barbéris, *Balzac et le mal du siècle*, chaps. 8 and 9, particularly vol. 2, pp. 1417–1430, on the "école du désenchantement."

17. Stendhal, *Romans et nouvelles*, ed. Henri Martineau (Paris: Gallimard-Pléiade, 1952), vol. 1, pp. 787, 791. The celebrated *poire* was Philipon's invention (see Vincent, *Daumier*, p. 20). Louis-Philippe's misfortune was that his physiognomy so readily lent itself to the visual and verbal mockery of this extraordinarily influential satirical icon.

18. See particularly, Adhémar, *Daumier*, p. 81, commenting on the exposure of the staunchly bourgeois Flaubert family and their circle to the paper.

vari ceaselessly and so inventively mocked. Its satire thus helped to institutionalize *disaffection. Le Charivari* opened a space for important forms of cultural resistance to the dominant discourses of nineteenth-century liberal capitalism.

As with any parody bound closely to its conjuncture, much of the paper's material today seems drained of its critical force. But the *forms* of its intervention still retain their original virulence. In the face of the complacent self-satisfaction of those "in place," *Le Charivari* posited *difference.* The paper projected an alternative dimension from which critique of the social could be prosecuted. This development amounted to a founding attempt to employ mass-circulation and organization techniques, however primitive, to forge and consolidate a counter-hegemonic consciousness.

To be sure, this was not Daumier's or Philipon's intention at the outset. They simply wanted to bring back the Republic. In the period between the foundation of *Le Charivari* and its enforced change of satirical direction in 1835, which I will examine shortly, their polemic against the regime was almost constantly of a political character. Thus, of the 250 lithographs which Daumier published between July 1830 and the 1835 press law, which reimposed the censorship of images, only 9 diverge from this overtly factional mode of criticism.[19] But the explicitly political mechanisms of opposition and repression on the respective sides of the battle in this first period seem characteristic of a distinctly early stage in the long consolidation of liberal society and its internal ideological struggles.

And indeed (leaving aside the foundation of *La Charge*), the response of the regime to the opposition press was a traditionally political one. The decision was made in mid-1835 to bring the entire journalistic apparatus under much firmer control. From the beginning, the government had had nothing but trouble from the disaffected newspapers, whether explicitly satirical like *Le Charivari* or more serious in tone like Carrel's *Le National*. The frequency of judicial process against the opposition papers had become almost embarrassingly high. Between 2 August 1830 and 1 October 1834, Vincent has counted 520 press trials, 188 convictions, and penalties totaling 106 years in prison and 44,000 francs in fines.[20] During the period, Philipon himself had

19. See Passeron, *Daumier*, p. 88.
20. *Daumier*, p. 52.

accumulated 6 separate condemnations and 13 months served in prison.[21]

A more systemic solution than the piecemeal use of fines and seizures to induce the compliance (or, in the extreme, to cause the financial ruin) of offending periodicals seemed required.[22] This was particularly true because, in the early years of the regime, the juries which tried these cases were more sympathetic to the accused journalists than the authorities were happy to see. In his brilliant article entitled "Quelques caricaturistes français" (which focused particularly on Daumier himself), Baudelaire—living within the experience of much stricter Second Empire censorship—expressed his astonishment that the caricatural battle which Philipon and the members of his apparatus had waged against Louis-Philippe's regime had been allowed to continue for as long as it did.[23] But in September 1835 the government suddenly and decisively brought it to an end.

The pretext was Fieschi's attempt to assassinate the king with a bomb on the fifth anniversary of the regime. Though Louis-Philippe escaped unharmed, fourteen by-standers were killed. Manipulating a discourse of "law and order" and intending the sorts of repressive mechanisms which have since become familiar to us, the government capitalized upon the tragedy. The principal provisions of the new press law with which the government intended to solidify public order required, first, that all criticism directed against the person of the king or his family, against the form of government or the order of succession to the throne, and against the acts of the government to the extent that they had previously been approved by the king, was prohibited; second, that offenses against the new law were to be tried in the Chambre des Pairs (thus precluding jury trials and their relative indulgence to journalistic offense against the regime); finally—and most relevant to our discussion—that all images appearing in periodicals receive prior authorization from government censors.[24] It is instructive to note that in this new law, the distinctive status, and implicitly the particular opinion-forming power, of the image were officially consecrated. Iron-

21. See also *HGPF*, p. 103, and Vincent, *Daumier*, p. 66.

22. See Passeron, *Daumier*, p. 74.

23. See Baudelaire, *Oeuvres complètes*, ed. Y.-G. Le Dantec and Claude Pichois (Paris: Gallimard-Pléiade, 1961), pp. 999–1000.

24. See *HGPF*, pp. 113–14, and Passeron, *Daumier*, p. 112.

ically the sign of its difference was institutionalized by the very authorities who had been the objects of its mockery.

The new press law required an immediate reorientation of the content of the satirical papers, of their whole project. Most of what they had printed for five years, the very basis of their expression, was suddenly foreclosed. But paradoxically, the result of this prohibition of explicit political caricature and satire was to hasten emergence of the tendency toward more infrastructural critique of the social forces, practices, and discourses which sustained the self-proclaimed liberal regime. If the *government* of the nation could no longer legally be attacked, the dominant national *ideology* became open to the most corrosive ridicule.

Philipon's response to the new law was decisive. He folded the weekly *Caricature* (with the continuing success of *Le Charivari*, it was later refloated in 1838, and lasted until 1843).[25] On the other hand, the daily *Charivari* carried on, on the finest edge of formal legality. On 16 September, the day after the new censorship laws were promulgated, *Le Charivari*, prohibited from publishing a lithograph attacking the new law, appeared instead with a blank caricature page surrounded by a funereal border. In a newspaper economy (such as that discussed in the preceding chapter) in which page space exchanges for money, printing a blank is an immediately expressive gesture—here, of contemptuous protest. But despite the prohibition, the lithograph which would have occupied the caricature page was nonetheless given representation—printed, we might say, as a *virtual* image. For *Le Charivari* devoted a text page in the issue to a hilarious *verbal* description of the plate which it was prohibited from running in its habitual place on page 3. Thus the new legislation notwithstanding, the paper was able to keep faith at least with the spirit of its motto ("Journal publiant chaque jour un nouveau dessin"). And it found an expedient by which it could mock the ridiculous paradox at the heart of the new law and maintain the paper's stance of brilliant provocation.[26]

Such was what might be termed *Le Charivari*'s negative response to its new situation, its attempt to retain its ties to the modes of counter-discourse which Philipon had been developing since 1830. But *Le Char-*

25. See Delteil, *Daumier*, vol. 2, at no. 544.
26. See Wechsler, *Human Comedy*, p. 81.

ivari's positive responses to the new law are of greater moment for our purposes. With no possibility of criticizing the king or his government, Philipon shifted the focus of the paper's mockery to those of whom king and government in any case had always been the synecdochic representatives.[27]

Thus, on 23 September 1835, just a week after the press law went into effect, *Le Charivari* announced a new series of images by the members of its staff:

> *French types.* Daumier, under this rubric, proposes to reproduce the types of physiognomy, bearing and dress characteristic of the diverse classes which ornament society. This series, along with the gallery of Grandville's *Grotesques parisiens*, and Bourdet's *Béotismes parisiens*, will comprise, in *Le Charivari*, a complete physiognomy of the nation which is considered the wittiest and the best mannered in the universe.

In discussing the proliferation of Codes, Physiologies, and similar genres in Chapter 1, I observed how these representations of cultural signs and practices provided resources for comprehending a rapidly self-transforming society. To understand what was new in the satirical daily, we need to consider these forebears of the mode of caricature which began to emerge in 1830. No social discourse is an aerolite, falling fully formed and unexpected from the sky. In the stock of available gestures, practices, and formulations, each discourse locates the raw materials of what it will become when it is fully deployed. The physiologies represented a kind of ethnography of postrevolutionary France, a recension and a directory of the transformed social signs which constituted the new formation. The details they catalogued might seem to us to have been negligible. But Pierre Bourdieu has provided a suggestive account of why such apparently negligible de-tails of social behavior take on particular significance in transitional situations: "If all societies . . . that seek to produce a new man through a process of 'deculturation' and 'reculturation' set such store

---

27. This inflection to a more infrastructural social satire has long been noted (see for example Benjamin, *Baudelaire*, p. 36, citing Eduard Fuchs; and Adhémar, *Daumier*, p. 23). Already in 1865, under a regime whose political censorship of the press was fully as stringent as Louis-Philippe's became in its later phases, Ulbach had expressed the intimate connection between intense political repression and the more subtle, socially critical forms of counter-discursive irony (see *HGPF*, p. 265).

on the seemingly most insignificant details of *dress, bearing*, physical
and verbal *manners*, the reason is that, treating the body as a memory,
they entrust to it in abbreviated and practical . . . form the fundamental principles of the arbitrary content of the culture."[28] In other words,
beyond any of their specific contents, such signs communicate and
enforce the reality and the constitutive practices of a culture's internal
differentiation: older forms from newer, more socially valorized from
less, and—of primary importance in the period of concern to me
here—social stratum from stratum, class from class. The Physiologies,
the earlier Codes, can be considered early efforts to systematize knowledge of these details of a transforming social world.[29]

It would be impossible to establish any absolute distinction between
earlier "objective" Physiologies and later forms of corrosive caricatural
satire. The division between them, articulating around the change of
regime in 1830, was not systematic or rigid. Balzac's *Physiologie du
mariage* (published in 1829), whose socially critical intentions and techniques have been demonstrated by Barbéris,[30] already firmly establishes the new tonality before the July Revolution. But there was
nonetheless an evolutionary movement by which the earlier forms of
the Physiologies were superseded. This generic shift can be conceived
as an inflection progressively moving us away from the more neutral
stance taken by the Physiologies toward the objects of their mimesis,
and in the direction of overt satire. *Le Charivari* led the way. Passeron
provides a table showing the timing and the types of Daumier's par-
ticipation in this evolution, the long succession of series mocking the
French.[31] The "Types français" were the first; they were followed by
the "Bons bourgeois," the "Moeurs conjugales," the "Beaux jours de la
vie," the "Philanthropes du jour," and, in culmination, by the Robert
Macaire series in which Daumier brought the critical and corrosive
character of the representation to its highest intensity.

Over time such an inflection away from the relative neutrality of the
Physiologies had considerable consequences. Through the mobiliza-

28. *Outline of a Theory of Practice*, p. 94.
29. On the physiologies, see Melcher, *Monnier*, pp. 135–37; Barbéris, *Balzac et le mal
du siècle*, vol. 1, pp. 715–721; Stierle, "Baudelaire and the Tradition of the *Tableau de
Paris*," pp. 345–61; and Wechsler, *Human Comedy*, p. 32.
30. *Balzac et le mal du siècle*, vol. 1, pp. 715ff.
31. *Daumier*, pp. 124–25.

tion of mimetic techniques in the service of an increasingly pointed social critique, *description* slowly became *counter-discourse*. Certain representational techniques were borrowed from the Physiologies, but with an alteration in what we might term their metalinguistic resonance. An ironic attitude toward the objects of these representations, toward the middle-class here-and-now in general, was being organized and consolidated for the dissident readership which *Le Charivari* was simultaneously creating for itself.

The current of such satirical representation was very broad. This is the period of Traviès's Mayeux, of Monnier's Prudhomme; of Daumier's Macaire (borrowed from Frédérick Lemaître's well-known stage success); later, under Napoléon III, of his Ratapoil. All of these figures served as metonyms for what the new press law made legally or socially unrepresentable: for a government of swindlers who had somehow acquired the power to prohibit their counter-discursive representation; or, at the other end of the social scale, for that diffuse vulgarity which the caricaturists cast as the essence of bourgeois existence. With the progressive naturalization of these images among the dissident readership, the objects of the satire seemingly needed only to be framed and foregrounded for their degradation to become patent.

These early representations thus helped strikingly to define the attitude of disaffected intellectuals toward emerging middle-class society. Certain tones and expressive techniques which more than two decades later Flaubert would employ to convey his damnation of the bourgeois are already present in the lithographs and texts which *Le Charivari* was publishing within a few months after the new press law necessitated reformulation of the paper's satirical strategies.

Of course the consolidation of this counter-discursive attitude—like any significant inflection in cultural strategies—was not instantaneous. The first images which *Le Charivari* published in the period after the press law went into effect devote rather catholic attention to all the classes and stations of society, in a spirit which clearly recalls the broadly representational Physiologies. Clerks and bankers, tailors and cooks, succeed each other among the "Types français."[32] Daumier, particularly, was feeling his way into the new counter-discursive tonality necessitated by the altered legal and social situation in which his

32. See L.D., 260, 261, 263, 265.

images appeared. But as we read chronologically through the catalogue of his prints, slowly but unmistakably the characteristic tone of
sardonic contempt for the attitudes and practices of middle-class
France defines itself and emerges.

Thus, for example, the short series of four lithographs on orangutans (L.D. 318–21) which appeared in *Le Charivari* from September
through November 1836 (see illustration 2). While other classes and
stations of society are spared, the bourgeois are subjected to the corrosive comparison of their own physiognomies with the apes. The
tactic of the caricature functions to ridicule their pretensions. The
bourgeois would, of course, indignantly have refused imputations of
kinship with the orangutans which the figures depicted in these plates
all too conclusively resemble. But the suggestion of the satire is that
they would equally well have declined any suggestion of fraternity with
the human beings of the "inferior social orders" which their own class
increasingly dominated. Along similar critical lines from the same period, we might consider Plate 20 of the "Galerie physionomique" (L.D.
345), entitled "Contentement de soi-même" (the image even appeared
with an English translation of the title: "The Man who is satisfied with
Himself"). The lithograph is a masterpiece of class-specific characterization and critique: a middle-aged bourgeois, slightly dissipated in
appearance, is observed admiring with insufferable self-infatuation his
image in a hand-mirror.

Overall, Daumier drew nearly four thousand lithographs. It is evident that any discussion of them in a study like the present one
chooses—knowingly or innocently—the manner in which it will interrogate this corpus, and thereby the limited number of items which it
will select for display as evidence supporting its perspective. As against
such selectivity, a perusal of the ten volumes of Delteil's catalogue or of
a series of numbers from *Le Charivari* will demonstrate the breadth of
Daumier's representational interests, the generality of his social
subjects.

Yet to make sense of Daumier's production we need to seek some
more "oriented" perspective on his satire than is suggested by any
presumption of its social neutrality. What establishes the critical bearing of these diverse lithographs, and justifies the perspective I am
taking here upon them, resides in the realm of tone: in the specific
expressiveness of *la charge* which constitutes each image and trans-

2. Orang-outangs: "Voyez, M. Mayeux, cet animal . . ." 6 October 1836 (L.D. 319) (the Armand Hammer Daumier Collection)

forms our impression of it from one of simple intended reproduction of the social to a more or less profoundly judgmental and critical representation.

If we wished to identify a turning point in the consolidation of his strategies, and in his selection of their appropriate social object, the caricatures of Robert Macaire would serve well. Nothing quite like the *violence* Daumier directed against the person of his quintessential bourgeois swindler ever appears in the artist's depictions of members of other social groups or classes. Daumier had treated Macaire as early as 1834, before passage of the new press law. In an image from November 13 of that year, the crook and his pear-shaped king exchange comradely embraces while mutually picking each others' pockets (L.D. 95). But however effective such a single image might have been, the corrosive series of one hundred plates on Macaire which followed the press law (a series entitled, significantly, "La Caricaturana") redirected Daumier's critical energies decisively. It provided a paradigm for reading bourgeois reality which strategically transformed its appearance. "La Caricaturana" appeared from 20 August 1836 through 25 November 1838 (there was a second series of twenty Macaire plates published from October 1840 to September 1842). The series systematically reconceived the emerging bourgeois socioeconomy in terms of the most transparently cynical forms of larceny and fraud.

The first plate of the series introduced its two main characters, Macaire and his vaguely imbecilic sidekick Bertrand. For his opening shot in this campaign against the middle class, Daumier invoked the mechanism of rapaciousness which most tellingly characterized the historical moment.[33] In the liberation—or the licentiousness—of a social and economic conjuncture transformed by the change of regime, Macaire and Bertrand celebrate the pleasures of untrammeled financial speculation:

> [*Macaire*:] Bertrand, I love business. Why don't we found a bank, right, a real bank, a hundred million million francs of capital, a hundred billion billion shares—we'll sink the Bank of France, we'll sink the bankers, we'll sink everyone.

33. For the legal and institutional innovations by which the July Monarchy opened the realms of industry and finance to what we could politely term unrestrained development, see Rondo Cameron, *France and the Economic Development of Europe*, pp. 85–88. A

[*Bertrand*:] Yes, but what about the cops?
[*Macaire*:] Don't be silly. Do millionaires ever get arrested?[34]

This cynicism constantly characterizes Macaire's attitude toward the objects of his swindles. Of course with literary figures like Nucingen and Vautrin, Balzac was already focusing the portrayal of particularly modern forms of acquisitiveness and power hunger. Thus depicted, Vautrin, Nucingen, seem the epochal, the titanic representatives of early capitalism's dynamism and of its rapacity. On the other hand, the significance of Macaire as he was produced and circulated in the satirical newspapers was—in the spirit of the dailies themselves—to seize the *quotidian* character of the bourgeoisie's activity. If Vautrin may be counted a figure in something like capitalism's foundation myth, Macaire is its daily life: the constantly recurring reminder just over the horizon of middle-class good conscience of the corrupted Other that the bourgeoisie bore within itself.

In this regard, the extraordinary range of professional positions which Macaire successively assumes in the course of his unsavory career in "La Caricaturana"—banker, financier, shareholder, speculator, lawyer, industrialist, political candidate, newspaper editor, merchant, doctor, surgeon, dentist, oculist, hypnotist, pharmacist, magnetizer, journalist, and so on—generalizes his identity in a particularly significant way. The fact is crucial. A single print from the Macaire series cannot adequately disclose the authentic object, or the essential mechanism, of Daumier's satire. By itself each print castigates a local abuse, ridicules a limited area which, at most, one might be tempted to reform. But the setting of the images in a large-circulation periodical sold to continuing subscribers—who can be presumed to have followed the prehistory of each image, and who will be around to appreciate further developments in the story—transforms the mode in which they function. The repetition of the Macaire character in a great diversity of situations causes each individual evil depicted to appear to diffuse through the entire social landscape. Then it is not a specific

---

particularly strong evocation of the atmosphere of the period can be found in Marx's *Class Struggles in France*, pp. 33–40—esp. p. 36, where Marx calls Louis-Philippe "Robert Macaire on the throne." The spirit of the period is powerfully conveyed in the second part of Stendhal's *Lucien Leuwen*.
34. "Caricaturana," pl. 1; L.D. 354.

behavior but a systematic pattern of pathology which emerges as the real object of satire beyond the perspective of the isolated image.

The point of instituting such a "recurring character" was to assure that no one could take Macaire simply as a condemnation of the shadier members of an otherwise innocent—indeed beneficent—class. His appearance, sinister, often seedy, might have led to such an interpretation. But Daumier intended Macaire to personify an entire period and social system. And he achieved the generalization of his character's significance by boxing the middle-class compass with the figure of his swindler. *Every* social role in bourgeois society—and the most prestigious first of all—is successively occupied by his character. *Despite* the outwardly disreputable appearance which Daumier teaches us to see beyond, Macaire comes to represent not the con man he *looks like*, but the more mystifying one he authentically *is*: something like the corrosive spirit of capitalism in its early acquisitive phase, in its moment of what Marx termed primitive accumulation. That is the full and chilling resonance which develops, over the course of the series, around Macaire's "I love business."[35]

Baudelaire saw clearly this generalization and deepening of the figure's range and significance: "The *Robert Macaire* series was the decisive inauguration of 'caricature de moeurs' ["caricature of manners," or more broadly, social caricature]. From that time on, caricature took a new direction, and was no longer particularly political. *It became the general satire of the citizenry.*"[36]

Daumier drove the point home in plate 76 of the series (L.D. 431), in which a self-infatuated Macaire expresses to Bertrand his enthusiasm for the disciples whom they have educated in corruption (see illustration 3). With a broad sweep of his arm he indicates them: we recognize lawyers, artists, financiers, and a general group of scions of the bourgeoisie. Unlike their mentor, all of them are dressed neatly and well. Their figures are not unpleasing, and they seem the personification of middle-class respectability. Yet *they* are Macaire's disciples. Moreover,

---

35. In the second Robert Macaire play, which was produced on the crest of the figure's popularity in 1834, Frédérick Lemaître, who had created the original role, appeared in the final performance of the drama—it was closing because the government had banned it—in a parallel apotheosis: he made himself up as Louis-Philippe. See Wechsler, *Human Comedy*, p. 85.

36. *Oeuvres complètes*, p. 1005; my italics.

3. La Caricaturana: "C'est tout de même flatteur . . ." 11 March 1838 (L.D. 431) (the Armand Hammer Daumier Collection)

his success in initiating them into the workings of a capitalist economy, in reproducing his own essence in them, has created a characteristic problem. Their proliferation has constituted them as a sort of social overproduction crisis. The competition is rising. As Macaire puts it to Bertrand: "It certainly is flattering to have acquired so many disciples! but dammit, there are too many of 'em, the competition is ruining business, and if it goes on like this, we're going to go under."

No doubt the most brilliant satirical touch in "La Caricaturana" comes in plate 78, dated 8 April 1838 (L.D. 433). In this image the ideological combat between Macaire as personification of middle-class dominant discourse and Daumier's counter-discursive subversion of it becomes so intense that the code of the representation is itself transgressed. At last the social forces which have been in conflict from the outset of "La Caricaturana" confront each other directly, even if the conflict is displaced from overt struggle to the verbal sparring of a quintessential Macaire swindle. In this image the swindler himself steps out of the caricatural never-never land he has long occupied in order to visit Daumier himself in his studio (see illustration 4). Macaire has come to *compliment* the artist on "La Caricaturana"—on the series in which he has been corrosively depicted for a year and a half. His dialogue then stages a paradigmatic effort at mystification:

> Monsieur Daumier, your Robert Macaire series is delightful! It is the exact portrait of the thievery of our times . . . the faithful depiction of the collection of rogues we find everywhere—in business, in politics, at the bar, in finance, everywhere. The crooks must be furious with you. . . . But you have surely gained the esteem of decent people. . . . You say they haven't yet awarded you the *croix d'honneur?* Why, that's infuriating![37]

In Daumier's portrayal, Macaire's conduct is unmitigatedly amoral. This is what makes the representation of bourgeois morality which he personifies polemically effective. Macaire calculates *everything* in relation to himself, and nowhere does concern for the negative consequences of his actions upon others enter his logic. So in this plate his flattering exchange with Daumier—the artist who had been keeping

37. Here, as frequently in Daumier's captions, the ellipsis points appear in the original text.

4. La Caricaturana: "Monsieur Daumier, votre série est charmante . . ." 8 April 1838 (L.D. 433) (the Armand Hammer Daumier Collection)

him so painfully exposed before the public—implies new heights of manipulation. For Macaire has never given a disinterested compliment in his life. As with Nucingen (whom Balzac himself compared to Macaire in *Splendeurs et misères des courtisanes*), *everything* comes under the sign of middle-class rationality, of a precise calculus of the coldest self-interest. So a gesture as unexpected as Macaire's confrontation with his primary antagonist, under the guise of whatever admiring cameraderie, must cover an attempted con even more essential to his designs than any of the others which Daumier had depicted him as perpetrating.

Its project is evident in the double movement of his speech to the artist. First, Macaire attempts to limit the satirical range of "La Caricaturana" in order to gain control of its polemical referent. His object is to truncate the critique to the obvious cases of fraud—the "coquins"—about which no ethical or ideological disagreement among "decent" people could possible exist. He aims to exonerate the social order by denouncing its abuses and its abusers. Second, by dangling the possibility of a decoration, Macaire seeks to implicate Daumier himself in the circuit of self-interest which it has been the object of "La Caricaturana" all along to map and to expose.

Both of these, of course, are classic strategies of mystification: the facile concession that there are still some bad apples in the bunch; and the worldly insinuation that, after all, a little venality is only natural. Both of Macaire's tactics seek to trivialize and to marginalize effects which Daumier perceives as *systemic* in middle-class liberal capitalism. And in his turn, by representing these characteristic discursive tactics in this central confrontation of the series, Daumier seeks to outflank and to stigmatize them precisely because they are essential to the construction of the world which "La Caricaturana" seeks to subvert.

In this series Daumier invented a code by which a certain bourgeoisie might successfully be represented as other than it seemed. He put a face and a name to tendencies within the social formation which otherwise enjoyed the transparency of the everyday, which profited from the self-serving mystification of induced distortion. With Macaire—his particular syntax of bearing, gesture, dialogue, and conduct—Daumier sought to intervene in the depiction of a dominant fraction of the social world at a crucial moment in its implantation and consolidation. He defined the essence of strains of middle-class behav-

ior whose increasing domination of the social discourse was unprecedented. His lithographs thus focused and specified a counter-discursive formation: an image of the bourgeoisie which contested the
valence and the function generally attributed to them. In this early
period the defensive or self-celebratory apologia for middle-class discourses and practices was of course intense. Thus Daumier's propagation of a counter-image operated upon—and against—broadly circulated and widely credited representations. His own were thus wreathed
with the most profoundly sardonic irony: the rhetoric which Daumier
perfected in this series. Its characteristic tone would henceforth always
attach in some degree to his portrayal of the class which dominated his
society.

The elements of such a representation had been floating in the pool
of notations and perceptions which make up the cultural stock, the
storehouse of social signs, in any period. The characteristic gestures
and tactics which compose his depiction of Macaire did not emerge
from nowhere. But their appearance in Le Charivari, particularly in
"La Caricaturana," sharpened their lineaments, defined their configuration unforgettably. And this was particularly so because of the connection Daumier established between the images themselves and their
medium, constituted by exaggeration and ridicule. Of all his series, the
depictions of Macaire thus appropriately merit the name of the genre
itself, "Caricaturana," attributed to them by Le Charivari. Through the
portrayal of the swindler, Daumier and Le Charivari established these
images of the bourgeois as unavoidable critical elements in cultural
consciousness. Daumier confronted the hegemonic norm, the received
idea of an entire class, and by *force of image* he skewed it toward a new
counter-hegemonic perception. With Daumier, these corrosive depictions of the middle class do not so much come into existence as they
enter the realm of cultural power and social effectiveness.

This effectiveness was possible in large part because of the way in
which Daumier's images were put into circulation. We need to remind
ourselves that the combat was waged in a medium—the daily newspaper—which might almost have *defined* the power of the very forces
against which Daumier, Philipon, and their associates were struggling.
However paradoxically, the field and the object of their battle was
"newspaper culture." I will return to this central contradiction below.

But we have already seen how such a struggle for control of a social language is ceaselessly exposed to efforts of reenvelopment and out-flanking by strains of the dominant discourse. Macaire's imagined visit to Daumier constituted one such tactical attempt; and as I argued, Daumier in his turn contrived to fold the process of mystification which sought to reabsorb his criticism back into the representation itself.

A similar interrogation of the process by which the combat of counter-discourse and dominant plays itself out under the new cultural conditions of liberal capitalism is at work in another of Daumier's most interesting images from this period (see illustration 5). The plate depicts two comfortable bourgeois perusing a lithograph in Philipon's relaunched *La Caricature* (L.D. 561). The one holding the paper seems indignant at what we may imagine to have been another in the paper's long series of scurrilous attacks upon middle-class values. In contrast, his companion contemplates the image in the paper with nothing more than a patronizing smile. Such disengagement is more disturbing, for it puts into question the effectiveness of any counter-discursive critique. The image's caption records words which could belong to either of the bourgeois depicted or to both; its ambiguity can as easily carry the anger of the one as the untroubled superiority of the other: "Pas fameux? n'est-ce pas!" ("Not very good, is it?"). This reflection from within the medium upon the process of its own circulation—and possible neutralization—is of exceptional interest.

Another perspective on the same configuration can be found in L.D. 792: two bourgeois, their faces invisible behind an opened copy of *Le Charivari*, peruse the paper (see illustration 6). They discuss one of the humorous texts on page 2 and the caricature on page 3. They find these entertaining; indeed, one of them is so amused that he decides to purchase a copy of the paper. Yet despite their indulgent appreciation, we sense that the satire has not touched them, that in their contemplation they have employed a tactic to *avoid* implication in it, to maintain themselves exempt from its corrosive energy.

The twist, of course, is that in its turn their attitude of superior distance becomes the *charge* of the caricature which *we* peruse just as *they* are examining the one in the paper they hold before them. There is even an additional layer to the play of critical envelopment and reenvelopment which this image stages. For we too confront *Le Charivari* as we consider the image in which two disengaged bourgeois face this

5. Types parisiens: "Pas fameux? n'est-ce pas!! . . ." 7 April 1839 (L.D. 561) (the Armand Hammer Daumier Collection)

6. "La lecture du *Charivari*," 1 April 1840 (L.D. 792) (the Armand Hammer Daumier Collection)

intensely engaged newspaper. There is a risk that our contemplation may imitate their own. And if our reading should tend toward the same detachment as theirs, the satirical hook to the caricature is present to expose it to the challenge to which they are themselves subjected. The embedded metalanguage of the representation thus seeks to devaluate an attitude toward the image by which the consumers of a critical artifact manage, *in the very exercise of their power to acquire it*, to absorb or evade its ideological implications and the threatening bearing of its mockery.

The Chinese-puzzle exchange of efforts to undo or outflank the discourse of the Other is thus particularly complex in this representation. But the configuration of this "mise en abyme" is really that of the termless struggle to reenvelop the opponent which constitutes *all* discursive combat. Indeed, the play of opposing efforts to achieve symbolic domination resembles nothing more than the childhood fantasy (or the topological enigma) of two predators each of which is intent upon devouring the other, absorbing the substance of its rival into itself.

In the case of the struggle figured in Daumier's lithograph, it is particularly difficult to say which of the competing sides has the final word. For as I have suggested, one could easily imagine the very lithograph under discussion, whose corrosive counter-ideological implications seem so clear, indulgently "appreciated" (that is, dismissed) by a member of *precisely the class which it depicts*, schooled as they have been to the assumption of superiority which permits their self-serving detachment. They express their superiority, they *practice* their non-implication, according to the most characteristic paradigm of middle-class relation to the subversive energies which are constantly released within the cultural realm: by *purchasing* the object which has afforded them such amusement, thereby containing it in the quintessential middle-class reflex of consumption.

What Daumier maps and mocks are the corporeal attitudes and ideological practices characteristic—one might say *diagnostic*—of the bourgeoisie. Baudelaire expressed the impulse exactly. Concerning Daumier's *capture* of the bourgeois, he wrote: "All of the stupidities, all of the vaingloriousness, all of the desperation of the bourgeois are there. Daumier knows the shape of his nose and the construction of his head, he knows the mood which dominates his house from top to bottom."[38]

Essentially Daumier sought to figure and to ridicule a class language (or, more accurately, a complex of multiple, interdependent, socially specific languages). Beyond their individual contents, and to the extent that they inscribe and express the *differentiation* of social groups, such languages inevitably refer us to the arena of social struggle. In their designation of the practices particular to one competing group, as a sign of the *exclusion* of the Other, they implicate the conflicted relations *between* classes and the determinants of this conflict.

A long tradition of Daumier scholarship has privileged (or fetishized) the visual—the "artistic"—side of his production almost to the exclusion of the other signifiers which it carries. This view has tended particularly to disjoin the complex of *image and caption* which composes nearly all of Daumier's plates. But the notion of the diverse languages of a social group as interdependent codes, signifying class-specific physical appearance and habits of mental behavior, re-fuses this complex of languages in a single representation. A proper reading of these images would seem to require such resynthesis. For the critical tendency toward estheticization of the image violates the essential characteristics of the process by which Daumier's plates were produced.

To be sure, the factual situation seems relatively complex. It seems established that Daumier did not compose most of the captions for his lithographs himself (an exception is made for the very late plates whose legends consist only of a word or two). Rather they were written by one of the journalists on Philipon's staff at *Le Charivari*. With their customary doggedness, scholars have sought to determine exactly what role the different figures in Philipon's shop might have played in composing the captions.[39] And, finding that Daumier did not write the

38. "Quelques caricaturistes français," *Oeuvres complètes*, p. 1005.

39. The idea that Daumier did not compose his captions has led a diffuse existence, but seems traceable to an article by one of the staff journalists on *Le Charivari*, Albert Wolff, which appeared at the time of Daumier's death ("La mort de Daumier," *Le Figaro*, 13 Feb. 1879; see Vincent, *Daumier*, p. 252, n. 8). In 1934 Jean Adhémar made a detailed examination of the problem, and concluded that the longer the caption, the smaller the chance that Daumier composed it himself. This perspective is recapitulated in Adhémar's book on Daumier (p. 27), where he specifies the details of the process the plates went through on their way to publication. The lithographic stone which

actual texts, critics have tended to depreciate them and their importance in the plates on the assumptions that texts produced, as these were, by diverse and probably distracted hands, under such chaotic conditions, could hardly aspire to much esthetic dignity, and that the genius behind the lithographs was of a *visual* character, that Daumier was not much interested in words anyway.

Such abstracting separation of the different elements of a cultural artifact always suggests an ideological move. While the facts offered in support of such accounts of the caricatural production process may be accurate, the tradition has tended to interpret their significance in a manner which distorts them. This critical effort at estheticization is fundamentally reductionist.

The view which privileges the image to the extent of disdaining its verbal accompaniment (even preferring proofs "before the letter," whose rarity not so coincidentally has given them significantly more value on the art market) denies the real conditions surrounding Daumier's production and the protocols according to which his images were designed to be perceived. It transforms Daumier into something like the familiar—and politically innocuous—easel painter, rather than the committed critical journalist, which was his consistent cultural role. The scholarly tradition can speak of Daumier's steadfast republicanism, of his constant politics of opposition—indeed, it can hardly avoid doing so. But it contrives to evade their real implications. It treats his production as if it was salon material offered for the delectation of the esthete, and betrays thereby the counter-discursive project of his satire. Its stance is that of the indifferent bourgeois whose detached con-

---

Daumier prepared for the printer carried no printed text. Once the printer struck the proofs (the stage of the process known, for obvious reasons, as "before the letter"), the secretary of *Le Charivari* sent them to Daumier in his studio for approval. At that point, the artist would typically add, in the margin of the proof, an "idée," a rapid explication of his represented subject. When the proofs, thus annotated, were returned to *Le Charivari*, they went to one of the journalists who specialized in composing the actual texts of captions (Wolff, for example). At times, they found Daumier's telegraphic "idée" too vague or incomprehensible and sent a messenger back to him to get a clearer notion of what he might have had in mind (Adhémar, *Daumier*, p. 27; see also Vincent, *Daumier*, pp. 96–98). It was Baudelaire, in "Quelques caricaturistes français," who accredited the notion that the captions of Daumier's plates were more or less unnecessary: "The captions beneath his images hardly serve any purpose, for, generally speaking, one could do without them" (*Oeuvres complètes*, p. 1006).

templation of *Le Charivari* Daumier sought to outflank in the images I have been considering.

But we need to *credit* Daumier's method of working, and specifically the social *interaction* between members of *Le Charivari*'s staff which was integral to it. A vision of the plates as art objects comfortably insulated from social struggle has led to a romantic idealization of the mechanism by which they "ought" to have been produced—to an involuntary (and, in the context, deeply ironic) caricature of the solitary artist in his studio, driven in the isolation of his genius to accomplish everything alone. But Daumier worked for and through a large-circulation periodical, for a highly organized and influential counter-discursive *apparatus*. The way his captions came about reflects the real conditions of production in such a setting.[40]

The relation between caption and image thus needs to be seen differently. If there are captions in these images, it is because the protocols of Daumier's caricature, of the subversion which he sought by it, require them. *All* the languages of the bourgeoisie—and indeed, of the other classes depicted—are necessary for the critical work of the satire which it was *Le Charivari*'s object to put into circulation. So it seems conceptually satisfying that a particular lithograph may have been the result of a floating collaboration between the members of the Philipon network, a process of formulation, criticism, and redefinition as the object passed through the hands of those involved in bringing it before the paper's public, accumulating its sedimented representations of middle-class reality and, sustaining them, the diverse tactics by which this dominant here-and-now was daily mocked.[41]

---

40. The tradition has explained away Daumier's captions on the basis of a false historical and generic determinism. It is a fact that the styles of earlier caricature, in the late Restoration period, typically were less visually brilliant than Daumier's were to become. They required captions to point their meaning (Charlet was apparently the first artist regularly to employ them, after 1822; see Adhémar, *Daumier*, p. 71). After 1830, Daumier's visual talents rapidly eclipsed these earlier images. Traditional scholarship has implied that—had not the public become accustomed to them—Daumier might have preferred to omit the captions altogether. But such a view ignores the degree to which, in every *other* aspect of the material and conceptual invention of the satirical daily, Philipon and his associates had found it possible to be strikingly innovative, to overturn traditional assumptions concerning their medium and its modes of production and circulation.

41. Adhémar suggests that Balzac himself (with whom, we recall, Daumier had worked on *La Caricature*) may have been the source for a number of the satirical ideas

The effect of Daumier's lithographs is the result of their *collaborative* production. Both in their conception as an integral element of a mass-circulation periodical and in their diffuse and multiple authorship (itself an early example of the division of cultural labor), the expressive resources of these lithographs—which form one of the major counter-discursive apparatuses of the nineteenth century—are the result of modes of social cooperation which have increasingly generalized themselves in cultural production since that time (one thinks of the seemingly endless list of workers in the credits of a modern film).

Individualist forms of symbolic resistance sometimes seem alone to typify the range and the varieties of nineteenth-century counter-discourses. And in our cultural history their prestige is rightly high. But in one significant sense, of which their isolation is itself the sign, such individualist forms remained systemically underdeveloped. They contradicted the irreducibly *collective* character of all social discourses (particularly in the postromantic period) by failing to integrate it into the form of their production and circulation. This fact determined failure and resignation as their mode of being from the start. But the counter-discourses of *Le Charivari* were not haunted by such anticipatory capitulation to the power of the dominant. For them, for Daumier's plates particularly, the counter-hegemonic struggle and the social stakes were distinctly real. The discourses of the social world were still intensely contested.

It is thus particularly significant that the overwhelming majority of Daumier's captions report *speech*. They comprise an effort to record the class- and situation-specific utterances which—along with bodily at-

---

which Daumier transformed into socially caricatural plates ("lithos de moeurs") for *Le Charivari* (*Daumier*, p. 77). Just how indispensable the captions of Daumier's plates really are can be seen, by negation, in the small number of them whose production was for some reason arrested at the stage of proofs "before the letter"—for example, L.D. 1567, which was never titled and never received its caption. It depicts a bourgeois in a downpour, his umbrella folded under his arm. Those in the street around him are protected by their raised umbrellas; he alone stands there, an indefinable expression on his face, getting thoroughly soaked. Why does he not open his umbrella? We will never know: his conduct remains incomprehensible because he has been deprived of a language crucial to his conception. Of course Daumier must have meant the representation to signify *something*. But the integration of a caption and thereby the process of our understanding have been disrupted by some technical incident which no doubt will always remain an enigma for us.

titude, costume, facial expression, and the other nonverbal languages which could be represented in a drawing—carry the image of the satirized world. With a logic which parallels Balzac's perception that the multiple languages of a social formation are the levers by which one might seize its inner articulations, the languages of these lithographs—and the verbal, paradoxically, most powerful among them—are indispensable elements in the generic innovation which the caricatures constituted.

What in fact they are principally engaged in turns out to parallel the discursive strategies of the mass-circulation newspapers which I have already analyzed as a constitutive expression of the middle class, as a principal instrument of its consolidation. In bodying forth the dominant discourse, in displaying it insistently and with the fullest possible precision, the caricature snatches the everyday from the apparent invisibility of its ideological protection. Daumier's satire seeks to *pin* the individual specimens and moments of the dominant discourse. Embedded in the network of quotidian existence which collectively validates the factors constituting it, the diffuse elements of dominant practice—speech, manners, and attitudes—appear invincible. Daumier's tactic is to isolate such elements so that their ideological guarantee is stripped away and they stand exposed. The caricature seeks to seize them so tightly that they fall of their own weight.

"La Caricaturana" was a crucial turning point. With Macaire, Daumier had fixed the techniques by which the inner truth of a dominant class could be uncovered and exposed to judgment. Then the demystificatory process could be generalized by dispensing entirely with the exaggerated swindler's disguise and demeanor which had mediated the development of its early moments. The referents of the satire could at last be clothed in their own recognizable and respectable everyday costumes without thereby returning to the transparency of the everyday. This change opened strategies of subversion which had not previously appeared conceivable. For it turned out that one could take on the middle class *in its own language*. Then the bourgeois depicted in these corrosive plates almost seemed *themselves* to have authored the *charge*, the satirizing excess, which turned around to mock them. Their conduct could now be produced and revealed as its own *self*-caricature. It was as if the dominant formation, adequately represented, could be induced to deconstruct its own ideological disguise.

Yet this effort to imprison dominant discourse within the caricatural frame exhibits the same propensity to engender an endless *mise en abyme*, a limitless contest of discursive envelopment and reenvelopment, that we saw earlier in some of Daumier's richest lithographs. For, as I argued concerning Balzac's effort to master the power of the sign, in a counter-discursive situation the introduction of the dominant, the representation of the language of the antagonist, is always a perilous act. Rather than containing the dominant by the techniques of counter-discursive subversion, the gesture risks fostering the counter-discourse's own colonization from within, its contamination by the power of the dominant, and ultimately its neutralization.

The combat waged around this issue was intense. And such intensity reflects the conditions of representation which resulted from the project of the satirical daily itself: to contest or control or neutralize the power of the dominant within the confines of a medium whose global object was to subvert it. Specifically, the satirical daily wanted to be able to reproduce the discourses of its antagonist: to cite the speech, to depict the conduct and the practices, of the class it sought to mock. But in opening its space to these representations it risked becoming a text determined by them.

How could these fragments of dominant discourse be framed and confined to prevent *their* subversion of the subversion? As I have already suggested, there is no mechanism within the world of words which can guarantee the predominance of one text over another which it seeks to contain. The very nature of the combat makes this configuration precarious. A counter-discourse is counter-discourse because it presupposes the hegemony of its Other. It projects a division of the social space, and seeks to segregate itself in order to prosecute its critique. But such segregation can never be hermetic: consciousness of the antagonist's power inevitably implies that the practices by which it functions have *already* been internalized to some degree. The dominant surreptitiously turns out to have penetrated the counter-discourse which sought to control it.

Within the space of the satirical daily we might identify two orders of resistance to this project of counter-discursive subversion. The first of these is inherent in the nature of the nineteenth-century newspaper itself, in the practice of divisibility and precise calculation of space which virtually defined the medium. This practice reinforced a structure of social understanding in which all facts, whatever their specific content, are overdetermined by their relation to the principle of strictly calculated disposition of space. The "value" attributable to any "article" receives a precise, visible correlative in the page area granted to it in the paper. On the other hand, conceived in isolation one from another, the contiguity of disparate items on a page becomes nothing more than a meaningless spatial relation and is purged of any explanatory force. The form of the newspaper imparts to the practice of reading a logic of dispersion, of imposed incoherence.

The ideological content of such a mode of relation—or dissociation—was to become consciously foregrounded later in the century. To members of the avant-garde such a relation appeared intimately linked to the production of texts serving social and cultural interests which they were striving to contest. They began to question the assumptions of traditional typographical layout, the habits of regular disposition of words upon the page (I will return to these developments, and to Mallarmé's critique of the "column" itself, in Chapter 7). This avant-garde resistance depended upon the recognition that, in a textual economy in which page space was measurable in money just as readily as in column inches, the column functioned principally to afford the maximum amount of type, and thus of income, per unit area. So the column *itself* became readable as a machine to make money. Its disruption, on the other hand, came to signify a counter-discursive concern with integrity of thought and form, and an overt, programmatic refusal of paradigms of writing determined by the maximization of profit.

The sort of uneasy compromise with commercialism and its practices which *Le Charivari* was—more or less involuntarily—involved in would seem no longer tenable to dissident intellectuals later in the century. The fact suggests that, like the modes of penetration of the dominant, the conditions of counter-discursive production were changing fast. The avant-garde would seek to project a pure counter-discursive object. Daumier's lithos could never achieve such a purity, and in any case he would have rejected this sort of hermeticism. The mode he worked in presupposed an open struggle with the dominant: a conflicted inscription, and a simultaneous refusal, of its discourse which, by taking it on, his images intended to combat directly.

Such avant-garde developments belong later in the century. But *Le*

Charivari had already anticipated these "advanced" paradigms of opposition in some interesting ways. By moments the satirical daily did assert the subversion of the orthogonal—the regular, rectangular typographical layout so well suited to systematic fragmentation of the news, indeed of all social representation.

The classic case would surely be the paper's publication of the legal verdict which condemned it for its notorious depiction of the king as a *poire* (see illustrations 7 and 8). In France, publication of the court's verdict in the offending newspaper was generally decreed as part of the judgment itself. So in a gesture of brilliant derision directed against the regime and the repression it had deployed against them, *Le Charivari* set the text of the judgment itself in the outline of the July Monarchy's forbidden fruit (see illustration 8). Here at least they disrupted what Mallarmé was to call the newspaper's "insupportable colonne" and its attendant signification of middle-class "orderliness."

Yet in general, with the crucial exception of the page 3 lithographs, whose disruption of norms of newspaper appearance and layout I have already considered, the nineteenth-century satirical daily still looked very much like any other newspaper. However corrosive its content, its layout reproduced that of its antagonists, and to that extent it more or less involuntarily imitated the protocols sustaining their domination of the broader social text.

Yet to take accurate measure of the possibilities—and limits—of the sort of discursive contestation which *Le Charivari* attempted, we need to radicalize even this pessimistic observation. For there is a further ironic twist, a second order of resistance by the dominant to its neutralization within the satirical medium. It resides in the continued presence within the paper of another set of discourses constitutive of the social system which it was *Le Charivari*'s project to mock. As *newspaper*, as the institutional, material embodiment of that mechanism for selling products and images which the nineteenth-century discovered it had at its disposal almost before it knew how deep was its need for such an instrument, the satirical daily, even at its most corrosive, reproduces practices which functioned in complete harmony with the dominant modes by which the century was learning to conduct its affairs.

If we examine a Daumier lithograph as it was *meant* to be read, still in the paper and out of the frame to which collectors have generally

LES POIRES,

Faites à la cour d'assises de Paris par le directeur de la CARICATURE.

Vendues pour payer les 6,000 fr. d'amende du journal le *Charivari*.

(CHEZ AUBERT, GALERIE VÉRO-DODAT.)

Si, pour reconnaître le monarque dans une caricature, vous n'attendez pas qu'il soit désigné autrement que par la ressemblance, vous tomberez dans l'absurde. Voyez ces croquis informes, auxquels j'aurais peut-être dû borner ma défense :

Ce croquis ressemble à Louis-Philippe, vous condamnerez donc ?   Alors il faudra condamner celui-ci, qui ressemble au premier.

Puis condamner cet autre, qui ressemble au second.   Et enfin, si vous êtes conséquens, vous ne sauriez absoudre cette poire, qui ressemble aux croquis précédens.

Ainsi, pour une poire, pour une brioche, et pour toutes les têtes grotesques dans lesquelles le hasard ou la malice aura placé cette triste ressemblance, vous pourrez infliger à l'auteur cinq ans de prison et cinq mille francs d'amende ! !
Avouez, Messieurs, que c'est là une singulière liberté de la presse ! !

7. Philipon's *poire:* Defense exhibit at his 1834 trial, later reproduced as an *affiche* (the Armand Hammer Daumier Collection)

Le Charivari,

JOURNAL PUBLIANT CHAQUE JOUR UN NOUVEAU DESSIN.

Nous donnons ci-dessous, conformément à la volonté de nos juges, le dispositif et l'arrêt du jugement en dernier ressort qui a frappé le *Charivari*. Le jugement de nos derniers juges est absolument pareil à celui de nos seconds juges, lequel était lui-même la reproduction de celui de nos premiers juges. Tant il est vrai que les beaux esprits se rencontrent. Comme ce jugement, tout spirituel qu'il soit, risquerait d'offrir peu d'agrément à nos lecteurs, nous avons tâché de compenser du moins par la forme, ce qu'il pourrait y avoir d'un peu absurde au fond.

Louis-Philippe, roi des Français, à tous présens et à venir salut. La cour d'assises du département de Seine-et-Oise, séant à Versailles, a rendu l'arrêt suivant. — La cour, etc. — Considérant que l'opposition est régulière, — Reçoit Cruchet opposant à l'arrêt par défaut du 20 mars dernier. — Faisant droit sur son opposition, et statuant par arrêt nouveau. — Considérant que la question de compte rendu ne pourrait être examinée par la cour sans remettre en question la compétence irrévocablement fixée par l'arrêt de la cour d'assises de Seine-et-Oise du dix août dernier et celui de la cour de cassation le 19 octobre suivant. — Considérant d'ailleurs, que les articles incriminés relatant les interrogatoires des prévenus et les dépositions des témoins entendus dans les audiences de la cour d'assises de la Seine, des onze et douze mars dernier, renfermant ainsi, un véritable compte-rendu de ces audiences. — Considérant que de la comparaison des deux articles incriminés avec le procès-verbal dressé par les membres de la cour d'assises de la Seine le dix-neuf mars dernier, il résulte que le compte qu'ils contiennent, des audiences de ladite cour des onze et douze mars dernier, dans le procès, concernant Bergeron et Benoist est infidèle, qu'en effet les interrogatoires des accusés, les dépositions des témoins, les paroles prononcées par le président et par le procureur-général y sont pour la plupart tronquées et dénaturées, qu'on e même on y prête au président, au procureur-général et à plusieurs des témoins des paroles qui n'ont pas réellement été proférées. — Considérant que ces infidélités ont pour motif de jeter le ridicule et soit sur l'accusation, soit sur le président, et que d'ailleurs les deux articles dont il s'agit sont remplies de réflexions et de qualifications offensantes pour le président et le procureur-général ; d'où il suit que le compte-rendu l'a été de mauvaise foi, et qu'il est injurieux pour le président et le procureur-général. — Considérant que Cruchet a de son aveu signé lesdits articles comme gérant responsable. — Déclare Cruchet coupable d'avoir, dans le journal le *Charivari*, qu'il est gérant, imprimé, vendu et distribué, rendu de mauvaise foi un compte non seulement infidèle des audiences de la cour d'assises de la Seine des 11 et 12 mars dernier, mais encore injurieux pour le président et le procureur-général, ce qui constitue le délit prévu par les articles 7, 16, de la loi du 25 mars 1822 ; 26 de la loi du 26 mai 1819 ; 11 de la loi du 9 juin 1819, et 14 de la loi du 18 juillet 1828, lus à l'audience par le président. — Faisant application de ces dispositions de lois. — Condamne Isidore Mathias Cruchet, en un mois d'emprisonnement et en 5,000 fr. d'amende. — Interdit pendant un an aux éditeurs du journal dit le *Charivari* de rendre compte des débats judiciaires. — Condamne ledit Cruchet aux frais du procès. — Ordonne en exécution dudit article 26 de la loi du 26 mai 1819 la destruction desdits numéros du journal le *Charivari*, qui pourraient être ultérieurement saisis. — Ordonne que dans le mois, à partir de ce jour, le gérant du journal le *Charivari*, sera tenu d'insérer dans l'une des feuilles dudit journal qui paraîtront, un extrait contenant les motifs et le dispositif du présent arrêt. — Ordonne que le présent arrêt sera exécuté à la diligence du procureur du roi, conformément à la loi. — Fait et jugé à Versailles en audience publique au Palais-de-Justice le lundi 9 décembre 1833 en présence de M. Salerai, procureur du roi, par MM. Antoine AiméMarie Lefebvre, conseiller à la cour royale de Paris, président de la cour d'assises, Louis Claude Mirofle, vice-président du tribunal de première instance de l'arrondissement de Versailles, et Arnould Teissier, juge au même tribunal composant la cour d'assises du département de Seine-et-Oise, qui ont signé avec Jean Marie Fontaine, commis greffier assistant. — En foi de quoi la minute du présent arrêt a été signée par le président et le commis greffier ainsi signé Lefebvre Mirofle, Tessier et Fontaine.

---

8. *Le Charivari,* 27 February 1834, p. 1: Verdict against the paper for having represented Louis-Philippe as a *poire* (the Armand Hammer Daumier Collection)

relegated it; if we turn our object over to discover *its* own verso, *its* underside, what we find is "la quatrième page du journal," the page 4 advertising. This was the page which, owing to its intent devotion to the business of business, Mallarmé deemed the newspaper's most degraded *and thereby its most characteristic* element (see Chapter 2). Indeed, as anyone who has examined an original Daumier lithograph from *Le Charivari* has noticed, the surface of the plate is itself disrupted by the print-through of the page 4 advertisements, which under the conditions of nineteenth century letterpress technology was extremely difficult to prevent. A phantom, palimpsest presence of the medium's commercial side thus floats on the surface of its satire. And the presence of this *involuntary* representation and reproduction of dominant practices threatens the apparatus of satirical corrosion in a fundamental way.

I am not arguing that the staff of *Le Charivari* should have known better than to print advertising. Such an analysis of the political economy of oppositional media would surely have been anachronistic in the early 1830s.[42] The point is not to indict Daumier and his colleagues for ideological blindness, but to suggest how deeply implicated in the structures of dominant discourse even the most concerted strategies of resistance cannot fail to find themselves. And when, as was the case here, the apparatus in question was *public*, required to sustain itself within a given social economy, then the extraordinarily restricted range of alternatives to dominant practice available to those who seek divergence from normalized paths becomes particularly evident.

There is no doubt that the analysis of the mechanisms of nascent capitalism performed by *Le Charivari* was partial and was to some degree restrained by the involuntary opportunism characteristic of any institution which is seeking to survive. The paper did provide a constant critique of the practices of advertising puffery, which Daumier and his collaborators repeatedly associated with the swindles of Macaire.[43] On the other hand, *Le Charivari* happily accepted and published advertising. What is crucial is that this dissonance never led to

42. Bellet, however, has commented upon the acute consciousness on the part of the opposition and satirical press around midcentury of the pernicious effects of advertising upon the public—particularly of the psychological conditioning which it induced (*Presse et journalisme*, p. 194).

43. See, particularly, numerous plates from "La Caricaturana," e.g., L.D. 356, 360, 374, 387, 436, 446, 447.

any significant effort to alter the *form* of the paper's disposition of its space, or of its internal economy.

This latter, of course, depended upon advertising precisely because the paper sought to propagate, to publicize, its contestation. Unlike the internal emigrés whose more solitary forms of disaffection would characterize a later period in the century, *Le Charivari* was not satisfied to frame its dissent in the form of more or less impotent, and certainly isolated, cries of rage. On the contrary it sought to be socially *effective*, to intervene positively in the cultural field. Its staff members risked (and went to) prison because they conceived their struggle as taking place in the public sphere, and they believed that their action had significant implications in this realm. Indeed the repressive reaction of the regime to their activity only serves to confirm our perception that their dissidence transcended the idiosyncratic and the private.

But in a longer perspective, the entire adventure of this satirical counter-discourse serves to demonstrate how broad are the blind spots in any alternative vision, however dedicated, however brilliantly prosecuted. When we say that the dominant discourse is ubiquitous, this is a strong claim. The modes of domination penetrate to places where they could hardly themselves have known that they could succeed in gaining a foothold. And the habits learned in the atmosphere which they establish demonstrate a persistence which may make us wonder if discursive combat, if the war of words alone, can ever truly alter the forms of social existence or personal experience.

As time went on, the fourth page of *Le Charivari* slowly became indistinguishable from the corresponding page in the "straight" dailies we have considered, even those most thoroughly committed to the values which the satirical daily exerted itself to subvert. But business is business in capitalist society. And for all the ingeniousness expended in the characterization and the exposure of a bourgeois stand-in like Macaire, or of the class whose social practice he turned out to represent, the last page of a nineteenth century daily still paid the freight.

In the early years, the quantity of advertising carried in *Le Charivari* was still very small.[44] A timid squib in the last column gave the rates:

---

44. Though volumes reproducing Daumier's plates are numerous, it is harder to find intact copies of *Le Charivari* itself. Fortunately, a one-volume reproduction of entire selected issues has been published; see Rossel, *Un journal révolutionnaire*. From it we can get a sense of the physical reality, and the "dailiness," of the paper.

"Annonces du *Charivari*—1 fr. la ligne" ("Classified ads in *Le Charivari*—1 franc per line"; see, for example, the issue of 23 May 1834, p. 4). Later the advertising linage grew substantially; the seductions of display type were offered to the advertisers who chose to patronize the paper (see, for example, the *réclames* in the issue of 16 July 1842—like the one formerly cited, reprinted in *Un journal révolutionnaire*—with their profusion of distinctive type styles). But for the satirical daily, the paradox of the advertising presence was irreducible. It was not simply a question of opening the paper's columns to paid publicity in the familiar form of page 4. Embedded as it was within a social formation whose pressures propagated willy-nilly even to those who sought to resist them, the paper printed *pro domo* puffery hawking the productions of its own writers and artists. In doing so it found it perfectly natural to employ tones which, had they been attributable to others, *Le Charivari* would have subjected to merciless parody.

Consider this text which ran in the page 4 *annonces* during January 1843:

MARRIED LIFE

Album of 60 lithographs, by H. Daumier

Parisian married couples have a tireless adversary in Daumier's pencil. The disadvantages of marriage, its minor absurdities, its trivial unhappinesses, are recalled with that comic truth, that pitiless frankness, which are the attributes of our artist's talent. Examine *Married Life*, you who are considering leaving the single state. This album consoles bachelors and makes everyone laugh, even married men.—Price: bound, 32 francs.[45]

To be sure the text, in the mock-heroic exaggeration of its own claims, still seeks to maintain a distinct parodic edge. But there is nothing counter-discursive about the line advertising the price. And indeed, even the *charge*, the excess in the tone of the whole text, would be hard to distinguish from the consciously manipulative advertising methods which arose very early in response to widespread public skepticism about the institution of publicity in general: "a knowing, sophisticated, humorous advertising, which acknowledged the skepticism and

45. Quoted in Delteil, *Daumier*, vol. 2, at no. 683.

made claims either casual or offhand or so ludicrously exaggerated as to include the critical response. . ."46

The protocols of dominant discourse thus more or less effortlessly reenveloped even these ingenious efforts to turn them to account without entirely becoming their dupe. And so the satirical paper discovered itself involuntarily circulating the adversary's speech because inevitably it was implicated in—was to some substantial degree *defined by*—the adversary's practice.

Within the discursive space of *Le Charivari* which thus reveals itself as unexpectedly heterogeneous, indeed contradictory, we find three modes of discourse which coexist there, but in acute conflict one with another. The first of these is that determined by the material form of the large-circulation daily itself—practices of the orders we have considered: page layout, advertising, and the associated considerations of economic viability, which inevitably flow over into the diverse discourses of the paper itself and must be accommodated within them.47

The second of these conflicted modes of discourse in *Le Charivari* was the representation, consciously caricatured and deformed by the weight of *la charge* but still fully recognizable despite the excess, of the fragments of the middle-class languages framed as objects of depiction

46. Raymond Williams, "Advertising," p. 181. For another example of *Le Charivari*'s puffery, see the long introduction to the series of Daumier plates entitled "Histoire ancienne" (Dec. 1841 to Jan. 1843), reprinted in Delteil, *Daumier*, vol. 3, after no. 924. There is in addition a curious Daumier lithograph which appeared in *Le Charivari* on 1 May 1839 (L.D. 558) and which was widely circulated as an *affiche*, an advertising poster. It catalogued at length the joys of a subscription to *Le Charivari* itself: "Suivez tout le monde! Passez au bureau!" ("Join the crowd! Come by our office [to sign up]!"). The details of price and terms then followed.

47. Considerations of this order affected the material appearance of *Le Charivari* in the most concrete ways. In 1851, for example, the effort to reduce the production costs of the paper led to the replacement of the lithographic stones by metal plates (the process known as "gillotage"). A substantial degradation in the density of the inked tones and the fineness of the image's surface resulted and can be noticed when one compares lithographs from before and after this date. Subsequently, in 1870, a further technical "advance" (or economy) intervened: "single-printing," which permitted the entire paper to be run off on one mechanized press (that is, the separate operation of printing the page 3 lithograph was dispensed with). Further visible degradation in the images resulted. For anyone who valued the sumptuous blacks and grays of Daumier's earlier plates, these technical modifications must inevitably have been read as the internalization of paradigms of cost-cutting which characterize a bourgeois economy. On these developments, see Passeron, *Daumier*, p. 288; and Mongan, *Daumier*, p. 13.

through satirical and critical protocols which were mobilized here for the first time.

In turn the final mode of *Le Charivari*'s conflicted content is the explicit discourse of contestation—parody, political and social protest—by which the paper sought to restrain the osmotic power of the dominant discourse it had installed within its space, but which, once there, threatened to permeate every level of its representation. I have argued that the ceaseless struggle of each discourse to envelop the other is the most characteristic element in any social situation characterized by competing class languages and social perspectives: for every hegemony, a counter-hegemony seeking to absorb and neutralize it; for every counter-discourse, a dominant discourse striving to colonize it from within, to co-opt it, or, *in extremis*, to repress it by the sorts of mechanisms which we observed in the press law of 1835.[48]

The central problem which emerges was that of enforcing the *difference* of the satirical newspaper and of its discourses from the discourse which it installs within itself in the project (or the fantasy) that a corrosive operation directed against such elements of bourgeois speech, manners, and modes of thought might somehow expunge them. As time went on, Daumier's satirical plates sought increasingly to represent elements of middle-class discourses and practices *without* loading upon them the traits of a specifically marked and grotesque exaggeration.

Indeed a clear tendency exists in Daumier's images to move from obviously deformed and markedly caricatural figures like Macaire to less overtly distorted representations. Such a movement tended to draw the counter-discursive effort toward new expressive strategies, based on altered assumptions concerning the *modes* of relationship which could be asserted between dominant discourses and counter-discourses themselves. This dynamic of development within Daumier's work leads beyond his own practice toward even more radical forms of resistance to the dominant in the nineteenth century, to the production of even more intransigent counter-discourses, whose protocols will be the concern of my next chapter.

The inflection could be summarized in this way: over the course of

48. Cherpin, *Daumier*, p. 94 outlines the different phases and strategies of press restriction and censorship in the period.

the nineteenth century, dissident artists and intellectuals began to conceive that the realistic mimesis of fragments of middle-class reality could be framed or staged in such a way that they would suddenly unmask themselves. Under these new conditions of representation they would emerge as elements in what Champfleury had termed "the inexhaustible repertory of middle-class stupidity."[49] The project (or the fantasy) implicit in this new counter-discursive paradigm was that through certain special textual protocols, the lanugages and the practices of the bourgeoisie might be induced to *subvert themselves*.

In one sense such representation might be said to have stemmed from the "petit réalisme" of the Physiologies. But as it developed after midcentury, this new counter-discursive mode was to prove more culturally influential than such early avatars of its practices could ever have suggested. The hallucinatorily accurate imitations of bourgeois behavior and discourse which we associate with figures like Henry Monnier or with Stendhal's hilarious miming of "César Bombet, fournisseur de l'Armée pour les bas et les bonnets de coton" at Madame Ancelot's salon;[50] were to lead ultimately to epochal inventions: Villiers de l'Isle-Adam's Tribulat Bonhomet and Flaubert's Garçon, those obsessive and seemingly involuntary anthologists of the stupidities of a class and its period. In turn, the tradition no doubt points beyond these creations to the even more exaggerated figure of Ubu, whose imbecilic elucubrations—"S'il n'y avait pas de Pologne, il n'y aurait pas de polonais"—would strikingly epitomize the gems of middle-class speech which Monnier, and later Villiers and Flaubert, had taken such perverse delight in accumulating.

This tendency to inflect representation *away* from the stylized and parodic to something like the realistic is of central importance in the evolution of Daumier's career, and in a sense he may be said to have been the first to intuit and systematically to exploit the corrosive resources it could afford.[51] This newer counter-discursive mode needs to

49. See Melcher, *Monnier*, p. 140.
50. See ibid., pp. 58–59.
51. By "realistic" I do not intend any naively transparent or unproblematic copy of the social referent, but only a representation which, unlike the parodic, does not overtly *mark itself* as deformation or grotesque stylization: a representation which for its bourgeois audience—however disenchanted with their own class and period—might have been counted as falling within the norms of observed or observable behavior or expression.

be distinguished from the excesses and exaggerations of traditional caricature and overt parody. In practice, however, its paradigm developed slowly as Daumier and the *Charivari* apparatus struggled with the paradoxes of discursive interpenetration and contamination which I have already discussed. They sought a mechanism which might preserve, within the space of their representation, the *difference* from its social object which alone could establish the possibility of its critique. The grotesque stylization of traditional caricature provided a basis for such difference; but in its absence how could the critique be distinguished from its object?

Daumier began, as we have seen, with more traditional modes of opposition: his images grounded themselves in obvious caricature, the *charge* laid on unmistakably in the form (say) of grotesque noses and facial features. Such a protoexpressionist paradigm led him to the easily readable rapacity which he rendered in Macaire, or to the animalism of his depictions of the figure dominating the early July Monarchy. Of such an overtly parodic order, the depictions of the royal "poire" would be privileged examples; the celebrated and virulent "Ventre législatif" (L.D. 131) would no doubt stand as the masterpiece of Daumier's early paradigm for caricatural satire.

Later, however, such caricatural markers tended to disappear. Daumier was reaching toward something new, toward a subtler expressive system, one whose corrosion was more infrastructural. Thus with the post-Macaire depictions of the middle class, his drawings (and indeed their captions) increasingly attain effects which are based on strikingly different and, I will argue, more modern protocols of representation. They seek to achieve their deconstruction of the figures depicted not so much by an immediately recognizable *distortion* of their physiognomies or their reported speech but by a selection of referents for representation which locates the critique not in the manner of their deformation *but in their surface reality itself.* The implicit assertion sustaining the new mode is simple: that if the viewer will only look, it will become immediately apparent how *preposterous* these bourgeois figures, and the entire social formation they dominate, really are.

In effect, Daumier was training us to read the degradation of bourgeois culture even in its own eyes; he was developing the expressive means to depict a society positively eager, in its profound guilt and self-embarrassment, to unmask itself. His representations thereby project, in a devastating polemic, the systematic consciousness of nine-teenth century middle-class *false* consciousness.

The lithographs then become effects, we might say, not so much of caricature as of *intensification*.[52] And this movement, by which "real-ism" is imagined to achieve something like the effect of a penetratingly corrosive *surreal*, becomes (as I will argue in the next chapter) a tech-nique for opening up contemporary social existence from the inside such that the critique of middle-class discourse can be pursued from the very heart of middle-class society.

These techniques for the mimesis of dominant discourse and prac-tice—which in the next chapter I will term re/citation—thus paradox-ically place the counter-discourses of the satirical newspaper at both extremes of the dialectic of their recuperation by the dominant. On the one hand, as these representations seek more and more closely to mime ordinary, everyday recognition and reproduction of the middle-class real, they tend to exaggerate the movement by which the satirical text is turned inside out by dominant discourse and is colonized despite itself by the endless propagation of middle-class representation. But, at the other end of the scale of discursive struggle and envelopment, and in a vertiginous reframing which recalls the combat of discursive en-velopment staged in Daumier's most brilliantly self-reflexive plates, such apparent neutralization of the satire by its dominant antagonist is suddenly and unexpectedly forced to invert itself again. This final per-ipeteia produces what is arguably the most powerful technique yet devised within the world of words for subverting the discourses of the bourgeoisie.

52. Cf. the Goncourts on Daumier, quoted in Vincent, *Daumier*, p. 236: "With Daumier the bourgeois reality reaches an intensity which is fantastic."

CHAPTER 4

Counter-Humorists: Strategies of Resistance in Marx and Flaubert

The cynicism is in the facts.
—KARL MARX, *Poverty of Philosophy*

L'avenir est ce qu'il y a de pire, dans le présent. [The worst thing about the present is the future.]
—GUSTAVE FLAUBERT,
letter to Ernest Chevalier (24 Feb. 1839)

L'Ironie est fille du temps. [Irony is the daughter of time.]
—LUCIEN FÈBVRE, *Le problème de l'incroyance au 16e siècle*

Marx and Flaubert are the canonical humorists of the nineteenth century. These two great contemporaries—principal antagonists of their own period, originators of what have come to be paradigmatic strategies for opposing its prolongation into our own time—gathered their devastating anecdotes at the same source. For both, the world was filled with, might almost be said to have been constituted by, material for their sardonic comedy.

Humor is intensely counter-discursive. I have argued that the discourses of contestation deploy an extremely broad spectrum of techniques and demonstrate great tactical inventiveness. Among these counter-discourses we might have supposed Flaubert's and Marx's strategies of resistance to bourgeois ascendency to have been irreconcilable. Surely each is associated with a different subversive strain— what we might term the "esthetic" and the "political" alternatives which were opened (in large measure through their respective efforts) to nineteenth-century dissidence. But Marx and Flaubert unexpectedly join in projecting against such domination the corrosive force of a unique species of comedy. Their tactics suggest reflections concerning the historicization of ideological and counter-ideological discourse— the fundamental insight which generated the comic text that weaves in common through their writing—and in turn concerning the functional limitations of such comic textualization.

The counter-discursive is always protodialectical. It asserts alternative structures for conceiving the real in the expectation—however naively hopeful—that their intervention will induce some fissure or slippage in the apparent seamlessness and solidity of the dominant. But it is a curious fact that in the realm of what we might take as strictly "literary" prose, nowhere was the theory of what was at work and at stake in the counter-discursive dynamic pushed to a thorough dialectical understanding. In this perspective it seems particularly pertinent to compare Flaubert's counter-discursive practice with that of Marx himself. The comparison has the advantage of demonstrating how closely the two track with each other up to the point—enthusiastically embraced by Marx; intensely rejected by Flaubert—at which the antinomic passes over into authentic dialectical contradiction. The limits of what I am calling the "counter-discursive" begin to be mapped at the point of this divergence.

Marx and Flaubert were born, and they died, within a few years of each other; the most important of the works they published during their lifetimes appeared almost simultaneously (the first volume of *Capital* in 1867; *Sentimental Education* in 1869). Beyond such chronological parallels, the two came together in their object, as Flaubert put it, of *sinking* their civilization. They seem not to have heard of each other, or at least no trace of any mutual recognition has been found. All the better: investigation of their respective compendia of the stupidity, cupidity, and morbidity in which they felt their period was drowning them can proceed without fear that the convergences in their tactics might have had a merely anecdotic source. On the contrary, their intertextualities *signify*. And their peculiar castigating humor stands as a central sign of such signification.

The protohistory of the counter-discursive strategy Marx and Flaubert deployed has been sketched in my discussion of Daumier in the preceding chapter. Flaubert and Marx were neither the first nor the only collectors of the absurdities and idiocies whose analysis will occupy me here. Henry Monnier's Monsieur Prudhomme lives thoroughly in such discourse. It was Prudhomme who authoritatively expounded the principle of the communitarian interdependence which sustained nineteenth-century liberal civilization: "Take man from society, you isolate him."[1] In turn, beyond Prudhomme, we would find the triumphant, semilegendary figure of Calinot, whose dicta the Goncourt brothers delighted in collecting. According to them it was Calinot who first asserted of Napoléon that "if he had remained a captain of artillery and Josephine's husband, he would still be ruling France."[2] And as the preceding chapter argued, the retextualization of such absurdities forms the heart of one of the most characteristic entertainments and most celebrated subversive apparatuses in the nineteenth century: the popular lithographic caricature, and particularly its caption.

Nor were Marx and Flaubert without their contemporary rivals in the anthologization of idiocy. Baudelaire explained the joys which such masochistic researches might offer the aficionado: "The intelligent man, who will never find himself in agreement with anyone, must apply himself to delighting in conversation with imbeciles and to reading bad books. He will find bitter pleasures therein."[3] And Lautréamont populates the world of *Maldoror* with glowing icons drawn from frequentation with the sententious and the asinine: "Sauver la vie à quelqu'un, que c'est beau!" ("Saving somebody's life, what a wonderful thing"); or, "Il revenait dans ce pays fatal" ("Thus he returned to that place of doom").[4] But in Flaubert and Marx the procedure of such

1. See Prudhomme's *Mémoires,* passim, and Melcher, *Monnier,* p. 200.
2. Melcher, *Monnier,* p. 198.
3. Baudelaire, *Oeuvres complètes,* ed. Y.-G. Le Dantec and Claude Pichois (Paris: Gallimard-Pléiade, 1961), p. 1298.
4. Examples cited by Suzanne Bernard, *Poème en prose,* p. 224.

textualization of idiocy achieved an intensity and a coherence which their forerunners and competitors could hardly have imagined.

Humorists such as concern us here, of course, are not custard-pie comedians or pantaloons. Their stimulation of the laugh reflex, by means of a singular set of textual strategies, suggests no lack of gravity in their enterprise. On the contrary: theirs was a mode of jesting intent on annihilating social existence as they had come to know it. Through its operation, and in the effort to devastate, in effect they designated what we have come to know as the *realm of the ideological*. In part through the operation of the textual strategies I want to consider here, this intractable and elusive area of existence has come to be seen as subtending all modern social formations—indeed, as constituting a central dynamic within them which fosters their domination of individual lives and even of entire competing social systems which may increasingly come under their sway.

The highest form of the ideological is the assertion that its content is *nature*, that its appearance is reality. All ideological discourse strives to approach the transparency of such totalization of the real. In this regard Marx's and Flaubert's counter-ideological strategies are of extreme interest. Independently they discovered that it was possible, under certain conditions, to array fragments of contemporary discourse in such a way as to mediate their apparent *self*-destruction. What had previously been agreed to as socially effective language, carrying the unmistakable cachet of authority, upon retextualization in their texts comes to be perceived in its grotesque intellectual poverty; it then becomes licit—indeed, imperative—to withdraw our assent to its truth.

The arena for such discursive self-destruction is an intensely social world. And the process by which such annihilation is made to occur cannot be understood if it is severed from the conjuncture, the context, which frames it. This is important because Flaubert's name and particularly his signifying practices have been taken as a founding and privileged case—what Barthes baptized the "flaubertization" of writing[5]—of some imagined *transcendence* of history by an "Art" which, finding itself powerless in the face of the "bourgeois state,"[6] defensively decid-

5. *Degré zéro*, p. 58.
6. Ibid., p. 56.

ed to transport its operations "elsewhere." But there is no such place. The counter-discursive procedures under discussion here were intended—not only by Marx but, scandalously for certain contemporary formalisms, by Flaubert as well—as ideological resistance, as social subversion. Flaubert's writing may represent a practice of estheticization. But then we are constrained to reconceive the esthetic as a mode of struggle.

The practices common to Marx and Flaubert can be thought of as the realization of a dynamic implicit in all parody. Jonathan Culler puts the general situation well: "Parody must capture something of the spirit of the original . . . and produce through slight variation . . . a distance between the vraisemblance of the original and its own."[7] But it is the specific *modes* of production of such variation, of such "making strange," which are at the center of Marx's and Flaubert's procedure and which determine the means of their intense counter-discursive engagement.

In the classical formulation, the satiric text attains its effect by exaggerating traits of an individual argument or style in such a way that we experience the deformation, but as one still consistent with characteristics recognizable in the original. The apparent stability and adequacy of the source text are interrupted and upset; eccentric potentialities obscured within it become the content of its parodic retextualization. As simultaneously *adversative* (through its opposition to its original) and *citational* (through reincorporation of the original by the very fact of its parody), the satire effect might be understood as a productive yoking together of these two antithetical dynamics, one tending toward differentiation, the other toward identity. In turn, however, the textualization enacting this identity-in-difference is possible only because the parody reveals that the satiric object is itself fragmented, incomplete and dissonant. It is the purpose of satiric production to unfold such dissonance, such potentiality for internal contradiction, in its "original."

Such a dialectical notion of satire has the advantage of permitting us to integrate Marx's and Flaubert's innovations in satirical production with a fundamental preoccupation of nineteenth-century discourse, the

7. *Structuralist Poetics,* pp. 152–53.

operation of history. For it then becomes possible to situate historical change itself as one source of the variation, the difference, which constitutes the satire effect. Transformed social structures, altered class perspectives, political revolutions, all become potential conditions of possibility for the displacement that opens a text which appeared unimpeachable to our perception of its absurdity. Not the figure but its ground is altered. But with such reframing, the content of the figure itself can be conceived anew—in these cases, with results which destroy the impression of authority which it had appeared an inherent function of the text to convey.[8]

If history can produce the difference which founds the satiric text, then history should be readable within it. But as is well-known, the project of mid-nineteenth-century ideological discourse was to figure history such that its operation—which still had not been entirely obscured for middle-class consciousness—was at least enlisted in support of a specific rationality of class itself in the process of formation and stabilization. Consequently, to invoke history as the productive mediation in Marx's and Flaubert's satire of contemporary discourse amounts to saying that the arena of their satirical production is that of ideological critique. And it suggests that we need to theorize the modes by which such techniques intervened in and disrupted the transhistorical assertions of the ideological discourses which they sought to extirpate. So the counter-ideological impulse in Flaubert and Marx to situate history itself as producer of the satiric text is crucial. The strategies which independently they devised inscribe within the circuit of textual production and reception the variations mediated by time and social change by which the failures of former certainties could be displayed and their authority deflated.

The displacement by which this devaluation occurs seems at first to take the form of an astonishment: that only so little time ago such transparently deficient perspectives should have appeared unquestionable—*monnaie courante,* legal tender. The psychosocial process by which such values were devalued was an entire generation's sentimental education. It learned from its own history that the self-celebratory promises of the bourgeoisie proved fraudulent when tested against the

---

8. Along similar lines, see the argument by Daniel D. Fineman, "The Parodic and Production," pp. 69–85, esp. pp. 71–72.

realities of midcentury social life. This was thus a generation which came to Marx's and Flaubert's counter-ideological texts having already interiorized irony as the supreme rhetoric of the real.

But such a figure is the textual projection of a displacement of a rather different kind: a historical defection *within* the middle class which determined the critical perspective from which Marxian and Flaubertian humor was generated and from which it could be understood. The class as a whole was increasingly hegemonic; but a certain segment of it emigrated internally, into the stance of negation and refusal whose varieties define the social existence of intellectuals in the period. It is from this perspective that—by no more powerful demystificatory procedure than their simple reiteration—certain characteristics within contemporary utterance could be foregrounded and made to destroy the texts within which they were found: a peculiarly noisome self-satisfaction; a tolerance for logical solecism complacently sanctioning just the irrationalities and inequities profitable to the dominant class; and so on.

In a first movement, our humorists had an easy time. Instead of striving to refine their pastiches of contemporary utterance, they found that history and social existence had already composed their texts.[9] They needed only to *compile them*—what we might term the hunting-and-gathering phase of counter-ideological production. Here are some gems collected at this stage of their counter-discursive researches:

> During the English manufacturers' revolt of 1848–50, "the head of one of the oldest and most respectable [manufacturing] houses in the West of Scotland . . . " wrote a letter printed in the *Glasgow Daily Mail* of 25 April 1849 . . . : "Let us now . . . see what evils will attend the limiting to 10 hours the working of the factory. . . . They amount to the most serious damage to the mill-owner's prospects and property. If he . . . worked 12 hours before, and is limited to 10, then every 12 machines or spindles in his establishment shrink to 10, and should the works be disposed of, they will be valued only as 10, so that a sixth part

9. It is interesting that Marx's strategy of reproducing contemporary discourse was felt to be so devastating that in 1872 a campaign accused him of having falsified certain passages which he had cited. The polemic over this charge continued well after Marx's death—and well after evidence had demonstrated that his citations were perfectly accurate. See Engels's preface to the fourth edition (1890) of *Capital*, volume 1, pp. 115ff.

would thus be deducted from the value of every factory in the country."[10]

"Wherever they may be, fleas always land on light colors. This instinct has been given them in order that we may catch them more easily." (Bernardin de Saint-Pierre, *Harmonies de la nature*)[11]

It is not possible to bring out the cretinous character of [Ganilh's] standpoint except by quoting his own words: "The classes which are condemned to produce and to consume grow smaller, and the classes which direct labour and bring relief, consolidation and enlightenment to the whole population increase in size . . . and appropriate all the advantages which result from the reduction in the cost of labour, from the abundant supply of commodities and from the low prices of consumer goods. Under this leadership, the human species rises to the highest creations of genius, penetrates the mysterious depths of religion and establishes the salutary principles of morality . . . , the laws for the protection of liberty . . . , and power, of obedience and justice, of obligation and humanity."[12]

"But why, we might ask, could not a frank discussion put an end to everything the next day? Why did the King not understand the fears of the people? Why did the people not understand the difficulties facing the King? But why are men men? At this last question, we must stop, submit, resign ourselves to human nature, and continue our sad tale." (Thiers, *Histoire de la révolution française*, 1823)[13]

At this stage of directly citing the words of their contemporaries and near-contemporaries in order that they might be annulled, the very angularity of the punctuation they employed to set off the passages which they had pirated for embalming within their prose (and which can be clearly seen in reproductions of their manuscripts) seems the marker of an aggressive sectioning not only of the textual but of the social space. It is the sign of a primitive, brutal deconstruction of the consecrated forms of midcentury rationality.

My sampling here can only seek distantly to recall the frequency of such derisive quotation within Marx's and Flaubert's texts. The pro-

10. Marx, *Capital*, vol. 1, pp. 425–26.

11. Cited in Flaubert, *Bouvard et Pécuchet*, in *Oeuvres complètes*, ed. Société des Etudes Littéraires Françaises (Paris: Club de l'Honnête Homme, 1972), vol. 5, p. 422.

12. Marx, *Capital*, vol. 1, p. 575, n. 48.

13. Cited in Flaubert, *Bouvard et Pecuchet*, in *Oeuvres complètes*, vol. 6, p. 477.

cedures of this satirical mechanism are characteristic of the compilation long known as Flaubert's "sottisier."[14] But such a collection as the "sottisier" material—which had its precise parallel in Marx—represents only an initial stage in the development of a counter-ideological strategy which could engage dominant discourse by citing it, and through the process produce the atmosphere of "terror" which (as Flaubert dreamed of it) might shut off stupidity forever.[15]

Marx and Flaubert are unexpected bedfellows. They will part company in the course of their counter-discursive development—but not yet. To this point they seem to have been on exactly the same track. They framed samples of the dominant discourse like those just cited in such a way that the *cretinism* of such texts (the same word occurs to both) revealed itself as their deep-structural signified—a kind of stupidity effect to put alongside Barthes's reality effect. In doing so they seemed to have a parallel realization. It became clear that such attributed texts constituted only an infinitesimal proportion of what we might call the set of ideological discourse. In a later stage of this evolution, the relationship of the sample lifted out of the set to the set itself will pose a crucial theoretical difficulty, and in their efforts to resolve it Marx and Flaubert will adopt profoundly differing strategies. But at this point their tactics concurred: they began to generalize the attribution of the satirized text, and thereby sought to broaden the sweep of its self-annihilation.

For Marx this move represented an essential moment in conceptualizing the ideological itself. But its effects are most easily perceptible in a kind of generic slippage within the material which was to become Flaubert's *Bouvard et Pécuchet*. The requoted text whose stupidity has required only the passage of a little time to come to light (the stage of the "sottisier") gives way to the compilation and citation of an unattributed (and unattributable) discourse, of a body of anonymous utterances whose origin has disseminated through the whole social formation. Its status as always-already constituted text even more completely mystifies the process of its production.

14. The term, however, was not his; see *Bouvard*, vol. 5, p. 279.

15. See the letters to Louise Colet, 16 Dec. 1852, *Correspondance*, ed. Jean Bruneau (Paris: Gallimard-Pléiade, 1977), vol. 2, p. 208; to Turgenev, 25 July 1874, *Oeuvres complètes*, vol. 15, p. 328; and to Madame Brainne, 30 Dec. 1878, ibid., vol. 16, p. 116.

This move is prefigured in the broadcast distribution of Marx's and Flaubert's counter-ideological scorn in the "sottisier" stage, in the stage of attributed discourse. There we witnessed the wild proliferation of our humorists' opponents, until between them Marx and Flaubert had subjected *hundreds* of authors, *thousands* of individual utterances, to their mocking retextualization. Already the locus of stupidity was beginning to lose its definition. It was beginning to seem endemic.

The implication of the strategic move *beyond* simple reproduction of identified fragments, and toward textualizing a generalized social voice, then becomes clear. The text attributed to another individual can never circulate with complete freedom. This is particularly true within a social system which defines identity as a form of ownership. The attributed text is like entailed property. It remains anchored in a foreign subjectivity, an unalienable alterity, which determines that though I may receive it, it can never be *mine* because it has to be shared, say, with Ganilh or with Thiers. Thus its existence *as exchange value* can never be fully realized—nor, more to the point of any counter-ideological strategy, can it ever be fully annulled. But when such a text is severed from any sign of its ownership, when it no longer gives itself out as a text of Thiers or of Ganilh and enters the public domain, then, under its guise of universal currency, it can be conceived as *ideology* talking. And thereby it becomes available for generalized ideological critique and, potentially, for radical nullification.

Just such a conception founds Flaubert's "Dictionary of Received Ideas" along with its annexes (the "Catalogue of Stylish Ideas" [*Idées chic*]; the "Album of the Marquise"). And it is characteristic of the intention to produce this discourse as "general," as atmospheric, that Flaubert made no distinction in the manuscript he was preparing for the "second volume" of *Bouvard* between those items in the "Dictionary" which he had himself collected, and those which were compiled by his friend Laporte.[16] The lesson seems clear: *ideology talks to everyone.*[17]

In Marx, the passage between what we have called the stage of the

16. See *Bouvard*, vol. 6, p. 528.
17. See on this subject Michel Foucault's remark concerning language in the modern period: we talk only "à partir d'un langage déjà parlé" ("on the basis of an already-spoken language"; *Les mots et les choses*, p. 341).

"sottisier" and the more complex "dictionary" stage is less cleanly marked than in Flaubert. No single text in Marx's work mobilizes one of the counter-ideological protocols to the exclusion of the other. But conceptually this second movement is even more significant in Marx. In the earlier formation ideological utterance had been exemplified by an attributed text whose pompous self-certainty could be humorously punctured. But now ideology becomes conceived as systematizable, as *systemic:* derivable not from the idiosyncrasies of individual perception (or failure of perception) but rather from the need in situations characterized by social contradiction to fashion—or to fabricate—socially acceptable sense. Ideology *functions.* And in this second movement it begins to be possible to imagine a *logic* to the absurdities which occupy and seem to dominate the social space and which thereby block access to more authentic forms of understanding and of communication.

Marx and Flaubert found that the anonymous utterances produced within such a system could be retextualized no less effectively than those of individually attributed discourse. For Marx, assumption of bourgeois perspective and voice, through what might be termed a heuristically useful travesty, became a frequent counter-ideological procedure. The protocol worked just as with attributed discourse: the text generated and retextualized in this fashion destroyed itself, again seemingly from within. An interesting example occurs in a pastiche fragment from the projected fourth volume of *Capital (Theories of Surplus Value),* in which Marx adopted as momentary identity the uncritical self-confidence and infuriating sententiousness of the bourgeois political economist:

> A philosopher produces ideas, a poet poems, a clergyman sermons, a professor compendia and so on. A criminal produces crimes. If we look a little closer at the connection between this latter branch of production and society as a whole, we shall rid ourselves of many prejudices. The criminal produces not only crimes but also criminal law, and with this also the professor who gives lectures on criminal law and in addition to this the inevitable compendium in which this same professor throws his lectures onto the general market as "commodities." This brings with it the augmentation of national wealth. . . .
>
> The criminal moreover produces the whole of the police and of criminal justice, constables, judges, hangmen, juries, etc.; and all of these different lines of business, which form equally many categories of

the social division of labour, develop different capacities of the human spirit, create new needs and new ways of satisfying them. Torture alone has given rise to the most ingenious mechanical inventions. . . .

The criminal produces an impression, partly moral and partly tragic, as the case may be, and in this way renders a "service" by arousing the moral and aesthetic feelings of the public. He produces not only compendia on Criminal Law, not only penal codes and along with them legislators in this field, but also art, belles-lettres, novels and even tragedies, as not only Müllner's *Schuld* and Schiller's *Räuber* show, but also *Oedipus* and *Richard the Third*. The criminal breaks the monotony and everyday security of bourgeois life. In this way he keeps it from stagnation, and gives rise to that uneasy tension and agility without which even the spur of competition would get blunted. Thus he gives a stimulus to the productive forces.[18]

But though he does not often allow it to extend as far as in this extraordinary parody, Marx's stinging mimic impulse provides a constant comic obbligato to his dissection of the solemn theorems of bourgeois political economy: the theory of abstinence, of "The Last Hour," of the liberation of the workers by machinery, and so on.[19]

In Marx as in Flaubert the divorce of broader ideological discourse from the specific attributions of the "sottisier" stage enables such discourse to circulate more freely and thus permits a more powerful reincorporation (and potential subversion) of these voices within larger textual systems. But there is a contradiction in the act of such reframing and quotation. This is what makes the gesture of counter-discursive citation both interesting and inherently problematic. I have already commented on the adversative/citational ambiguity which underlies the parodic impulse. This ambiguity looks very much like the contradiction which constitutes counter-discourses in general, and simultaneously sets the limits of their effectivity.

The character of the ambiguity within this form of parodic quotation needs to be clearly specified. The textual process of what I have

18. *Theories of Surplus Value*, vol. 1, pp. 387–88. Lacking any overtly satirical or ironic frame in the fragmentary state of the manuscript, this passage upon occasion has been taken as straight by commentators and compilers; it is reproduced in the collection *Marx/Engels on Literature and Art*, pp. 154f., in a way which seems to attribute the absurdities of the position taken to Marx himself. Flaubert would have been enchanted by this grotesque slippage.

19. *Capital*, vol. 1, pp. 298, 338, 792.

termed the "dictionary stage" couples the predetermined *reproduction* of the automatized language of ideology—the contents which a culture demands that its members naturalize within their speech—with the simultaneous *ridicule* of such dominant discourse. To mark the coupling of this involuntary *duplication* of the other's discourse with the willful *mockery* intended in parroting it, I want to rename the procedure which Marx and Flaubert were beginning to deploy *re/citation*. The pun is only half jocular.

The discourse subject to re/citation then turns out to be *everywhere*. It is the speech of the cliché, the language of the received idea, the discourse whose domination resides in its appearance of ubiquity and inevitability. In reaction, re/citation projects transforming its banality into an *event*. The discourse of idiocy, of stupidity, of *Bêtise*, would seem to be characterized by the fact that in it what pass as "ideas" are exchanged without in any way being *changed*. What infuriates—and to some degree disorients—both Marx and Flaubert in the process is its inertness. It appears that the discourse of ideology traverses entire social networks without the slightest alteration. In effect it desubjectifies the subjects who only imagine that they are speaking it.

Thus in Bêtise, consciousness encounters that mystified domination by language, by the code, which we first observed in examining Balzac's frustrated effort to gain control of signs. And it could be argued that *Bouvard et Pécuchet* or the *Theories of Surplus Value* stand in relation to the earlier paradigm of the roman d'éducation as its radical counter-discourse—as epics of semiotic and discursive *counter*-education. Their function might seem to be to uncover the mechanism of the domination paradigm inherent in the sign by experimenting with its radical proliferation. Marx's and Flaubert's texts then demystify such domination by staging it—obsessively—as a *scandal*.

The tactic of re/citation thus attempts to introduce *difference* within an infuriatingly constant return of the same. The discourse of ideology, as Marx and Flaubert both encounter it in the social world, represents iteration without origin. It is the always-already said, the always unproblematically speakable. So the process of re/citation represents a meditation on recurrence which can only achieve its effectiveness by introducing some principle of alterity into the discursive circuit, by forcibly interrupting its apparent seamlessness.

Such naturalization of ideological discourse might at first appear to render "citation" (or "re/citation") theoretically impossible—for who could determine whether, in uttering an idiocy, one is taking distance from it or rather involuntarily adding one's own authority to its self-evidence. So inscription of some principle of differentiation is essential; only in this way can any critique be generated at all. Thus as Ranier Warning has observed, the very fact of *citing* a cliché—rather than simply uttering it mindlessly—signals that the "citing subject is an eccentric one" with respect to the cited discourse. Citation, Warning argues, "presupposes a break in identity in the history of the ironic subject, a break in identity that in turn reflects a situation of fundamental historical change."[20]

It was such an effort to establish a stance of difference with regard to the dead language of the cliché, of ideology, of dominant speech, which (around the same time as Flaubert's and Marx's preoccupation with similar discourses) had motivated Baudelaire's perverse fascination with the "poncif": "Créer un poncif, c'est le génie. Je dois créer un poncif" ("Creating a cliché is an act of genius. I need to create a cliché").[21] In thus projecting *control* over automatized language, Baudelaire fantasized an antidote to involuntary and endless reproduction of the banal. In turn, and again at the same moment, the deeply critical stance of such a relation to the cliché is summarized most clearly in a remark of Monnier's, whose Prudhomme represents one of the most influential early examples of the battle against dominant discourse in this particularly intractable form. "Prudhomme," he wrote in a letter of 1863, "was a vengeance."[22] The intensity of the emotion which motivates this ridicule of the contemporary world's banality is unmistakable in such a statement.

The tradition of such mocking mimicry, Bahktin tells us, is very old: "The most primitive mime . . . , a wandering actor of the most banal sort, always had to possess . . . two skills: the ability to imitate the voices of birds and animals, and the ability to mimic the speech, facial

---

20. "Irony and the 'Order of Discourse,'" p. 270.
21. "Fusées," *Oeuvres complètes,* p. 1260.
22. See Melcher, *Monnier,* p. 185. Something like the same perception (though in a much more complex form) might be found in a letter from Flaubert to Louise Colet (25 Feb. 1854): "Have you not sensed that all the irony with which I attack feeling in my works was just a cry of the defeated, or perhaps a song of victory?" *Correspondance,* ed. Bruneau, vol. 2, p. 526.

expressions and gesticulation of a slave, a peasant, a procurer, a scholastic pendant and a foreigner."[23] Re/citation codes its critique by embedding it in the scorn for the inferior social figures to which Bakhtin's restoration of the history of such corrosive mimesis refers. Each intervention of the re/cited humor characteristic of the "dictionary" stage thus produces a little exemplum of corrupted utterance— what we might term a fundamental syntagm of ideological analysis. For each exemplifies how *not* to write or speak; each seeks to make manifest the inferiority of those who might unthinkingly utter them. In turn such cautionary exempla of the vulgar and the grotesque can be integrated into higher structures of social representation or critique. In Flaubert particularly the divorce of the generalized discourse of stupidity (Bêtise) from the specific attributions of the "sottisier" stage allows these now-disembodied voices (including those cast in *style indirect libre*) to be re/cited within the mimetic system of a text whose constant impulse is to eradicate them.

Such a satirical projection of dominant discourse is inseparable from (and provides crucial imaginative solidity to) an effective concept of class. Once it is liberated to unfold its recombinatory potential as a free social sign,[24] the fragment of unattributed ideological discourse becomes an element in the representation of a *class-specific* subjectivity. In it we hear the class it exemplifies speaking, and the speech is a self-indictment. Such a discourse becomes the raw material for social analysis and critique; it manifests itself as a lexeme in the conflicts which stress a social totality.[25]

In Flaubert there are traces of citational tactics lying between the stage of the "sottisier" and that of the "dictionary." For a moment, as part of the joke in *Bouvard,* he conceived a plan to provide fictitious attributions of invented citational texts ("Give false bibliographical references as if they were true").[26] But such hybrid forms disappeared

23. *Dialogic Imagination,* p. 57. Fredric Jameson comments on a striking modern example of the use of such corrosive mimicry as "a conduct of *ressentiment*" which Gissing directed against the dominant class; see *Political Unconscious,* pp. 202–3.

24. See Derrida, "Signature événement contexte," p. 381.

25. Concerning the terms of this semantic analogy, intended here only in an informal sense, see Greimas, *Sémantique structurale,* pp. 50–54.

26. *Bouvard,* vol. 6, p. 607.

with the development of the more powerful strategy of the "diction-ary."

Just how powerful Flaubert may have conceived this strategy to be has become clearer with the complete publication of *Bouvard*. As the editors of the edition cited here plausibly reconstruct the material of the "second volume,"[27] it appears nearly certain that a division into successive stages of counter-ideological critique parallel to those I have already considered was to have shaped the compilation of Bouvard's and Pécuchet's own "Copie"—the collection of inanities with which Flaubert planned to end the novel. The two copyists were to have proceeded through the development of these strategies, from the chance incorporation of disparate texts ("They copy at random"; vol. 6, p. 607), through an increasing classification and hierarchization of attributed idiocies (concluding with anthologies from history, science, and literature). The process was to have culminated by transforming them into the prosecutors of a conscious ideological critique: they were to have concluded by compiling the famous "Dictionary" *them-selves*. After long hesitation Flaubert, it now appears, had determined to credit *them* with its authorship.[28]

The phylogenetic development of their "copy" from "sottisier" to "dictionary" was thus designed to mime the progressive refinement of a sophisticated counter-discursive campaign. At the end, in the pro-jected final chapter of the novel, the two copyists were to have dis-covered that the authorities—in the person of the Préfet as symbol of post-Napoleonic bourgeois "rationality"—had considered having them imprisoned for what our counterpart guardians of public order today would no doubt have termed their "socially deviant behavior." The threat of such repression rehabilitates Bouvard and Pécuchet. However hapless—and to some degree *because* they are so hapless—they begin to seem the heroes of a counter-ideological underground.

But the story as we may reconstruct it concealed a final brilliant twist. Through an ultimate re/citation it was to have sought to out-flank the consummate, *explicitly sociopolitical* idiocy of the here-and-now epitomized in the Préfet's surveillance of the copy clerks. They were to have recorded even this devastating stupidity: Flaubert's imagined

27. See ibid., vol. 5, pp. 283–86.
28. See ibid., p. 286.

them incorporating *in extenso* into their own "copy" the documents concerning their near-incarceration at the hands of the authorities (vol. 6, pp. 760–61). It was a quintessential strategem—and a desperate one. For it projected recontaining the deliberations concerning their subversion—a fantasized neutralization in language of the hegemonic power of the bourgeois state which, on another level, of course, the stratagem could neither interrupt nor deny.

Our understanding of *Bouvard* thus needs to be revised. The text projects an effort to situate within the social world represented in the text itself a standpoint from which critique of dominant ideology could be prosecuted. The realm of *positive* values—the "art" world—no longer seems completely discontinuous from the "real" world of social action and experience. Tentatively but definitely, in *Bouvard* the two realms establish relations with each other which might have seemed unimaginable in Flaubert's earlier texts.

The critical energy and the totalizing impulse of the dialectic thus force themselves into a body of work which Marxists and formalists alike have tended to conceive as aspiring to their effacement.[29] And this insertion *within* the representation of the Other of dominant ideology, however undeveloped in the state of the texts and fragments left at Flaubert's death, permits us to trace out an extension into the period after 1848 of the modes of analysis of material, social, and ideological production for which dialectical criticism has long valued the earlier realists.

Such structures, explicitly *thematizing* the generation of dialectical perspective, represent the imaginative counterparts of the effort undertaken by Marx to formulate the experience of historical change and to conceptualize as intrinsic elements of the realm in which such change occurs the determinations which drive it forward. Based upon such structures, the unexpected symmetry between Marxian and Flaubertian counter-discursive practices can be pursued one step further before they diverge.

The problem was to define a stance of *critique* which could be distinguished from that of the hegemonic discourse whose subversion

29. As a personal example of this long-received view, I might cite my own article, "Flaubert formaliste."

was sought. A perspective from which ideological utterances can be retextualized—without so thoroughly contaminating the subject who re/cites them as to appear to absorb *all* subjectivity—necessarily projects a space dissociated from the realm of ideological hegemony. Like its provisional manifestation set off by the aggressive quotation marks which Marx or Flaubert employed in the "sottisier" stage, the discourse of ideology must be systematically divided, *and be seen to be divided,* from the discourse of its contestation.

But the problem becomes particularly acute in the case of unattributed ideological discourse. For Flaubert this is the case of the "Dictionary" to begin with, and beyond it its disseminated recapitulation in the voices of virtually all his characters. For Marx it is the discourse of the bourgeoisie to whose historical role and celebratory self-justification he gave expression in the first part of the *Manifesto,* in the analyses of the *Grundrisse* and of *Capital,* in the detailed historical investigations of *Class Struggles in France* and *The 18th Brumaire.* Both Marx and Flaubert insist that such discourse was no more their own creation than were the explicitly attributed texts of the "sottisier." What is re/cited must necessarily be *someone else's* language. Flaubert put this clearly in a latter to Louise Colet (17 Dec. 1852) concerning his project for the "Dictionary." "In the entire book," he wrote, "it would be essential for there *not to be a single word of my own [pas un mot de mon cru]"*[30]

Whose words were they to be, then? That Flaubert and Marx should castigate as "bourgeois" the imputed subjects of their re/cited utterances seems at first to represent no more than a commonplace coincidence, a received idea for midcentury intellectuals. Sartre has provided an exhaustive analysis of this shared perception, the product of what he identifies as an objective neurosis of defensive reaction against middle-class domination.[31] But in the common perception, based in large part on Flaubert's exasperated broadcast usage, the recurrent imprecation "bourgeois" has been neatly depoliticized. An entire tradition of criticism since Flaubert has understood it to inscribe little more than

30. *Correspondance,* vol. 13, p. 267; my italics.
31. *Idiot,* vol. 1, pp. 612–13; vol. 2, pp. 133–443.

Flaubert's signifier for negative values. "Bourgeois" has thus been transformed into a term for blanket depreciation, with no specific historical or class referent whatever.

But this construction has the problem backward. A re/citational work like Flaubert's "Dictionary" codifies a discourse which has *already* become hegemonic, and which by the fact of its domination threatens to block the articulation of other discourses. Such a threat is anything but abstract: it is a specific conjunctural danger. In reaction, Flaubert projects a transhistorical fantasy of *negation* itself, of antiphrasis prosecuted as rarely before in literary history: "This apology for every aspect of human vulgarity [*canaillerie*], ironic and strident from start to finish, full of quotations and proofs (which would prove the contrary) and terrifying texts (this would be easy) has as its object, I would say, to put a stop once and for all to eccentricities, whatever they might be."[32]

But Bêtise is always *situated* speech. Even in denying the conjunctural, such a work of retextualization always reinscribes it.[33] So the "Dictionary" does not so much seek to prove the existence of paradigms specific to bourgeois reality-construction as it fundamentally presupposes them.

Or to put it even more strongly: an understanding of the discursive mechanisms of bourgeois class domination defines the counter-discursive strategy of Flaubert's "Dictionary," and indeed of all the re/cited ideological discourse in his novels. Without it they would not exist, for in the mid-nineteenth century it was the bourgeoisie which was engaged in constant and massive manipulation of ideology toward attainment of its hegemony. At that period no other class could possibly have structured itself in such a position.

The "Dictionary" was thus not conceived to represent or exhaustively to analyze some fully articulated and internally consistent structure of bourgeois consciousness. Sartre and following him Jonathan Culler demonstrate the ideological incoherences in Flaubert's text.[34] But they find them more puzzling than may be necessary. For the object of the "Dictionary" is to record the isolated fragments, the elements, of a class-specific ideology, of dominant discourse *in its domi-*

32. Letter to Louise Colet, 16 Dec. 1852, *Correspondance,* ed. Bruneau, vol. 2, p. 208.
33. See on this point Françoise Gaillard, "Petite histoire du bras de fer," p. 84.
34. Sartre, *Idiot,* vol. 1, pp. 633–40; Culler, *Flaubert,* pp. 158–60.

nation. In a real historical class, in a real historical conjuncture, these are never fully systematic, never completely integrated into the structures of hegemony which determine (even in their internal tension) the social formation.

At this point, then, it matters very little whether Flaubert believed himself to be combating the ageless tradition of human inanity or on the contrary was a closet Marxist. His "Dictionary of Received Ideas" functions by recording that which *has been received,* that which *is experienced* as ideological construction in its own time: a kind of pervasive Saussurian *langue* always transparent to itself, necessarily asserted as natural and as timeless, and which the act of framing and re/citing denaturalizes and seeks to situate, against such conservative assumptions, as social and as contingent.[35]

Still, as a strategy for revolutionizing the world of discourse, the Marxian/Flaubertian operation described here must be reckoned as rather naively hopeful. Living today within the unparalleled shadowing of real social relations under advanced capitalism, almost inevitably we experience these satiric texts as a kind of armchair terrorism, as would-be provocative acts doomed to absorption within the mystificatory structure which seems to define the imaginative horizon of the present. Under such conditions the counter-discursive efforts of Marx and Flaubert, as I re/cite them here myself, might well appear to have suffered the same self-demolition that they attempted to organize for the victims of their own primitive deconstructions.

The experience of historical and social movement which constituted Marx's and Flaubert's re/cited texts as satires was still—marginally, fleetingly—imaginative reality for their generation. Their counter-discursive procedure can be understood in precisely this way: re/citation figures perspectival and historical change from a point of vantage still close enough to experience of such change that the combative assertiveness, the contemptuous passion, of their polemical humor are mobilized. The objects of their critiques seem dangerously near them—one would hardly imagine them deriding Ptolemy for his errors the way they did Malthus or Cuvier. Thus, fundamentally, the crime of which they worked to convict the objects of their re/citing operation was a

---

35. The movement is analogous to the socialization of *parole;* see Saussure, *Cours de linguistique,* chap. 2.

species of false consciousness: a culpable apologetics which strove to mask the contingence—indeed, the *precariousness*—of middle-class hegemony. In Marx this was explicit:

> With the year 1830 there came the crisis which was to be decisive, once and for all. In France and England the bourgeoisie had conquered political power. From that time on, the class struggle took on more and more explicit and threatening forms, both in practice and in theory. It sounded the knell of scientific bourgeois economics. It was thenceforth no longer a question of whether this or that theorem was true, but whether it was useful to capital or harmful, expedient, or inexpedient, in accordance with police regulations or contrary to them. In place of disinterested inquirers there stepped hired prize-fighters; in place of genuine scientific research, the bad conscience and evil intent of apologetics.[36]

Flaubert's attitude was more ambiguous, for in his moments of depression and exasperation he was wont to call for plague on everybody's house. "Absurdity," he wrote, "does not shock us at all, we only want it *exposed;* and as for fighting it, why not fight its opposite, which is equally stupid."[37]

But absurdity exists in Flaubert's world, and as he organizes them to re/cite it, the practices of his novels make it clear he did not believe it was innocent. If he refused to conclude what is right, his counter-ideological strategies demonstrate that his instinct for what was wrong—and *guiltily* wrong—was unerring. The theme of prostitution which haunted him as the constitutive degradation of his period can be understood in no other way.

So "false consciousness" as Marxists have understood it names the object of the parallel critiques I have been investigating here. Such a situation is implicit in the conjuncture in which these strategies developed. For surely *false consciousness must itself be understood as a historical category*. It represents an early form of ideological mystification, one still susceptible to the tactics of humor mobilized by Marx and Flaubert. Their demystificatory operation amounts to a kind of surveyor's triangulation of the ideological through change in perspective, demonstrating the inauthenticity of would-be transparent discourse.

---

36. "Postface to the Second Edition" (1873), *Capital*, vol. 1, p. 97.
37. Letter to Louise Colet, 31 March 1853, *Correspondance*, ed. Bruneau, vol. 2, p. 295.

In our own period, on the other hand, for good historical reasons, it is far from clear that the members of the dominating class, or of the derivative segments within it which administer managerial capitalism or even produce cultural theory, bear the inauthenticity of their situation as some repressed and threatening element on the guilty edge of consciousness. Through the penetration and stabilization of bourgeois structures since the mid-nineteenth century, in contemporary life the concept of false consciousness has come to seem empty. And contestation now must operate on different territory, with different strategy, if it operates at all.

Yet even in Flaubert's and Marx's own period there was something brittle in the laughter evoked by re/citation. Following Sartre, we might understand such laughter as projecting our dissociation from a threat or danger.[38] In any case some sort of defensive mechanism is operating here: a peculiar flinching from the proffered representation at the very moment it is tendered haunts this strategy. In Flaubert particularly it is clear that the terror and demoralization he longed to induce in others by his counter-ideological practice introjects back and transforms itself into a generalized pessimism.

No counter-discursive strategy ever carries guarantees. Notwithstanding the efforts which our humorists put into this one, the bourgeoisie carried on. Our determination of the range of effectiveness of re/citation, and of its limitations, thus needs to take explicit account of our impression here of a capitulation *in advance*. This secret defeatism seems determined by the same conditions which motivated the textual practices Sartre termed "black literature" (*littérature noire*).[39] Such production seems already to inscribe, in the earliest phases of capitalism's consolidation, the neutralizing power which is the most damnable capacity of a liberal ideological system.

This capacity to neutralize counter-discourses is the frustrating element which contrives to assure that even as each of the utterances composing dominant discourse is undermined by re/citation, paradoxically the space for an alternative discourse shrinks in the same proportion, until finally it almost seems that the greater the success of the counter-ideological campaign, the more it is thrown on the defensive.

38. *Idiot*, vol. 1, pp. 681–82.
39. Ibid., vol. 3, p. 83.

Whence a persistent strain of submission in advance to the limitations which impose themselves upon any counter-ideological strategy—both in Flaubert: "If ever I take an active part in the world, it will be as . . . *demoralizer*"; and in the Marxist tradition: "The socialist problem novel . . . carries out its mission if . . . it shakes the optimism of the bourgeois world, and . . . instills doubt."[40] Concerning operations like the re/citational tactic considered here, we thus need to determine how such limitations were folded back into the system of a discourse which, *not yet* resigned to the impossibility of adequating itself to the dominant reality of the nineteenth century, continued to seek means for understanding its incoherences and undoing its contradictions.

The material which was to have become the second volume of *Bouvard et Pécuchet* repudiates the traditional distinction between our two authors' attitudes toward the social world—between a supposed Flaubertian "pessimism" and a Marxian "revolutionary enthusiasm." This is most deeply true because strategies for representing the real are never seamless mind-sets, rigid *prises de position*. They represent evolving phases of a search for adequate comprehension and expression. In the theoretically endless variety of strategies which might be mobilized, no absolute necessity arrests development at any predetermined point. Flaubert and Marx join in seeking to establish for their discourse a position of alterity, a stance of positivity, from which the ideologized structure of the real might be situated and denaturalized. And if at this point their improbable yoking finally fragments, their divergence can best be understood in terms of the articulations available within the discourse of each to deal with the limitations inherent in their common re/citational strategy.

In Flaubert's practice, re/citation posits a fragment of discourse as alien, hence as laughable for the subject who attempts to confirm his or her own self-identity in the reflection of its alterity. But then Flaubert is constrained to watch this otherness bleed back, until it becomes impossible to define the position from which the alternative voice had

---

40. Flaubert to Ernest Chevalier, 24 Feb. 1839, *Correspondance*, ed. Bruneau, vol. 1, p. 37, my italics; Engels to Minna Kautsky, 26 Nov. 1885, *Marx/Engels on Literature and Art*, p. 88.

been designated.[41] The locus from which the distance of alien discourse was to have been measured then itself dissolves. Any negativity evokes a positivity which constitutes the dialectical complement of its deconstructive activity. *But this positivity is largely unarticulated in Flaubert:* his dystopia seems to project no compensatory utopia, at least in social life. His work might be seen as the totality of a series of denials; but the totality remains imprisoned in a space continuous with that which it opposes. Its own self-infection continually haunts it.

Even so, it might prove instructive to fantasize with Flaubert the consummation of re/citational strategy: the final elimination of the incoherence, the social fraudulence, the intellectual depravity sustaining the structure of dominant discourse in his period. What discourse then would become speakable? Let us place the most generous construction upon the traces of Flaubert's intention in *Bouvard et Pécuchet* to adumbrate even such an underdeveloped voice of reason as that of his two copy clerks. In such a vision they become, like their creator, the therapeutic encyclopedists of their civilization's inanities, the lexicographers of a debased social language which, as Sartre put it, Flaubert intended not simply to record but to annihilate.[42] But even so, with the imagined completion of the re/citational "monument" of which Bouvard and Pécuchet become so proud,[43] we face nothing less than the exhaustion of imaginable discourse. Even if the whole of the bourgeois world could be re/cited, the result would only be an epochal emptiness. And this fantasized self-silencing would then take its place in the typology of a certain set of nineteenth-century counter-ideological strategies which (adapting Peter Verkhovensky's description of Stavrogin in *The Possessed* [part 1, chap. 5]) we might characterize not quite yet as nihilist but as cosmically *sarcastic (nasmešlivyj).*

But *The Possessed* surely demonstrates that such "sarcasm"—the hori-

---

41. The experience, pushed to its extreme, becomes that of the critic's horrifying *possession* by the supposed object of criticism; of being spoken by its language. His discourse *becomes* the clichés he seeks to deride or to expunge. In Chapter 6 below I will argue that this experience is at the center of Mallarmé's "Démon de l'analogie" and that its horror arises in the nineteenth-century perception that the instrument of labor increasingly threatened to dominate the work process, to automatize the worker.

42. *Idiot*, vol. 1, p. 965; vol. 2, p. 1618.

43. *Bouvard*, vol. 5, p. 286; vol. 6, p. 752.

zon toward which Flaubert's counter-discursive tactics point—is not a stable strategy. We must seek the traces of its inevitable slippage, and the outlines of its possible inflections toward new means of conceiving the relationship between the critical text and the social world. Compared with Marx there is no doubt that Flaubert's procedure, adhering to the comedian's rule of never explaining the joke, exhibits a more rakish style. Marx comments laboriously on the processes of textual self-annihilation which he is at pains to exhibit (as comic examples, consider his footnote exploding J. B. Say's conflation of production and exchange,[44] or his refutation of Senior's concept of productive labor).[45] At such moments Marx appears more doggedly professorial. But, ranging from the most delicate deflation of the absurdities hiding within a text[46] to the display of others whose crushing inanity seems only to require our laughter for them to be erased forever,[47] his practice points to an opening toward further discursive production, *beyond* the self-dispossession of "sarcasm," which remains undeveloped in Flaubert.

Marx's response to such blockage of the discourse hardly requires rehearsing here. Rather than pursuing a Flaubertian *exhaustion* of the endless chain of ideological utterance, he posited its *subsumption*. Within the structure of the here-and-now it appeared impossible to eradicate the degraded discourse which sustained contemporary hegemony. Marx imagined overturning the structure itself.

Such projection of an alternative created theoretical space for a metadiscourse which it became the task of historical materialism to generate. The dominant discourse which had been the object of re/citational strategy was thus not to be erased at all. Rather it would be reinscribed as the *dominated*, as the overdetermined predicate of another discourse to which access could now be opened: the discourse of

44. *Capital*, vol. 1, p. 755, n. 48.

45. *Theories of Surplus Value*, vol. 1, pp. 287–88.

46. Consider the devastating Gallic interjection by which he punctuates Storch's celebration of the working class: "'The progress of social wealth,' says Storch, 'begets this useful class of society . . . which performs the most wearisome, the vilest, the most disgusting functions, which, in a word, takes on its shoulders all that is disagreeable and servile in life, and procures thus for other classes leisure, serenity of mind and conventional' (*c'est bon, ça*) 'dignity of character'" (*Capital*, vol. 1, p. 801).

47. "It is impossible to pursue this nonsense any further. We, therefore, drop Mr. Bastiat" (*Grundrisse*, p. 893).

social history which, though it had subtended the counter-ideological practices we have examined, nonetheless had remained in unarticulated principle of their existence. History's demystificatory capability here transforms itself into the principle founding a discourse for comprehending the social *rationality,* the class-specific *utility,* of the illusions which the re/citational strategy had sought with such constantly frustrated vengeance to extirpate.

The resources of such a discourse Flaubert never utilized. But the closure of his response to dominant discourse should not be seen as absolutely disconnected from other contemporary counter-discursive practices. It is not simply the contrary of Marx's. Rather it identifies an unexploited opening, a lacuna in his development of the strategies for opposing the contradictions of mid-nineteenth-century reality of which re/citation represents a stage he shared with Marx. The rupture implicit in this arrested movement, the determined absence which has opened Flaubertian discourse to its appropriation by contemporary neo-Heideggerian critiques of representation, is an enigma which Sartre seeks to penetrate in *L'idiot de la famille,* and it situates the limiting question of any psychosocial investigation: why was a certain thing *not* done, a certain discourse *not* generated? We cannot comprehend Flaubert unless we penetrate the interrupted striving in his work toward constitution of the particular protodialectical discourse whose *absence* concerns me here.

Two incipient tactics for generating such a discourse are discernible in Flaubert. The first, so well known as to require only to be named, is the canonization of the Beautiful, which Sartre exhaustively explicates in the third volume of *L'idiot de la famille.* It represents the negation of dominant contemporary values, but it is more than this. We need to conceive it as a projective alternative to the hegemonic, as the utopia which both stigmatizes and responds to dystopia. Such an alternative might be counterposed against, undermine, and replace the rapaciousness and the vulgarity of midcentury socioeconomic existence.

The other tactic has been less attended to.[48] This is the constant presence within Flaubert's writing (but, like the theory of the Beautiful, confined largely within the "private sphere" of his correspondence) of an alternative discourse of *indecency,* of Bakhtin's "carnival-

---

48. Bakhtin had hinted at its importance for Flaubert in *Rabelais,* p. 422n.

esque," which represents a simplified but gratifying return of the repressed, an assertion of those potentialities in human existence which submission to the dominant discourse within capitalism (as Flaubert had good reason to know from his trial)[49] seemed to require one to sacrifice.

These two counter-discourses suggest those which, under the names of "art" and "folk tradition," Marcuse situated as the principal categories within which the counter-ideological dynamic in the cultural sphere attempts to formulate its expression and solidify its critique.[50] But neither of these projections produces any extensive body of discourse within Flaubert's "public" writing. This rather remains preoccupied with the generalization and exhaustion of the ideological critique of which the re/citational strategy provides the fundamental form. The dual subversive textual practices for which Flaubert prepared the conceptual space were exploited not by him but by Mallarmé and the symbolist tradition on the one hand (as I will argue in more detail in Chapter 7) and by a rich pornographic tradition from Sade to Bataille on the other. In the meantime, Flaubert continually and insistently returned to the tactic of kidnaping from their context, and holding captive within his own text, snatches of a hegemonic discourse whose overall *systemic* power he could never effectively counter.

Such a gesture, whose repetitive character marks it as intrinsically incompleted, stands as the trace of an arrested dialectical formulation. Just over the horizon of Flaubert's practice it implies its own completion in a more powerful and more radical response to the ideology against which it sought to serve as counter-discursive strategy. This perception is what authorizes our own rereading, our own re/citing, of Flaubert's text to detect not its self-annihilation but on the contrary its phantom *development* of that palimpsest textualization of the social about which Claude Duchet has written.[51] This unrealized text is an insistent dynamic within Flaubert's writing. In what we might term the mode of virtuality, it records the history of his attempts at discursive intervention. And thereby it inscribes a repressed relation to the

49. See LaCapra, *"Madame Bovary" on Trial.*
50. See *Counter-Revolution and Revolt*, pp. 79–80.
51. "Signifiance et in-signifiance," p. 362.

conjuncture to which the explicitly dialectical strategies which might have been unfolded out of them, but never were, could have given more adequate access. It suggests how we might undo his erasure of the social determinants by which his writing came to celebrate its own freedom from determination by the social.

Flaubert ignored such determination; Marx conceived it as the key to understanding the real. But we need to acknowledge that even the fully developed discursive strategy which Marx devised quickly encounters its own limits. No discourse—as Marx himself was at pains to insist—can totalize history, if only because the sociohistorical dialectic to which discursive strategies are responsive is not played out within the closure of language, within the world of words, alone. For the material world, which we have seen to be the referent—indeed, the obsession—of the counter-discursive practices which Flaubert shares with Marx, retains its relative autonomy and, with it, its capacity to pressure the collapse of the symbolic structures both of dominant discourse and of the counter-discourses which seek to contest it.

Still, short of such collapse these antagonistic discourses demonstrate an awesome staying power, and with the immense weight they acquire over time can appear to us as locked in a ritual struggle, an endless and eventually objectless controversy, in which the old contents have been bleached out and only the forms remain. It has sometimes been difficult for our contemporary critical and analytic discourse not to be absorbed into the enclosure of this seemingly termless disputation. Such absorption always threatens. In a series of monographs, dictionaries, treatises, and compendia, as if they were *miming each other,* Marx and Flaubert both sought to turn bourgeois techniques of rationalization against the bourgeoisie itself. But for them the most obvious form of danger was that of being drowned by their own collections, which neither was able to complete nor to circumscribe.

These monuments both writers left behind unfinished at their deaths. And one can imagine them—the one with the immense dossiers of *Theories of Surplus Value,* the other with the overflowing folders of the "copy" destined for *Bouvard*—losing their way in the registers of their civilization's intellectual underdevelopment and its venality, accumulating still further specimens of that dominant discourse which haunted them, by a kind of atavism returning again and again to that project of endlessly re/citing ideology which beckons in perhaps the most poignant sentence Flaubert ever wrote: *copier comme autrefois* ("copy like we used to do").[52]

The collections accumulated by our humorists are the most terrifying we possess of the dominant discourse which threatens to envelop us. Yet simultaneously they record a succession of strategies for its annihilation—even, at least incipiently, for its replacement with less degraded paradigms for understanding and for transforming our reality. In seeking to disentangle and to develop the strategies by which this early counter-discursive battle was fought out, our own discourse mobilizes as well against its absorption in the denser ideological nexus of contemporary capitalism. For certain recent theoretical work, the apparently seamless circuit of symbolic exchange in which we appear immersed has mediated conceptualizing out of existence altogether the social referent against which Marx and Flaubert had still been able to exert their humor. It is harder to be humorous today. But the counter-discursive, the authentically *critical*, remains as it was under an earlier capitalism a necessary field for discourse in any larger struggle to sink the civilization of Bêtise and revolutionize the real.

52. *Bouvard*, vol. 5, p. 275.

CHAPTER 5

Ideological Voyages: On a Flaubertian Dis-Orient-ation

Amer savoir, celui qu'on tire du voyage. [It's a bitter
knowledge that one gains from traveling.]
                              —BAUDELAIRE, "Le voyage"

If the dominant discourse was the speech and writing of a France
resolutely middle class, self-absorbed, and certain of its self-sufficiency,
then in our period one of the most prominent and most influential of
the counter-discourses mobilized to subvert it was what we might term
the discourse of *everywhere else:* texts about the imagined or actual trips
which would *remove* one from the place where the dominant so
effortlessly exercised its domination. Beyond the horizon of the
hegemonic, other horizons were thus projected with a fervor which
can hardly have been exceeded in the most intently devout epochs of
medieval religiosity: "N'importe où! n'importe où! pourvu que ce soit
hors de ce monde!"—"Anywhere," as Baudelaire put it in his memora-
ble prose poem, "out of *this* world."

I want to examine one of the most sustained of the texts reflecting
upon—indeed, attempting passionately to grasp—another world:
Flaubert's *Voyage en Orient,* in which Flaubert recounts his 1849–51 trip
to the Middle East, through Egypt, Syria, Lebanon, Turkey, Greece,
Italy, and back again to France. The stakes in an ideological analysis of
these pages on the trip would seem uncommonly high. For even
among the profusion of nineteenth-century voyages (and fantasies

227

thereof), these texts project a *particular* psychological and ideological intensity.[1]

For Flaubert, as for most of the nineteenth century's literary travelers, the trip and the texts narrating it were undertaken to answer a peremptory need. But such needs were more than personal. They defined themselves against a background of ideological and cultural structures around midcentury which transcend the peculiarities and susceptibilities of any of these writers as individuals. Through the mediation of a political, scholarly, and social institution—Orientalism—which played an important role in constituting the mentality of the period in Europe, these structures seem to have determined the literary project to depart France for the East, and thereby at the same time the conditions of its internal contradiction.

The biographical reasons behind Flaubert's own decision to take his trip are well known, and seem at the outset to pose no problem. Flaubert expressed them in a letter (6 May 1849) to his friend Ernest Chevalier:

> I have some news to tell you, dear Ernest. Next October, or at the end of September, I'm taking off for Egypt. I'm going to take a trip throughout the Orient. I will be gone around fifteen or eighteen months. I can imagine you goggle-eyed, wondering how I managed to arrange to go. Be informed that it appears your friend is ravaged by a pox whose origins are lost in the depths of time. It's no good treating the symptoms which may go away, it comes back somewhere else. The nervous problem which I still suffer from sometimes, and which can't be cured in the milieu I'm living in, may have no other cause than this. Anyway, everything I'm surrounded by exasperates me so much, I feel so worn out, so gloomy, so sad, that I pretty much felt myself going the way of Hamard [his brother-in-law, who had recently gone mad]. Dr. Cloquet and Achille [Flaubert's brother, who was a physician] have recommended a warm climate. He even claimed it was urgent. I believe him much more on the moral than on the physical level, because I have to get some air.

1. The texts relating to Flaubert's Orient trip can be found in volumes 10 to 13 of *Oeuvres complètes*, 16 vols., ed. Société des Etudes Littéraires françaises (Paris: Club de L'Honnête Homme, 1972). The completeness of this edition makes it convenient for quotation here.

I have to get some air, in the broadest sense of the term. My mother, seeing that it was necessary, has agreed to the trip, and there you are. [Vol. 12, p. 630]

What is striking in this text is the curious slippage in designating the illness which Orient will be called upon to cure: a mobility between the "physical" and "moral" realms which, beyond the microbe which torments him, seems to textualize the psychological and ideological overdetermination of his trip. Such a slippage opens an interpretive space—like the one opened by Sartre in his analysis of Flaubert's nervous crisis of January 1844, which had likewise strategically permitted Flaubert to evade the desires of his parents—which may help us penetrate the relation between Flaubert's individual depression in 1849 and more broadly social, more material, and more persistent structures of desire, of need, and of representation.

On the personal level, to be sure, Flaubert's melancholy resulted from rather clear determinants: the death of his friend Alfred Le Poittevin in April 1848, the mental illness of Hamard in June, and underlying everything, the constant difficulties he was experiencing with the writing of the first *Tentation de Saint-Antoine*. Benjamin Bart is clear on the point: he writes that after 1847 Flaubert's relations with his family and his surroundings began to seem to him virtually impossible.[2]

In Flaubert, these sorts of difficulties unleashed a persistent escapist dynamic: an intense desire to transcend the resistances and the conflicts of his life, to substitute for them other scenes, other occupations, and finally, *other texts*.[3] The geography of these visionary alternatives—a choice of other words clearly deriving from romantic formations—is

2. See Bart, *Flaubert*, p. 168, and the letter to Chevalier (3 Oct. 1848; *Oeuvres complètes*, vol. 12, p. 628). Flaubert goes so far as to say that, having been drafted, he hopes to go to war, "since I have got to get out of here, say goodbye to my charming entourage, get some air." This last expression reappears and repeats itself in the letter to Chevalier already quoted, written seven months later.

3. For the period of Flaubert's youth, Jean Bruneau has retraced this tendency, and Bruneau quotes more than two dozen passages drawn from texts preceding the Orient trip in which Flaubert evokes, in an evident compensatory enthusiasm, the imagined "elsewhere" which figured the negation of his immediate reality and something like a series of antidotes for what he found unlivable there. See Bruneau, *Le "Conte oriental,"* pp. 38ff.

familiar. The Orient (what we would call the Middle East) was central to this iconography of escapism and to the voyages it determined. Thus Bruneau quotes a passage on the "fantastic" by Nodier dating from 1830 in order to compare it with characteristic texts of Flaubert: "The penchant for the marvelous is the essential instrument of our imaginative life, and may even be the sole compensation for the miseries which are inseparable from social existence."[4] The first *Education sentimentale* invokes the same strategy of escape: "Jules's desire soon having acquired ideal proportions, modern life began to seem too restricted to him, and he returned to Antiquity to find subjects for pleasure and objects of desire."[5] The resonances of another 1845 text bring it even closer to our problematic here; the text comes, however, not from Flaubert himself, but from a letter written to him by his friend Le Poittevin: "I think of nothing but getting away somewhere, to Egypt or Greece, to console myself with what used to be for what is now."[6]

By this point in European history, the Middle East had of course been rather thoroughly studied: it was concretely known despite its place at the heart of the romantic and postromantic "elsewhere." Yet within critical consciousness this geographical reality has remained abstract, as if it were nothing but the product of an antinomic formation—one wanted to get *away;* the Orient *was* away. In this guise, as nothing more than the negative reflection of a detestable reality, these territories of the romantic voyage give rise to no imaginative density, to no critical specificity. They seem almost to have been chosen at random, and to that extent they appear to raise no problems. Conceived as the space of compensation, they appear as sterile utopias of a pure imaginative reaction.[7] Understood in this way, these distant "elsewheres" are simply silenced.

But the preferred territories of writers in the romantic and postromantic periods—Flaubert's Orient particularly—carry a much less

4. Ibid., p. 56.

5. *Oeuvres complètes*, vol. 8, p. 139.

6. Quoted by René Descharmes, *Alfred Le Poittevin: une promenade de Bélial, et oeuvres inédites* (Paris: Presses françaises, 1924), p. xxxvi.

7. Such a *negative* ideology concerning the voyage is expressed in the well-known lines of Baudelaire which conclude *Les fleurs du mal:* "Mais les vrais voyageurs sont ceux-là seuls qui partent/Pour partir" ("But the only true travelers are those who depart simply for the sake of traveling").

rarefied content than such a conception would imply. Their reality resists reduction; their symbolic constitution and their textual representation inscribe determinants much more concrete and conjunctural than those projected by such an idealizing reading—itself profoundly romantic in its tendency—of the distant geographic referent. And by that fact, however unwillingly, these texts speak a historical context whose constituents have been forgotten, or disguised, or denied in familiar criticism of romanticism and of its ideological descendents. Such criticism renders inaccessible to interpretation the sociohistorical reality of Western contact with the Oriental referent, and the ideological and material modalities of such contact.

Edward Said's *Orientalism* suggests the necessity of restoring the specific context and content of that therapeutic, touristic, and artistic operation which Flaubert's trip to the Orient represented. Said's study incites us to define, within the network of their ideological and material determinants, the specific contradictions which Flaubert's trip sought—however unsuccessfully—to resolve. For Said, the European formation of an Orientalist "idea" and "institution" in the nineteenth century depended first of all upon the existence of a power relationship linking West and East in a manner profoundly less innocent than certain literary texts of the period (notably the earlier "voyages" of Chateaubriand, Lamartine, and Nerval) might have suggested.

There is of course some truth to the notion that these trips were taken in the spirit of a pure denial of Europe. Said acknowledges the fact that these literary pilgrims were seeking "an exotic yet especially attractive reality," a "locale sympathetic to their private myths, obsessions and requirements"; in sum, a "salutary *dérangement* of European habits of mind and spirit."[8] But at the same time *Orientalism* suggests how these dreams of escape and of renewal presuppose the quite concrete political domination of the territory ideologically invested as the "elsewhere" of romantic imagination. These dreams, and these texts, silently inscribe that domination in a manner which stresses them from within, and threatens to empty them completely.

The Western need for an "elsewhere" registered in the profusion of texts from Flaubert's period to which I have already referred becomes

8. *Orientalism,* pp. 170, 150.

translated in Flaubert himself as the coming to consciousness of a blockage of his textual production. It was convenient for him to impute the responsibility for it to that pervasive and crushing banality of his own society which was soon to become a central theme in his writing. It was as if the referent of writing had simply become emptied out, as if there was nothing—*and therefore nothing to write about*—in France.

We need only examine the text of the *Voyage en Orient* itself. At its opening it seems intent on justifying Flaubert's departure by minute attention to the profound vacuity of the country he was leaving behind: "From Paris to Nogent, nothing; a gentleman in white gloves seated opposite me in the railway car"; "From Paris to Marseille, nothing worth speaking about."[9] Such insistent triviality formed the dominant discourse in which Flaubert felt he was drowning, textualized the *ennui* which constantly threatened to overcome him. He meditated obsessively upon it in numerous texts from this period. And this same dominant discourse, in this particularly insistent form, would seem to have been the most important determinant of an earlier tactic of escape, of an alternative counter-discourse—imaginary and literary rather than concretely touristic—which directly preceded his real voyage, and for which the first *Tentation de Saint-Antoine* is the immediate textual evidence. Antoine's anguished exclamation is characteristic: "What sadness! what misery! will I never be able to free myself from this colossal *ennui* which is crushing me?"[10]

The similarity between this mood and Flaubert's own as he left France for the East is striking. The trip to the Orient was decided before Flaubert received Bouilhet's and Du Camp's depressing judgment concerning *Saint-Antoine*. But in a sense it anticipated their opinion. The implicit project was clear: the voyage to the East was to have functioned as a counter-experience, the texts relating to it were to have mobilized a counter-discourse, from which the *ennui* and the banality characteristic of Flaubert's life and his consciousness for a long time would have been banished.[11] The trip was supposed to expunge the

---

9. *Oeuvres complètes,* vol. 10, pp. 434, 442.
10. Ibid., vol. 9, p. 229.
11. See, after his return from the trip, his letter to Louise Colet (early Nov. 1851): "At school we were a group of young rascals [*jeunes drôles*] who were living in a strange world. We oscillated between madness and suicide. Some of us killed themselves, a

dominant discourse which was drowning him. In the presence of a
new referent (and we need to emphasize that of all of Flaubert's texts
the *Voyage en Orient* is the most intensely referential), in this Orient
geographically and culturally situated as *other*, Flaubert's textual practice was to have restored and liberated itself:

> When we were two hours from the coast of Egypt, I went forward
> with the chief helmsman and I saw Abbas-pacha's seraglio looking like
> a black dome above the blue of the sea. The sun was beating down on
> it. I perceived the Orient through it, or rather, in a bright melted silver
> light on the sea. . . . I was gorging myself with colors [*je me foutais une
> ventrée de couleurs*] like a mule gorges itself with oats.[12]

The metaphor of absorption is characteristic, and it helps to diagnose
Flaubert's project at this early stage. He seems to have intended his
passionate digestion of the exotic referent to alter what we might term
the metabolism of his writing. Indeed the *Voyage* was initially to have
been written as a journal—"paragraph by paragraph, in the form of
little chapters as I went along [*au fur et à mesure*]" (vol. 10, p. 437). The
effect of such a project was to key his text intimately to the referent
itself, maximizing its chance of receiving a full and unadulterated dose
of this medicine which the Orient represented in Flaubert's mind, of
capturing *immediately* the counter-discourse of the East which was to
revivify his own Occidental discourse.

This search for counter-discourses responsive to an exotic or exceptional referent is constant in Flaubert. It is the source of a dialectical
dynamic within his writing whose existence some critics (Lukács first
among them) have called into question, but which produces his texts
(and produces itself within them) as the constant, repeated, and multiform exercise of an opposition to dominant discourse. In this perspective, certain aspects of the 1849 *Saint-Antoine* begin to appear like

---

number did themselves in with debauchery to drive away the boredom. I could write a
whole book on that unknown generation who grew up like mushrooms swollen with
boredom" (ibid., vol. 13, p. 149). See also Sartre's discussion, *Idiot,* vol. 2, pp. 1107ff.
The association between *boredom* and death is constant: it is immediately after having
spoken the words about *ennui* quoted just above that Antoine is tempted by Death,
who promises him the end of the discourse which is exhausting him: "you will not
think about anything, you will not feel anything" (*Oeuvres complètes,* vol. 9, p. 232).

   12. Letter to his mother, 17 Nov. 1849, *Oeuvres complètes,* vol. 12, p. 645.

elements of the same formation upon which Flaubert was to draw just a few years later in his Orient texts. In *Saint-Antoine* the parade of the heresiarchs—founders of a series of counter-discourses privileged by the fact of their status as utterances effectively *threatening* to the established order—seems comprehensible as an effort to generate a principle of difference. Only such a heterological principle, it seemed, might withstand the absorption of *all* discourse by the dominant. In the *Voyage en Orient*, on the other hand, this exorcism of the dominant discourse was to have occurred more directly, through its displacement by the continuously renewed "ventrée de couleurs" with which Flaubert sought therapeutically to fill himself in Egypt.

But the tactic to produce these texts as *other* failed. Looking closely at the *Voyage en Orient* or in Flaubert's parallel correspondence from the period of the trip, we would have difficulty distinguishing any trace of a renewal of his writing, of a supposed "Oriental renaissance" (the notion of such a rejuvenation of the West from the East had become a commonplace of the postromantic period).[13] In fact, aside from a few sparse indications of a search for new forms and modes of textualization, Flaubert's Oriental texts read like . . . *Flaubert*. And that fact defines their problem. Despite the plenitude which stems from a constant reference to places, monuments, terms, and mores which were exotic for him, these texts really represent an *absence of rupture* from the protocols of dominant discourse. On the contrary: these protocols are unexpectedly inscribed at the center of a mode of writing whose mission was precisely to exclude them. The result is a profound sense of disappointment which floats over these pages on the Orient every time Flaubert comes to reflect upon his own writing activity and on the texture of his texts. My object will be to detect in Flaubert's writing concerning the trip the structures by which the discourse which he would so fervently have wanted to expunge from his own nonetheless persisted within it.

In the perspective defined by Said's study, the Orient of Western travelers needs to be understood less as a geographic region of the globe than as a topos in Occidental discourse, a discursive region

---

13. The term "Oriental renaissance" is Edgar Quinet's, and dates from 1842. See Bruneau's discussion, *Le "Conte oriental,"* pp. 23, 32–33.

whose consistency and content were propagated by the Orientalist institution.[14] Orientalism thus exhibits all the attributes of an ideological apparatus, including the will to totalization and transparency, the ability to naturalize its own content, which in the operation of such an apparatus represent the most tenacious and the most infernal elements.

Of course Flaubert's text is hardly reducible to a simple reproduction of the structures of Orientalist discourse. Flaubert transforms and re-works them—but he cannot obliterate them. They inform important aspects of the *Voyage en Orient* in a manner which Flaubert cannot master despite the intense desire on his part to liberate himself from the constraints of a preformed ideology. We feel this, for example, in the anti-ideological exasperation of the following passage from the *Voyage,* which still registers the full power of the ideological structures which it would have wished to eliminate: "Oh necessity! Always to be obliged to do the right thing; always to have to act, depending on the situation—and despite the fact that your disgust in the moment [*la répugnance du moment*] moves you to desire something entirely different—the way a good young man, the way a good traveler, the way a good son, the way a good citizen is supposed to act!" (vol. 10, p. 504). Such necessities always bear upon conduct and consciousness—overtly at times, but sometimes (as here) much more subtly and elusively. For the practical force of Orientalist discourse is not confined to a certain vulgar and guilty colonialist mentality: it is inscribed in an objective sociopolitical situation in which Flaubert participates despite his manifest desire to escape from it, and which really constitutes the irreducible condition of possibility of his own text.

My analysis of this Orientalist apparatus is based on three linked notions concerning the structure of this ideological system which can help to identify the determinants of the textual dead end at which Flaubert discovered himself in the Orient.

1. Since Orientalism is a *European* representational apparatus, necessarily it figures its referent by means of just the degraded conceptual system from which Flaubert was trying to escape.

2. This ideological system, imposed upon the Oriental referent, and

14. See Said, *Orientalism,* pp. 42 and 177. On Flaubert's extensive education in "Orientalism," see Bruneau, *Le "Conte oriental,"* p. 37.

authorized by the dominant culture to represent it adequately, leaves little room for an intrinsic discourse of the Orient itself, which thus remains not simply heterogeneous, but *inaccessible.*

3. These relations in their turn are framed and determined by another discourse subtending any possible representation of the Orient: that of European hegemony. For Western travelers in the Middle East, this framing discourse imposes its privileges in the form of a fundamental social and cultural barrier which impedes the articulation of any exterior discourse, any authentically heterogeneous system of representation.

These were the structures which seem to have determined both the project Flaubert set himself in leaving France and the impossibility of its practical realization. Both his departure *and* his failure thus begin to appear prescribed within the larger system which conditioned imagination and conduct in his period. We need to see in just what ways, and within what limits, we can legitimately designate as truly "foreign," as truly heterogeneous, the geographical and cultural referent which, in so many dreams and desires, Westerners had constructed.

Chateaubriand, Lamartine, Nerval, Flaubert: such is the lineage of important French writers who traveled to the Orient, and transformed their voyages into texts. It is hardly surprising that representations possessing the power of theirs influenced those who followed them to the East. As an apparatus determining the relation with these foreign territories, Orientalism propagated through these works to the point of becoming one of the immanent formations of nineteenth-century cultural consciousness. Victor Hugo put it clearly: "During the age of Louis XIV they were Hellenists; today we are Orientalists."[15]

Of course there is an inherent paradox implicit in this *institutionalization* of Orientalism. Through it this region, which for these writers had value because it could be imagined as unknown, was impregnated by a textual network so dense that it threatened to exhaust its own referent completely. Thus the land which Nerval had characterized as the very "place of dreams and illusions"[16] would rather

15. *Oeuvres politiques,* ed. Pierre Albouy (Paris: Gallimard, 1964), vol. 1, p. 580.
16. Quoted by Said, *Orientalism,* p. 182. Cf. Lamartine: "I dreamed constantly of a trip to the Orient, as a major act of my inner life" (quoted by Said, *Orientalism,* p. 177).

appear uncannily *familiar* to Flaubert: "Everything I discover here I *rediscover*. . . . I pity the poor devils who still have to lose their illusions."[17] And this experience of reproducing representations which have already been interiorized, this encounter with the paradoxical banality of the exotic, is constant in these texts: "I take our boat up river to the village of Manhatta. . . . Clumps of palm trees surrounded by little circular walls, with two Turks smoking beneath them; it was like an etching, a picture of the Orient in a book."[18]

Flaubert thus seems situated at the intersection of two conflicting representations: an original fantasy project of personal re-creation and liberation in the Orient on the one hand, and on the other a textual realization which inscribes clearly conventional, predetermined structures and protocols. Of course the initial preconscious project could not openly articulate itself without losing its status of fantasy. But it nonetheless finds representation. The implicit structure of Flaubert's fantasy appears as the dream, not so much of naturalizing within his own writing (in the form of some sort of curative antidote) the discourse of the Orient, but much more radically of absorbing himself—almost *obliterating himself*—in this other discourse.

This fantasy of absorption of the self is a characteristic impulse in Flaubert, one often elicited at the height of a personal crisis. We might recall, for example, the final impulse of the last version of *Saint-Antoine:* "être la matière!" ("to become matter itself!").[19] The same dynamic is already perceptible in the following passage from Flaubert's *Voyage:* "A tartan-colored native boat floats by . . . : truly that's the Orient [*voilà le vrai Orient*], a melancholy and lulling effect; you vaguely sense something immense and pitiless within which you disappear."[20]

The representations of relationships between East and West constantly take the figural form of such metonymies. And indeed this

17. Letter to Bouilhet, 4 Sept. 1850, *Oeuvres complètes,* vol. 13, p. 77.

18. Ibid., vol. 10, p. 495. This *pre*figured representation is also what makes possible the exclusion, from the image thus contemplated, of an element whose existence is registered at the beginning of the following paragraph. With a logic which is constant in these texts, and which retraces the formative influence of the Orientalist institution, the disagreeable detail in question succeeds in being both *visible* and *invisible* at the same time: "In the dust a child with rickets was crawling around."

19. Ibid., vol. 4, p. 171.

20. Ibid., vol. 10, p. 455.

metonymic operation inscribes within itself the full meaning which the Orient bears for orientalizing Europe: the womb, the origin. But—as we might put it—the trope was a trap. For in some obvious sense, the complex movement which it projected simply could not be realized in practice. Established as *other* for each other, West and East could not be stably or productively combined. *They produced no text*—or rather, they produced only the text of an arrested production, the figure of a trope which could neither be abandoned nor sustained. Thus when Flaubert's hoped-for absorption in the Oriental referent shows itself to be unrealizable, an alternative discursive figuration of the contact between Occident and Orient comes strategically to replace it. This new strategy inverts the original metonymy. It produces a more dispersed tropology, but one whose elements still inevitably inscribe within themselves the original dynamic of assimilation.

The character of Flaubert's Oriental texts depends upon the successive transformations of this tropology. And in their turn the two principal metonymic movements which will symmetrically provide their structures appear as the figures of a discourse from which it has proven impossible to expunge the inscription of an oppressive, reifying, vulgar, irreducibly *French* imperialism. At the heart of Flaubert's Oriental discourse, France thus comes to occupy the place which the sociohistorical conjuncture has established as its own despite the whole apparatus of Flaubert's efforts to obliterate it.

In his original fantasy, it was the objective conditions of colonialism itself which were to have been systematically inverted: the dominated Orient would fruitfully and beneficently have come to dominate its dominators, liberating them from themselves and from their own history. On the other hand, the substitute rhetorical figures at work in the texts themselves trace the reinscription of precisely this same history and of its principal institutional mediations: family, nation-state, Orientalist ideology and, in general, the bourgeois system of social meaning itself—precisely those complexes which the original fantasy had had the ambition of neutralizing.

So beyond his reciprocal fantasies of self-dispossession and absorption, the texts of Flaubert's trip to the Orient—of this intersection of two socioeconomic and signifying systems—can be conceived as organized by two versions of the original metonymy, two symmetrical figures for representing real historical confrontation with the Other.

These might be termed *penetration* (the projection of the dominant subject into the object, the forcible imposition of the dominator and of his discursive system within the dominated space) and *appropriation* (the seizure on the part of the subject of elements belonging to the object, the consumption enforced by the dominator of what belongs to the dominated). These tropological operations impregnate the most fundamental aspects of these texts, beginning with the thematic, and penetrating to rhetorical, semantic, and even syntactic levels.

Colonialist texts in general demonstrate the twin metonymic structures in question here. The fundamental transaction which characterizes such regimes of unequal exchange is *necessarily* a tropological appropriation. Its object is never the authentic totality of an economic or cultural system (for the colonialist never "really" intends to "become an Oriental," to lose himself in the East), but rather a series of detached, reified elements drawn from it. Their status is defined by their fragmentary quality, precisely by the possibility of *extracting* them from the whole. On the other hand the "whole" is incapable of resisting this violation, given the structure of relative power which establishes the transaction to begin with. Its content thus depends upon the conceptual and ideological *exteriority* of the determining subject (and of the system of needs which in its turn determines him) in relation to the system which finds itself the object of his decisions. His discourse will have the structure of a reduction or a separation precisely on account of such exteriority. This is what makes it fundamentally metonymic.[21] In these Flaubertian texts, the two movements which characterize such representation of the heterogeneous will be determined by the same logic.

If Flaubertian discourse could not attain its hoped-for discontinuity in relation to the territory of Western ideology, if (despite itself) it found itself involuntarily produced as an extension of the discourse of European hegemony, this was because, in the first place, the traces of such hegemony were omnipresent in the Orient. Flaubert sought obsessively to track them down. But the West he was trying to flee

21. See Said, *Orientalism,* p. 20, and Hayden White, *Metahistory,* introduction, esp. p. 34. I might add that it is in the course of such a rhetorical operation, determined by forces outside itself, that a sociocultural system may discover its own divisibility: whence the examination by a member of the culture in question (Said) of the phenomenon of Orientalism itself.

pursued him right into the desert, and in one of its archetypal guises: as that particular form of Occidental stupidity he named *Bêtise*. Thus in Jerusalem, directly opposite the Holy Sepulchre itself, he discovered a full-length portrait of Louis-Philippe. Flaubert's cry of mortification is pitiful: "Oh Grotesque, you are thus like the sun itself, dominating the world with your splendor; your light shines even into Jesus's tomb!" (vol. 10, p. 566). The figure of *penetration*—the colonization of a text which seeks desperately to represent itself as Oriental by an Occident whose ridiculousness is only heightened by its heterogeneity—could hardly reveal itself more strikingly. But these moments are everywhere in these texts. The following scene, described in a letter to his mother (23 February 1850), depends upon the same structure:

> From Benisouëf we made a trip to Lake Moeris and into the province of Fayoum. . . . For four days we slept on mats on the ground, and lived completely like Arabs. . . . We were invited to dinner by a Christian from Damascus. . . . During dessert, our host, heated with enthusiasm concerning Napoléon, got a bit drunk. Can you possibly guess what he had on the walls of his living room? A picture of Quillebeuf and one of Graville. [Vol. 13, p. 17]

In the end, this repetition of the incongruous, this ubiquity of the detestable, leads to a nearly paroxysmic protest: "L'Europe dans l'Asie! elle y pénètre par le billard, par l'estaminet, par Paul de Kock, Béranger et les journaux. Comme ça se civilise!" ("Europe in Asia! it penetrates in the introduction of billiards, in the introduction of bars, in the introduction of Paul de Kock, Béranger, and newspapers. How civilized everything is becoming!" vol. 10, p. 594).

Disillusionment—mediated by the constant intrusion of the signs of the West—imposes itself immediately. Arriving in Alexandria, Flaubert is treated to the sight of Pompey's column. It bears literal inscription of the penetration by Europe which is destined to undermine his text from start to finish. He describes the experience in a letter to his uncle Parain on 6 October 1850:

> Dear old friend, have you ever reflected upon the utter serenity of imbeciles? Stupidity [*la bêtise*] is something unshakeable; nothing comes up against it without being destroyed. It's like granite, hard and resistant. In Alexandria, a certain Thompson, from Sunderland, has

inscribed his name on Pompey's column in letters six feet high. You can read it from a quarter-league away. You can't even see the column without seeing Thompson's name, therefore without thinking of Thompson. This cretin has incorporated himself into the monument and perpetuated himself with it. It's even worse than that: he has outdone the column by the splendor of his gigantic inscription. All imbeciles are more or less like Thompson of Sunderland. And they always defeat us [*ils nous enfoncent toujours*]; they are so numerous, there's no way to stamp them out, they are simply too healthy. You meet a lot of them while traveling. [Vol. 13, p. 82]

Flaubert went on carefully collecting the traces of this exasperating persistence of the inappropriate. At the top of the Great Pyramid: "I discovered a piece of white paper pinned to the stone, and what was written on it? HUMBERT THE POLISHER. It was Max [Du Camp] who had contrived to get to the top before I did and prepare this sublime surprise for me."[22] Here, of course, the inscription of the West was consciously amusing. But the joke was based on less comic realities: in the same spot, at the top of Cheop's Pyramid, "one is infuriated by the quantity of imbeciles' names written everywhere: there is one Buffard, 79 rue Saint-Martin, who identifies himself in black letters as a manufacturer of wallpaper; an English admirer has written Jenny Lind's name; what's more, there's a pear representing Louis-Philippe." Inside the Pyramid of Chephren, carved into the stone, Flaubert finds the name of "M. Juste de Chasseloup-Laubat," a member of the French Chambre des Députés (vol. 10, p. 463). Flaubert finds the monumental head of Abousir "covered with the names of travelers"; he judges that one inscription, "Belzoni 1816," must have taken three full days to cut into the stone (vol. 10, p. 501). Upon arriving at the celebrated Cedars of Lebanon he discovers a doubly imbecilic graffito: Lamartine's name, recording the earlier writer-voyager's trip, has in turn been "covered over by the name of some perfectly ordinary person" who had followed Lamartine to the spot.[23]

22. Letter to his mother, 14 Dec. 1849, *Oeuvres complètes*, vol. 12, pp. 600–1. See also vol. 10, p. 462 and vol. 12, p. 672. The name is that of a "scieur-frotteur" who had a shop in Rouen in 1849 and who apparently formed a part of the comic mythology of Flaubert and his friends; see Naaman, *Lettres d'Egypte*, part 3, p. lxxviii.

23. *Oeuvres complètes*, vol. 10, p. 606. Since he didn't care to make the trip himself, Chateaubriand recounts how he sent a servant to carve his name on the Pyramids; see his *Oeuvres romanesques et voyages*, ed. Maurice Regard (Paris: Gallimard, 1969), p. 1148.

But these reactions—conscious, carefully organized within Flaubert's texts, defined by the anger which such scandalous penetration of the Oriental referent by the European signifier regularly and repeatedly elicited—mark only the beginning of the process I am retracing here. What seems to be happening is that the West is imposing itself within the Orientalist text, the dominant discourse is colonizing what had been conceived as an *antidote* to domination. The West, having preceded Flaubert to the East, is obliging him to record it there, like an unanticipated referent which forces its representation upon the text whose function had nominally been to evade it.

The process invades these texts even further. Flaubert's writing about the trip at times constructs itself as an almost obsessive series of comparisons linking terms chosen from the two worlds in presence. What occurs is a confrontation of their difference. On the semantic level it creates a sort of montage which perpetuates and institutionalizes the Occidental signifying system at the heart of Oriental representation.

A few examples: in Benisouëf, Flaubert sees some bleached bones lying flush with the ground; he is struck by the resemblance to the surface of a slice of fine Parisian pâté (vol. 10, p. 480). Along the Nile some children diving from the tops of palm trees into the river remind him of classical bronze statues (vol. 10, p. 494). In Abu-Simbel the noise of the animals makes him think of the farms of Normandy "in high summer, when everyone is in the fields, around three o'clock in the afternoon" (vol. 10, p. 504). In Djenin, on the west bank of the Jordan River, he watches a woman drawing water "a little in the style of a Mignard painting" (vol. 10, p. 581). In Damascus the decoration of the hotel where he and Du Camp stay is "so tortured that it rivals Louis XV style" (vol. 10, p. 588).

The montage of disparate elements which these examples typify is constant. Flaubert gets to the point of seeking to regain control of his text by rethematizing the force which disrupts it. He does this through an appeal to one of the commonplaces of touristic Orientalism: the notion that the East which one has come seeking is disappearing under the weight of Western penetration. The feeling affects him early on: "the temples of Egypt bore me stiff. Are they going to end up like Breton churches?" (vol. 10, p. 504). And the impression increases as he continues on his trip, constantly evoking the paradox at the heart of the entire touristic operation which he has undertaken—the hoped-for renaissance of his writing and his spirit by a passage through that which is dying: "They're going to abolish the harems, the example of European women is contagious; one of these days the women in the East are going to begin reading novels. . . . All around us the whole thing is collapsing of decrepitude" (vol. II, p. 49). In another letter, written on 13 August 1850, he urges Gautier to leave Paris and join him and Max on their trip: "It's time to hurry. In a little while the Orient will have ceased to exist. We may be its last witnesses. You can't imagine how much it has already been ruined. I've seen harems go by on steam boats" (vol. 13, p. 66).

But the determinants of this experience of disillusionment were much more structural and ideological than chronological. To be sure, the intensity of the need Flaubert felt to discover a source for the counter-discourse he was striving to produce explains why he believed he would have done better to come East even earlier than he did. But on another level the contradiction structured by his need and his effort to satisfy it suggests that in his search for a revivifying Oriental counter-discourse *he would always have been too late.*

Thus it is that Flaubert's text registers its contamination by Europe as a systematic and more or less conscious critique of this mode of intervention and domination. It organizes itself in the form of a network of tiny points of European infection, distributed over its pages as they seem to have been over the map of the Orient itself. Such contaminated geography it takes as its model. It was as if, in the effort to ground its representation in definite, localizable places in Oriental territory, his text had sought to divest itself of any internally determined organization, to ensure that its structure would become the expression of Oriental reality itself. But since the Orient which Flaubert could visit was already objectively penetrated, his account of it opens itself to the ineluctable discourse of Europe.[24]

24. One of the most surprising indications of this involuntary penetration occurs in the text entitled "A bord de la cange." It is the only example within Flaubert's *Voyage* of a text which *presents itself as contemporary* with the events it describes. It was written "on the spot" in Egypt (between 6 and 20 Feb. 1850). (The rest of the *Voyage,* of course, was composed in France after Flaubert returned, on the basis of the summary notes he took day by day.) Consequently, in "A bord de la cange" we expect *l'actualité,* "current events," Egypt "live and direct." But the reality of this fragment is unexpectedly differ-

The figure of *penetration,* and the textual consciousness of its parasitic presence in the discourse of Flaubert's trip, might well be interpreted
as a consciously thematized irony. It would then appear as the trace of
colonialist false consciousness which Flaubert allowed into his text
precisely because, thanks to certain satirical techniques, he could conceive it as containable. As in the writing considered in the preceding
chapter, Flaubert retextualized imbecility here with the intention of
seeking, by evoking it, to bring it down of its own imbecilic weight.
He allowed European stupidity to speak within his text in order to
mark his text's difference from it.

His aim would then have been to found his counter-discourse in the
face of the dominant discourse's downfall, contrived by re/citing it
within his own text. He adopted the voice of imbecility, he constructed
outrageous mini-narratives out of it: cautionary tales which, through
their archetypal ridiculousness, functioned to demystify a degraded
consciousness. In France, he had invented his celebrated Garçon.[25] In
the Orient, it is the turn of his *sheik:*

> As far as we're concerned, we've never been less bored on a boat
> even though we have nothing to see or do any more. We have books
> but don't read them. We don't write anything either. We spend nearly
> *all* our time playing *sheiks,* that is, old men. The sheik is the old, inept,
> well-off, well-respected, well-established, ancient gentleman who asks
> us questions about our trip, something like this:
> "And in the cities where you have been [in Egypt], have you made
> contact with polite society? Is there at least a club where you can read
> the newspapers?"
> "Are they constructing railroads there? Do they have any major
> lines?"
> "And socialist ideas, good heavens, I hope they haven't made their
> way into those territories?"
> "Do they at least have some good wines? Are there any famous
> growths, etc.?"

---

ent. It is a text of *displacement;* its logic is purely associative and transchronological; it
makes one think of Proust. The text was written on the Nile, but speaks almost
exclusively of *other* voyages, of memories of home, of the trip from Paris to Marseille
which Flaubert had now taken three times. "A bord de la cange" is a text *about France.*
Such displacement appears as the emblem of the referential difficulties which I am
discussing.

25. See Sartre's *Idiot,* part 2, book 2.

"Are the women agreeable?"

"Do they have any decent cafés? Do the employees there dress well?"

All this delivered in a trembling voice, in an imbecilic manner. From single sheik we've passed on to double sheik, that is to say, to dialogues.[26]

But the coordinate figure of *appropriation,* the tropological and sociohistorical counterpart of this structure of penetration, alters this paradigm in a significant way. For with regard to this second figure and the entire rhetoric it organizes, for the first time the text seems *unaware of its presence.* Consequently its self-critical power suddenly risks inadequacy. It seems unconscious of its own immersion in the ideological, which nonetheless it bears along with it and insistently stages for us.

If this is so, it is because *appropriation* objectively represents the condition of possibility both of Flaubert's own voyage and of writing concerning it. Consequently, traces of this second figure are rendered transparent, become mystified in this text which, nonetheless, it structures in the most fundamental ways. An analysis of its presence can locate within Flaubert's Oriental texts the mode of existence of the ideological operating in its most refractory disguise.[27]

This paradigmatic figure of appropriation really arises in the paradox of referentiality which we have already observed: in the subject's ambiguity with regard to foreign reality, to the reality of foreignness. Such ambivalence surfaces in Flaubert's oscillations between a sentimental, almost religious, reverence concerning the cultural system to which he had appealed to purge him of his Occident, and on the other hand a rather methodical exploitation of the same system. In the latter mode he seems to have wanted to *absorb* the Orient in his text rather than seeking to *absorb himself within it* as he had in the early fantasy to which I have referred. The result is that despite Flaubert's more enlightened intentions, the pages of his *Voyage* appear as the *text of his consumption* of the Orient: as a carefully composed instruction manual for the

---

26. Letter to his mother, 24 June 1850, *Oeuvres complètes,* vol. 13, p. 50.

27. This mystified centrality of the ideological—masked for the text itself, but essential to its structure—betrays the methodological difficulty which confronts any purely idealist or structuralist analysis of colonialist discourse. The historical and conjunctural *charge* upon a text's signifiers necessarily remains invisible for such a methodology.

proper exploitation of a foreign culture. This *other* culture is conceived as inferior on account of its very availability for such exploitation, its powerlessness, its subjection.

There were prestigious models of this attitude, much less obsessed then was Flaubert's own text by aversion to an imperialist false consciousness. For example, Lamartine's own *Voyage en Orient:* "[The domination of the Western Powers] sanctioned as a European right will consist principally in the right to occupy specified portions of territory. Each [European] Power will exercise an armed and civilizing guardianship over its protectorate; it will guarantee its existence and the basis of its national integrity under the flag of a stronger national authority."[28] As Said has observed, such a guarantee was what made it possible for Flaubert to *be in the Orient at all* and made it impossible for the Orient to resist his presence there.[29] Flaubert's text clearly registers this attitude: "I note that we Franks are highly respected [here]; our military force and the memory of Napoléon have a great deal to do with that."[30]

The reference to Bonaparte is significant. For Napoléon's expedition to Egypt in 1798 inaugurated what could stand as the first modern effort on the part of one culture scientifically to appropriate another: to dominate it systematically, to render it totally accessible, to transform it into a subdivision of French knowledge and erudition. The monument to this project of controlling Oriental reality is the celebrated *Description de l'Egypte:* twenty-three enormous volumes which appeared between 1809 and 1828, whose pages—as if they were the concrete objectification of the rationalist means by which the Oriental referent was to have been mastered—each measured exactly one meter square.[31]

In theory Flaubert's and Du Camp's trip itself had a scientific and scholarly object in the spirit of this original will-to-appropriation. In approving the project which Du Camp had proposed to them, the Académie des Inscriptions et Belles-Lettres encouragingly stated that they expected the trip would produce "conquests on behalf of phi-

28. *Voyage en Orient* (1835; Paris: Hachette, 1887), vol. 2, pp. 526–27. Said discusses Flaubert's implicit belief in the superiority of the Westerner in *Orientalism*, p. 15.

29. *Orientalism*, p. 15.

30. Letter to his mother, 14 Dec. 1849, *Oeuvres complètes*, vol. 12, p. 661.

31. See Said, *Orientalism*, pp. 42, 83–86.

lology, archeology and art."[32] And in line with this ideological sanctioning of an essentially exploitative project, a first trace of what we might term the "appropriative attitude" can be perceived in an intermittent but repeated preoccupation in Flaubert's texts with two modes of symbolic absorption of the referent which stand in cultural history to the decided credit of his and Max's expedition: the detailed architectural and archeological description of Oriental monuments ("This temple is 33.70 meters long, 16.89 meters wide; the circumference of the columns is 5.37 metres, their total height is 11.37 metres. An Arab climbed up to the capital of one of the columns to drop the tape measure for us"; vol. 10, p. 491) and, above all, the photographs they took.

Flaubert's and Du Camp's photographic activities represented a good deal more than simply taking snapshots. Their images of Egypt, which are celebrated in the annals of photography just as much as in those of Orientalism, would have caused their trip to be remembered even if the voyagers themselves had been less famous. For (with the exception of a few daguerreotypes which Horace Vernet had made during his voyage in 1839–40) these were the first photographic images which revealed the visual elements of Egypt to a Europe eager to acquaint itself with them.[33]

But in the context of my argument here, such an imposition in the foreign country of paradigms for seizing it is striking. No doubt the paradox was invisible to the travelers themselves. But through their very objectification of the "foreignness" of Egypt, they caused an alien system to intervene in and ultimately to determine its representation. They captured it in images and surveyed it in archeological notebooks—correct to four significant digits. However involuntarily, their procedures functioned to render accessible, permeable to Occidentals an Orient portrayed as mute, powerless, lacking any consciousness of itself, any desire to record its *own* monuments, write its *own* history, derive its *own* meaning. The Europeans were thus obliged to carry the East home with them and to speak on its behalf. It became *their* text.

This ideology of permeability is perceivable everywhere in Flaubert's pages; indeed for him it defined the material and subjective conditions

32. See Naaman, *Lettres d'Egypte,* p. 17.
33. See ibid., p. 16.

surrounding his trip. With the self-satisfaction of those who know themselves to be highly placed, he instructed his mother as follows: "Write me in Cairo. All you need are my name and my title plus: Cairo, Egypt." Such gratifying centralization of the European is the very meaning of his status in the Orient: "We seem like princes, I'm not joking. Sassetti [their servant] keeps saying: 'At least for once in my life I can tell people that I had ten slaves to serve me, and another to chase the flies away.'"[34] And such a hierarchical distinction, which makes even their servants seem like masters compared to those who serve *them,* can be perceived clearly in what we might term the travelers' touristic economy. Flaubert spent twenty-seven thousand francs during his twenty months in the Orient—just about the same amount he earned during his entire career as a writer.[35] Upon arriving in Alexandria, he had more than twelve hundred pounds of baggage; but it took a bribe of only fifty sous to persuade the customs agents to let it through without a search. The boat on which they made the trip up the Nile had a crew of ten, none of whom earned more than fifteen francs a month (vol. 12, p. 659). Under such conditions, repeated everywhere along their way, it would have seemed extraordinary if our travelers had not experienced their European superiority as a virtual fact of nature. And the text of Flaubert's *Voyage* is studded with little details in which that attitude makes itself apparent in the relative absence of any self-critical commentary on the author's part:

> The [Nile] cataract is as straight as a canal. Five men dive into the water, to entertain me. [Vol. 10, p. 495]

> *Saturday morning.*—I purchase two women's tresses with their ornaments; the women whose hair is cut off weep. . . . It must have been very upsetting for them [*Ça a dû être une désolation pour ces pauvres femmes*]; they appear to have cared a good deal about their hair [*paraissent y tenir beaucoup*]. [Vol. 10, p. 510]

> 26 [December 1849], visit to the Mosques with Delatour and *Mister* [*môsieur*] Malezieux: frock coat, high collar, hat, yellow gloves, pitifully dumb manner, not at all interested in Arab architecture. On the other hand, he got excited when we were passing near the slave

---

34. Letter to his mother, 22 Nov. 1849, *Oeuvres complètes,* vol. 12, pp. 651 and 647.
35. See Naaman, *Lettres d'Egypte,* p. 29, and Bart, *Flaubert,* p. 188.

market: "Get your guide to tell her to take all her clothes off" concerning a poor black woman who was displayed before us. [Vol. 10, p. 470]

In their turn, these passages seem to define from the outside the fundamental appropriative theme of the *Voyage:* sex and prostitution. The question has been frequently discussed, especially with regard to the celebrated night Flaubert spent with Kuchuk-Hânem. But the problem needs to be placed in the context of the dynamic of consumption of the Oriental referent which, as I have been arguing, involuntarily organizes the text of Flaubert's *Voyage*.

The theme of Oriental sexuality was traditional within the Orientalist atmosphere, had already institutionalized itself (above all, perhaps, in Lane's 1837 *Account of the Manners and Customs of the Modern Egyptians,* which Flaubert had read.)[36] What was at issue was the sexual *availability* of the Oriental female (and indeed, of the Oriental male). The impulse to profit from the situation thus projected makes itself felt at the very beginning of the Egyptian adventure which Flaubert's text recounts: "We had hardly landed [in Alexandria] when the infamous Du Camp got turned on [*avait des excitations*] by a black woman who was pumping water at a fountain. He is also turned on by the little black boys [*les négrillons*]."[37] The letters which Flaubert wrote from Egypt to his friend Bouilhet are (among other things) a catalogue of the travelers' erotic exploits. Particularly, they detail Flaubert's observations concerning the sexual peculiarity of the Orientals, one of the essential—and deeply ambiguous—components of Orientalist ideology. In this category we might place Flaubert's descriptions of a boy pimping for his mother in the street (vol. 12, p. 654); of public copulation (vol. 12, p. 654); of homosexual encounters (vol. 12, p. 674; vol. 13, p. 48); of several orgies (for example, vol. 13, p. 69), and so on.

At a later point in the trip, out of a sense of something like *noblesse oblige,* and after frequent paid experiences of his own with Oriental

36. See the letter to his mother of 8 Mar. 1850, *Oeuvres complètes,* vol. 13, p. 22. Said discusses the essential theme of Oriental sexuality in *Orientalism,* pp. 87, 103, 106. Flaubert speaks about it in a bitter jest in one of his letters to Bouilhet, wondering about the origin of the venereal infection he contracted during his trip: "I suspect a Maronite of having given me this gift, but it may have been a little Turk. . . . This is one aspect of the Oriental question which *La Revue des Deux Mondes* has failed to consider" (14 Nov. 1850, *Oeuvres complètes,* vol. 13, p. 94).

37. Letter to Bouilhet, 1 Dec. 1849, *Oeuvres complètes,* vol. 12, p. 653.

prostitutes, Flaubert even treated his servants to women (vol. 10, pp. 474–75). The lesson would seem to be that *everyone* ought to get his piece of an Orient which could not resist being the object of European desire and of its enforced satisfaction. After a time the rhythm of such enjoyment almost begins to seem to have been measured in *industrial* terms: "At Esnèh I got off five times in one day"; "I screwed three women and got off four times—three times before lunch, once after dessert."[38] Thus the text and the appropriative dynamic which energizes it moves from spectacles to entertainments to women's tresses to whole women: everything is made the Occidentals' lawful prize in that accelerating absorption of the foreign which structures the *Voyage*.

In relation to this objectification of the Oriental recipients of such European desire, the celebrated episode with Kuchuk is surprising. On the one hand the scene is played as the epitome of the exploitation of one culture's representatives by the privileged members of another: Kuchuk's dance leads automatically to the "baisade" Flaubert had contracted for, and so on. At the critical moment the musicians in attendance are blindfolded; the sailor Fergalli and one of his companions "who were there to bring out the *grotesque* of the scene" (vol. 11, p. 689; see also vol. 10, p. 489) are asked to depart. The Occidentals, quite properly displaying their authority, take their pleasure in an intimacy from which all inferiors are excluded.

Yet an ambiguity in the relationships depicted inverts the configuration. For with Kuchuk, Flaubert falls, if not in love, then at least into the state of availability, even of *subjection,* which characterizes the colonialist relationship that frames the *Voyage* both as experience and as text. But this time it is the Westerner who experiences dependency: "What satisfaction [*douceur*] one's pride would experience if, upon leaving, one could be sure one would be remembered, and that she would think of you more often than of the others, that you would remain in her heart!" (Vol. 10, p. 490). But Flaubert's dream of romantic acceptance by Kuchuk turns the conditions of his relationship with her upside down.

It would seem to have been projected at the price of his conceiving, *against all sociocultural logic,* that she might have freely chosen him exactly as he had himself acquired her. The problem is that *this* form of

---

38. Letters to Bouilhet, 13 Mar. 1850 and 20 Aug. 1850, ibid., vol. 13, pp. 27, 69.

Western desire—the desire to win hearts and minds, not just bodies, to recall a more recent usage—takes a form whose satisfaction European power can simply not compel. Indeed in this case it would seem that the exercise of such power would rather ensure the contrary. In a revealing detail, lying next to Kuchuk, Flaubert thinks of Judith and Holophernes in bed together (vol. 10, p. 490). In the image the repressed threat of violence that is the inseparable counter-condition of his own domination seems for a few seconds to demystify itself, to surface as a powerful fantasy of the revenge of the oppressed.

There are other indications of this fantasy of annihilating the social and political givens which determined relations with the Oriental "Other," and which in turn made Flaubert in the Orient inevitably seem to exercise dominion over its reality. Sometimes he plays at refusing the gesture of appropriation offered him: "We return to the prostitutes' street, I stroll through there on purpose; they call to me. I give money first to one of them, then to another; some of them grab me to take me off with them, but I refuse to screw them [*je m'interdis de les baiser*] so that the melancholy of the memory will better remain with me."[39]

Yet it is clear that this self-denial is exercised in the service of another kind of satisfaction, of another and more fundamental variety of appropriation whose substance brings me back to the fundamental problem with which I began: the reenergization of Flaubert's *writing*, the need to utilize the trip to the Orient to liberate a counter-discourse which might annihilate the dominant discourse he felt was so painfully blocking him. But this seems far from having been achieved in these texts.

It is not only that Flaubert never attempted the sort of radical Orientalism on the linguistic level which Pound later exploited in his experiments with ideograms, his practice of a poetic system which seems authentically inter- and pluri-cultural. In Flaubert's pages we occasion-

---

39. *Oeuvres complètes,* vol. 10, p. 485. To Bouilhet he recounts his return to Esnèh: "I saw Kuchuk-Hânem again. It was sad. She had been ill. I looked at her for a long time, to keep her image in my head. When I left, we told her that we would return the next day, and we didn't return. But I savored the bitterness of the whole thing, that's the main point." Further in the same letter, on an analogous theme, we read: "That's one of the sadnesses of the trip, which may in fact be one of the most profitable things about travelling" (2 June 1850, ibid., vol. 13, pp. 46–47).

ally find traces of an effort to conceive, even beyond the exoticism of the Orient which began to seem insufficient to him, a *totally* fantasized referent, a sort of "alternative world" which might have produced the renascent text he sought: "Could one imagine a forest in which the palm trees would be as white as bouquets of ostrich feathers?" (vol. 10, p. 516). But such attempts remain sterile, as indeed all his production during this period would come to seem to him:

> I have to tell you seriously that my intelligence has declined enormously. It alarms me, *I'm not joking in the least,* I feel completely empty, completely deflated, completely sterile. The business with *Saint-Antoine* was a real blow to me, quite honestly. I tried in vain to make something out of the "conte oriental" [see vol. 12, pp. 143ff.]. I thought for a couple of days about the story of Mycerinus in Herodotus (the king who screws his daughter). But it all evaporated. The first days [in Egypt] I tried to write a little, but thank God I quickly realized how inept it all was.[40]

In the same vein, he writes his mother a commentary on what was surely the most continuous mode of his literary production during the period of his trip, his letters home: "My poor old friend, I realize that the letters I'm sending you are pretty worthless" ("*je te cadotte d'une correspondance passablement nulle*").[41] And in that perspective, Flaubert's continual lamentation concerning the inadequacy and the imperfection of his writing seems much more than a rhetorical flourish.[42]

Yet despite such pessimistic assessments, if we look closely, the whole form of the *Voyage,* of the letters, of the notebooks most of all, appears like a frantic series of attempts to transcend these limits and these inadequacies, to seize (if nothing else) at least the representational plenitude of a collection of objects observed, of sites explored, of women possessed. In spite of his intense dissatisfaction concerning the results of this effort to absorb the exotic reality, he could not give it up. Yet its symbolic appropriation resisted him systematically. He could not evade the implication of his writing in the social structures determined by the West's domination of the East.

40. Letter to Bouilhet, 13 Mar. 1850, ibid., vol. 13, p. 25; cf. vol. 13, p. 75.
41. 8 Mar. 1850, ibid., vol. 13, p. 21.
42. See, for example, ibid., vol. 10, pp. 547, 596–97, and vol. 11, p. 93.

Flaubertian criticism has repeatedly—if somewhat vaguely—claimed that the Orient trip opened Flaubert's way to the realization of his authentic writing style.[43] The suggestion is that the mature Flaubert emerged somehow from his passage through the desert. This is to accept something like the same ideology—or fantasy—with which the writer himself went to the East. Of course it can hardly be denied that, upon returning from his voyage, he set to work on *Madame Bovary,* whose credentials as "authentic Flaubert" are sufficiently persuasive. But the process of the breakthrough mediated by the Orient trip remains obscure. Perhaps some understanding of what may have occurred may be possible through recognition of the overall *failure* of the textual paradigm which, I have argued, was at the origin of Flaubert's desire to leave France: the faith that somehow contact with an exotic referent would reenergize his writing.

A curious dialectical reversal would then take the place of the imagined "discovery" opening the way to "Flaubertian" writing about which critics have spoken. The path Flaubert found himself following once he returned from his trip really denotes the *absence* of an "Oriental renaissance." And the *Voyage en Orient* stages this negativity. For this text which carries so many objects, so many places, so many people along with it finds itself empty, exhausted, in the face of its own accumulation. The foreign referent never succeeds in liberating Flaubertian discourse, in driving out of it the degraded Western contents and paradigms whose domination was driving him to fury—on the contrary.

The two metonymic operations which were supposed to have incorporated the foreign into the body of European representation in fact produce nothing the least bit satisfactory. Indeed, there is a disabling interference between the two tropes themselves, the first ("penetration") consciously satirizing the hegemonic presence in the Orient of the hated discourse of the West; the second ("appropriation") involuntarily *reproducing* the very same discourse. Thus subverted, the renewal seems to disintegrate, the text seems to undo itself in the very process of its making. Flaubert had begun with the desire to mobilize the

---

43. Naaman gives a list of the critics making this sort of assertion (Bertrand, Thibaudet, Dumesnil, Carré) in *Débuts de Gustave Flaubert,* p. 256n.; see also his *Lettres d'Egypte,* p. 35. To this list must be added the most recent of Flaubert's biographers, Benjamin Bart; see his *Flaubert,* p. 184.

referential power of writing in order to displace a dominant discourse by means of that which the sociohistorical conjuncture had established as its Other. But the text which sought to found itself as counter-discourse reveals that the desire which drives it along is inscribed as a constitutive element in just the order of meaning which it sought to transgress.

With the perspective our temporal and political situation makes possible, we are able to see that, despite all his efforts, Flaubert had gotten himself caught in the most banal sort of misunderstanding: in a naive and unconscious idealism which ignored the profoundly *directional* nature of the exchange between two unequal societies. In effect Flaubert sought magically to abolish the objective constraints in the relationship between sign and referent within any real discursive formation. Such relationships can never be reduced to the reversible, nonhierarchical, antihistorical, and fundamentally complacent structure which modern theory has termed "communication."[44] *Domination* is part of what dominant discourse carries along with it, no matter where it travels.

The preceding chapter has already suggested how powerfully the project of constituting and sustaining a counter-discourse was to continue in Flaubert's career. Indeed he would never abandon it. But what makes possible its persistence in his later texts is the inscription at the very heart of his writing of a constant recognition of the immanent ideological power of hegemonic discourse. This is what his writing about the Orient had unconsciously sought to evade. Flaubert's later texts *erase* his romantic fantasy of discursive liberation—a fantasy which is itself the ancestor of the utopia of free language which so powerfully attracted Barthes in *Le degré zéro de l'écriture*. Since that time, of course, such a projection of a language liberated from the real has attracted other theoreticians, not all of whom have been as conscious as Barthes concerning the conjunctural determination of the fantasy project itself. This utopia has thus reappeared in the form of a notion of textual productivity imagined as autonomous, as a free play of signifiers to which is attributed the privilege of transcending all referentiality, all external or material or conjunctural determination.

The content and strategies deployed in such a projection will con-

---

44. See on this point Bourdieu and Passeron, *La reproduction*, book 1, sec. 2.1.2.

cern me in Part 3 of this study. An analogous dream is already inscribed everywhere in Flaubert's Oriental texts. *But these texts are also the place where the fantasy is obliterated.* It is this already-canceled utopia of free and radical counter-discourse which some critics have conceived as the ideal of the writing practice which would later characterize Flaubert. On the contrary: in the Orient, Flaubert discovered that such a pure counter-language, annihilating the immanent discourse of an entire sociohistorical formation, was unsustainable. That is the point, then, when Flaubert *reoriented* himself toward other forms of transgression of the dominant, and thereby toward an authentic dialecticity of writing.

That reorientation will comprise not the radical subversion of the prosaic—this (as I will argue in Chapters 6 and 7) will be Mallarmé's project—but rather an explicit contestatory representation. Traces of it are already present in the celebrated letter written from Damascus to Bouilhet in which Flaubert first speaks of the *Dictionnaire des idées reçues*.[45] The constant referent of such a strategic reorientation will be the degraded, French, middle-class reality from which Flaubert had sought to free himself in departing for the East, and which once there he discovered had ineluctably accompanied him. In the conjuncture in which he found himself, his object (as my preceding chapter argued) would no longer be some imagined purification of the Western discursive system but, rather, its corrosive reinscription within his own writing. This is the movement which, from this point on, would release his textual production.

Later the realization that the Orient trip had solved nothing inscribes itself in other Flaubertian texts which deal with the Orient, with the exotic, and with traveling: for example, in the disappointment experienced when at last the Veil of Tanit is attained in *Salammbô*;[46] in the flat laconicism of the celebrated "Il voyagea" ("He traveled") near the conclusion of *L'éducation sentimentale*;[47] in the derisory and sardonic fantasy of the regeneration of Europe by Asia which we find in the plans of *Bouvard et Pécuchet*.[48]

But toward the end of the Orient trip itself, as the travelers journey

---

45. 4 Sept. 1850, *Oeuvres complètes*, vol. 13, p. 76.
46. Ibid., vol. 2, p. 194.
47. Ibid., vol. 3, p. 392.
48. Ibid., vol. 5, p. 273.

back to Europe, the dream still doggedly persists: "I assure you that I'd like to keep going by land as far as China"; "Well, yes, I've seen the Orient and it's not enough [*je n'en suis pas plus avancé*], since I want to go back. I want to go to India, to lose myself in the pampas of America and go to Sudan."[49] As France approaches, and with it immersion in the discourse which the exoticism of the East could not displace, Flaubert still feels tormented—by the uncertainty of what direction to follow in his work, by the decadence of his profession and his period which he knows awaits him upon his return: "La littérature a mal à la poitrine. Elle crache, elle bavache, elle a des vésicatoires. . . . Il faudrait des Christs de l'Art pour guérir ce lépreux. En revenir à l'antique, c'est déjà fait. Au moyen-âge, c'est déjà fait. Reste le présent. Mais la base tremble; où donc appuyer les fondements? . . . Tout cela m'inquiète tellement que j'en suis venu à ne plus aimer qu'on m'en parle."[50]

Nonetheless a conviction of the practical uselessness of any strategy of evasion or escape—whether geographic or discursive—seems to emerge as the basis of the writing choices which upon his return to France Flaubert was close to being able to make and to sustain for the remainder of his career. In the midst of his lamentations concerning the future, such a conviction is perceptible in the bitter realization which he expresses in another letter to Bouilhet. In Flaubert's own voice it can provide our final diagnostic word concerning the Oriental therapy which he had attempted in his own case:

> Où prendre notre point d'appui, en admettant même que nous ayons le levier? Ce qui nous manque à tous, ce n'est point le style, ni cette flexibilité de l'archet et des doigts désignée sous le nom de talent. Nous avons un orchestre nombreux, une palette riche, des ressources variées. En fait de ruses et de ficelles, nous en savons beaucoup, plus qu'on n'en a peut-être jamais su. Non, ce qui nous manque c'est le principe intrin-

49. Letter written from Damascus to Dr. Jules Cloquet, 7 Dec. 1850, ibid., vol. 13, p. 80; letter written from Rome to Ernest Chevalier, 9 Apr. 1851, ibid., vol. 13, p. 137.
50. "Literature is dying of consumption. It's spitting, and drooling, and on its last legs. You'd need an artistic Jesus to cure this leper. We can't go back to ancient times, it's already been done. The middle ages have already been done. The present is all that's left. But the base is shaky; what can we use to prop it up? The whole situation upsets me so much that I've gotten to the point of not wanting to talk about it any more at all" (Letter to Bouilhet, 14 Nov. 1850, ibid., vol. 13, p. 95).

sèque, c'est l'âme de la chose, l'idée même du sujet. Nous prenons des
notes, *nous faisons des voyages,* misère, misère.[51]

In the discourses of the later nineteenth century, we could expect to
discern the same dynamic within numerous other fantasies seeking
liberation through exoticism and escape. The burden of the lesson here
would seem quite pessimistic. Yet Flaubert became productive. He
returned from his trip to the same France which had generated the
dominant discourse he had discovered himself unable to elude. In his
confrontation with it his writing began to deploy an immense—and
deeply subversive—cultural power, one which no other figure in the
second half of the century quite matches. Orientation to the counter-
discourse which was to become Flaubertian discourse depends upon
the negative realization of his voyage East—upon this painful and
productive dis-Orient-ation.

51. "Where can we find a fulcrum, even assuming that we had a lever? What we all
lack is neither style nor that suppleness of bow work and fingering which people call
talent. We have a profusion of tones, a rich palette, numerous resources. We know a lot
of tricks and devices, indeed we may know more of them than anyone has ever known
before. No, what we lack is the inner principle, the soul of the thing, the very idea of a
subject. We take notes, *we take trips,* but it leads to nothing, to nothing at all" (2 June
1850, ibid., p. 41; my italics).

PART THREE
ABSOLUTE
COUNTER-DISCOURSE

CHAPTER 6

The Paradoxes of Distinction: The Prose Poem as Prose

L'homme de lettres est l'ennemi du monde. [The writer is
a public enemy]
— BAUDELAIRE, "Mon coeur mis à nu"

Dans les domaines de la création, qui sont aussi les
domaines de l'orgueil, la nécessité de se distinguer est
indivisible de l'existence même. [In the realm of creation,
which is also that of pride, the necessity of distinguishing
oneself is indivisible from one's very existence.] —
VALÉRY, "Situation de Baudelaire"

The prose poem needs reexamination *from the side of prose:* as a strategy
for intervention in the dominant discursive apparatus of the nineteenth
century. At just the historical moment when the term "prosaic" was
mutating into a pejorative,[1] the prose poem sought to reevaluate the
expressive possibilities, and the social functionality, of prose itself.
Nothing in the second half of the century situates this institution more
acutely, nor puts it into crisis more decisively, than its reinscription in
the project of the *poème en prose.* From this perspective, the reflection
on the discursive which the prose poem constituted by problematizing
the entire realm of discourse appears as a sophisticated—and deeply
subversive—scrutiny of its mechanisms of control, and of their points
of potential fracture.

---

1. *Oxford English Dictionary,* s.v. "prosaic," para. 2.6.

Two elements are conjoined in theoretical reflection concerning the prose poem: the complex adversary relationship between the new medium of expression forged by avant-garde writers and its hegemonic discursive object; and the conjunctural pertinence of the confrontation between the two strains of discourse. Their resonances are recoverable in one of Mallarmé's richest characterizations of the genre, in which by that time he had been engaged for more than thirty years: "une forme, peut-être, en sort, *actuelle,* permettant, à ce qui fut longtemps le poëme en prose et notre recherche, d'aboutir, en tant . . . que *poëme critique*" (a form may then emerge, *contemporary,* allowing what was for a long time the prose poem and our study finally to manifest itself . . . as *critical poem*).[2]

Mallarmé narrates the genesis and the development of these twin preoccupations in "Crise de vers" (pp. 360–68). The contingency of cultural forms upon their moment (the "exquise crise" of the text, p. 360) structures this piece in a manner which has perhaps not been adequately accounted for. Multiple elements of the text express this

2. From the "Bibliographie" (1896) of Mallarmé's collection of his prose, *Divagations;* in *Oeuvres complètes,* ed. Henri Mondor and G. Jean-Aubry (Paris: Gallimard-Pléiade, 1945), p. 1576; my italics. Further references are to this edition. The translation of Mallarmé's prose texts would seem a desperate enterprise. The English versions here are my own. They seek a more or less literal rendition, both of syntax and (as far as possible) of vocabulary. The relation of the medium of criticism (Mallarmé's prose poem) to the object of its critique (prose) evokes a complicity to which I have already referred (in my Introduction, and in discussing the roman d'éducation): the uncomfortable difficulty of disengaging the discursive signifier from its signified, the medium from its object. Such complicity is inherent in any self-reflexive investigation of discourse, but here it is particularly acute. "Le langage se réfléchissant," as Mallarmé put it in notes to himself (p. 851): "Dans le 'Langage' expliquer le Langage" (p. 853). For the purposes of my analysis, strict generic distinction between the prose texts Mallarmé explicitly called "prose poems" ("Poëmes en Prose"; pp. 269–89) and others (particularly from "Variations sur un sujet," where the trope of generic hybridization refers to the musical realm rather than the poetic) has not seemed necessary. The intention to intervene in the dominant prose discursive apparatus is uniform in all of these texts. Much of Mallarmé's own reflection tending to deconstruct such generic distinctions would seem to sustain this methodological choice. In "La musique et les lettres," Mallarmé suggests that the designation "poëme en prose" has already in some sense been transcended in the internal logic of development of nineteenth-century expressive institutions ("L'épanouissement de ce qui *naguères* obtint le titre de poëme en prose"; p. 644). And it should be noted that the 1897 *Divagations* joined together the "Poëmes en Prose" with the other short prose texts—what are ordinarily called Mallarmé's "critical" pieces. Distinction between them here seems a barrier to understanding the counter-discursive functionality common to all of these texts.

preoccupation with cultural and social time: "à date exacte," "le fait d'actualité," and so on (p. 360). Thus this text projects *history* in the precise materialist sense in which it evokes mediations between the apparently timeless, abstract formality of esthetic institutions on the one hand and the denser, more socialized patterns of historical change on the other. It would seem that such projection is conscious, at least in Mallarmé's comparison (even if figured here under the aspect of difference) between this literary crisis and the social revolution in France a hundred years before: "on assiste, comme finale d'un siècle, pas ainsi que ce fut dans le dernier, à des bouleversements" ("we are witnessing as the century's finale, [though] not like it was in the last one, upheavals").

So "Crise de vers" situates *its crisis and its critique* in the specificity of a determinate moment: as the production, driven by historical time and change, of new forms for cultural expression, of new mappings of the realm of discourse. These are conceived as responsive not only to some internal logic of the esthetic, but in dense relation to its Other, to the structures and contents of the broader social discourse and to all their sustaining institutions. From its opening phrases—"Toute à l'heure," "le mauvais temps"—"Crise de vers" plunges us into the multivocality of time and of the conjunctural—esthetic *and* social— which will orient my examination of the prose poem as counter-discourse.[3]

The counter-discursive resonances of "Crise de vers" surface in refer-

---

3. If we join to the denotative level of "Crise de vers" the figurative, semantic, and etymological strata to which a hundred years of reading Mallarmé have sensitized us, the density of the text's engagement with the historical appears more strongly still. "Crise" and "vers" both resonate with these sorts of sedimented meanings: "crise" carrying its sense of distinction, of separation and sectioning within reality, and of particular conjunctural intensity; "vers" still transmitting from its origins the figure of inflection, of redirection of time's directionality. Then homonymy with the preposi- tional *vers* ("toward") reinforces the sense of willed reorientation, and joins with the larger project of "notre recherche" in the field of prose which Mallarmé evoked in the framing "Bibliographie" he composed for *Divagations* (p. 1576). With relation to "La musique et les lettres," Barbara Johnson has explored parallel resonances; see *Défigura- tions du langage poétique*, pp. 176–77. Her work provides a model for recovering the effects on other levels which sustain the denotative effects in Mallarmé's prose texts. Even the abandoned title for some of the paragraphs included in the final version of "Crise de vers" ("Averses ou critique") maintains within its signifiers the double evoca- tion (*vers/critique*) whose presence developed in the definitive title.

ence to two dynamics within bourgeois imagination which the text projects and simultaneously seeks to disrupt. First, in the notion of "crisis," it subverts what Walter Benjamin termed the *Immergleiche* (always-the-sameness), or Sartre the *practico-inert*, of bourgeois time.[4] Second, "Crise de vers" maps a complex relation (one of exclusion, of refusal) with the realm of the extraliterary, the nonesthetic—with the concrete social world. The text strives to divide what Mallarmé elsewhere calls the larger "reserve of Discourse" (p. 375) by "reserving" or privileging only the poetic. The remainder is banished into irrelevance. But of course what the text seeks to section off by that very gesture is evoked as an inevitable term of relation.

These twin efforts to interrupt constitutive elements of the dominant discourse become dual assertions of the *contingency* of the poetic and the literary. The first operates in the diachronic, evoking the inflections of cultural time; the second in the synchronic, suggesting the tensions within social space. These referents are conceived as secrets repressed within the social formation's discourse concerning itself, repressions enforced by the dominant discursive institutions against which Mallarmé's texts, and the prose poem in general, counterpose themselves.

These institutions against which the prose poem deploys its critical energy are not explicitly characterized as "prosaic." It is as if Mallarmé wished to avoid taking notice of the opponent. Rather, he allows the aura of the "prosaic" to play dismissively over the dominant prose apparatus which confronts his texts with its own infuriating self-satisfaction. Through Mallarmé's tactical assumption of superiority, the discourse of the dominant is made to seem a vast accumulation of linguistic and cultural slag against which the *poetic* then subversively intervenes.

The bipolar pairing *prose/verse* had long figured a varied set of distinctions in the natural and esthetic worlds. In the prose poem this antinomic structure becomes more conscious of its capacity to express tensions within the social formation itself. Earlier (in a text which could stand as the emblem for many such), Hugo had availed himself

---

4. See Martin Jay, *Dialectical Imagination*, p. 209; and Sartre, *Critique de la raison dialectique*, book 1.

of the older form of the opposition, in which the comparison analo-gized *poetry* and *nature* on the one hand, *prose* and *culture* (or social existence) on the other. In Nature, Hugo wrote, everything is cadence and measure: "And one could almost say that God made the world in/of verse [*en vers*]."[5] But any distinction which conceives one term in a pairing as "natural" implicitly condemns itself to passivity. It accepts a state of affairs over which the descriptive discourse expects to have no power.

For the prose poem, on the other hand, the generic distinction which the hybrid existence of the genre evokes will map explicitly *social* contradictions. Whatever valorization may be carried in the structure of distinctions which the prose poem projects cannot be conceived as natural or as given once for all time. As a cultural artifact conscious of its contingency and its historicity, the prose poem carries an awareness of its ambivalent status in the interstices of more traditional "natu-ralized" genres. It understands the social realities it takes as its refer-ents, and the representational instrument it devises to figure them, as determined, thus as *transformable*. In this way we might say that the new genre *internalizes* certain analytical structures which had animated the counter-discourse of novelistic realism in the first half of the cen-tury. It carries the critical functioning of this older instrument in its very constitution.

This is how we might understand Suzanne Bernard's characteriza-tion of the prose poem less as an "object of beauty" than as an "instru-ment of power."[6] In turn Julia Kristeva sees this transformative project at the heart of the dynamic of development, and of functionality, within the genre: "It is true that earlier texts, those of Baudelaire, Nerval or Rimbaud . . . , already suggest the mutation which Lautréa-mont and Mallarmé will achieve. But these earlier texts still remain tied to the requirements of estheticism [*l'exigence esthétique*], and their negativity appears rather as an anarchic and individualist revolt than as an *attempt at social intervention*."[7]

The prose poets had not worked out this configuration on their

5. "Tas de pierres," *Oeuvres complètes*, vol. 9 (Paris: Imprimerie Nationale and A. Michel, 1943), p. 469.
6. *Poème en prose*, p. 765.
7. *Révolution du langage poétique*, p. 617.

own. Here as elsewhere, the dominant opposition played its determining role. As early as Balzac's depiction in *Illusions perdues* of Lucien de Rubempré's degradation from lyric poet to novelist and eventually to corrupt journalist, lines of generic distinction which really expressed a structure of social power were already becoming clear.

Around the same time as *Illusions perdues,* Musset composed a short text ("Le poëte et le prosateur," 1839) constructed around a series of oppositions between poetry and prose. He took them to reflect two fundamentally different personality types, alternate sensibilities. Musset insists he has no intention to rank these in order of value: "My object is not to draw a parallel and prove that the prose writer is a pedestrian, the poet a mounted knight. I contend that they are of two entirely different natures."[8] Yet, as in the Hugo passage, beneath the objective language which asserts two "natures" the entire text reflects a naturalized hierarchization. Later in the century, however, the hierarchical implication of such distinctions could no longer be repressed. Eric Hobsbawm cites the French critic and député Eugène Pelletan in 1877: "Why do you write in verse? No one cares for it now. . . . In our age of skeptical maturity and republican independence, verse is a superannuated form. We prefer prose, which, by virtue of its freedom of movement, accords more truly with the instincts of democracy."[9]

The equation "politician equals philistine" is so ready in our consciousness that we may not grant this assertion the cultural force it merits. But the position was very widely held. It is harder to dismiss a variant of it when we find it in Flaubert: "Prose is a newborn, that's what we have to tell ourselves. Verse is the form par excellence of *older* literatures. All the rhythmic structures of verse prosody have been tried, but those of prose, far from it."[10] Along the same lines, Michelet argued in his *Introduction à l'histoire universelle* (1831) that the contemporary passage from verse to prose signaled a welcome increase in intellectual egalitarianism.[11] And if these paeans to the up-to-date

8. Alfred de Musset, *Oeuvres complètes,* vol. 10 (Geneva: Cercle du Bibliophile, 1969), p. 131.
9. *Age of Capital,* p. 307, citing E. Dowden, *Studies in Literature, 1789–1877* (London, 1892), p. 404.
10. Cited in Bernard, *Poème en prose,* p. 87, n. 395; my italics.
11. See ibid., p. 176, n. 146. There can be no doubt concerning the sociopolitical identity of the group Michelet designated as his "contemporaries." Already in 1801, in

democratic suppleness of the prose apparatus—pleadings admittedly *pro domo* for these prose writers—were not sufficient, Mallarmé himself argued the identical point in "Crise de vers": "The remarkable thing is that, for the first time in the literary history of any people . . . anyone with his individual touch and ear can create an instrument for himself" (p. 363).

The distinction between the genres was thus more than historicized: it was firmly *socialized,* we might even say politicized. It designated a structure of social power organized around the competition for class hegemony; it valorized a set of political ideals still vigorously being struggled over. Of course on one level Mallarmé was enthusiastic about the literary democratization which prose made possible. But on the other hand, the discovery that the traditional distinctions between poetry and prose (and the entire esthetic circuit in which it had long been implicated) had suddenly taken on intense extraesthetic implications began to appear clearly menacing. The emotion which accompanies this realization can be perceived in the avant-garde's insistence upon the *independence* of the esthetic realm from any extraliterary contamination. Its members refused to acknowledge that literature might play any role whatever in arguments beyond the world of letters.

On the other side of the traditional generic boundary, the phenomenon of the *poète maudit* is too familiar to require rehearsing here. Poets felt they had *been* damned. The perception, its apparent cultural diffusion and influence, thus denote the activity of a social force with the authority and the motivation to *enforce* the poet's malediction. The configuration in which such a repressive structure operated is evoked in a quip from Baudelaire's "Fusées": "If a poet requested of the State the right to keep a few bourgeois in his stable, it would be thought surprising, whereas if a bourgeois ordered up some roast poet, it would seem perfectly natural."[12] But the passage from "poète rôti" to "poète maudit" requires only that the discourse of social power diffuse

---

his *Néologie,* at the height of middle-class revolutionary optimism, Sébastien Mercier was writing: "*Prose* is ours; its rhythm is free; it is up to us to produce in it a more lively character. Prose writers are our true poets" (cited in Bernard, *Poème en prose,* p. 33; my italics). The self-satisfied, socially dominant bourgeois "we" is striking in both of these texts.

12. *Oeuvres complètes,* ed. Y.-G. Le Dantec and Claude Pichois (Paris: Gallimard-Pléiade, 1961), p. 1257. Further references are to this edition.

hegemonically through the social formation. What is figured is the transition of the mode of domination from overt brutalization (Baudelaire's fantasized cannibalism) to more distinctly modern, more subtly ideological forms of oppression and control.

Baudelaire's jest concerning roast poets has as its subtext the discovery that certain cultural distinctions had become caught in even denser structures of social hierarchization and power. The value system of the dominant liberal, republican, egalitarian world in which prose was the "natural" means of expression and exchange had unexpectedly left nothing in the literary value system innocent or unimplicated. But Baudelaire's anecdote does more than simply register envelopment of the esthetic structure by the social. It introduces a crucial—if more abstract—third party to his burlesque dialogue: the state. The state is the embodiment of the relations of power which are suddenly discovered to determine all social possibilities and cultural behaviors. It imposes itself as leading actor in the plots out of which literary production emerges, and in which the tensions which such production attempts to master are formed and articulated. The state appears as that collective, immanent presence which functions, not to mediate the tensions inscribed within oppositions like poetry/prose, literary/everyday language (leaving aside more overtly political struggles and social contradictions), but rather to impose the predominance of the dominant discourse itself.

There is a brutal gratuity, a bewildering circularity to its impositions. They are enforced with an institutional weight so massive, deploying collective apparatuses so apparently irresistible, that the celebration of the "individual" which became the sign of so much counter-discursive cultural production in this period appears almost as if it had been invented in pure reaction against the dominant discourse which the state regulated and represented. Individuals—the men of letters, the poets, the opposition intellectuals—seem to have experienced their existence as a pure "effet de structure." Their refusal of the dominant discourse almost appears designed to guarantee its stability in the same way that for Foucault the postulation of madness assures the dominant configuration of sanity. Such a vision of the individual's *production,* and of his implication in esthetic innovations that turn out to signify much more than themselves, makes the grotesque devaluation of the poetic realm in Baudelaire's "roast poet" anecdote an expression of something crucial.

The prose poem intervenes in this structure by exploding its anti-nomies and its polarizations. Barbara Johnson has demonstrated how intricate a maneuver is involved in the new genre's strategic displace-ment—its proto-Derridean deconstruction—of generic difference and distinction. Moving beyond the image of an external opposition be-tween two more or less fixed and "natural" forms, the prose poem's realm of representation becomes that of an *internal* necessity for differ-entiation within language itself.[13] It is this difference constitutive of linguistic *and social* systems that the prose poem registers, prob-lematizes, and seeks to inflect.

Because it refuses to conceive the oppositions which it represents as immutable, because it inscribes history as determinant not only in its own constitution but in all elements of social reality, the prose poem functions as a dialectical structure. In contrast to the organicist nar-rative systems which had dominated literary representation in Europe from the late eighteenth century onward, the discursive paradigm un-derlying the prose poem does not seek the resolution within the text of some set of oppositional terms which it registers. In an earlier period, organicist notions of form had played a decisively progressive role. As the first significant modern theorization of the social world as con-stituted by contradictions, as an expressive system permitting their inscription within the texts by which culture conceived itself, organic-ism can be thought of as an effort to accommodate within literary representation the growing experiences of dissonance characterizing social existence since the Enlightenment. As such, organicism is best understood as a product of bourgeois thought in its still-revolutionary phase.

But though organicism represents the social world as multiform, and thinks of dissonance in this world as literature's irreducible refer-ent, it conceives the work of the art object to be *resolution* of this multiformity. It both sanctions but at the same time requires the con-tainment of the experience of conflict. At the limit of its esthetic canons

13. See Johnson, *Défigurations*, p. 10.

it inscribes the idealist dream that the stresses of social life might be canceled in the realm of thought, that (as Friedrich Schiller once claimed) politics might resolve itself in esthetics.[14]

The temptation of such idealist positions is constant in the avant-garde prose of the later nineteenth century. But the texts themselves—whatever they may thematize about the relationship of social to intellectual and artistic life—*practice* a different vision of contradiction and of its role in determining cultural forms. The perception of social existence which constitutes these texts opens up, as still persistently problematic, the resolution of works which earlier paradigms had seemed to reduce to satisfyingly integrated—and harmless—coherence. The prose poem conceives such harmony as the false closure of dominant ideology. For it the genre substitutes a determined and positive heterogeneity which is the text's specific mode of existence in the face of its contradicted referents.

The organicist paradigm had sought to subsume the tension of the world in an oxymoron: Hamann's *coincidentia oppositorum* or Coleridge's "Multëity in Unity."[15] But the prose poem—its hybrid name itself pugnaciously oxymoronic—foregrounds the constitution of the tropes by which the contradictions of social and cultural existence are textualized. It makes them its explicit theoretical and representational concern. Its task, then, was not to contain contradiction but to *radicalize* it in representation and thereby to render its social existence, and its mode of social reproduction, positively scandalous.

Specifically, by turning the language of dominant discourse *against itself,* the prose poem devised a strategy for counter-discourse which could begin to situate the oppressive character of the dominant itself. The prose poem's critique is thus by no means exercised from some imagined space of "objectivity." Rather the locus and the means of critique are to be found *within* the realm of the dominant, but at its most distant edge, its point of greatest fragility. The dialectical force of the prose poem's practice, and the intensity of its engagement with its antagonist, proceed from this turning of prose, of its self-evidence and its solidity, inside out.

---

14. See *On the Aesthetic Education of Man,* trans. Reginald Snell (New York: Ungar, 1965), Second Letter.
15. See Abrams, *The Mirror and the Lamp,* p. 220.

Such a project carried immense risks. The most obvious, and histor- ically the most consequential, was that by situating itself at the furthest border of a dominant social apparatus while resolutely declining to cross it, the prose poem came close to rendering its own discourse inaccessible. It condemned its critique to political impotence. This is no doubt the reason why so much more attention has been given to the genre *from the side of poetry*. Usually such attention has taken the form of scholastic definitional squabbles which only the most recent work on the prose poem—notably Barbara Johnson's—has transcended. Whether intended or not, such estheticization of the genre has a- mounted to what Fredric Jameson calls a "strategy of containment."[16] For the structure of generic distinction which was being determined for literature in part from outside itself began in just the period of the prose poem's flowering to situate the "poetic" as socially irrelevant.

Faced with this imposed marginalization, the avant-garde sought to turn it into a virtue. Whence its consistent celebration of the difficult text, and its self-selection of an elite audience (see particularly Mal- larmé's early "Hérésies artistiques—l'Art pour tous" [1862] and, at the other end of his career, "Le mystère dans les lettres" [1896]). In his well-known discussion of the prose poem in *A rebours*, Huysmans (himself telegraphing the pleasure in his wordplay) called the prose poem "une délectation offerte aux délicats, accessible à eux seuls" (a delectation offered to the delicate, accessible to them alone).[17] And for a long time the critical tradition has not only consented to this margin- alization, it has positively enforced it.

A second danger inherent in the project of the prose poem might be seen as the obverse of the first. This is the genre's difficulty in repress- ing the final moment of its own status as a dialectical discourse, the moment which would have driven it over the "border" I projected

16. *Political Unconscious*, pp. 10, 53–54, 210–212.
17. *Oeuvres complètes* (Paris: Cres, 1927), vol. 7, p. 301. Baudelaire completed the implicit comparison in the following way in "Le chien et le flacon." He addresses his dog: "Thus, you yourself, unworthy companion of my sad existence, resemble the public, to whom one must not present delicate perfumes, which they find irritating, but rather carefully chosen garbage [*des ordures soigneusement choisies*]" (*Oeuvres complètes*, p. 238). The perspective remains the dominant one on the genre: a number of the ex- tremely interesting essays in the most recent reflection concerning the prose poem implicitly accept—or explicitly celebrate—such social marginality; see Caws and Riffaterre, *Prose Poem*.

above, beyond its strategy of intervention in the sociopolitical system and into some imagined *transcendence*. Against every impulse within itself, the prose poem posed a limit of practice and of ideology which it would not transgress. It remained intensely critical of the social formation and of its institutions, powerfully negative and reformist. But it never issued into the authentically revolutionary stance (save in its projection of an *esthetic* revolution) which would have fulfilled essential dynamics within its project. These were dynamics of which it was itself clearly aware. "Crise de vers" evokes the revolutionary, but only to differentiate its own mode of opposition from it. The association of the prose poem and the entire avant-garde with anarchism, which Julia Kristeva has carefully studied,[18] is closely linked to this ideological limit, as is the thematic fascination in a succession of important avant-garde prose texts with class conflict in its most openly adversative forms. I will examine this phenomenon in my concluding chapter.

Revolutionary discourse, I argued in my Introduction, is always the repressed Other of counter-discourses, and defines their functional limit. The prose poem sustained its critique at the price of respecting the ideological barrier posed, in a century of revolutions, by the revolutionary impulse itself. Thus constituted, the genre might be conceived as standing at the margin of a mode of bourgeois consciousness turned against itself all through the nineteenth century: the consciousness of the internal emigré or of the "secret agent" (Benjamin's characterization of Baudelaire).[19] The aficionados of the prose poem of course were fully aware of its dissident implications. Around the time he was composing *A rebours,* Huysmans wrote to Mallarmé: "More than poetry perhaps, the prose poem *terrifies* people like Homais [Flaubert's quintessential bourgeois], who makes up the largest proportion of the public."[20]

18. See *Révolution du langage poétique*, Book B, chap. 3.
19. *Gesammelte Schriften,* ed. Rolf Tiedemann and Hermann Schweppenhäuser (Frankfurt-am-Main: Suhrkamp, 1972), vol. 1, part 3, p. 1167.
20. Letter of Nov. 1882; cited by Henri Mondor, *Vie de Mallarmé* (Paris: Gallimard, 1941), p. 21. The verb "terrify" recalls others which Flaubert himself was employing around the same time to characterize the effect he hoped another counter-discursive attempt—*Bouvard et Pécuchet*—would have on the public: "ahurir tellement le lecteur qu'il en devienne fou" ("confuse the reader so completely that he will lose his mind"; letter to Madame Brainne, 30 Dec. 1878, *Oeuvres complètes,* ed. Société des Etudes Littéraires Françaises [Paris: Club de l'Honnête Homme, 1972], vol. 16, p. 116). See also

The problem is that, thus situated on the *near* side of the revolutionary impulse, it was exceedingly difficult for the writers of the prose poem to define clearly—for themselves or for whatever public might read them—the basis of the internal distinction within dominant discourse which permitted constitution of the genre's own adversative position while still remaining "within" prose. What within the prose apparatus established the possibility of a *poème critique?*

Distinction was a characteristic sociocultural gymnastic of the later nineteenth century. We need to interrogate the practice if we are to understand how the prose poem functioned in its conjuncture. Of course the nature of distinction changed substantially with the passing of a society of estates in the political and social revolution which Mallarmé had evoked as the predecessor of literature's own. In the older sociopolitical structure, the signs of distinction appeared more or less permanently imprinted upon the social formation itself, in the form of a hierarchy of fixed statuses. Each bore its own unambiguous signifiers. But the inception of liberal society in the nineteenth century profoundly changed the givens of the problem and the means by which distinctions staged themselves.

Citing E. H. Gombrich and Norbert Elias, Pierre Bourdieu argues that an intimate relationship between esthetic objects and the practice of social distinction has been constant since the Renaissance.[21] Yet

---

the letter to Turgenev, 25 July 1874, ibid., vol. 15, p. 328; and my *Dialectics of Isolation,* p. 82.

21. *Distinction,* pp. 250–51. Bourdieu's study is of considerable relevance to my discussion here. His approach, both empirical and theoretical, goes well beyond the positivist mapping of shifting status groups and their self-perceived characteristics typical of American sociology of the Parsonian school. Bourdieu locates socially and culturally significant behavior—taste, style, group and individual choice, etc., as distinguishing practices—in relation to exhaustive knowledge of a concrete society (contemporary France) and its constitutive patterns of privilege and deprivation, economic power and coordinate exploitation. The main divergence between my own approach and Bourdieu's (connected with his focus on the question in a period a hundred years later than the one which concerns me here) is that he tends to take the phenomenon of distinction (like that of interclass conflict) as a constituted fact; he then works out its specific modalities. On the other hand, imitating to some degree the status of the question a century earlier, my own analysis seeks to understand how distinction could arise *at all* within and between fragments of the dominant class grouping in later nineteenth-century society.

within the frame of such constancy, the problem of distinction is deeply dependent on the sociohistorical moment—because the social fractions against whom distinction was asserted have shifted substantially over time. Distinction is exquisitely sensitive to the evolving configuration of social forces and to their shifting patterns of conflict. It maps the intricate pattern of a culture's symbolic affiliations and exclusions. In doing so, distinction becomes the model for all social practice in complex societies.

I argued in my Introduction that since Saussure the analysis of cultural systems has been influenced by his doctrine that language is constituted as a system of abstract differences. But social systems do not operate in the realms of semiotic abstraction alone. Differences once semiotized inevitably take on social resonances which cannot be ignored in their analysis. We might recall Baudrillard's insistence that even the arbitrary relation between signifiers and signifieds is founded within a specific system of sociality, a specific historical conjuncture (see Chapter 1). These in turn are necessarily inscribed within the institution of any sign.

The opposition between "poetry" and "prose" might have remained abstract, purely descriptive, and theoretically reversible in some imaginary conjuncture. But in the nineteenth century it carried a highly charged and irreducibly *normative* signification. It was implicated in a structure of power which was anything but abstract for those who experienced its determinations. This fact recalls the doctrine of Bourdieu and Passeron in *Reproduction* that each time use is made of a sign inscribed with the sort of differential, hierarchical meaning that has as its source and referent a specific structure of social power, such use both reinforces the inscription of the structure of power within the sign and legitimizes the power deployed within the system (see above, Chapter 1).

Such differential structures cannot be adequately theorized with the notions which Saussure deploys for the analysis of "langue" (nor would he have expected that they could). Such abstraction makes it impossible to seize within the sign the determinants by which social configurations are structured and their contradictions expressed. That extra, *socialized* element of meaning must be restored if our theoretical apparatus is to be able to grasp the conflicts carried in the semiotization of any cultural element. What Vološinov/Bakhtin called the sign's "value accent" (see my Introduction) becomes pertinent at this point. It is through these evaluative significations intrinsic to its social use that the sign plays out its role in social conflict.

Bourdieu's work in *La distinction* advances efforts to socialize the theorization of cultural difference, to understand its semiotization. One of his most important notions holds that *any* cultural element can express distinction.[22] No practice or apparatus within a given formation can be insulated from implication in such process of difference. For Bourdieu, distinction is a *structural requirement* within any social formation. It is involuntary and independent of any individual intentionality.[23]

On the basis of such a model, two things become clear. The first is the process by which an apparatus as seemingly neutral as prose discourse could have been discovered to be an element of social struggle. It was unexpectedly caught in a circuit in which it turned out to signify something—middle-class democracy and ideological egalitarianism; assent to fundamental dogmas dominant within the new liberal social formation—to which adherence seemed *automatically* guaranteed by the very pervasiveness of the apparatus to which the meaning had become attributed.

Bourdieu's work clarifies the fact that such unexpected and logically unpredictable implication is perfectly normal. The ubiquity of the particular signifier—prose—which had thus been invested did, however, create an interesting new configuration. Essentially we can understand this *trapping* of the prose apparatus as an early experience of the process of involuntary co-optation of cultural elements by dominant power. At a much later stage of its penetration, Marcuse was to theorize this process in *One-Dimensional Man*. Its manifestations can be detected everywhere in the discourse of the dissident intellectuals in the mid–nineteenth century, but nowhere more strikingly, perhaps, than in this passage from one of Flaubert's letters to Louise Colet (cited in part in my Introduction, but worth a further look now):

> If nothing changes in the next few years, a confederation will grow up among intelligent people tighter than any secret society. Separated from the mass [*la foule*], a new mysticism will arise. . . .

22. Ibid., p. 249.
23. See ibid., esp. p. 274.

ABSOLUTE COUNTER-DISCOURSE

But a truth seems to me to emerge from all this. It is that we have no
real need of the common people [*le vulgaire*], of the populous elements, of majorities, of approval, of ratification. 1789 demolished the
monarchy and the aristocracy, 1848 the bourgeoisie, and 1851 the *people*.
There's *nothing* left except an imbecilic and vulgar mass.—We are all
driven down to the same level in a common mediocrity. Social equal-
ity has spread to the Mind. We produce books for everyone, art for
everyone, science for everyone, like we build railroads and public waiting rooms. Humanity is rabid with moral degradation.—And I'm
furious with humanity, because I belong to it.[24]

This text is characteristic of the way in which their own situation
increasingly appeared to intellectuals in the period. In it the forces
determining the social changes which formed the dominant social narrative of the period are completely desubjectified; subjectivity retreats
and takes refuge in a practically impotent fragment of the social formation. What is even more striking in Flaubert's letter is the perception of
a pervasive dominant antagonist controlling *not only* the apparatuses
which have already been conceded to mass society (the railroad, the
public waiting rooms) but the world of *culture,* of distinction itself.
This is experienced as a grotesque invasion of privileged space. At the
nightmare end of such a conception of the hostile social world by
intellectuals whose self-consciousness was increasing precisely in relation to the threat they felt was deployed against them, we find Flaubert's vision of the mass state: "some kind of enormous monster absorbing within itself all individual activity, all personality, all
thought."[25]
   We could understand the prose poem as the quintessential product
of the avant-garde whose defensive mysticism Flaubert's text foresaw.
In relation to it Bourdieu's notion of structural distinction, of the
potential colonization of the entire field of discourse by the struggle
playing itself out within any social formation, is crucial. For it helps to
explain the *urgency* of counter-discursive production in this period. In
connection with Flaubert's anxious analysis of the absorption of discursive apparatuses within the emerging modern state, the source of

24. 22 Sept. 1853, *Correspondance,* ed. Jean Bruneau, vol. 2 (Paris: Gallimard-Pléiade,
1980), p. 437.
25. Letter to Louise Colet, 15–16 May 1852, ibid., pp. 90–91.

the apprehension experienced (not only by him but by nearly all the writers whose works compose the cultural canon of this period) becomes clearer. What haunts their efforts at expression is the fear that the dominant discursive apparatuses, the increasingly pervasive and powerful languages of everyday life which confront them, will block and swallow *all* efforts to differentiate. The fear is that distinction, even signified in the consecrated and previously protected medium of the esthetic object, may *already* have become impossible.

Mallarmé's celebrated self-interrogation in "La musique et les lettres" (1894) concerning the status of the literary takes on its full sense in this atmosphere of menace weighing upon the possibility of cultural expression itself: "Dans des bouleversements, tout à l'acquit de la génération, récente, l'acte d'écrire se scruta jusqu'en l'origine. Très avant, au moins, quant au point, je le formule: —A savoir, s'il y a lieu d'écrire." ("In the upheavals, all to the credit of the recent generation, the act of writing examined itself back to its origin. Very far, at least, with regard to the issue, as I formulate it: To discover whether [1] there is any reason to write [2] there is a place for writing"; p. 645.) My translation necessarily separates out in parallel, alternative versions the strategic ambiguity of Mallarmé's question. Has the flow of our own history made writing *useless*? Has it made it *impossible*? Mallarmé's answer—"La Littérature existe et, si l'on veut, à l'exception de tout" ("Literature exists and, if one wishes [it], to the exception of everything else"; p. 646)—then resonates with a certain determined desperation. It is as if, in the face of the threat of total envelopment, the only possible counterattack is to *threaten total absorption of the threat*. Mallarmé thus projects the radical elimination ("à l'exception de tout") of the entire configuration which had determined his question to begin with and had made it so urgent.

In consequence, texts like "La musique et les lettres" attempt to establish and enforce a distinction internal to prose itself. They are produced as a direct response to the anxious fantasy of total envelopment by the dominant, which Flaubert had projected forty years before. Of course the threatened counter-absorption, really a tactic of pure denial, is transparently reactive. Mallarmé even acknowledges himself that his response to the question of writing's possibility is an exaggeration (p. 646).

For us, however, his answer measures the disquiet concerning whether a social and cultural space still existed for the production of counter-discourse, for the postulation of any distinction whatever. The sort of text in which the question came to be asked and answered, then, is offered not only as the place in which Mallarmé expresses his response but as an exemplification of it. The prose poem is intended as a concrete representation of the truth of Mallarmé's assertion. The text thus seeks to appear radically self-reflexive, self-referential, to speak of and for itself only. But even this denial of external referentiality is part of its process and is recoverable as such.

The mechanism of distinction thus becomes a principal means of mapping the interdeterminations of the cultural realm and the broader, more refractory, realm of socioeconomic fact. But the struggle to produce distinction is inhibited by more than empirical or conjunctural resistances. The defining trait of the dissident intelligentsia, of the avant-garde particularly, was its situation *at the absolute limit* of consciousness of a class ideology, of a dominant discourse, while never transgressing it. The impulse to distinction from the dominant ideology which framed their very existence proved by nature contradictory.

The numerous apostasies among these figures (one thinks of Huysmans, of Lautréamont, and in different senses of both Baudelaire and Rimbaud) are one form of evidence of the stresses in their borderline situation, of its inherent instability. But within the paradigm of distinction there are elements even more contradicted and more refractory. The critique of the dominant discourse which these figures attempted to prosecute sought to define a space of social meaning and value *heterogeneous* to that occupied by the dominant power of the bourgeoisie and by all of its apparatuses of social and cultural determination.

Such space is necessarily situated in relation to the dominant and appears surreptitiously parasitic upon it, almost as its emanation, as its creature. Its heterological status is always incomplete, derivative, or arrested. The paradox of any social distinction is that the heterogeneity sought is determined by that which it excludes: situated thus, one never gets outside. And as I argued in the preceding chapter, even the desire to escape, to find the authentic "elsewhere"—a desire intensely thematized in all of these figures—is itself perversely generated by the power one is seeking to deny. So the will toward establishing some absolute difference *within* the prose apparatus (the counter-discursive project which defines the prose poem) is inherently subverted—not least by its incomplete knowledge of its own determinants.

As hybrid genre, the prose poem registers its multiple Others, the systems against which it seeks to found its difference. But because it is constituted as a denial of their force, it cannot represent its own *generation* out of them. An analytical language figuring social and individual development, a rhetoric of process (whose growing force in the bourgeois period I first remarked on in connection with the roman d'éducation) might have represented these determinants. It could have made it possible for the avant-garde to understand the causality of its own practices. Under such conditions the self-consciousness and self-reflexivity of its discourse, which it so intensely sought, would *authentically* have been achieved. But such comprehension was ideologically quarantined for just the reasons that had led the avant-garde to define its project as absolute counter-discourse to begin with: because the discourse of process, of determination, of sociohistorical analysis, *belonged to the enemy*. Indeed, as we will see, Mallarmé defined it as the only significant alternative to the discourse of literature itself.

Absolute counter-discourse thus blocked its own self-understanding and inhibited its own self-realization. The would-be subversion subverted its own practice. The paradox of distinction was inherent in the situation out of which these texts were produced, inherent in the very choice of discursive medium (prose) in which the contestation was conducted, and in the acceptance of the contamination which this necessarily entailed. It thus came to be reinternalized within these texts. It fed back into the prose poem as a dissonance which the genre could neither acknowledge nor overcome. Its status *as prose*—as signifying the dominant apparatus even in its struggle against it—bore this contradiction from the start.

The strategies and the internal contradictions of avant-garde prose counter-discourse on the one hand and of counter-discursive re/citation on the other are symmetrical and reciprocal. The two projects can be seen as mirror images of each other. Each has at its heart an absolutizing dynamic for subverting dominant discourse. Re/citation seeks this by radically *reappropriating* the dominant, by framing, forcing, and thereby estranging its inanity. On the other hand the strategy of the prose poem might be termed "*de*/citation." It seeks a total *exclusion* of dominant discourse. It treats its antagonist in precisely the opposite way from the re/citational dynamic which I examined above in the texts of Flaubert and Marx.

The two projects seek through complementary means to denaturalize the self-evidence of the dominant and to attain the status of the heterological. But in their attempts to subvert it, both experience the damnable staying power of their antagonist: the contaminating presence they had sought to contain irresistibly bleeds back into their own substance. Thus neither strategy is able to enforce the distinction through which each had set out to contest the domination of its Other. Neither can succeed in canceling the hierarchical structure from which it had attempted to abstract itself and in which it remains inscribed.

But the dynamic which emerges as so troublesome and so urgent here did not stage itself only for the misprized intellectuals and accursed poets with whom we associate its most articulated forms. On the contrary, *every* group within the legally homogeneous social formation that came into being after the 1830 revolution experienced the need to define its value and its standing differentially. The paradoxes of distinction awaited each such attempt. I first commented on such a project in examining the calculus of self-promotion and self-realization in the roman d'éducation. But the resistance experienced there was encountered universally.

In his study of the cultural formation in France between 1848 and 1945, Theodore Zeldin examines the mechanisms by which diverse social and professional groups attempted to define and to enforce perception of their own value during this period.[26] This investigation provides for the period which interests me here a wealth of fact and specific analysis comparable to what Bourdieu provides for the France of our own period. But it turns out that all the massive detail represents the exhaustive working out of a relatively simple figure: the bipolar mechanism of distinction. Its familiar antinomies seem everywhere. For each successive status group they represent a constant stra-

26. *France*, vol. 1: *Ambition, Love and Politics*; vol. 2: *Intellect, Taste and Anxiety*.

tegic reduction of the chaotic pattern of social tension, the better to focus its energies for essential combats.

Such a reductive tendency is what makes each group's tactic appear as a strategy of opposition directed against a single adversary, against one specific target chosen out of the confusion of the social whole. It is this subjective dynamic which renders each moment of the combat strangely simple in its conjuncture. This narrowing of diffuse social struggle through the binary mechanism of distinction tends to organize the consciousness of participants according to the protocols of some naive protostructuralism.

Two things need to be said about this appearance of geometrical clarity which dominates the representations by embattled groups of their combats. First of all, such representations are inherently ideological and mystified. Because of their reductionism, they are unable to figure the determinants of their form or of the object of their struggle. But they do reflect a fundamental truth, which leads to a second observation concerning the paradigm of distinction as it operates in concrete situations of conflict. The familiar bipolar, "protostructuralist" configuration into which it forms itself *is* the authentic image of the tension within postrevolutionary social formations. For the confrontation between workers and bourgeois is the model for all social representation and social struggle in this period, and the ultimate source of all social apprehension. The hermeneutic moments of 1848 and 1871, at which the antagonisms within the social formation burst out in quite unmystified ways, became a profound structure within nineteenth-century consciousness. And such a structure, *authentically* bipolar, underlies all the varied microcombats by which shifting class fractions oppose each other and by which they seem incessantly to be rehearsing for the real struggle.

By elucidating the varied combats of competing status groups, Zeldin helps us to notice elements of the problem which remained vague in the avant-garde's understanding of its own isolation. Zeldin examines numerous class practices for enforcing distinction: for example, the necessity of eating the evening meal (however frugal) in a room *exclusively* reserved for dining; or the refusal by certain large wholesalers and brokers *ever* to receive retail merchants (who by the nature of their trade were obliged to *handle merchandise*) in their homes. These social practices express their exclusions with a brutal openness: "The bourgeois gave much effort to distinguishing himself *from the masses*."[27] But applied to this more open competition for status, Zeldin's analysis uncovers the double-bind irreducible in the contradictory imperatives within the configuration: "Do as others do: that was the level that [the bourgeois] worked up to. Do not be common: that was the barrier he had to maintain."[28] The attempt to sort out such irreconcilable injunctions understandably led to complex psychosocial gymnastics.

We have already encountered these positive and negative moments of the practices by which distinction needed to be sought and achieved. But the inherently precarious structure of difference-within-unity which defines the social horizon of bourgeois consciousness, the double-think whose mutually exclusive dynamics needed somehow to be conciliated, carry their contradictions wherever they appear. The dangers are reciprocal: if the dynamic of *homogenization* should become too powerful, then distinction becomes impossible. The menace of absorption into the "imbecilic and vulgar mass" which haunted Flaubert in the letter I quoted earlier lies at this end of the structure. On the other hand, if the impulse to *difference,* the struggle pitting the fragments of an already unstable formation against each other, were to break the bounds of a certain politicosocial decorum, then the specter of real revolution always lay at the edge of consciousness to organize such adversative impulses and to give them a terrifyingly effective model for working out their energies.

The gymnastics of distinction, like the struggle of all against all, had therefore to be contained within the space defined by these extremes. No wonder then that, with the uncovering of the structures of his construction of the world, the bourgeois—whether intellectual or tradesman, poet or industrialist—begins to look like a particularly trepidant dialectician who would happily have erased the implications of his own model of social existence as soon as they appeared. His stance was mirrored in that of certain reactionary Hegelians of the same period, who wished to retain of history only what had con-

27. Ibid., vol. 1, p. 15; my italics. On the essentially diacritical, differential function of "distinction" and of symbolic power in general, see Bourdieu, *Ce que parler veut dire,* pp. 133–34.
28. Ibid., p. 16.

stituted it to date but who denied for the future the functioning of the very energies which had created their present.

This determined structure of historical arrest may be the quintessential form of the figure of distinction in our period. But it can be perceived in much less exalted loci. As an example we might take a social choice characteristic of nineteenth-century captains of industry. It exhibits a rather scandalous resemblance to certain exclusions practiced *against* these same bourgeois figures in the avant-garde prose texts which concern me here. The writers of the prose poem notoriously emphasized their contempt for the rationalist, analytical, manipulative discourse of science, technology, and material production which underlay the bourgeois revolution. But curiously a moment came when bourgeois industrialists themselves began in their practice of distinction to express the same apparently self-denying choice:

> The industrialists . . . were . . . abandoning their support for science in the schools. This can be seen in a particularly striking way at Mulhouse [a city which had become the symbol for enrichment through industrial production of consumer goods, chiefly textiles] where, early in the nineteenth century, they had established a school for their children. . . . During the Second Empire they gradually increased the literary content [of the curriculum], and henceforth they preferred to obtain the literary *baccalauréat,* as a surer mark of respectability.[29]

For poets as for industrialists, *culture*—in the honorific sense—thus could figure, not so much a refuge as a polemical symbol marking distance from the degradation of the social whole.

The drawing of the line of distinction in the prose poem, in prose discourse itself, is problematized by such developments elsewhere within the middle class. As middle-class tactics of distinction evolved, they shifted the locus at which differentiation from the middle class itself became enforceable. They thus possessed the potential to radicalize the counter-discourse of the avant-garde adversary even if the bourgeoisie as a whole remained largely unconscious of these dissidents. But this forced radicalization had considerable consequences for the prose poem. Its own practice of distinction became a kind of *mise*

29. Ibid., vol. 2, p. 247; cf. vol. 1, p. 16.

en abyme, subject to unlimited and uncontrollable slippages, to a potentially infinite and disorienting regress.[30] Such a figure foregrounds yet again the unwitting determination of any counter-discourse by its Other. In mutual ignorance, both seek to occupy the same ground of differentiation; and their subterranean interdependence, the contamination of difference itself by the apparently inevitable return of the same, are illuminated thereby.

An opening toward the mystified social content of all such distinctive operations within the nineteenth-century bourgeoisie—of whatever stratum—then becomes possible. The repressed but constant referent of the distinction paradigm is *social class:* the confrontation of the elements within an inherently unstable totality. The subtext of distinction is a structure of apprehension and antipathy inscribed in every social act, in every cultural practice, in all social and esthetic representation. The tension which surrounds its exercise flows from this.

In such a perspective, we can say that semiotics becomes the register of class struggle itself; distinction (to quote Marx in a celebrated passage) becomes the science of the "ideological forms in which men become conscious of this struggle and fight it out."[31] In the exclusions from his dinner table enforced by the industrialist, such content was expressed in a manner less ethereal than we find it in the prose poem.[32] But it is the common ground of both. Bourdieu's work makes evident its implication in the functioning of even the most apparently autonomous esthetic object or the most apparently disinterested exercise of critical judgment. The principle is fundamental for his analysis: "*Nothing distinguishes different classes as rigorously* as the disposition objectively required by the legitimated consumption of legitimated art works."[33]

La distinction thus helps to restore the reality of this relation between the avant-garde esthetic and its social ground which our critical ab-

30. On the practical determinants and consequences of such a situation, see Hobsbawm, *Age of Capital,* p. 107.

31. *Contribution to the Critique of Political Economy,* p. 21.

32. However, as we will see below, the prose poem by no means entirely ignores it. It is of great significance that in their prose poems both Baudelaire and Mallarmé powerfully represent encounters with the threatening reality of the *other* class.

33. *Distinction,* p. 41; my italics.

sorption in the self-conception of its originators has at times tended to obscure. Bourdieu's penetration of this structure both seizes its fundamental elements and insists upon the recovery of suppressed social meanings indivisible from them. The key passage is worth quoting at length:

> In order to explain the growth, along with the level of education, of the propensity for, or at least the pretense of, appreciating a work "independent of its content," as the most culturally ambitious subjects often say, and more generally, the propensity for making the "free" and "disinterested" investment appropriate for legitimated works, it is not sufficient to invoke the fact that educational apprenticeship furnishes the linguistic instruments and the references which permit expression of the esthetic experience and its constitution in such expression: what is affirmed in such a relation is the dependence of the esthetic disposition upon the material conditions of existence, past and present, which are the condition both of its constitution and of its exercise, and at the same time the conditions of the acquisition of a level of culture (whether certified by formal education or not) which can be acquired only through a sort of withdrawal from economic necessity. The esthetic disposition which tends to *put into parentheses the nature and the function of the represented object* and to exclude any "naive" reaction . . . or any purely ethical response, and only to consider the mode of representation, the style, perceived and appreciated by comparison to other styles, is one dimension of a global relation to the world and to other people, of a style of life, in which are expressed, in a disguised form, the effects of particular conditions of existence: . . . these conditions of existence are characterized by the suspension and the deferment of economic necessity and by objective and subjective distance from practical needs, which found the objective and subjective distance from groups which are subject to these determinisms.[34]

As a *class privilege*, in the nineteenth century estheticism was inevitably deployed as such. In their battle to distinguish themselves from the fragments of their own class to which their esthetic attitudes firmly, if surreptitiously, relinked them, a mystified bourgeois *class solidarity* was thus affirmed by the avant-garde. The positive moments of the dynamic of distinction were inseparable from the negative ones. In this histor-

---

34. Ibid., p. 56.

ical conjuncture, the poet is inescapably contaminated by the merchant whose discourse he has striven to expunge from his own; the avant-garde text is inescapably contaminated by the detested texts of journalism and advertising. The paradoxes of distinction play themselves out in this cultural quicksand.

The esthetic doctrines of the avant-garde, the practices of the prose poem in particular, then appear as reflexes of efforts to maintain differentiation from the "bourgeois" in the face of a surreptitious *similarity* between the two antagonistic systems. The traces both of such similarity and of the effort to disguise it needed to be eradicated in the avant-garde's self-representation and in its understanding of its sociocultural situation. In turn, the tactical requirements of such eradication determine much of the content of avant-garde counter-discourse, beginning with the stance from which it is uttered. Mallarmé is very direct about the latter:

> Il importe que dans tout concours de la multitude quelque part vers l'intérêt, l'amusement, ou la commodité, de rares amateurs, respectueux du motif commun en tant que façon d'y montrer de l'indifférence, instituent par cet air à côté, une minorité: . . . or, posé le besoin d'exception, comme le sel! la vraie qui, indéfectiblement, fonctionne, gît dans ce séjour de quelques esprits, je ne sais, à leur éloge, comment les désigner, gratuits, étrangers, peut-être vains—ou littéraires.[35]

Such disengaged superiority is deflated in a blunt remark by Walter Benjamin. He displaces the self-characterization the avant-garde would have wished to enforce: "Among the upper classes," Benjamin writes, "cynicism was part of the accepted style."[36] And the repressed content

---

35. "It is important that in any confluence of the multitude in whatever direction toward interest, amusement or practical need, some rare *amateurs*, respecting the common motif precisely as a manner for demonstrating [their] indifference, institute by their disengaged air a minority: . . . given the need of exception, as of salt! the true [exception] which, indefectibly, functions, lies in this resort of a few minds, I don't know, in their praise, how to designate them: as gratuitous [or "free"]; as outsiders; perhaps as useless—or as literary" ("La musique et les lettres," *Oeuvres complètes*, p. 652).

36. "The Paris of the Second Empire in Baudelaire," in *Baudelaire*, p. 24. Benjamin's analysis of the tactics of distinction inscribed in the conduct and the self-description of the *flâneur* is relevant to any attempt to restore to the social attitudes of the avant-garde their full conjunctural meaning. He conceives the apparent disengagement of the

of such pretenses of uninvolvement, of such exclusive and seemingly autonomous exercises of taste, is clarified in Valéry's well-known remark: "Le goût est fait de mille dégoûts"("taste is the product of a thousand distastes").[37] The history which underlies the formation of such attitudes, fundamental for the esthetic which was emerging as the strategic arm of that effort toward distinction practiced by the avant-garde, begins to be recoverable within such a structure.

The preeminent values of this esthetic—*individuality* (or originality) and *difficulty* (or obscurity)—demonstrate the contradiction that has characterized our examination of the distinction paradigm from the beginning. In his interview with Jules Huret, Mallarmé addresses the first of these values as follows: "In a society without stability, without unity, no stable, no definitive art can be created. From this incomplete social organization . . . is born the unexplained need for individuality of which present literary manifestations are the direct reflection."[38]

The prescription of such originality can easily be understood as reaction against the standardization and massification of culture in a rapidly industrializing France. The extent to which this may have been true I will consider later on. What needs to be observed at this point is that, though usually posed as absolute criteria for evaluating cultural objects, as an intense exigency motivating their creation to begin with, originality, individuality, are *here* comprehended (in a quite protomaterialist manner) as *misreadings*: essentially as fetishes in Marx's sense.[39] What is experienced by individual creators as a pure cor-

---

flâneur—for Baudelaire an expression of living what Mallarmé later systematized as "indifférence," as that "air à côté"—as the only sustainable mode of their *involvement* in bourgeois socioeconomic relations: "As *flâneurs,* the intellectuals came into the marketplace"; "Paris, the Capital of the Nineteenth Century," in ibid., p. 170.

37. "Choses tues" in *Oeuvres,* ed. Jean Hytier, vol. 2 (Paris: Gallimard-Pléiade, 1960), p. 476. For matters of taste compare Bourdieu's analysis (recalling both Spinoza and Althusser) of the process of determination as negation (*Distinction,* p. 60).

38. "Sur l'évolution littéraire," pp. 866–67.

39. The figure of misreading here would essentially be *metalepsis*—the trope in which the relation of cause to effect is upset. A fetish is an object whose real determinations are obscured, and which therefore comes to be invested with a power which in fact derives from some other complex of social realities: a contingency mistakenly endowed by thought as an absolute. The classic Marxian analysis of the fetish uncovers the disguised determination of the commodity (see *Capital,* vol. 1, part 1, chap. 4). Gerald A. Cohen discusses the mechanism of fetishization in *Marx's Theory of History,* chap. 5.

relative of their own personal distinction, as an absolute, in Mallarmé's understanding turns out to be a *production*. The organization (or disorganization) of the social world is as significantly the author of these "literary manifestations" as is the writer himself. What seemed a value absolutizing the individual and the text on the contrary is asserted to be *a contingent effect of social determination*. A crucial dissonance within avant-garde esthetics is revealed thereby: contradictions which had been suppressed within the paradigm of distinction here surface. We need to play the strategy of their unmasking back into elements of the esthetic itself in order to illuminate the foundations of their apparent absolutism.

The deconstructive rhetoric of such an insight must particularly be applied to Mallarmé's own production—much of which, in his prose at least, is devoted to the self-reflexive expression/exemplification of the esthetic canons associated with the avant-garde. We can begin with his assertion of language's autonomy and self-sufficiency. It is this which serves as the conceptual underpinning of the entire system.

This claim subsumes both positive and negative moments which we will need to consider in succession. The former is the will to expunge the normalized—referential, instrumental—use of language characterizing dominant discourse: the moment of Mallarmé's "notion pure" (p. 368), that magic hypostatization of the *poetic* flower as "l'absente de tous bouquets" (p. 368) whose diaphanous delicacy is grounded only in the tenuousness of fragile signifiers (in the voice, in printed words on paper).

Yet such objects as Mallarmé's imaginary flower, and indeed the language which could figure the theory of their constitution, can be expressed only through negation of the dominant mode of referentiality. The use of signifiers must continually be policed for Mallarmé because the dominant threatens constantly to reinsinuate itself into the discursive circuit and to contaminate its operation. His "absente de tous bouquets," his "palais . . . hors de toute pierre" (p. 366), exist through their denial of more material palaces and flowers. Mallarmé jokes touchingly about this condition of their "existence," noting that the stones of which *his* palace is—not—built would fit awkwardly between the pages of the book in which it alone has being ("pierre, sur quoi les pages se refermeraient mal," p. 366). But the same text defines this idealist purging of all materiality as the essential tendency of the avant-garde: "an Idealism which refuses natural material and, owing to its coarseness [*comme brutale*], [refuses] the exact mode of thought which would organize them" (p. 365).

Yet the language which Mallarmé projects as *absolute* counter-discourse is still haunted by the negative determinants of its own constitution. Clearly the disjunction from the mode of ordinary language and everyday referentiality fantasized in his idealist reveries is impossible. For it projects the constitution of a hermetic linguistic system which would be inaccessible to any protocols of competence or understanding: a *sui generis* state so radical as to make any such counter-discourse theoretically meaningless. This would be a kind of ultimate philological nightmare, the absolute *hapax logomenon*. But however great its temptation for him, the line beyond which such meaninglessness would lie is one Mallarmé does not and cannot cross.

In its rejection of its antagonist Mallarmé's language continues to inscribe the power which its antagonist retains. His prose exists in the mode of denial of its Other, *but never of its annihilation;* the referentiality of his language is—we might even say—*radically* maintained. In the final paragraph of "Crise de vers" itself (p. 368), the presence of this involuntary referentiality becomes patent. A word like "refait" ("remakes") implicitly denies the constitution *ex nihilo* of *any* discourse; "isolement" ("isolation") paradoxically evokes the field of discourse from which such isolation must be sought. The social context of the text is represented—even in the "neuve atmosphere" (the "new atmosphere") created by the counter-discourse itself. Indeed this latter phrase-form itself (an unaccustomed inversion of substantive and attribute, but one composed of the most familiar words) expresses the contingence of any counter-discourse even as it seeks to obscure or to evade it.

Mallarmé grudgingly acknowledges as a condition of the creation of avant-garde discourse the existence of the referent whose discourse he would wish to separate from his own: "Les choses existent, nous n'avons pas à les créer" ("Things exist, we do not have to create them"; p. 871); "La Nature a lieu, on n'y ajoutera pas" ("Nature occurs/has its place, we cannot add to it"; p. 647). What seems distressing about the real object whose discourse the avant-garde esthetic would bracket resembles the phenomenon of reification with which a whole tradition of dialectical thought has familiarized us.[40] The concrete object—the object for dominant, instrumentalized discourse—in Mallarmé's construction appears not only dead, *but capable of inducing morbidity in its contemplator.*

The alternative to it is what Mallarmé calls "creation": the consciousness within the text of its power to form its own effects, as if no concrete trace, no fixed, dead object were thereby left behind. The notion counterposes immobility against movement, dumb existence against the brilliance of self-reflexive generation of the new. This structure is reproduced on the level of naming itself. If Mallarmé recommends that we depict "not the thing, but the effect it produces,"[41] this would seem to be because direct naming can produce the same chilling reification, the same severing of the object from its *life,* that the avant-garde esthetic ascribes to the petrified "thing."

Yet this seems a fundamental metalepsis. The semiautonomous activity out of which these esthetic objects are produced depends upon the increasing abstraction of all social life under emergent capitalism even as they react against it. In *The Political Unconscious,* Fredric Jameson considers the surplus capacity of sense perception liberated in this period by profound alterations in modes of work and of social interaction. Such capacities began to float free within the culture's network of signs (pp. 229–30). Developments of this sort define the preconditions for conceiving esthetic objects as autonomous totalities; but thus conceived, the *production* of such conceptions is strategically bracketed. The self-understanding of such abstracted esthetic objects is thus constitutively limited. They would seem more powerfully understood from outside their own paradigm as breakdown products of traditional unities and social forms—as an effort to reform and recuperate what Jameson calls the "broken bits and pieces" of older social capacities.[42]

But then it is the hypostasis and autonomization of *language itself* which appear reified: as if the avant-garde were applying to the esthetic realm the very protocols of abstraction, of fragmentation, which capitalism applies to all social production and reproduction. Reification

40. The classic text is Lukács's "Reification and the Consciousness of the Proletariat" (1923), in *History and Class Consciousness,* pp. 83–222.
41. Letter to Cazalis, October 1864; quoted by Bernard, *Poème en prose,* p. 261.
42. *Political Unconscious,* p. 63.

has not been outflanked, only displaced—indeed, it has been granted control of the signifying system at its very heart. Benjamin put this perception bluntly when he claimed in "The Paris of the Second Empire in Baudelaire" that, under the conditions of the avant-garde esthetic, "the poet for the first time faces language the way the buyer faces the commodity":[43] in the mode of exchange value, as an object so deep within a circuit of abstraction that its fetish character can no longer be figured in its conscious discourse at all.

These ideological reversals are radicalized in the prose poem. Its generic indeterminacy, its peculiar discursive uncertainty, not only mirror the play of inclusion and exclusion, of reification and dialecticity, of autonomy and contingence, they positively *produce* this indeterminacy as a subliminal signified with which the genre's hybrid status is somehow homologous. So the truth of the social constitution of these texts remains *somewhere* inscribed within them. To put this in terms reminiscent of an earlier phase of my discussion, the prose poem fetishizes itself. But in doing so it reproduces the conflicted process by which it ceased to be able to figure its own determinations—and thereby retains them on the edge of its referential horizon.

At the limit of his esthetic, Mallarmé attempted to enforce this paradoxical fetishization of the text. He repeatedly described the esthetic object as totally autonomous—requiring neither author ("the pure work implies the elocutory disappearance of the poet"; p. 366) nor audience ("depersonalized, the volume, just as one separates oneself from it as author, requires the approach of no reader"; p. 372). Thus as Mallarmé says, the work "a lieu tout seul: fait, étant" ("occupies a place/takes place completely by itself: fact, being"; p. 372).

Reification could hardly be preached in more admiring language. Since it so clearly represents one of the most characteristic moves of their own antagonists, we might have thought the avant-garde would have done everything in their power to *avoid* it. But the reversal can be understood as a measure of social calamity—a calamity so grave that it led its critic to fantasize as esthetically indispensable the total annihilation of the social. The suspicion experienced with regard even to the most enlightened subjectivity, imagined to exist in the circuit of the

43. *Baudelaire,* p. 105.

work *only* as contaminant, would seem to derive from a crisis of individual self-conception determined by the alteration of the nature of social process under capitalism.

We thus perceive two contradictory patterns of assertion within Mallarméan thinking: the one projecting as indispensable the radical conquest of individuality; the other just as radically dreaming of de-subjectification of the esthetic. And we can speculate that such perturbations around the concept of the individual and around his or her role in the production of cultural objects may derive ultimately from a more fundamental, infrastructural disorder in the circuit of social reproduction, perceptible particularly in a broadly experienced reversal of control in the work process itself.

For the first time in the incipient capitalist period the experience of historical change permitted conceptualizing the role played by the structures of social life in the formation of consciousness. With change in such structures, with their relativization, it became possible to model human consciousness differentially—to historicize it. From the time Hegel first theorized the dialectic of work and subjectivity, it has been clear how alteration of the structure of productive activity can determine new modes of experience, new conceptions of social existence. If the individual subject realizes his or her identity through work upon the materials of nature, then the radical alienation of this relationship—in our period, the instrumentalization of the worker, the apparent transfer of subjectivity to the tool—will accordingly determine a profound revision of consciousness.

Such a reversal—the sense that the world is living me—is thematic in much avant-garde writing. One thinks of Rimbaud's celebrated letter to Izambard (13 May 1871): "C'est faux de dire: Je pense: On devrait dire: On me pense" ("It is wrong to say: I think; one ought to say: I am thought").[44] And I will argue shortly that Mallarmé's "Démon de l'analogie" textualizes an equally alarming (dis-)possession of the self by the instrument.

For consciousness, such a reversal becomes the equivalent (and exhibits the inverted structure) of the fetishization of the commodity which occupied us earlier. Again, the real determinants of a social

44. Rimbaud, *Oeuvres*, ed. Suzanne Bernard and André Guyaux (Paris: Garnier, 1981), p. 346.

phenomenon—here, the relations of the work process, between its instruments and the subjectivity of the producer—are made unavailable for consciousness. The worker's activity is projected beyond and against him or her; the work of others (the previous social labor which has produced the tools with which the work is done) appears as a dead structure (Marx's "constant capital") imposed blindly upon consciousness, automatizing labor and worker at once.

The mediations between the high-cultural crisis of subjectivity in avant-garde writing and the social production process as a whole may seem obscure. But encounters between worker and poet, which one might have conceived as unimaginable for the avant-garde in their mode of ethereal idealism, turn up with surprising frequency as a theme in their prose. I will have occasion particularly to consider Mallarmé's "Conflit." And many of Baudelaire's prose poems explore parallel identifications between the poet and the instrumentally manipulated and dominated: with the poor, with the crowd, and so on. It is as if the instinct to track down the determinations which provided the mystified logic of the social formation had led these writers to such thematic identifications.

For it would be a mistake to think of the striking presence of the workers and the poor in these texts simply as the result of social guilt, as a gratuitous humanitarianism or a utopian romanticization of the underclass. It is rather an effort to achieve theoretical understanding of a crisis which threatens *all* nonautonomous social actors under capitalism: the domination by the structure in its apparent anonymity and irresponsibility which is conveyed in one of Marx's striking formulations: "[Under capitalism] it is not the worker who employs the instruments of his work, but rather the reverse, the instruments of work employ the worker."[45]

Much later the crisis of subjectivity engendered by this reversal, that complication of the notion of subject itself, was to be formalized as the "theoretical antihumanism" of Althusser, or its Lacanian and Foucauldian structuralist equivalents.[46] But the Lacanian "effet de structure" is the *content* of the crisis with which the prose poem struggled. In it

45. *Capital*, vol. 1, p. 548; translation adapted.
46. See Jameson, *Political Unconscious*, pp. 124–25. Bourdieu has traced the prolongation of the social phobia about instrumentalization in a brilliant polemic concerning Heidegger. See *Ce que parler veut dire*, part 3, chap. 1.

arises the urgency of the counter-discursive dynamic in the nineteenth century, the new situation in which independent discourse and thought were obliged to fight for space within a formation which appeared to exclude them.[47]

Anxiety attaches to any dispossession of a subject's power of speech. Any substitution of some depersonalized source of language performance for our articulatory capacity, our enunciative competence, signals the danger to the self which arose as a characteristic nineteenth-century preoccupation. With Flaubert the obsession with Bêtise flows from this anxiety; his fascination with re/citation is its textual reflex. With Mallarmé the discourse of the Other insinuates itself more mysteriously, its source is less clearly designated. At times he projects an autonomous poetic capacity inherent in language itself, independent of any poetizing will. (At other moments, he locates the production of dominant language which he seeks to eliminate from his own in the same degraded elements of the social formation that appeared as its source in Flaubert.) But both figures register the crisis of subjects who feel their self-possession slipping away.

This is the rhetoric of "Le démon de l'analogie."[48] The entire text communicates the anguish of possession by an utterance not your own: *the anxiety of involuntary re/citation*. Most readers of the text have concentrated upon the effort to domesticate the infuriatingly meaningless phrase, the "cursed words" (p. 272) which sing on the poet's lips. The effort to interpret this alien language finally fails: as if this

47. Benjamin observes that although Baudelaire apparently had not the slightest notion of industrial work, he was "captivated by a process whereby the reflecting mechanism which the machine sets off in the workman can be studied closely, as in a mirror, in the idler" (*Baudelaire*, p. 134). In other words, the dominant social organization of experience is apprehendable in its contrary; it appears *in its negation* in Baudelaire's consciousness and in his texts. Benjamin suggests to what degree the choice of the idler and of the *flâneur* was bound to the problematic under consideration here, and pertinent because of it. But Baudelaire's closest approaches to the reality of these social processes occur in the prose poems (which Benjamin does not extensively discuss). It is these texts which represent his most explicit penetration into the world of modern capitalism, into its discourses and its dissonances, which he re-situates in the counter-discourse of *Le spleen de Paris*.

48. Ursula Franklin discusses this prose poem in some detail, and reviews previous criticism, in *An Anatomy of Poesis*, pp. 52–66. One of the most interesting analyses is in Barbara Johnson's *Défigurations*, chap. 8.

experience of the irrational—this "anguish under which my formerly sovereign mind agonizes" (p. 272)—could ever have been rationalized.

The text's title itself can be forced to a disruption of its terms. They break down (as if under the pressure of the crisis of de-subjectification) into semantic elements whose presence within them they register and express perhaps for the first time. The vocable "démon" then fissions to signify nullification of the quintessentially subjective (*mon* = my) by the quintessentially privative (*dé*). But in terms of the characteristic nineteenth-century anxiety in question here, if *mine* is taken away, what is left of me is *theirs*. So what is experienced is the annihilation of the counter-discursive. And this is a fair image of what demonic possession could be said to do: to alienate my identity, annex my existence, disposses my *self*.

The preposition *de* linking the two substantives of the text's title seems to redouble this privative dynamic. Finally, "analogie" undergoes a parallel division. The incomprehensible phrase which obsesses consciousness in the text takes on the resonance of *excrement speech* (*anal-logie*), completing alienation of that supreme guarantor of subjectivity—the "words of our mouth"—and representing the mind's colonization by the degraded products of the other, nether, end of the discursive circuit through whose operation the subject is constituted *as subject*.

This problematic of the dispossession of the speaker, of the inversion of the work process, of the domination by alien discourse and ultimately by ideology, leads us back to consideration of the most immediate problem posed by the prose poem: the problem of its genre and of its intervention in the pervasive, apparently sovereign prose apparatus itself; its attempt to disclose an unsuspected fissure, a concealed crisis of non-self-identity, within dominant discourse.

To understand this counter-discursive intervention, we need to consider how the generic system was reformulated after midcentury. The genre of the prose poem refers us to the larger question of institutional disruption and redistribution which framed its production. The prose poem necessitated a critical resituation of its parent genres, a mutation in their role within cultural expression. Critical discussion of the new hybrid genre has tended to concern itself with its effect upon verse. But the resituation it determined was as profound in the case of prose. The prose poem is a counter-discourse to *each* of its generic antecedents, and its intervention signals a general reorientation of the entire question of literary genre.

What happened in the revolution which produced the prose poem can be seen as simple. There was an earlier cultural pairing, the ideological antithesis which set *verse* (clearly marked as a literary form in what Flaubert, we recall, had termed "littératures anciennes") against *prose* (which had not yet fully acquired its high-cultural credentials). This pairing was then displaced by another version of the differential which sanctioned serious literary expression. This new form was no longer defined along formal lines but rather operationally, functionally. It reflected a deeper recognition of the facts and the theoretical necessity of specialization in the intellectual and cultural realm, of the mental division of labor characteristic of a more complex socioeconomic formation.[49] So a pure literary language came to be counterposed to everyday speech, to the discourses of instrumentality. The theory of this division was most elaborately developed by the Russian and Prague School Formalists.[50]

This reorientation permitted the absorption of certain forms of prose production into the honorific category of the "literary." Its con-

---

49. On these questions, see Mary Louise Pratt, *Speech Act Theory,* pp. 26, 129.

50. Indeed, this body of theory—particularly in the rigidity of its insistence upon characteristic forms of distinction—formalizes the principles of differentiation which Mallarmé was working out thirty to forty years earlier in the texts of "Variations sur un sujet" and in "La musique et les lettres," with the adjunction of Saussure's semiotic formalism (itself a model harmonious with the enforcement of the antinomies which are the foundation of the system). The Prague School theses of 1929 demonstrate the configuration clearly: "In its social role, language must be distinguished according to its relation to extralinguistic reality. It has either a communicative function, that is, it is oriented toward the signified, or a poetic function, that is, it is oriented toward the sign itself." (*Travaux du Cercle Linguistique de Prague* 1 [1929], p. 14; my translation; see also Roman Jakobson, *Essais de linguistique,* p. 218.) The same strategy of distinction persists, for example, in Todorov's work: "Literature . . . exists precisely as an attempt to communicate what ordinary discourse cannot and does not say. . . . It is only through this difference from everyday discourse that literature can come into being and exist" (*Introduction à la littérature fantastique,* p. 27; my translation). Jakobson coined the term "literariness" (*literaturnost*) to name the distinction concisely; see Victor Erlich, *Russian Formalism,* p. 172. The devaluation of the "prosaic" by Sklovskij and others is coordinate with it. Recently the entire basis of the theory has come under critical attack; see Pratt, *Speech Act Theory,* chap. 1. Bakhtin expressed doubts about the specificity and stability of *literaturnost;* see *Dialogic Imagination,* p. 49.

sequences are of great interest here. First of all, the specialization of function—or what we might call a division of discursive labor—which such a development renders explicit has long been identified with the coming of the market system. There were now to be *two* kinds of writing, differentiated not by the presence or absence of rhyme and versification, but by *how* and *for what* they were used. Indeed, they were distinguished according to who could legitimately use them to begin with.

But a second consequence of this redistribution of the contrast is more pertinent to the present discussion. It was *explicitly* to problematize the notion of prose discourse itself. The status of such discourse had not been less conflicted within the older structure of distinction, as the contradictions uncovered in Balzac's exploitation of an instrumental model of sign and discourse in the roman d'éducation have already suggested. But in an earlier period when the apparatuses of the market economy had had less time to penetrate and solidify themselves, these problems could still avoid coming to consciousness as such. After midcentury, on the other hand, the prose apparatus was forced to self-reflection concerning its own utility and concerning its relation to the fractions within the society for which considerations of utility formed a dominant mode of thinking.

Out of this necessity that the prose apparatus *position* itself socially, the counter-discursive mechanisms under consideration here came into existence. They did so against the background of involuntary identification between prose as a mode of writing, on the one hand, and on the other, social interests (however much they may have been striving to mark themselves, like prose, as *neutral*) motivated by deeply partisan, fundamentally *differentiated,* concerns.[51]

Fredric Jameson has argued that "a genre is essentially a socio-symbolic message, or in other terms . . . form is immanently and in-

---

51. The notions of "marked" and "unmarked" units in linguistics attempts to seize the metalinguistic difference between a standard or accepted member of a paradigm (akin to an element which is ideologically naturalized) and the nonstandard or noncanonical case; see Lyon, *Introduction to Theoretical Linguistics*, p. 79. Barbara Johnson remarks on the status of prose as the "unmarked case" in standard usage (*Défigurations*, p. 37). Within such a model, we could say that the effort of the prose poem is to *restore* the marking of its discourse, to "make it strange," as the Russian Formalists argued was necessary for any literary use of language; see Erlich, *Russian Formalism*, pp. 176–79. The analogy with hegemonic and counter-hegemonic formations is clear.

trinsically an ideology in its own right."[52] If so, the interests which it seeks to naturalize will always be " 'oriented': partisan . . . , consonant with certain social interests" (see Chapter 1). But what is true of genre needs also to be predicted of that suprageneric apparatus which is the institution of prose discourse itself. The new principle of functional differentiation according to which generic structures were reorganized after midcentury became a means of disrupting the apparently neutral hegemony over prose discourse on the part of these same social forces. The avant-garde effort to establish a distinction *internal* to prose served as the ground of a strategy to recuperate the prose apparatus for contestatory expression.

Because in the older version of the antithesis the specifically "literary" form was marked as *verse,* we can understand why poetry remained the normal analogon of explicitly *literary* prose expression. We might examine in this regard two characterizations by Baudelaire of the *Petits poèmes en prose.* First, from a letter to Troubat (19 Feb. 1866): "In sum, it [the *Petits poèmes en prose*] is the *Fleurs du mal* again, but with much more freedom, detail, and mockery [*raillerie*]."[53] Baudelaire's description argues in the same direction as Mallarmé's later account of the prose poem's evolution toward the status of "poème critique." Exaggeration of the explicitly subversive, counter-discursive aspect—of mockery—becomes the key element of contrast between the prose poems and his own verse writing.

On the other hand, in the dedication to Houssaye published in 1869 with the *Spleen de Paris,*[54] Baudelaire goes at defining the nature of his accomplishment from the opposite angle. His ironic self-deprecation overlays a more serious point: "My dear friend, I send you a small work of which one could not say without injustice that it has neither beginning nor end [*ni queue ni tête*], since on the contrary everything in it is at once beginning and end, alternatively and reciprocally. I beg you to consider what admirable advantages this combination offers to all of us, to you, to me, and to the reader. We can cut wherever we wish" (p. 229). Here, it is the distinction from the older formal neces-

---

52. *Political Unconscious,* p. 141; cf. pp. 105–6.

53. *Correspondance,* ed. Claude Pichois and Jean Ziegler (Paris: Gallimard-Pléiade, 1973), vol. 2, p. 615.

54. For Baudelaire's hesitations between this title and *Petits poèmes en prose,* see the Pléiade edition's notes, p. 1598.

sities of verse—the advantage of a certain structural abandon counter-posed both against the formal rationality of verse and against the linearity of explicitly *instrumental* prose—which Baudelaire appeals to as the *differentia specifica* of the new genre.

But accommodation of the new genre implied some serious changes in the ideological system which presides over response to all cultural expression. For resistance to reformulation of cultural systems like those defining the interplay of genres does not arise only from the seemingly transhistorical inertia of social structures, from their tenden-cy to reproduce themselves unaltered, and along traditional lines. It depends as well upon conjunctural conditions which determine the manner in which literary prose could be perceived.

As my discussion of the role of the newspaper has already suggested, the competition between explicitly high-cultural expression and jour-nalism inevitably intervened in any attempt to define the expressive capacities of prose. Almost at the moment Baudelaire was working on the *Petits poèmes en prose,* the Goncourts entered the reflection which I considered in connection with my discussion of the newspaper (see Chapter 2) in their own (ironically named) *Journal.* It is worth repeat-ing here: "Our age marks the beginning of the destruction of the book by the newspaper, of the man of letters by the journalism of the literati" (22 July 1867). The cultural pervasiveness of the newspaper, this creature of the market economy—and of that economy itself, which the newspaper in its turn functioned to textualize—could per-haps be denied, but not overcome.

The facts of this penetration by the market system are well known, but a few examples of how its operation must have appeared to the writers who have concerned me may help to situate the pressures defining the conjuncture. Thus we might note that Baudelaire earned no more than 500 francs from the first edition of *Les fleurs du mal;* Flaubert got 800 francs for *Madame Bovary,* plus a later bonus of 500. Verlaine's *Poètes maudits* (1884) sold exactly 253 copies.[55] At the same

---

55. Concerning the profits from *Les fleurs du mal,* the calculation is based on sale of 1,300 copies at 3 francs, with one-eighth to Baudelaire. The fine which he was con-demned to pay on 20 Aug. 1857 amounted to 300 francs, or more than half his profit; see Duchet, *Manuel d'histoire littéraire,* pp. 38–39; and Zeldin, *France,* vol. 2, pp. 357–58. Concerning Flaubert's income from *Madame Bovary* and Verlaine's sales, see the sources just cited. Zeldin puts Flaubert's profit at 400 francs, (*France,* vol. 2, p. 376).

period, Millaud's *Petit journal* was printing 300,000 copies a day. Earlier (in 1844–45) *Le Constitutionnel* had increased its readership from three thousand to forty thousand by serializing Sue's *Le juif errant.* In response to the disproportionate sales of the *feuilletons,* publishers began dropping the price of novels: Charpentier to 3 francs 50; Michel Lévy to 2 francs; Jacottet to 1 franc.[56] In 1870, with the fall of the Second Empire, the right of *brevet,* or privilege, for booksellers was abolished, resulting in a proliferation of sales points where book trade was mixed with newspapers, stationery, and so on—the forerunner, we might say, of modern merchandising of drugstore paperbacks.[57]

So the anger or the anguish perceptible in this complaint in Baudelaire's *Fusées* had a solid experiential basis: "Qu'est-ce que l'art? Prostitution" ("What is art? Prostitution"; p. 1247). Mallarmé's reflection on the problem was more prolonged and profound, situated as it was at a considerably later point in the process of market penetration. In his resignation he defined what seemed the only possible stance of that figure we have come to call the "artist": "A quoi bon trafiquer de ce qui, peut-être, ne se doit vendre, *surtout quand cela ne se vend pas*" ("What good is it to trade in something which perhaps shouldn't be sold at all, *especially when it doesn't sell anyway*"; p. 378, my italics).

Under the pressure, a divorce from the market economy itself became the quintessential distinction identifying particular production as *literary.* The Mallarméan esthetic begins to take form in systematic exclusions of the characteristic accoutrements of this economy. In such a situation the equation presupposed by Mallarmé's doctrine concerning ordinary language—"speech" as opposed to "writing"—becomes not only comprehensible, but deeply diagnostic of the crisis: "Parler n'a trait à la réalité des choses que commercialement" ("Speech only relates commercially to the reality of things"; p. 366).

The avant-garde thus refused to concede control of the dominant prose instrument. They could hardly prevent the commercial uses to which it was being put, but they sought to develop techniques to quarantine them, to relegate them to the realm of some degraded necessity having nothing to do with literary language. It became a

56. See Zeldin, *France,* vol. 2, p. 356.
57. See Duchet, *Manuel d'histoire littéraire,* p. 40. On this and the related question of the market for visual art, see Hobsbawm, *Age of Capital,* pp. 312–16; and, in more detail, Reitlinger, *Economics of Taste.*

police operation. Because the social formation hardly divided itself as systematically as the new form of distinction establishing the realm of the literary required, maintaining the segregation necessitated meticulous purificatory rites.

Mallarmé's "Etalages" ("Display Windows") is probably the most significant text for the analysis of this process. It names the institutions whose banishment the preservation of distinction would require: *journal* (newspaper), *feuilleton* (serial), *placard* (advertising poster), *texte politique* (political text), *presse* (press), and of course the display window itself: "Commerce, the sum of enormous and elementary interests, those of the mass, employs printing for the distribution [*la propagande*] of opinions, the narration of news items [*fait divers*], and that becomes plausible, in the Press, limited to advertisement, it seems to me, [but at the cost of] omitting art" (pp. 375–76). At the conclusion of Mallarmé's brilliantly suspenseful period, the element—"art"—which defines distinction shyly shows itself, as if mortified to be named (even under the mode of negation) in such degraded company.

Even ordinary narrative prose comes under the doctrinal interdict because of the difficulty of imagining how it might be differentiated from the frankly instrumental, manipulative, propagandistic, ideological prose of the advertising blurb, the instruction manual, the bill of sale. Again from "Crise de vers": "Narrer, enseigner, même décrire, cela va et encore qu'à chacun suffirait peut-être pour échanger la pensée humaine, de prendre ou de mettre dans la main d'autrui en silence une pièce de monnaie, l'emploi élémentaire du discours dessert l'universel *reportage* dont, la littérature exceptée, participe tout entre les genres d'écrits contemporains."[58] Again, high literary culture hides uncomfortably in the interstices of this haughty sentence. Even books themselves eventually come under suspicion because of their colonization by instrumental prose: "avert your eyes before the degradation [*encanaillement*] of the sacred format, the volume" (p. 377).

So the daily spectacle of liberal, market society which will thoughtlessly go on producing its epiphenomenal effects is consigned to an

58. "Narration, teaching, even description, they are normal and may even perhaps suffice everyone for exchanging human thought, for silently taking from or putting into someone's hand a piece of change, the elementary use of discourse serves the universal *reporting* in which, literature excepted, all among contemporary genres of writing participate" (p. 368).

outer darkness of grotesque abomination: "Jaunes effondrements de banques aux squames de pus et le candide camelot apportant à la rue une réforme qui lui éclate en la main, ce répertoire—à défaut, le piétinement de Chambres où le vent-coulis se distrait à des crises min-istérielles—compose, hors de leur drame propre à quoi les humains sont aveugles, le spectacle quotidien."[59] Again, "Crise de vers" demon-strates the most programmatic understanding both of the tactic at-tempted here, and of its inherent arduousness: "An undeniable desire of my period is to separate as if destined for different attributions the double state of the Word, here gross [*brut*] or immediate, there essen-tial" (p. 368).

The difference internal to prose was thus to be enforced by a kind of generic border patrol. In the face of the difficulty implied by this attempt to sustain it, Mallarmé was tempted to experiment with a more radical solution to the problem. Its audacity was breathtaking. Under the pressure of maintaining the distinction which enabled literature to exist within the same discursive space as the market economy, Mal-larmé fantasized abolishing "prose" altogether. By centering attention upon form in the characteristic avant-garde reification of language, he found it possible to discover verse *everywhere:* "Verse is everywhere in language where there is rhythm. . . . In truth, prose doesn't exist" (p. 867). The troublesome equation was thus solved by the simple elimina-tion of its problematic term: "a majestic unconscious idea, that the form called verse is simply Literature itself" (p. 361).

But the excised growth regenerated—or, to change the image, real-ity bled back. And the momentarily triumphant passage on the ubiq-uity of verse quoted just above runs aground by rediscovering the contaminant whose presence returns the problem to its previous state. Verse is everywhere, Mallarmé writes, "except in advertising posters and on page 4 of the newspapers" (p. 867). As I observed earlier, the

59. "Yellow failures of pus-scaled banks and the ingenuous [or "white"] tabloid bringing to the street a reform which explodes in its hands, this repertoire—or in its absence, the plodding of the Assembly where the breeze amuses itself with ministerial crises—composes, outside their own drama to which humans are blind, the daily spectacle" (p. 414). Kristeva suggests that the explosion in question here was that on 9 Dec. 1893 of an anarchist bomb in the Assemblée Nationale; see *Révolution du langage poétique,* p. 434, n. 10.

fourth page of French newspapers was par excellence the locus of advertising.[60]

So the attempt to carve out a protected space for literary discourse remained futile. The difficulty of the conjuncture undid the most sophisticated efforts to produce the disjunction cleanly. And in this it only underlined the reality of an intricate *interpenetration* of the different moments and movements of the entire cultural process which it had been the purpose of avant-garde esthetics to refuse.

In the face of this attempted eradication by the avant-garde of the entire emerging "public sphere," we recall that Baudelaire a quarter century earlier had emphasized a conception diametrically opposed to Mallarmé's concerning the determination of the prose poem:

> Quel est celui de nous qui n'a pas, dans ses jours d'ambition, rêvé le miracle d'une prose poétique, musicale sans rythme et sans rime, assez souple et assez heurtée pour s'adapter aux mouvements lyriques de l'âme, aux ondulations de la rêverie, aux soubresauts de la conscience?
> C'est surtout de la fréquentation des villes énormes, c'est du croisement de leurs innombrables rapports que naît cet idéal obsédant.[61]

The notion that from new social formations new genres arise has a pleasing shape to it. But the specific functionality, in *this* social situation, of *this* new genre (whose birth *this* prefatory text announces), needs to be elucidated. Two points seem essential.

First, there is a disquiet peculiar to life in the capitalist city. The threatening quality of its social relations and of their disorienting combination of density and emptiness which Benjamin discusses,[62] the resistance by the social referent of discourse to knowledge and mastery by *any* discourse—in sum, the determined alienation of the city dweller from the elements of his or her own experience—appear in con-

---

60. See above, Chapter 2, and Zeldin, *France*, vol. 2, p. 513.

61. "Which of us, in his moments of ambition, has not dreamed of the miracle of a poetic prose, musical though without rhythm and without rhyme, sufficiently supple and articulated to adapt to the lyric movements of the soul, to the undulations of reverie, to the sudden starts of conscience. It is above all from the experience of great cities, from the intersection of their innumerable relations, that this obsessive ideal is born' (p. 229).

62. *Baudelaire*, p. 40.

sciousness as essential conditions for the internal emigration of the writer and intellectual which necessitated the complex distinctions of the prose poem.

Second, in Paris particularly, this structural consideration was coupled with a more immediately conjunctural one. The transformation of the city by Haussmann beginning in 1859 uprooted even those elements of comfortable familiarity with which easy association might have been maintained. The continual meditation on the appearance and disappearance of their city by Parisians of all classes reflected perception of the fragility of the city in relation to the tissue of social existence—one thinks for example of Du Camp's multivolume description/memorial of the capital after midcentury, or of the depiction of the city in Meryon's etchings which Baudelaire admired.[63] Of course such portrayal of the moods of the city, particularly those reflecting customs and social forms which could already be perceived as doomed, defines one of the primary impulses of the prose poem in its earliest major incarnation (Baudelaire's title was, after all, *Le spleen de Paris*).

But this depiction of what was threatened, whether the physiognomy of a social landscape or the consciousness of an individual, had a critical, angry subcurrent. Long before Mallarmé asserted that this was its inner dynamic, the prose poem demonstrated its propensities toward becoming the *poème critique*. The structures against which its critique directed itself were those of the middle-class city in its early capitalist phase, its most brutal period of what Marx called "primitive accumulation."[64] Benjamin recalls Jules Laforgue's remark that Baudelaire was the first person to write of Paris "as someone condemned to live in the capital day after day."[65] Baudelaire's identification of his prose poem with the city seizes a fundamental truth of the new genre's determination.

What appeared an incompatibility between Baudelaire's identification of the new genre with the new middle-class social formation, and Mallarmé's intense refusal of *any* extraliterary referentiality, turn out to be connected moments in the development of the genre's own self-

63. See Zeldin, *France,* vol. 2, p. 624; Baudelaire, "Salon de 1859," *Oeuvres complètes,* p. 1083, and "Peintres et Aqua-Fortistes," ibid., pp. 1147–50; and Benjamin, *Baudelaire,* pp. 86–87, 174.

64. See *Capital,* vol. 1, part 8.

65. *Baudelaire,* pp. 54–55.

consciousness. The prose poem's concept of relation to what we might call its social base had simply evolved under the pressure of nineteenth-century social reality. A continuously inflecting strategy of distinction brought both notions to expression and produced the later out of the earlier.

So the problem of the city is inseparable from the conditions under which the critical function of the prose poem became pertinent and urgent. Yet with further development of the dynamic which had brought the "ville énorme"—Paris and the Parisians of all levels—into these texts, the social stresses which they registered began to show themselves as completely refractory, as unmasterable. And the city—as privileged signifier for the new social formation which was solidifying its hegemony, and more and more effortlessly demonstrating its capacity to deflect critique—began to seem an inappropriate, an ignoble, ultimately a dangerous referent.

The movement of the social process itself had thus outflanked the moment at which the city could appear under its own name in the dialectic constituting avant-garde prose. At a certain point, no doubt strongly influenced by the disaster of the Paris Commune and its repression only two years after *Le spleen de Paris* had appeared, it began to be apparent that *the city could no longer be tackled*. To preserve the critical distinction that sanctioned the prose poem's co-tenancy of the prose apparatus while not being swamped within it, reference to the city simply had to be eliminated. So new versions of pastoral—transparently reactive, nostalgic counter-discourses—took the place of Baudelaire's attempt to represent the urban formation directly as the locus and the determinant of a cultural crisis. But the logic of determination, though it could be denied, could not be suppressed. The formation which Mallarmé's complex purificatory practices sought to expunge from avant-garde prose texts erupts even at the center of such compensatory pastoral landscapes. This is the critical burden of Mallarmé's remarkable "Conflit," which I will consider in my concluding chapter.

The prose poem thus expressed itself differently at different moments in the development of the network of practices and discourses against which it counterposed itself. But the fact of such relation, which I now want to examine more systematically, is irreducible.

305

CHAPTER 7

The Dialectics of the Prose Poem

Combien . . . tonne, peu loin, le canon de l'actualité.
[How close the guns of reality sound.]
—MALLARMÉ, "Bucolique," p. 404

The Labyrinth of Referentiality

In his 1859 essay on Gautier, Baudelaire enunciated as clearly as any-where the central principle of the esthetic developing within what we have come to know as the avant-garde: "La Poésie," Baudelaire wrote, "n'a pas d'autre but qu'Elle-même" ("Poetry has no other object than Itself").[1]

What this doctrine might mean is clarified by reference to more contemporary models of discourse: it intends to simplify the circuit which embeds the literary text by denying it (to use Jakobson's term) any *referential* purpose.[2] Such a text would be the radical contrary of a "counter-discourse" as I use the term here. Understandably, then, the

---

1. *Oeuvres complètes*, ed. Y.-G. Le Dantec and Claude Pichois (Paris: Gallimard-Pléiade, 1961), p. 685. Page numbers of Baudelaire's works given in my text refer to this edition.
2. Indeed, in the quotation, Baudelaire's term "but"—implying intentionality or directionality pointing beyond the text itself—could plausibly be translated as "referent." See Jakobson, "Linguistics and Poetics," pp. 350–77, and Ducrot and Todorov, *Encyclopedic Dictionary*, p. 341.

perspective I have taken has involved a systematic negation of this doctrine of self-referentiality. The prose poem wants to be understood as referring to nothing but itself. I have argued that in fact it functioned to inscribe the operation of precisely the elements in the social formation whose dominance threatened its own existence. This was a precarious strategy for achieving local mastery of the socially hegemonic. The mechanisms of such surreptitious or displaced referentiality need to examine more carefully.

In analyzing forms of social initiation in the period after the Revolution, deployed particularly in the roman d'éducation, I speculated on the process by which the sign came to consciousness as a discrete concept. I argued in Chapter 1 that "there is no process of institution in social life without a preceding, and determining, destitution." In the world of the conceptual, it does indeed seem as if nothing is ever given without first appearing to have been taken away. Along the same lines, I would argue that the notion of referentiality became focused just as the referential image itself began to dissolve.

As long as some unproblematic relation between word and thing persisted, as long as mimesis posed no social challenge and its mechanisms remained naturalized for cultural consciousness, the practice of representation itself hardly needed to exist as a concept. Still less did it need to attend to the theoretical possibility of its own operation. But social life "uncovers" problems by instituting conditions in which previously functional modes of solution begin to fail. Then it is as if philosophy and theory come along to figure out what might have gone awry in the areas of experience which they take as their preoccupations. This centering "after the fact" is one of the important resonances of Hegel's famous dictum concerning the Owl of Minerva.

But the process by which referentiality became denaturalized, and its concept simultaneously asserted itself, is recoverable as a means to understand *what is designated in the avant-garde's refusal to designate.* Then the eclipse of the *practice* of referentiality in the prose poem might plausibly signify emergence of the referentiality *problem* which has preoccupied cultural theory more or less constantly since that time.

Mallarmé's poetics of suggestion and allusion, his exclusion of the real "because it is vulgar," and more generally his strictures concerning the naming of the object, are the fundamental model for his effort to disrupt the process of any referentiality directed outward.[3] Yet even from within Mallarmé's own esthetic, as within the general code of *L'Art pour l'Art*, the literary object sustains at least a restricted, purposive signification: it is meant to mean *at least itself.*

The problem is to penetrate the closure of this self-conception, to expose the operations which are the means by which *these* objects are produced in the from we know them. We need to observe that even self-referentiality is irreducibly transitive. It would appear that a slogan like *L'Art pour l'Art* and the entire esthetic to which it refers assert a tautology: Art is Art; A equals A. The form of such a proposition seeks to assure atemporal, transhistorical stability; to guarantee, we might say by analogy with real processes of labor, that the subject of the relation will do no work upon its predicate. In turn the predicate—Art, self-identical and indistinguishable from the proposition's subject—is meant to remain unchanged across the copula, unaffected by the process of its own predication. Thus such a proposition attempts to evade inclusion within instrumental discourse, linked irretrievably to fundamentally economic notions like *production* and *power.* Its only instrumental purpose is to assert itself as resolutely *non*instrumental.

But in the conjuncture in which this esthetic sought to project its vision of the literary, the situation of such self-referentiality appears quite different. For even an object constituted as its own unique referent must nonetheless *be constituted,* must be produced by a process of signification which (no more than the object itself) is not "given" or "already present" in some fixed, positive, transhistorical notion of its unchanging identity.

So as a conception of the function of texts at a particular historical moment, *L'Art pour l'Art* does not simply assert a tautology. For the texts created within its protocols must establish their self-referentiality by communicating a quite different, and quite contradictory, signified: their own disjunction from the larger world of degraded social dis-

3. On these points see particularly Mallarmé's "Sur l'évolution littéraire," p. 869, and "Toute l'âme résumée . . . ," *Oeuvres complètes,* ed. Henri Mondor and G. Jean-Aubry (Paris: Gallimard-Pléiade, 1945), p. 73. Page numbers of Mallarmé's works given in my text refer to this edition. Barbara Johnson's claim that reference in Mallarmé is not denied but suspended seems to argue in favor of the same point; to the extent, however, that her position ratifies a fundamental Derridean "undecidability" of reference, it might be more difficult to reconcile her perspective with mine here; see *Critical Difference,* p. 65.

courses. They seek to "mean" this just as deeply as they "mean" themselves; but such assertion is no easy feat. The preceding chapter examined the work of distinction by which the space for avant-garde texts was created and their protocols constituted. But the analysis demonstrates that the intensely instrumental production of this possibility of self-signification entails the expenditure of considerable ideological labor. Particularly, this work takes the form of a system of repressions and transformations whose existence must itself be repressed in its turn if the fiction of self-referentiality is not to collapse under its own weight of denial.

A tension is thereby internalized within the avant-garde text. For, as I argued, its hybrid generic status acutely registers the text's self-consciousness of its own process of formation. It needs to repress what constitutes it in order to constitute itself. The ideal of the supremely beautiful at the heart of the doctrine of *L'Art pour l'Art* is achieved at the price of eternalizing this unresolvable contradiction. And the traces of the expenditure can be detected everywhere in the effort to sustain the line separating artistic text and social world.

The precondition for this tense conundrum is a world in which separation of use value from exchange value allows (and probably necessitates) the discontinuities of utility and referentiality which are in question here. Fredric Jameson puts the situation clearly: "We can think abstractly about the world only to the degree to which the world itself has already become abstract."[4] There is thus nothing paradoxical about the consequent inscription, deep within the signifying practices of the avant-garde, of the rationalized structures of dominant discourse against which their own writing produced itself.

This may seem ironic, given the avant-garde's efforts to eliminate such inscription. But to think they might have succeeded would be to give in to a version of abstraction more radical still, the notion that a cultural practice or object might simply *evade* the contradiction which brought it into being. Such a view projects a vision of the text which is as mystified as the contrary one which ascribes to art direct responsibility for changing the world. The relationship of the literary object with the real is one neither of total submission (in which the real somehow penetrates the text unchanged and perseveres inertly within it), nor of

4. *Political Unconscious*, p. 66; cf. p. 26.

total domination (according to which the text might somehow transform or transcend the real altogether). The traces of contradictions in the social world persist in the form of internal dissonances which the text can attempt to repress or to disguise, but which it can never erase. They are the determinants of its own formation. In this way these traces of dissonance constitute an irreducible element of the text's own *referential* network, of its resources of intelligibility. Ultimately the literary object signifies that which it denies—both objects *and* process of repression—because such denial is the detectable trace of its own production. If the traces disappear, *it* disappears.[5]

The chain of mediations by which social contradiction became textual dissonance can be recovered; the abstracted object can be restored to the complex of social acts and interests which produced it under its guise of autonomous object. In "La double séance," Derrida asserted that a shifting series of *relais* or transfers of signifiers along an illimitable chain—rather than any definable structure of dialectical opposition or contradiction—provides the fundamental access to the system of meaning in these difficult texts.[6] And in the spirit of such a deconstructive perception I have attempted to demonstrate how the avant-garde texts themselves problematize any simple antinomic structure (*workers/ruling-class; prose/poetry; literature/journalism;* and so on). But there is a sense in which to center on the differential structure of Mallarméan prose relative to its network of reference is to pass alongside Derrida's influential assertion.

For the significance of a text is surely not exhausted by its *internal* attempt to evade, to recast, or even to absorb the contradictions within the meaning-system upon which it works to create its own order. Mallarmé cannot avoid his texts' implication in a network which establishes terms, such as those confronted above, *as* binary opposites, however much he might have wished to have evaded such an engagement, to have defined on his own autonomous terms the grounds of any contestation.

Even the most fervent deconstructionist would have to concede that though we may put such contextual oppositions under erasure, their

5. I have discussed aspects of these questions in "Materialist Imagination: Notes Toward a Theory of Literary Strategies." The perspective derives from the work of Pierre Macherey; see his *Theory of Literary Production.*

6. *La dissémination* (Paris: Seuil, 1972), pp. 199–317, esp. pp. 216–19.

ability to frame our own meaning (and their propensity to be signified by our text production) subsists. An example discussed above comes immediately to mind: Mallarmé's abortive attempt to put under erasure the opposition *prose/verse*. We observed its immediate, *culturally determined* failure. The text is free to register socially instituted oppositions in any way that it can frame them, even by displacing their confrontation or denying their pertinence. But it cannot *not* register or inscribe them. It is in relation to this principle that the choice of prose for the Mallarméan "poème critique" becomes absolutely strategic. It is the precondition for any strong meaning in these texts, the precondition for the display of their referentiality. They cannot evade their status as counter-discourses because they engage dominant discourse in the operation of its own most fundamental apparatus.

In relation to Derrida's notion of a limitless displacement of meaning, Bakhtin's concept of the *ideologeme* is worth raising again.[7] Jameson defines the ideologeme as "the smallest intelligible unit of the essentially antagonistic collective discourses of social classes."[8] The play of Mallarmé's texts occurs within a definite set of ideologemes. One could no more evade them than one could ignore the phonemic binaries which are the basis of a given language's intelligibility. Thus though Mallarmé may work upon and transform them, the inherent oppositions of his own culture's shifting set of ideologemes represent the zero degree, the ground level, of his semiological (or even semioclastic) activity. An example would be the opposition between *journalism* and *literature* which, in the historical conjuncture within which Mallarmé found himself writing, subverted that between *poetry* and *prose*. Oppositions like these are never created ex nihilo. This one had already been broadly institutionalized (and had thus been constituted as an unavoidable social meaning) as early as *Illusions perdues*.

Within such a context, the terms of Mallarmé's contestation of dominant discourse by the substitutions of the relevant counter-discursive element are already determined and cannot fully be made new. They inscribe a sedimented history which reinvocation of the opposition between them only reproduces. However long or tortuous the series of *relais* which maintain meaning within the text, necessarily a moment

7. See Bakhtin, *Dialogic Imagination*, p. 333.
8. *Political Unconscious*, p. 76.

comes when *contextual* referentiality reasserts itself as the ground on which even the internal play of displacement can be read. In this sense, Derrida's understanding of the process of meaning, however subtle, can function in part as a subtle "strategy of containment." The effect of such a move, in Jameson's terms, is to "project the illusion" that its protocols of reading are sufficient and thereby to forestall any re-grounding of the successive displacements internal to the text in its contextual structures of conflict.[9]

Barbara Johnson argues persuasively that a deconstructive reading "does not proceed by random doubt or arbitrary subversion, but by the careful teasing out of warring forces of signification within the text itself."[10] The characterization demonstrates the pertinence of such a tactic of reading within any strategy of ideological analysis and critique. But then inscription within the text of the terms from the conflicts which inform it must surely be completed by a transitive, referential movement back *outside* the text, to designate the presence in the social world of those oppositions and contradictions which became the transformed traces of its social determination.

However hermetic the disengagement it claims for itself, it is thus in no sense reductionist to attribute to any text the sort of counter-discursive project which has occupied me throughout.[11] Contestation, polemic—these are essential horizons of *any* imaginative production, and they always entail a definite and directive referentiality. This is so because contestation always already supposes the existence of a cultural and sociopolitical nexus in which it is embedded and in which it seeks to intervene. So in the most telling ways the prose poem in the second half of the nineteenth century implicates the world and the social practices of even so vulgar a referent as industrial capitalism. The genre's condemnation of the ideological values, political representations, and cultural institutions sustaining the social formation in which it arose is too systematic to be explained in any other manner.

9. Ibid., p. 10.

10. *Critical Difference*, p. 5.

11. Bakhtin's analysis here is straightforward and useful. Having asserted the dialogized reality of *any* literary language, he observes that strains of literary "aestheticism" would emphatically deny it. He notes the consequent presence within certain texts of a doctrinal "ideologue for aestheticism" who sustains such an argument, but whose very existence within it violates the norms of the "art" itself, and thereby immediately undermines them (*Dialogic Imagination*, p. 333).

In this sense, Sartre's judgment in his unfinished 1952 essay "L'engagement de Mallarmé" that the poet's cultural identity was essentially that of the "Negator," that Mallarmé's project was to "refuse everything," needs to be modified.[12] The general bearing of Sartre's essay, that Mallarmé must be seen under the category of "poète engagé," has of course informed my entire treatment of him. Yet the structure of his oppositions to the dominant is substantially more selective, more politically sensitive, than Sartre's suggestion of totalizing negation would lead one to believe.

Ultimately the referent of Mallarmé's texts is a highly specific and thoroughly historicized complex of social control. I will examine some of its fundamental structures in more detail shortly. My purpose will be to sustain the perspective upon which this examination of the structures of referentiality in avant-garde texts has already insisted: that the *poème en prose,* if it is a poem at all, is intensely *social* poetry.

Social Poetry

Mallarmé was haunted by *reading*. How can *we* read his obsession?

> [Un infortuné] récuse l'injure d'obscurité—pourquoi pas, parmi le fonds commun, d'autres d'incohérence, de rabâchage, de plagiat . . . , ou encore une, de platitude; mais, celle-ci, personnelle aux gens qui, pour décharger le public de comprendre, les premiers simulent l'embarras.
>
> Je préfère, devant l'aggression, rétorquer que des contemporains ne savent pas lire—
>
> Sinon dans le journal; il dispense, certes, l'avantage de n'interrompre le choeur de préoccupations.
>
> Lire—
>
> Cette pratique—[13]

Traditionally, Mallarmé's anger has been comprehended—or contained—as protest against the vulgar model of language consumption

---

12. The draft was published in *Obliques,* nos. 18–19 (1979); the judgment in question is on p. 188.

13. "[An unfortunate reader] condemns [with] the insult of obscurity—why not, among the common store, others too, of incoherence, of drivel, of plagiarism, or

which valorized facility over seriousness—here, journalism over literature. Such an attitude became naturalized as a habit of mind in the second half of the century, in step with the increasing penetration of middle-class practices of production and reproduction. And on its face, it would seem clear that such a practice of "easy" or unproblematic reading would be consonant with the functioning of dominant discourse in the conjuncture. As I argued in Chapter 2, by the reading practices they induce, newspapers challenge no fundamental element of an ideological construction of the world, of that "universelle entente" ("universal agreement")[14] by which the dominant reproduces and sustains itself. Indeed, newspapers reinforce such a construction through the implacable insistence of their dailiness.

Mallarmé's "Un spectacle interrompu" takes as its founding trope the fantasy of a *counter-journalism* which might upset this self-satisfied mechanism of reproduction. The tradition has understood Mallarmé to be arguing for a certain difficult text, a certain mode of deep reading: for the valuation of that dense and powerful language use—"literariness"—which might counter the prosaic. But necessarily such opposition implicates the *social* hegemony of the dominant discourse.

Traditional understanding has marginalized the intense contestatory function of the literary objects which Mallarmé argued we must learn to read—to "practice"—adequately. We have been induced to ignore the political charge, the social stress, inscribed within these difficult texts which we now observe to have been conceived as somehow strangely contentless, as already neutralized. The mode of interpretation prescribed for them by the tradition would seem to purge them of just the energy which would have made composing them pertinent to begin with. The intensity of the conjuncture in which these texts, and the entire genre, were instituted argues for recovering this sociopolitical charge in connection with which the prose poem defined its project.

---

another, of platitude; but this one, [directed] personally to the people who, to relieve the public from [the effort of] understanding, are the first to simulate incomprehension. I prefer, in response to the attack, to reply that some contemporaries do not know how to read—Except the newspaper; it purveys, of course, the advantage of not interrupting the chorus of preoccupations. Reading—That practice—" ("Le mystère dans les lettres," *Oeuvres complètes*, p. 386).

14. *Oeuvres complètes*, p. 276.

These tensions were more evident in the earlier incarnations of the prose poem, particularly in Baudelaire. There they are often overtly represented as the stresses within the social formation. In *Le spleen de Paris,* the poor do not appear as long-suffering objects of compassion but as a social force bearing latent consciousness of its power. They are capable of inducing conflict even between their more privileged fellow-citizens. Their threat is open.

Baudelaire consciously thematized the historical dialectic around midcentury. Of course he was well placed to understand it, having fought alongside the insurgents in the June Days of 1848. His later comprehension of that conflict—traces of which appear for example in "Mon coeur mis à nu" (p. 1274)—demonstrates what became a tendency to marginalize after the fact the importance of the confrontation in which he had taken part. But "Assommons les pauvres!"—*the* prose poem on 1848—stages the dialectic openly. And the text surrounds it with a bitter atmosphere of sarcasm directed at the bourgeoisie, whose quasi-Flaubertian re/cited discourse the text's title stigmatizes. Not all commentators have registered these resonances in their interpretations.[15]

I want to note some elements bearing on representation of the conjunctural and the social in "Assommons les pauvres!" The speaker in the text is a comically disoriented intellectual, more at ease treating abstractions than encountering experience. His voice sabotages its own reliability by emphasizing the dumb stupor into which a stack of political treatises has thrown him: "in a state of mind close to confusion or idiocy" (p. 305). Something like a *class* devaluation is at work here.

The speaker's escape from his books and his subsequent encounter with the beggar induces an impulsive and hilarious mock-utopian experiment. Its purpose is revealed in two successive moments of an inseparable social action. In the first of these moments, the protagonist engages in a burlesque Hegelian remake of the master/slave dialectic. He strives to induce self-consciousness through the beating he administers to the decrepit beggar. In the second moment the social force potential in the class opponent rebounds, and the punishment is returned double upon its bourgeois instigator. With a bewilderment

---

15. See, for example, Jeffrey Mehlman, "Baudelaire with Freud", and Leo Bersani, *Baudelaire and Freud,* pp. 138–140.

which anticipates the perpetual perplexity of Bouvard and Pécuchet a decade later, the bourgeois in "Assommons les pauvres!" can comprehend only *theoretically* the drubbings given and received. He understands them only as the return of pride and vigor to his now fraternal opposite number. In grotesque caricature of an unavowed tenet of the dominant self-conception, subjectivity thus becomes defined as the power to *thrash* one's adversary. The succeeding revolution, which was to shock France out of the realm of theory only two years after "Assommons les pauvres!" was published in 1869, gives a kind of retrospective guarantee to Baudelaire's prescience.

A single word in "Assommons les pauvres!" appears not to have been filtered through the induced stupefaction of the bourgeois speaker. The unmistakable signifier of the energy driving the entire process is the *hatred* (p. 306) which registers in his consciousness just before he is flattened by the underclass. Then the grotesque satire of social harmony, the devalued dream of a certain fearful bourgeoisie no less stupefied than our philosopher and theoretician, concludes the text. But the conclusion falsely closes off a narrative which for ideological reasons could not continue to the authentic endpoint which awaits it just over its own ideological horizon. (One might almost speculate whether the position of "Assommons les pauvres!" as the *forty-ninth* item in the collection of Baudelaire's prose poems might not have represented an oblique numerological warning of an inevitable movement to follow 1848.)

It is well known that Baudelaire omitted a final sentence in "Assommons les pauvres!" It referred directly to Proudhon.[16] The reasons for the omission no doubt were tonal: a reference to the author of *The Philosophy of Poverty* would have unmasked the irony which constantly flickered in the poem's speaking voice. For Proudhon had made it impossible to ignore the conditions which produced the condition of the beggar who confronts the text's narrator. Consider this passage from his 1851 *Idée générale de la révolution:*

> When the worker has been stupefied by the division of labor, the indenture to machines, the ignorance-producing educational system, when he has been discouraged by the minuteness of his salary, demor-

16. See the notes in *Oeuvres complètes,* p. 1619.

alized by unemployment, starved by monopoly, when he no longer has bread, nor meat, nor a penny to his name, nor a place to lay his head, then he begs, he plunders, he cheats, he steals, he kills. . . . Is this clear enough?[17]

Indeed, it is far *too clear*—which is why Proudhon's lesson about the *reality* of poverty and its determination by the practices of the dominant class had to be avoided by suppressing his name at the conclusion of "Assommons les pauvres!" Baudelaire's prose poems can thematize the conflict of the classes, but not *that* openly. Referentiality, we sense, is beginning to be problematic.

An earlier piece in Baudelaire's collection, "Les yeux des pauvres," expresses the propagation of this stress more obliquely, but with consequences no less dire. The text recounts a misunderstanding between two middle-class lovers who encounter the "disadvantaged" while they are out for a drink. Confronting the destitute father and his children, the male speaker experiences a vague feeling of shame at the difference in what the nineteenth century would have called their respective class "conditions." And naively he seeks in the eyes of his beloved the reflection, the confirmation, of his own social guilt. But his mistress is only exasperated by the poor, by the representation of social tension which in their presence could hardly be suppressed. So the class difference between bourgeois and proletarian is displaced. It transforms itself into a lovers' quarrel. We can interpret the process as the propagation through the social formation of inequalities which surface in the divided consciousness of the dominant class itself, in an intraclass conflict which destroys the harmony of the day and the pleasure of privilege.

The third of the poems in *Le spleen de Paris* which overtly textualizes social tension by inscribing the poor in their titles ("Le joujou du pauvre") renders the confrontation all the more naked by staging it as the encounter of two children incapable of articulating the symbolic and the politico-economic distance which separates them as definitely as the "symbolic bars separating two worlds" (p. 256) that the text explicitly names. The final sentence resonates with particular bitterness: "And the two children laughed fraternally at each other, showing

17. Cited by Louis Chevalier, *Classes laborieuses,* p. 324.

teeth of an *equal* whiteness" (p. 256; Baudelaire's italics). The parody of the most famous of revolutionary slogans, the italicization of *equal* and its consequent ironic deconstruction, inscribe the potentiality of social conflict, the *reality of inequality,* in a representation of class relations which the text understands all the more powerfully because it is ideologically incommunicable for the actors themselves.

Such are a few of the more explicit representations in the *Petits poèmes en prose* of the struggle which invests not only the social formation but all of its discourses, all of its languages. It is present in more microscopic loci. In an acute exegesis in *Défigurations du langage poétique,* Barbara Johnson considers the presence within Baudelaire's prose "Invitation au voyage" of the curious notion of a "poetic cuisine." Her purpose is to deepen her deconstruction of the generic play which engenders the prose poem's own possibility.[18] But a different subresonance of this unexpected attribution of the term "poetic" to the culinary realm may equally well be disengaged. We note the surprising repetition within the first three paragraphs of the text of a series of adjectives characterizing the fantasyland to which the poet is extending his invitation. The string echoes twice, once on either side of the strange trope which Johnson so strikingly unpacks: "un vrai pays de Cocagne, où tout est *beau, riche, tranquil et honnête*" ("a true land of plenty where everything is *beautiful, luxurious, tranquil and honest*"); and "il est une contrée qui te ressemble, où tout est *beau, riche, tranquil et honnête*" (there is a land which resembles you, where all is *beautiful, luxurious, tranquil and honest;* italics mine).

What is evoked by this repetition in the course of a fantasy is the reality against which the fantasy counterposes itself. For example, the reduplicated presence of "honnête" produces by its very insistence a spectrum of virtual contraries like "mesquin" ("shabby," "mean," "stingy"), which help situate the dystopia against which this utopia sought to generate its counter-discourse. Then it begins to become clear why "poetic" cuisine becomes the object of fantasized desire—or rather, to what sort of conjunctural deficiency it represents the imaginary solution. The bourgeois social formation and its deformations

18. See *Défigurations,* chap. 5. "L'invitation au voyage" is in *Oeuvres complètes,* pp. 253–255. The passages discussed here are on p. 253.

come into focus as the absent determinants, as the specific forms of the plague to be fled by taking this trip.

To suggest the logic of such a contrast with the "culinary poetry" of this fantasized "pays de Cocagne," let us compare another text:

> The French chemist, Chevallier, in his treatise on the "sophistications" of commodities, enumerates, for many of the 600 or more articles he passes in review, 10, 20, 30 different methods of adulteration. He adds that he does not know all the methods, and does not mention all that he knows. He gives 6 kinds of adulteration of sugar, 9 of olive oil, 10 of butter, 12 of salt, 19 of milk, 20 of bread, 23 of brandy, 24 of meal, 28 of chocolate, 30 of wine, 32 of coffee, etc. . . .
>
> The adulteration of bread, and the formation of a class of bakers who sell bread for less than its full price, are developments which have taken place . . . since the beginning of the eighteenth century, i.e. as soon as the corporate character of the trade was lost, and the capitalist stepped behind the nominal master baker in the shape of a miller or a flour factor [broker].

This passage from the first volume of *Capital* (pp. 358–61) describes an unpoetic state of affairs indeed. The dialogic content latent in the repeated string of adjectives in Baudelaire's text begins to clarify itself in the conjuncture whose culinary habits—or perversions—are unmasked thereby.[19] Historicized, Baudelaire's fantasy seems less random or capricious; it begins to become readable. The charge upon its vocabulary makes possible an analysis of the tensions and conflicts which are coded so intimately within it that we might risk overlooking or dehistoricizing them altogether.

Still, the symmetrical structure of the dialogical in Baudelaire's writing, like the explicit representation of bipolar social stress, remains relatively unmystified. Such a network of antinomies propagates through the representational system of this self-proclaimed *homo duplex* (p. 658). And the whole associated complex of Baudelairean oxy-

19. Louis Chevalier discusses the significance of variations in the price and quality of bread for the maintenance (or disturbance) of social order in Paris in the period which concerns me here; see *Classes laborieuses,* pp. 315–21. And from another family of texts, we might recall the astonishing analysis of what by contrast with Baudelaire might be termed the "cuisine prosaïque" in Balzac: in Madame Vauquer's pension in *Le Père Goriot;* in Flicotteaux's restaurant in *Illusions perdues,* etc.

moronic structures[20]—the ambiguous postulation toward Satan and God (p. 1277); the "thyrse" which in its doubleness becomes the generically undecidable analogue of the prose poem itself (pp. 284–85)[21]— all register the existence of a relatively open conflict, at a stage which precedes its neutralization in the defensive protocols of dominant ideology.

Overtly thematized representation of conflict in Baudelaire is consonant with the presence of conflict in other elements of the prose poem's discursive system. It is important because it gives access to a fundamental dynamic while it is still visible as such. But the possibility of such thematic clarity was not to last long. The evolution followed subsequently by the prose poem seems to parallel that in other genres, and for parallel reasons. For example the explicit thematization of social stress in, say, Balzac, transmutes into the ubiquity of an internalized atmospheric tension in Flaubert whose sources (because they are dethematized) are unclear but whose propagation through the entire fabric of representation is the indispensable mark of this later writing. The passage from Baudelaire to Mallarmé is similar.

By the moment of Mallarmé, the oppositions so clear in Baudelaire will have tended for the most part to become more disseminated, more obscurely registered. Their interpretation will require a "practice of reading" which can track down social contents despite their disguise, displacement, or transformation.[22]

Even these more subtle inscriptions still remain accessible to decoding in the light of the dialogic structures active in the conjuncture. This is how we can understand Kristeva's observation that Mallarmé's "musical" metaphors (which for him had the value of distinguishing poetic language) radically counterpose themselves against the "*oratio* parlementaire*."[23] For this latter is the discourse which figures essential prosaic utterance—degraded both owing to its etymological resonance of exclusively instrumental speech (*oration,* from Latin "to pray or plead"), and because, along with all politics, the avant-garde experienced it as mystification or as cacophony. The opposition between the

---

20. See Johnson, *Défigurations,* pp. 59–61.
21. See Johnson's analyses in ibid., chaps. 3, 7.
22. Compare the passage in "Le mystère dans les lettres," *Oeuvres complètes,* p. 386, quoted earlier.
23. See *Révolution du langage poétique,* p. 402.

poetics of suggestion and the practice of literal denomination can be comprehended similarly. The referential delicacy prescribed in avant-garde poetics marks differentiation from a dominant discourse characterized by overbearing confidence concerning referentiality, by a sense of nonproblematic adequacy to instrumental language use. If, as seemed true, the language of the dominant controlled reality, in response the avant-garde would simply decline to refer to it at all.

These two examples begin to map a fundamental split within the codes of Mallarmé's representational system. He puts it clearly in "Magie": "Il n'existe d'ouvert à la recherche mentale que deux voies, en tout où bifurque notre besoin, à savoir l'esthétique d'une part et aussi l'économie politique." ("There exist open to mental research only two paths, in all, where our desire bifurcates, that is, esthetics on one side, and also political economy"; p. 399). This complex distinction resonates in a number of directions.[24]

One of the most important of these resonances counterposes the instrumental precision of political economy—what with Marx we might call the science of capitalism—against the poetic domain, which, I am arguing here, is close to being *capitalism's counter-discourse*. It defines itself contrastively as a realm of mystery and evokes the aura surrounding the fragility and the gratuity of the Beautiful. Consider this characterization of money from "Or": "Le numéraire, *engin de terrible précision,* net aux consciences" ("specie, *a mechanism of awful precision,* clear for consciousness"; p. 398; my italics). Money is conceived here as the quintessence and privileged signifier of the precision tool, and beyond it of the entire industrial apparatus. But however precise or powerful, such an instrument cannot manufacture "the fantasmagoric Sunsets when alone the clouds collapse" (p. 398). Poetry alone produces these and makes them available for circulation.

The question of utility thus comes to stand as the criterion around which a structure of distinction—what we can now identify as a fundamental ideologeme of the later nineteenth century—establishes itself. For this was not simply Mallarmé's problem. It was a contradiction

24. Compare, from "La musique et les lettres," "The whole divides into [*se résume dans*] Esthetics and Political Economy" (*Oeuvres complètes,* p. 656). My discussion is complemented by that of Barbara Johnson, *Défigurations,* chap. 5 ("L'économie de la poésie"), pp. 132–39; and by that of Bonnie J. Isaac, "'M'introduire dans ton histoire,'" chap. 4.

which propagated through consciousness and social discourse and which invested the language of process with its dialogic tensions. Consider François Arago's well-known expostulation (1837): "It is not with fine words that one manufactures beet sugar."[25]

Zeldin goes on to consider how, in the reigning atmosphere of a campaign for the instrumentalization of the social field, early capitalist France dealt with the polarization between languages of "precision" and of "evocation," between the practical and the poetic. He recounts how Duruy, Napoléon III's minister of public instruction, attempted to reform the lycée curricula by diminishing the role of theory in what students were to learn: "No metaphysics, no abstraction: let the word concrete be held in honour."[26] So the impulse to "evocation," and indeed the whole range of textual dynamics which we have seen constituting the paradigms of the avant-garde, cannot be conceived as self-generating, as autonomous. In however uncomfortable a way, they were determined by their contrary. The structure of distinction organizing these texts thus reaches outside of them to inscribe, by reversal, dominant ideology's valuation of the term which avant-garde writing so insistently depreciates.

The avant-garde thus rewrote the social world in defense of a threatened mode of conceiving it. But like all such reversals of social facts attempted in the world of words, the operation inevitably breaks down. The logic of Mallarmé's division of the "reserve of Discourse" between poetry on the one hand and political economy on the other would seem to have been that they invoke, each on its own side, fundamental and crucially distinct paradigms of human *production*. Thought of in this light, they become comparable and counterposable; they seem to stand, as we might say, on equal terms. And to that extent, each may legitimately seek the reconception in its own mode of the world mastered by the discourse of the other.

But from the side of poetry, this operation collapsed when the effort was made to inscribe the circuits of *exchange* into the paradigm of *production* (human, esthetic on the one hand; economic, instrumental on the other). Such attempted prolongation of the encounter between the paradigms brings to light a scandalous inadequacy of communication in the literary realm compared with the economic. In the face of

25. Cited by Zeldin, *France*, vol. 2, p. 243.
26. Ibid., pp. 248–49.

the well-ordered functionality of exchange in the market system, in the face of the *numéraire* and its brilliant precision, in the face of political economy as it operates with an apparently increasing effortlessness in an apparently growing fraction of the divided world of social consciousness, the prose poem encounters the shock that, outside of this regulated and totally rationalized realm, communication appears to function very badly.

Mallarmé puts this clearly: "a contact can, I fear, not establish itself between people" (p. 358); or "two people have perhaps . . . never conversed for the length of several words about exactly the same object" (p. 408); or "the best of what passes between two people always escapes them, insofar as they are interlocutors" (p. 411). The projected confrontation of discursive paradigms, of poetry and political economy, thus reveals itself as deeply unequal. On terrain which turns out to be that of its opponent, situated irretrievably in relation to the social world which frames the mode of its production, poetry awkwardly seeks its justification.

The line to follow in the face of this failure of the poetic has already been suggested: it is to draw back the defenses of would-be noninstrumental language to territory more easily protected, that of the individual text—written, not spoken; mediated, not immediate; gratuitous, not instrumentalized. The literary object is thus *abstracted* from the network in which it might circulate. Such abstraction, undertaken in defense, proves damaging nonetheless. The tactic leads in a direction we have examined: it ends up by prescribing the total desocialization of the language object—by promoting reification.

In a grotesque sublation, the logic of the counter-discourse thus rejoins and is absorbed by its antagonist at the heart of the antagonist's power, and on his terms. The attempt had been to situate the word—in poetry—as the quintessential noncommodifiable element of the social world. But it leads to the discovery that the word can then be exchanged only with the gravest difficulty, and finally, in a terrifying and paradoxical reversal, that it becomes, in its reification, the ultimate symbol, the nightmare representation, of the commodity itself: an object with *no use value whatever*.

For readings such as I have been attempting here, Mallarmé's "Conflit" appears a crucial text. I have already suggested how social stress invades the bucolic setting of the abandoned house in the country which is its locus. What needs to be examined now is the thematized encounter with the working class itself: Mallarmé's pendant to "Assommons les pauvres!" about thirty years later, and trailing behind it a certain atmosphere of the aftermath of the Commune.

The striking thing about this confrontation with the proletariat is that it *changes* something significant. It has the atmosphere of a *conversion* ("Je fus pris de religion" ["I was struck with religion"; p. 356]). As the intervention of the contextual into the text and into the ideological system which sustains it, "Conflit" registers a moment of referentiality as intense as any in Mallarmé's writing. In it the esthetic of the autonomous object comes under considerable stress.

"Conflit" is thus a text of transformations. These occur not only in the inner concept ("idée") of the artist's relation to realities beyond his own esthetic existence, which he had thought exempted from any conjunctural "accident" (p. 355), but in transformations of the socioeconomy and of the landscape, of the atmosphere of a place of substantial importance to him, and ultimately of social relations in the broadest sense. The forces mediating this complex of change are themselves complex. What is striking is the degree to which they depend upon the movement of the social itself.

The agent of change is the railroad—that quintessence of the evolving capitalist economy, both as means of investment, and as a medium of circulation and distribution. The extension of the railroad figures the penetration of the system beyond its centers, the conquest of the periphery, which is capitalism's law of development. "Progress," the colonization of the countryside, is what turns the abandoned house where the poet had been accustomed to finding refuge into a cacophonous worker's "tavern" (p. 355). Without such infrastructural change the encounter would never have taken place: the workers would never have been there, the pastoral would never have been invaded. (Of course, without such change there would never have been a working class for the poet to encounter—or, indeed, a middle-class poet to encounter it.)

Suddenly, though, the classes *are* thrown together, and the effort in the text is first to displace the normal discourse in which such a confrontation might be figured. Thus class identity becomes a problem.

For the workers, the poet is necessarily a bourgeois. What else could he be: for they know by looking that he is not one of them. There is a strange sublimation in the text's depiction of the scene—nothing ever really happens, and in characteristic Mallarméan fashion what occurs is conducted purely in the realm of imagination. Yet the peculiar conditions of the encounter are nonetheless motivated vigorously and unexpectedly by the real. The argument over class identity proceeds indirectly. From the window above, the poet overhears the workers: "'Yes, the bourgeois,' I hear, hardly involved at all, 'want a railroad.' 'Not me, anyway'" (p. 358). The poet's refusal of bourgeois status is explicit and even prideful. He feels himself moved by what he calls "some singular instinct to possess nothing" (p. 357)—a status as odd as that of poet, and perhaps indistinguishable from it. It appears that such a distinction needed obstinately to be insisted upon, as if bourgeois acquisitive desires were a microbe which might infect you if your vigilance faltered.

The relation to work also becomes problematic in the oblique colloquy of this text—silent on the part of the speaking voice, boisterous on that of his proletarian interlocutors. With a trace of familiar middle-class guilt, the poet imagines telling the laborers that he too may be considered a worker: "'Peut-être moi, aussi, je travaille'" ("'Perhaps I [might be said to] labor also'"; p. 358). He even imagines that they might have taken a man of his class, dressed as we must imagine him to be dressed, as somehow involved in the labor process (an accountant? a middle manager?): reflexes of the modern structures of production ("general exchange," p. 358).

Yet the gambit of fantasizing identification with their mode of social activity aborts. Unlike some free play of purely mental signifiers, the difference of which the represented workers are aware here firmly resists deconstruction. Try as he may to sublate it or to displace it, *this* clash reads out *only* as "conflict." It remains irreducible. The poet takes no part in "general exchange"; for him work is "a scourge" (p. 358) which exhausts the men who strew themselves on the ground below his window. He stands, contemplates, reflects, almost as if he believed that only his own subjectivity guaranteed that the scene and its proletarian *dramatis personae* had any substance at all.

Yet on another level there is something comparable in the oblivion sought by these railway laborers and the poet's attempt to find some quiet in this pastoral setting, some relief from the stresses of the city. The sorts of fatigues they experience are very different, but all here are simply trying to get some rest. Thus what occurs is a complex and awkward *rapprochement*. The poet's instinct for alienation from this complex of social forces which name themselves "progress"—an alienation which he has *worked* at producing—is also what brings him, as he puts it, closer to the proletarians ("me rapproche, selon que je me fis, de prolétaires"; p. 357).

Nonetheless, despite such a fraternal coming-together of poet and worker in opposition to the bourgeois force which dominates the social formation, group fusion is far from the desire of anyone in this text, far too from the possibilities inherent in the configuration itself. One of the workers who sees the poet at the window screams an insult. The poet plausibly fantasizes that a brawl might break out between them (p. 357). The threat here is very real. And it would be a mistake to attempt to elide the tension represented. For this text is dealing with *explosive* material. The hostile atmosphere of "Assommons les pauvres!" has by no means evaporated.

Lexical elements like "ressentiment," "animosité," "violemment," which appear within "Conflit," are only comprehensible in relation to a structure which situates the conflict between these individuals as one transcending their individuality. Their battle is not for control of an abandoned house where they desire to spend a few hours. Rather, this local and trivial conflict really refers to the epochal struggle which invests *every* interclass contact, every social meaning, every linguistic object with its tension.

The poet characteristically registers this contextual determination as a restraint upon his freedom to manipulate representation of the scene: "Très raide, il [one of the laborers] me scrute avec animosité. Impossible de l'annuler, mentalement" ("Very tensely, he scrutinizes me with hostility. [It is] impossible imaginatively to cancel him out"; p. 357). The worker kicks the fence (we recall the one in "Le joujou du pauvre") and thereby marks the division of a social space which has no third compartment where even a well-intentioned poet and his antibourgeois counter-discourses might take refuge. The bipolarity of such space positions all within it in a configuration beyond their own intentions. This violence has no individual basis: "je ne mesure, individu à individu, de différence" ("between us as individuals I detect no difference"; p. 357). The *conjuncture* determines this conflict and generates its inescapable configuration.

Thus the text discovers despite itself the irreducibility of meanings socially invested; thus the conversion which it began by registering with astonishment inscribes itself as the discovery that *class conflict* is a fundamental structure within consciousness. Indeed the phrase is present in the text in so many words: "la lutte des classes" (p. 357). Mallarmé knows the language in which this social action is figured because in his period such discourse was pertinent to a situation of great stress, perceived by everyone who lived it. Though somehow alien to the "poetic" fraction of the world, such language is perfectly at home in prose. And as such it comes to inhabit this prose text which takes as its purpose to explore the intersection of the two discursive continents. "Camarades," he imagines crying (p. 356): "comrades."27 Yet a very palpable sense of menace persists.

So we arrive at what appears an impasse, at an antinomy: the posing within a narrative configuration of a tension which none of the forces in presence can possibly overcome. Yet as Benjamin had argued with reference to Baudelaire's own antinomic structures of consciousness, such oppositions within a totality are always "the figurative appearance of the dialectic, the law of the dialectic at a standstill."28 The psychosocial impasse which "Conflit" narrates, the apparent textual aporia which leaves its denouement perpetually pending, represents an arrested dialectical formation. But the traces of its prolongation and possible completion are to be found—however displaced—in the very

27. This heavily charged word appears also in "Confrontation" and in "Action restreinte" (*Oeuvres complètes,* pp. 409, 369). Its political sense inevitably floats on the edge of Mallarmé's ambiguous usage, yet the word can always be taken neutrally if one wishes to avoid its full resonances. For his part Baudelaire explicitly refers to communism, though only in his personal works (see "Mon coeur mis à nu," *Oeuvres complètes,* pp. 1289, 1291, 1292). To understand the dialogical burden of any of these references, we need to recall that the period of the prose poem's genesis was equally one of intense working-class political activity: the time of Blanqui (who died in 1881 but left an active following) and Guesde; and of course the period of the Commune and its aftermath. The Party of Socialist Workers was formed in France in 1879 and adopted the strategy of the General Strike in 1892. On the evolution of the movement, see Zeldin, *France,* vol. 2, pp. 331ff.; Wolfgang Abendroth, *Short History of the European Working Class;* and David Caute, *The Left in Europe.*

28. *Baudelaire,* p. 171.

language of social conflict which the text admits—however tentatively—into itself. This historical stress, so delicately maintained, works its way nonetheless toward some form of resolution.

What is striking in the social material confronted in "Conflit" (in its unexpected place at the opening of the nominally musical, lyrical "Variations sur un sujet") is the struggle between the attempt to seize with sympathy the social force represented by the workers, and on the other hand certain strategies of containment which displace this perception. Admiration is what expresses itself near the end of the text: "These artisans of elemental tasks, I am free [*il m'est loisible*], looking over them, by the side of a flowing limpid stream, to conceive in them [*d'y regarder*] the people—a robust knowledge of the human condition bends their backs daily to produce, without the intermediary of grain, the miracle of life which assures presence" (p. 359).

Yet this lyricism and this sympathy encounter dynamics within the expressive system which deflect them. These dynamics resituate the relationship projected in the movement of sympathy, and recuperate it in controllable forms. Among the elements which function in this way is the vision of the laborers as an "aveugle troupeau" ("A blind herd"; p. 359), thanks to the superior position at the window overlooking them which the poet holds by virtue of his *social* situation; or the existence of the fence around the property which segregates the classes as long as the poet does not challenge the workers directly; and most significantly the transformation of the authentically dialectical language capable of articulating "la lutte des classes" (p. 357) into a traditionalizing Catholic rhetoric which recalls the reformism of Michelet. This rhetoric—this ideology—views and controls the antagonist not as the proletariat, the working class, but as "le peuple" (p. 359).

Elsewhere Mallarmé deprecates the language which might have comprehended the social totality whose contradictions surface in "Conflit." For example, in "Sauvegarde": "Society, the hollowest term . . . , is valuable and comfortable at least because, since nearly nothing [of it] exists in fact, to speak about it is the same as treating no subject at all or diverting oneself by remaining silent" (p. 419). But "Conflit" encounters an energy which such dismissive strategies cannot fully cancel. An opening of language, of form, to the social referent clarifies itself. But simultaneously, against its own central insights, the expressive system of avant-garde prose contradictorily argues for the neutralization of any such referentiality. Its evocative and instrumental impulses struggle as fundamentally—and as indecisively—as the classes confronting each other in "Conflict."

But the desegregation of these two discursive dynamics, their interpenetration—the *breakdown* in the structure of hermetic distinction which we have examined—is what constitutes the prose poem to begin with. To read it is to read *beyond* the contradiction through which it denies the conditions of its own production. And once we begin looking, the instrumental language of the market, the analytical language of political economy, the language of dominant *prose,* flows constantly back to occupy a significant part of the poetic domain.

The separation of its language from the practical, instrumental world formed a necessary element in the strategy of distinction which the avant-garde attempted to enforce. It was crucial to its self-conception. We have seen how politics in any form (symbolized by the parliamentary oration) was posed as the inadmissible. Thus Lautréamont: "[poetry] does not mix with political events."[29] Thus Mallarmé at the height of the Commune, considering the possibility of returning to Paris: "I must frankly admit to myself that [returning] to a mass which only thinks of tearing up cobblestones would be difficult." The divorce between the two discursive realms which is thereby ensured satisfies him—esthetically, one might say: "But precisely, there's no harm in the fact that politics has no need for Literature and settles its accounts [*se règle*] with rifle shots."[30] Thus one bizarre aspect of Mallarmé's response to the debacle of the Commune was to sketch a burlesque play, "discrediting Art and Science in the eyes of an attentive public for a considerable number of years. The joke might work very well."[31]

For a certain subjectivity, then, as "Sauvegarde" explains, self-realization could be conceived only outside the organization and reorganization of the social. These individuals seemed to inhabit an economy different from that of most people. Certainly they conceived

29. "Poésies," in *Oeuvres complètes* (Paris: Gallimard-Poésie, 1973), p. 302. Further quotations are from this edition.

30. Letter to Henri Cazalis, 23 Apr. 1871; *Correspondance* (Paris: Gallimard, 1959), vol. I, pp. 351–52.

31. Letter cited in the previous note. See Kristeva, *Révolution du langage poétique,* p. 409. The tone so parallels certain of Flaubert's letters describing his ironic intentions in the *Dictionnaire des idées reçues* or in *Bouvard et Pécuchet* it is hard to imagine that the two writers were not citing each other with sardonic delight.

it as separate from the world of those whose problems appeared resolvable by digging up cobblestones. We have seen how Baudelaire in 1848 shared what later came to seem to him (and to a whole tradition at whose origin he more or less presided) a hopelessly inappropriate enthusiasm for such social action: "My intoxication in 1848. What was the nature of that intoxication?"[32] Mallarmé's own sardonic relation to these earlier modes of action and of conceptualization are the subject of "L'action restreinte" (pp. 369–373).

So that stance of what I have called "internal emigration" became the discursive pose for the avant-garde in relation to everything that can be imagined on the other side of the line at which they sought to enforce distinction. Bejamin had called Baudelaire someone "who had already half withdrawn" from society.[33] But Mallarmé left such partial measures far behind: he sought to metaphorize society as the *radically nonexistent*.[34] Yet later, in the interview with Huret (1891) he found a strikingly different and inherently more contestatory, more effectively militant image to characterize the relation to the social. In a period like the present, he said, the poet is "on strike before society" ("en grève devant la société"; p. 870). The insights—what we might call the discursive innovations—of "Conflit" appear on the horizon of this language and evoke the time in the mid-1880s when the question of the strike was being intensely debated throughout the social formation.[35]

The language of the market and the economy thus reinvested a

32. "Mon coeur mis à nu," *Oeuvres complètes*, p. 1274.
33. *Baudelaire*, p. 59.
34. Such absolute *denegation* of the social—a strain we have already examined with regard to Mallarmé's reflections on the production and circulation of the literary text—was clearly a notion he took to heart. He referred to it in the letter he wrote to Verlaine (16 Nov. 1885), subsequently published under the title "Autobiographie." He suggests to Verlaine that the contemporary period must be considered an interregnum for the poet, "who ought to have nothing to do with it" ("qui n'a point à s'y mêler"). He continues by recommending that the only thing to do was, from time to time, "to send the living his visiting card, his stanzas or sonnet, so that they would not stone him *if they suspected that he knows they don't exist [qu'ils n'ont pas lieu]*" (*Oeuvres complètes*, p. 664; my italics). One of the earliest traces of the attitude leading to this denial of a world beyond poetry can be found in Mallarmé's 1862 polemic, "Hérésies artistiques: l'art pour tous," which concludes: "Ô poètes, vous avez toujours été orgueilleux; soyez plus, devenez dédaigneux" ("Oh poets, you have always been proud; be more, become contemptuous"; ibid., p. 260).
35. The history of trade union organization in France is marked by four major dates: In 1864 the Le Chapelier law was rescinded, and *coalition* (workers' combinations)

discourse which had sought to establish itself in *denial* of its Other's existence. The image of the strike begins to penetrate.[36] It registers the determined self-conception of the artist as a *producer,* constrained despite himself to investigate the conditions of his production, his relation with a public (however hostile it seemed), and obliged to inquire concerning the use value and the exchange value of his writing, the circuits of distribution in which it could move, and so on.

Even so, the ideology of absolute independence from the surrounding dominant discourse persisted, seemed ceaselessly to regenerate even in the face of its dissolution under the pressures of the reality it would have wished to deny. Perhaps its final incarnation lies in a further tactic of disengagement. It is a response to the dynamic which continuously restores the referentiality leading from within avantgarde writing to the external world of the market. Thus in certain figures and in certain moments we can perceive a kind of primitive will to overturn *everything:* to install systematic antiphrasis as the unique principle of text construction. The fear that the language of everyday life will swallow all efforts to differentiate engenders a mechanism of radical antinomy, the textual acting out of denial.

The monument to this tendency is the work of Lautréamont. He comments on the mechanism of negation-as-production at the heart of such a system: "A schoolteacher could produce a whole body of work [*un bagage littéraire*] by saying the contrary of what this century's poets have said. He would replace their affirmations by negations, and vice versa." And so in Lautréamont's "Poésies" *everything* is inverted: "Poetry should be made by everyone. Not by one person alone. Poor

---

ceased to be illegal. In 1884 the legal right to organize was recognized, and labor unions were granted explicit legal status. In 1890 the law governing industrial workers was modified to abolish the *livret* (the worker's registration book) which carried required recommendations by previous employers and facilitated surveillance and retaliation by owners in the case of "troublesome" employees. In 1892, as already mentioned, the Party of Socialist Workers adopted the strategy of the General Strike. Intense debates attended all these changes; see Zeldin, *France,* vol. 1, pp. 199–206 and 231–32.

36. The same metaphor is already at work in the first of Rimbaud's celebrated "Lettres du voyant," to Georges Izambard, [13] May 1871: "I'll become a worker: that's the idea I hold on to when wild anger pushes me toward the battle in Paris—where so many workers are still dying as I write you! Work [write] now, impossible, impossible; I'm on strike" (*Oeuvres,* ed. Suzanne Bernard and André Guyau [Paris: Garnier, 1981], p. 345).

Hugo! Poor Racine! Poor Coppée! Poor Corneille! Poor Boileau! Poor Scarron!"[37] So much, then, for Mallarmé's "Artistic Heresy."

This is the counter-discursive impulse in its most primitive, elemental form. Pushed to its extreme, it abstracts itself from *any* content: the text becomes an *inversion machine*. Its function is *to say the contrary*. The stance defines a position at the *end* of a trajectory because by nature it is formally sterile and can hardly sustain itself. And it stands in relation to the world of possible discourses at about the same place as (but at the opposite end of the spectrum from) the temptation to create a completely *sui generis* discourse, an entirely private language, to which I referred earlier.

In the radicalism of the position, one senses the potential for other reversals just as radical and just as automatized. The discourse of antinomy is rhetorically the close relation of the discourse of apostasy, of the palinode: instability is its intrinsic subtext. In our period the palinode is everywhere: Lautréamont's "Poésies" reacting against, denying, *Maldoror;* Huysmans's various Catholic novels undoing his decadence; and numerous other well-known conversions and reversals which punctuate the literary history of the nineteenth century's second half. We can understand the tendency as a universalized antiphrasis directed not against some discourse "out there," but against one's own *internal* discourse. One suddenly perceives that it, too, has been ideologically colonized; the inversion machine then is marshaled to extirpate it. In the language of a certain comic mechanization of the text-generation process, we could say that, functioning in its palinodic mode, the inversion machine seeks to produce absolute *de*/citation (see above, Chapter 6). But eventually, by virtue precisely of their own ultrarationalization and mechanization, by which they ironically come to resemble the modes of discourse and practice which they hold in greatest contempt, such textual procedures become *self*-canceling. Valences can be reversed only so many times before the system exhausts itself. The discourse of the inversion machine has no staying power.

Despite Sartre's characterization of him as comprehensive "Négateur," to which I have alluded, Mallarmé's relation to the problem was

---

37. "Poésies II," *Oeuvres complètes*, pp. 301, 311–12.

considerably more nuanced. We can best approach it by way of his reflection on *syntax,* which might be conceived as the elemental characteristic of socially instituted intelligibility in any discourse. Mallarmé's texts may seem difficult and obscure, may suffer thereby the most intense restrictions in their circulation in the general social field. But he never consented to the change of theoretical *unintelligibility* which would have been the result of creating his own private grammar.

Not that Mallarmé ever wished to recommend the pedestrian or the "prosaic"—what in "Le mystère dans les lettres" he calls "l'évidence moyenne nécessaire" ("mean required clarity," or what I might term "intelligibility in lowest terms"). This is the debased—dare we say "academic"—concern of "grammarians" (p. 386). The point is a familiar one: that freedom and the capacity for variation and innovation in any social system are licit and functional to the extent that their exercise remains within the framework of certain rules. This is what Mallarmé means by "syntax": *the structural principle of the totality,* ensuring the coherence of a social whole which sustains the intelligibility of even the most daring locution expressible within it:

> Quel pivot, j'entends, dans ces contrastes, à
> l'intelligibilité? il faut une garantie—
> La Syntaxe—
>
> (What balance-point, I mean, in these contrasts, for
> intelligibility? a guarantee is necessary—
> Syntax—; p. 385)

Mallarmé thereby declares a crucial refusal: he renounces the possibility of attaining *distinction* through *meaninglessness.* Despite its deeply eccentric, heterodox impulses, his writing remains within the same world as what it contests. Mallarmé thus identifies his production as constitutively counter-discursive. And he provides what can be a concluding description of its social functionality. The fundamental orientation of counter-discourse is toward the discovery and the expression of what (in the fragment just quoted) he terms "contrasts"— what I have been calling "distinctions"—in the sense of deviations from some stylistic or rhetorical or ideological norm. Such differences presuppose, play against, and seek to intervene in a discursive field that

333

the maintenance of essential rule-boundedness simultaneously serves to inscribe and to sustain.[38]

It is in this way—perhaps in this way alone—that Mallarmé can imagine the unification of the social totality whose expression had eluded him in the depictions of "Conflit": as an overarching framing principle which informs the antagonistic elements of the social whole even as their distinction is enforced. "Syntax" becomes the figure for the dialectical sublation of even the most intense contradictions— whose resolution in the discourses of social existence and of history Mallarmé discovered he was unable to represent.

Within the frame of such an ultimate, quasi-utopian reunification, an immense play of expressive idiosyncrasy became possible. In his own texts Mallarmé was able to joke gently about the world's perception of his discourse and his own attempts to distinguish it from theirs. In "Solitude" he fantasizes a journalist—Huret?—sent to interview the Master and bring back the Word. The newspaperman triumphantly discovers in the poet's conversation a clear statement, in a parsable sentence, of Mallarméan truth. But the poet, feigning shock and playing to his reputation, resists this accusation of clarity as the journalist tries to depart with his unexpected trophy: "'Serait-ce une phrase?' ou 'Attendez, par pudeur' il s'éloigne 'que j'y ajoute, du moins, un peu d'obscurité'" ("'You mean it's a complete sentence?' or 'Wait a minute, for decency's sake'—he is departing—'let me at least add a little obscurity'"; p. 407).

But the need to achieve distinction—to enforce the difference that is the sign of literature in general, and of antiprosaic prose in particular— is what determines the grammatical entrechats and syntactical caracoles which make Mallarméan prose recognizably his. *Alienation has gram-*

---

38. Mallarmé's fantasy is thus distinct from Rimbaud's impulse to overturn *everything*, even including syntax, in order to find a new language; see the letter to Demeny, 15 May 1871, *Oeuvres*, p. 349. Rimbaud seems to have envisaged the possibility of the "informe," of *breaking* with the claims of syntax. At this point his project (or at least its theory projection) diverges from the stance which sustained Mallarmé's production, and indeed from the realm of counter-discourse as I employ the term here. As a case beyond the limit of such counter-discursive protocols, it helps to situate their range and intentionality. Mallarmé's own version was crucially different: "Je suis profondément et scrupuleusement syntaxier" ("I am deeply and scrupulously syntactic"); cited by Bernard, *Poème en prose*, p. 299; see also Johnson, *Critical Difference*, p. 70, and her surrounding discussion of the problem of syntax.

matical consequences. A detailed study of Mallarmé's style would no doubt enable us to specify at least for certain characteristic patterns of expression and locution-types the absent norm against which his style establishes its difference. And we could probably detect what socially meaningful element signified by that normative usage is in these cases implicitly contested or refused.

A small example of the way in which syntax becomes counter-discursive will have to suffice here. The general utility of many of Mallarmé's stylistic deformations clearly is to break up the easily *consumable*, ideologically neutralized or naturalized construction of dominant prose. Thus Mallarmé regularly violates the canon of parallel structure—at least twice in the following sentence fragment from "La cour": "Loin de prétendre, dans l'assemblée, à une place, comme de fondation ou corporative, pour le producteur: il paraîtra, se montrant en l'anonymat et le dos convenables, je compare, à un chef d'orchestre" (p. 415). Both of the compound phrases in this extract have their parallelisms upset. The first ("comme de fondation ou corporative") constructs the attributive terms in two different ways; the second ("en l'anonymat et le dos convenables") forces into parallel positions substantives from radically separated semantic spheres whose coming together here—one solemnly abstract, the other comically concrete—ensures a minor shock effect at the heart of the process of their assimilation. Mallarmé rings changes on the expected and makes the reader reset the criteria of normalcy in locutions even as humble as these. The counter-discursive mechanism subtly undermines the primacy of the signified, the substantive instrumental message, and insists upon the defetishization of the content precisely by fetishizing the medium of its production and transmission.

What is enforced here on the microsyntactic level is sought equally in the syntax of more global levels of the discourse. Mallarmé's disinclination to produce *narrative* must be understood in this light. He puts it clearly in the preface to "Un coup de dés": "on évite le récit" ("narrative is avoided"; p. 455).[39] Thus if Mallarmé says (in "Les mots

39. It has perhaps not been sufficiently remarked that the typographic innovations of "Un coup de dés" have as repressed referent a discursive code at the antipodes of Mallarmé's own intention: the practices of the newspaper. There are basically only two places where type face and point size so systematically translate factors of relative importance, internal hierarchy, contrast or continuity of discourse, and so on: in the

anglais"): "trop de régularité nuit" ("too much regularity is harmful"; p. 1026), here as elsewhere we have to deduce the character of the counter-discursive project, and the repressed influence of its dominant referent, in order to understand *what* is "harmed" by the rationalized regularity of the discourse which Mallarmé refuses.

Conclusion: The Paradox of Instrumentality

In the intersection of social worlds which occurs most explicitly in "Conflit," there is a further element relating to the syntactic procedures and preoccupations just examined. With the grammatical and discursive denaturalizations characteristic of avant-garde prose, the possibility of any general consumption of the discourse is eliminated. Usually this inaccessibility is celebrated; indeed, Mallarmé himself tends to such applause. Yet "Conflit" deconstructs the apparent disjunction between *utility* and *value* and thereby renders such celebration problematic. In 1846 Baudelaire had hoped that the middle class would come to unite the appreciation of *beauty* to its possession of *power* (see his dedication of the *Salon de 1846*, "to the bourgeois"; p. 874). Events had proven otherwise. But the nostalgia for an audience persists. Mallarmé reacts with melancholy to the disjunction which makes his writing inaccessible to the workers in "Conflit": "Sadness that my production remains, to these people, essentially, like the clouds at sunset or stars, useless [*vaine*]" (p. 358).

In this reaction in "Conflit" to the distance which separates the poet's work from the work of workers, there is of course no desire to return to the commodity circuit in which other sorts of objects than poems—and labor first among them—are exchanged. Mallarmé has no commercial inclinations; he is unmovable on the issue of poetry's *salability*: "Nul vente ni qu'homme trafique, avec l'âme ou, sinon, il ne comprend pas" ("No selling nor can one trade with the spirit or else one fails to understand"; p. 412). Rather, what is problematized in this

---

make-up of the newspaper page (headlines, subheads, text, captions) and in "Un coup de dés." Mallarmé stipulates the parallel in "Le livre, instrument spirituel," articulating it around a distinctive "*Mais . . .* " (*Oeuvres complètes,* p. 381) which we might take as the surreptitious recognition of the relationship hidden within this difference.

rare expression of a touching subjectivity concerning the conditions under which his own work must remain isolated is the question of utility itself, or what I might term the paradox of instrumentality.

The oxymoron of the title, "Le livre, *instrument spirituel*" (p. 378; my italics), refers explicitly to this paradox. Much of the apparatus of distinction mobilized throughout Mallarmé's prose attempts to enforce the disjunction between the two worlds of the instrumental and the spiritual. Thus Mallarmé speaks in "Crayonné au théâtre" of "la gêne vis-à-vis de produits (à quoi l'on est, par nature, étranger)" ["the sense of unease in the presence of products (in relation to which one is, by nature, an outsider)"; p. 297].

The disjunction between poetry and utility might almost be said to have constituted the avant-garde: "Etre un homme utile m'a paru toujours quelque chose de bien hideux" ("To be a useful man has always seemed to me something extremely hideous").[40] Or: "En général dès qu'une chose devient utile, elle cesse d'être belle" ("In general as soon as a thing becomes useful it stops being beautiful").[41] And surely Mallarmé is not tempted to compromise, still less to vulgarize, in order to establish the contact with other people which might eliminate the sadness regarding his own work of which he speaks in "Conflit."

But the puzzle is why the ideological structure thus established conflates "usefulness" with "marketability," "communication" with "vulgarization." Under what conditions was the clear divorce between these two realms in the nineteenth century, between esthetic and practical perception, *enforced*?

What faced the avant-garde as the condition of their crisis was the progressive absorption of the world into the market economy, of all discourse into practical discourse. In response, their fundamental resource for maintaining distinction came to be a transformation of the old aristocratic doctrine that practical work is the attribute of inferiority.[42] An entire sea change in the metacriticism of language emerges from the avant-garde and passes through the Formalists to the more complex and self-conscious estheticism of our own day. But what

40. Baudelaire, "Mon coeur mis à nu," *Oeuvres complètes,* p. 1274.

41. Théophile Gautier, Preface to *Poésies complètes,* (Paris: Charpentier, 1919), vol. 1, p. xi.

42. For perhaps the most cogent and generalized account of this psychosocial tactic, see Max Horkheimer, "Feudal Lord," pp. 124–35.

looms behind it is the specter of instrumental determination of the whole social world.

The issue and the locus of the stress were clear to Mallarmé. He tests the problem by confronting representatives of its respective poles. Thus in "Etalages" he fantasized a convergence of writers and bankers: "On allait donc être, à la faveur de l'idéal, assimilé aux banquiers deçus, avoir une situation, sujette aux baisses et aux revirements, sur la place" ("We were thus, in the service of the Ideal, going to be conflated with disappointed bankers, to have a position, subject to declines and price reversals, in the market"; p. 373). Such assimilation is of course intolerable—but what the text detects is its secret *attraction*. The project of the prose poem as *absolute* counter-discourse emerges in the face of this intense ideological danger.

But its absolutism can never realize itself as total divorce from the operation of dominant ideology and from the dominant system which produces and reproduces it. If there is an admissible content to my characterization at all, what is absolute about the prose poem is the radicalism of its contestatory commitment, its constantly inventive refusal to consent to its own investment by the antagonist, to its own neutralization. Of course the flow of dominant language into its protocols and usages is uninterrupted; but in any case it can only contest them *in situation* and in the atmosphere of acute tension which is the genre's quintessential atmosphere.

A certain displaced image of another way of living and of thinking about the world, a project of the resolution of these intolerable deformations, is therefore implicit in the very existence of the prose poem and in its attempt to take on its antagonist in the realm of his ideological strength. It would be heartening to be able to claim some victories. Mallarmé essays such a claim in "Etalages." The text is framed by and refers to a crisis which is sapping the value of *everything:* a financial panic like so many which punctuated the economic and social life of developing capitalism toward the end of the century: 1857, 1873, 1882, 1893.[43] The market is dropping like a rock. Yet the products of the mind seem to be maintaining their value: "La mentale denrée, comme une autre, indispensable, garde son cours" ("The mental commodity, like any other indispensable, is holding its price"; p. 374). It would seem that, measured in the terms of the market itself, the desired

43. See Hobsbawm, *Age of Capital,* pp. 69–70; and Rondo Cameron, *France and the Economic Development of Europe,* pp. 96, 124–28, 133.

distinction had at last been achieved and stabilized, that literature might *at last* relax in the security of its status as an element of social life untouched by these periodic crises and depressions.

"Etalages" thus celebrates the stability of literature's value. But simultaneously Mallarmé's language betrays its contamination from within. It undoes its own assertion by adopting the very speech and ideology against which distinction was supposed to have maintained its exclusions—the parlance of the stockjobber and the commercial broker. This movement by which dominant discourses colonize their adversaries is familiar by now. Indeed, the struggle of counter-discourses is defined by such recrudescences of the combat, such reinfections, just when it had appeared ascendency had been attained. Such flare-ups and self-subversions are irreducible conditions of the counter-discursive process.

For such a process the field of struggle is that of language itself. The stakes are the system of meaning by which the social formation is reproduced, through which (as I have sought successively to show) it organizes its paradigms of initiation and socialization, of self-representation and self-criticism, of perception and of experience of the Other. Because such systems are never entirely stable, the discursive struggle—the policing of boundaries, the absorption or neutralization of adversaries—begins to appear theoretically interminable.

Ultimately this would seem to be why the counter-discourses I have been considering increasingly shun narrative: because, just as Baudelaire had sensed in his original characterization of the prose poem, there can be no decisive directionality in a guerrilla combat waged under these conditions. The only omnipresent, omnitemporal reality is the constancy of the struggle itself. Thus, no beginning, no middle, and surely no end to these texts, owing to the immersion of their protocols of contestation in a structure of social existence which would define itself as timeless, and which renders opposition apparently termless. Because they are determined by history, these counter-plots will be able to take the form of plots only when history itself legitimizes the representation of authentic difference, alters the conditions which by themselves counter-discourses never had the power to change but which they could uncover and incriminate.

The penetration of dominant discourse has only increased since the period which has concerned me here; the struggle of the figures who have occupied us has prolonged itself into our own time. Behind the succession of forms in which counter-discursive opposition has been organized—forms which have mutated but which could hardly be said to have advanced since the nineteenth century—lies a deeper continuity between our period and theirs. The process by which discursive hierarchies are produced and made to appear natural has become the object of a continuous and increasingly powerful analysis since the question of signs and discourses began to assume its modern configuration about a hundred and fifty years ago.[44] Within the field of such an investigation, a number of the problems which still fascinate us have come into focus. Our contemporary interrogations of ideology and control, of cultural resistance and historical change, arise within the problematic of difference and identity which the counter-discursive impulse really frames. Since the rise of liberal societies in the nineteenth century, such questions have been the true burden of its critical dynamic.

Mallarmé defined the terrain and the tone of such an investigation. "Magie" (pp. 399–400) focuses on the specificity of the contemporary as intensely as any nineteenth-century text. But strikingly, in a brilliant protodeconstruction of the canons of nineteenth-century reality, it does so by exploring a fantasmagoric persistence of the Middle Ages into modern times.

Specifically, the initial focus of "Magie" is the disconcerting survival of medieval *démonialité* (demonality)—the complex of a series of heterodox social practices (black masses, blasphemy, and so on)—in the nineteenth century. Mallarmé detected something crucial in this unexpected anachronism. It interests him because in its essential striving after *difference* it evades and subverts the normalized reason of his period, neatly undoing its claim of universality. Démonialité pluralizes a reality which had sought to represent itself as stable and internally unified. It opens into an otherness at a moment when such apertures seemed increasingly threatened and uncertain.

44. Again Balzac was prescient and premonitory. In *La rabouilleuse* (1842) he made an observation which would seem perfectly in harmony with important critical preoccupations today: "nothing in life requires more attention than the things which appear natural" (*Oeuvres complètes*, vol. 13 [Paris: Conard, 1913], p. 262). We have been working out the implications of this advice ever since.

The content and the function of such a heterodox social complex suggest that we read it in dialogue with Bakhtin. For nineteenth-century démonialité recalls the medieval *diableries* whose subversive, liberatory dynamic Bakhtin brought to light in his study of Rabelais.[45] The meaning of démonialité can be interpreted along parallel lines.

Along with the other multiform manifestations of the "carnivales-que," for Bakhtin diablerie represents an organized set of practices and discourses which are the figures for alternatives to official culture and its patterns of control. They strategically disrupt them. Understood in this light, nineteenth-century demonality becomes a crucial trace: one of a series of names for the *Other*—the excluded, the inadmissible, the scandalous—whose official disestablishment establishes the dominant forms of nineteenth-century consciousness and existence. The return of *this* repressed—in démonialité as in the other heterodox discourses which have occupied me in this study—bears a crucial truth about the establishment of culture itself. The deep political implications of the avant-garde's contempt for politics resituate themselves in such a perspective; the paradox of their texts' instrumentality discloses its logic here.

In this vision of Mallarmé's century, the demonic, magic, *poetry in general,* become the names for an essential *excess* which dominant discourse is unable to suppress. Even in the atmosphere of self-celebratory rationalism by which domination expresses its hegemony in the nineteenth century, the social continues to produce itself in forms which escape the control and resist the penetration of utilitarian intelligence. The function of Mallarmé's text is thus to search out the irreducible "disorder" which, though nearly concealed within our modern rational order of "finance," "credit," "capital" (p. 400), nonetheless underlies it.

"Modernity" is Mallarmé's characterization for the society founded upon such constitutive slippage, such suppressed internal difference. Like the formation itself, his judgment of it is ambivalent; he speaks of "cette vaine, perplexe, nous échappant, modernité" ("this vain, perplexing, us-baffling, modernity"; p. 399). We can recognize such ambivalence and such puzzlement as the signs by which ideology shows itself when it shows itself at all. In them is revealed the secret density

45. See *Rabelais,* pp. 265–268.

and inner complication of a dominant discourse which seeks above all to convey the appearance of a candid transparency, unreservedly delivering its unequivocal truths. It has no room for demonality, yet it cannot exist without it.

A second, perhaps involuntary resonance of Mallarmé's notion of the "Reserve of Discourse" is revealed thereby. For what emerges from the liberal pretense of openness under the unexpectedly baffling conditions of "modernity" is that discourse *always* holds something back. The problematic of the ideological is located in the space of that reserve. Its analysis—which has ceaselessly deployed its critical power from Marx to Derrida—then becomes the science of discursive densities and slippages, the practice of producing the unproduced determinants by which our modern reality occurs for us.

"Modernity" thus designates specific forms of discursive displacement and exclusion by which, in any utterance, more is always present than can be presented. Mallarmé sees this shortfall clearly—but as an openness of a different and more optimistic sort, as an opportunity. For him it creates the place for literature by establishing that a repressed *alternative* constantly doubles and complicates *all* discourse, however positive, however seemingly exhaustive. "Literature," then, becomes a prestigious designation for such displaced alternatives.

This is another vision—and perhaps the most general—of the counter-discursive, whose combined subversive and utopian resonances emerge clearly in it. And it permits us to approach the notion of an *absolute* counter-discourse from an altered direction. For if "modernity" is the name for a society increasingly regulated by discursive dominance, paradoxically the counter-discourse emerges as its crucially repressed secret, as the alternative whose exclusion defines the apparent stability of the social formation itself. As with so many of the reversals to which poststructuralist thinking has accustomed us, the marginal reveals itself as central. And such a notion redefines the ground upon which contestation—the conscious foregrounding of otherwise repressed alternatives in the discursive realm—might stage its struggle and attempt its subversion.

What is at stake in a structure like the counter-discourse which, however tensely stressed, has not changed much since Mallarmé? Across the adversative slash which punctuates my title—*Discourse/Counter-Discourse*—the figure of a suppressed historicity reasserts itself. If under the conditions of liberal society dominant discourse necessarily casts itself and its hegemony as timeless, as transparent, as proof against all corrosion and complication, the counter-discursive can be conceived as the present and scandalous trace of a historical potentiality for difference, as the currently realizable sign of a transformed future. The dynamism, the persistence, and the inventiveness of counter-discursive resistance ceaselessly recall to cultural consciousness the historical contingency of all forms of domination—what (adapting Bakhtin) we might term their "objective incompleteness."[46]

In such a perspective, counter-discourse designates the generalized impulse (however ambivalent and frustrated in the contemporary stage of combat) to pass beyond fixity, beyond closure. "Culture as a field of struggle": I began with this notion. The counter-discourse materializes such a conflict. However bound to the configurations of dominant discourse, the counter-discursive imagines the liberation of the whole realm of social discourse from such essentially defensive and oppositional structures. Its horizon—in Mallarmé's period as in our own—is the plenitude and the cultural richness of a freer discursive economy, in which something more like authentic democracy might prevail. The struggle continues.

46. Ibid., p. 127.

Bibliography
of Critical Works

ABENDROTH, WOLFGANG. *A Short History of the European Working Class.* New York: Monthly Review Press, 1972.

ABRAMS, M. H. *The Mirror and the Lamp: Romantic Theory and the Critical Tradition.* New York: Oxford University Press, 1953.

ADHÉMAR, JEAN. *Honoré Daumier.* Paris: Pierre Tisné, 1954.

ALLEN, JAMES SMITH. *Popular French Romanticism: Authors, Readers, and Books in the 19th Century.* Syracuse: Syracuse University Press, 1981.

ALTHUSSER, LOUIS. *For Marx.* Trans. Ben Brewster. New York: Vintage, 1970.

——. "Ideology and Ideological State Apparatuses (Notes toward an Investigation)." In *Lenin and Philosophy,* trans. Ben Brewster. New York: Monthly Review Press, 1971.

ARTLEY, ALEXANDRA, ed. *The Golden Age of Shop Design: European Shop Interiors, 1880–1939.* New York: Whitney Library of Design, 1976.

AUERBACH, ERICH. *Mimesis: The Representation of Reality in Western Literature.* Trans. Willard R. Trask. Princeton: Princeton University Press, 1953.

BAKHTIN, MIKHAIL M. *The Dialogic Imagination: Four Essays.* Ed. Michael Holquist. Austin: University of Texas Press, 1981.

——. *Esthétique et théorie du roman.* Paris: Gallimard, 1978.

——. *The Formal Method.* See P. N. Medvedev.

——. *Freudianism.* See V. N. Vološinov.

——. *Marxism and the Philosophy of Language.* See V. N. Vološinov.

——. *Problems of Dostoevskii's Poetics.* Trans. R. W. Rotsel. Ann Arbor: University of Michigan Press, 1973.

——. *Rabelais and His World.* Cambridge: MIT Press, 1968.

BARBÉRIS, PIERRE. *Balzac et le mal du siècle: contribution à une physiologie du monde moderne.* 2 vols. Paris: Gallimard, 1970.

——. ."Mal du siècle, ou d'un romantisme de droite à un romantisme de gauche." In *Romantisme et politique 1815–1851,* pp. 164–182. Paris: Armand Colin, 1969.

——. *Le monde de Balzac.* Paris: Arthaud, 1973.

BARBÉRIS, PIERRE, AND CLAUDE DUCHET, eds. *Manuel d'histoire littéraire de la France: 1789–1848.* 2 vols. Paris: Editions Sociales, 1972.

BARRETT, MICHÈLE, PHILIP CORRIGAN, ANNETTE KUHN, AND JANET WOLFF, eds. *Ideology and Cultural Production.* London: Croom Helm, 1979.

BART, BENJAMIN F. *Flaubert.* Syracuse: Syracuse University Press, 1967.

BARTHES, ROLAND. *Critical Essays.* Trans. Richard Howard. Evanston: Northwestern University Press, 1972.

——. *Le degré zéro de l'écriture* (1953). Paris: Gonthier-Médiations, 1965.

——. *S/Z.* Paris: Seuil, 1970.

——. .*Writing Degree Zero.* Boston: Beacon, 1970.

BATAILLE, GEORGES. *La littérature et le mal.* Paris: Gallimard, 1957.

BAUDRILLARD, JEAN. *Pour une critique de l'économie politique du signe.* Paris: Gallimard, 1972.

BECHTEL, EDWIN DE T. *Freedom of the Press and "L'Association mensuelle": Philipon versus Louis-Philippe.* New York: Grolier Club, 1952.

BECKER, HOWARD S. *Art Worlds.* Berkeley: University of California Press, 1982.

BELLANGER, CLAUDE, JACQUES GODECHOT, PIERRE GUIRAL, AND FERNAND TERROU. *Histoire générale de la presse française.* Vol. 2, *De 1815 à 1871.* Paris: Presses Universitaires de France, 1969.

BELLET, ROGER. *Presse et journalisme sous le Second Empire.* Paris: Armand Colin (Coll. "Kiosque"), 1967.

BEM, JEAN. "L'artiste et son double, dans la première *Education sentimentale.*" *Revue des Sciences Humaines* 53, no. 181 (1981): 11–19.

BENJAMIN, WALTER. *Charles Baudelaire: A Lyric Poet in the Era of High Capitalism.* Trans. Harry Zohn. London: New Left Books, 1973.

BERGER, PETER L., AND THOMAS LUCKMAN. *The Social Construction of Reality.* Garden City: Anchor, 1979.

346

BERNARD, SUZANNE. *Le poème en prose de Baudelaire jusqu'à nos jours*. Paris: Nizet, 1959.

BERSANI, LEO. *Baudelaire and Freud*. Berkeley: University of California Press, 1977.

BOURDIEU, PIERRE, *Ce que parler veut dire: l'économie des échanges linguistiques*. Paris: Fayard, 1982.

——. *La distinction: critique sociale du jugement*. Paris: Minuit, 1979.

——. *Outline of a Theory of Practice*. Trans. Richard Nice. Cambridge Studies in Social Anthropology. Cambridge: Cambridge University Press, 1977.

BOURDIEU, PIERRE, AND JEAN-CLAUDE PASSERON. *La reproduction*. Paris: Minuit, 1970. Trans. Richard Nice, under the title *Reproduction in Education, Society, and Culture*. London: Sage, 1977.

BRUNEAU, JEAN. *Le "Conte oriental" de Gustave Flaubert*. Paris: Denoël, 1973.

BUCK-MORSS, SUSAN. "Walter Benjamin—Revolutionary Writer." *New Left Review*, no. 128 (July–August 1981):50–75.

CAMERON, RONDO. *France and the Economic Development of Europe, 1800–1914*. 2d ed. Chicago: Rand McNally, 1961.

CAUTE, DAVID. *The Left in Europe since 1789*. New York: McGraw-Hill, 1966.

CAVALLARI, HÉCTOR MARIO. "*Savoir* and *Pouvoir*: Michel Foucault's Theory of Discursive Practices." *Humanities in Society* 3, no. 1 (Winter 1980):55–72.

CAWS, MARY ANN, AND HERMINE RIFFATERRE. *The Prose Poem in France: Theory and Practice*. New York: Columbia University Press, 1983.

CHERPIN, JEAN. *L'homme Daumier: un visage qui sort de l'ombre*. Marseilles: Arts et Livres de Provence, 1973.

CHEVALIER, LOUIS. *Classes laborieuses et classes dangereuses à Paris pendant la première moitié du XIXe siécle*. Paris: Plon, 1958.

COHEN, G. A. *Karl Marx's Theory of History: A Defence*. Princeton: Princeton University Press, 1978.

CRUBELLIER, MAURICE. *Histoire culturelle de la France, XIXe–XXe siècle*. Collection "U." Paris: Armand Colin, 1974.

CULLER, JONATHAN. *Ferdinand de Saussure*. New York: Penguin-Modern Masters, 1977.

——. *Flaubert: The Uses of Uncertainty*. Ithaca: Cornell University Press, 1974.

——. *On Deconstruction: Theory and Criticism after Structuralism*. Ithaca: Cornell University Press, 1982.

——. *Structuralist Poetics: Structuralism, Linguistics and the Study of Literature*. Ithaca: Cornell University Press, 1975.

DE CERTEAU, MICHEL. *La fable mystique*. Paris: Gallimard, 1982.

DE CERTEAU, MICHEL, LUCE GIARD, AND PIERRE MAYOL. *L'invention du quotidien*. 2 vols. Paris: Union générale d'Editions-10/18, 1980.

DE CERTEAU, MICHEL, DOMINIQUE JULIA, AND JACQUES REVEL. *Une politique de la langue: la révolution française et les patois*. Paris: Gallimard, 1975.

DELTEIL, LOYS. *Honoré Daumier*. Le Peintre-Graveur illustré (XIXe et XXe siècles). 11 vols. Paris: Chez l'Auteur, 1925–26.

DERRIDA, JACQUES. "De l'économie restreinte à l'économie générale." In *L'écriture et la différence*. Paris: Seuil, 1967.

——. "Différance." In *Marges de la philosophie*. Paris: Minuit, 1972.

——. *Positions*. Paris: Minuit, 1972.

——. "La question du style." In *Nietzsche aujourd'hui*. Colloque de Cérisy, pp. 215–29. Paris: Union générale d'Editions-10/18, 1968.

——. "Signature événement contexte." In *Marges de la philosophie*. Paris: Minuit, 1972.

——. "Signature Event Context." In *Glyph I,* pp. 172–97. Baltimore: Johns Hopkins University Press, 1977.

DESCOMBES, VINCENT. *Le même et l'autre: quarante-cinq ans de philosophie française (1933–1978)*. Paris: Minuit, 1979.

——. *Modern French Philosophy*. Trans. L. Scott-Fox and J. M. Harding. Cambridge: Cambridge University Press, 1980.

DREYFUS, HUBERT L., AND PAUL RABINOW. *Michel Foucault: Beyond Structuralism and Hermeneutics*. Chicago: University of Chicago Press, 1982.

DUCHET, CLAUDE. "Signifiance et in-signifiance: le discours italique dans *Madame Bovary*." In *La production du sens chez Flaubert,* ed. Claudine Gothot-Mersch. Paris: Union générale d'Editions-10/18, 1975.

DUCHET, CLAUDE, ed. *Manuel d'histoire littéraire de la France: 1848–1917*. Paris: Editions Sociales, 1977.

DUCROT, OSWALD, AND TZVETAN TODOROV. *Encyclopedic Dictionary of the Sciences of Language*. Trans. Catherine Porter. Baltimore: Johns Hopkins University Press, 1979.

ECO, UMBERTO. *A Theory of Semiotics*. Bloomington: Indiana University Press, 1976.

ENZENSBERGER, HANS MAGNUS. *The Consciousness Industry: On Literature, Politics, and the Media*. Ed. Michael Roloff. New York: Seabury, 1974.

ERLICH, VICTOR. *Russian Formalism: History-Doctrine*. 1965. 3d ed. New Haven: Yale University Press, 1981.

EWEN, STUART. *Captains of Consciousness: Advertising and the Social Roots of the Consumer Culture*. New York: McGraw-Hill, 1966.

FINEMAN, DANIEL D. "The Parodic and Production: Criticism and Labor." *Minnesota Review*, n.s. 18 (Spring, 1982):69–85.

FOUCAULT, MICHEL. *Language, Counter-Memory, Practice*. Trans. Donald Bouchard, Ithaca: Cornell University Press, 1977.

——. *Les mots et les choses*. Paris: Gallimard, 1966.

——. *The Order of Things: An Archeology of the Human Sciences*. New York: Random House–Vintage, 1973.

——. *L'ordre du discours*. Paris: Gallimard, 1971.

——. *Power/Knowledge: Selected Interviews and Other Writings*. Ed. Colin Gordon. New York: Pantheon, 1980.

FOWLER, ROGER, ed. *Language and Control*. London: Routledge & Kegan Paul, 1979.

FRANKLIN, URSULA. *An Anatomy of Poesis: The Prose Poems of Stéphane Mallarmé*. North Carolina Studies in the Romance Languages and Literatures, no. 16. Chapel Hill: University of North Carolina Press, 1976.

GAILLARD, FRANÇOISE. "Petite histoire du bras de fer, ou comment se fait l'Histoire." *Revue des Sciences Humaines* 53, no. 181 (1981), 79–89.

GEIST, JOHANN FRIEDRICH. *Arcades: The History of a 19th Century Building Type*. Trans. John H. Newman and Jane O. Newman. Cambridge: MIT Press, 1982.

GOULD, CAROL. *Marx's Social Ontology: Individuality and Community in Marx's Theory of Social Reality*. Cambridge: MIT Press, 1978.

GOUX, JEAN-JOSEPH. *Economie et symbolique*. Paris: Seuil, 1972.

GRAMSCI, ANTONIO. *Selections from the Prison Notebooks*. Ed. Quintin Hoare and Geoffrey Nowell Smith. New York: International Publishers, 1971.

GRAÑA, CÉSAR. *Bohemian versus Bourgeois: French Society and the French Man of Letters in the Nineteenth Century*. New York: Basic Books, 1964.

GREIMAS, A.-J. *Sémantique structurale*. Paris: Larousse, 1966.

——. "Structure et histoire." Reprinted in *Du sens*. Paris: Seuil, 1970. Originally published in 1966.

HAMON, PHILIPPE. *Texte et idéologie: valeurs, hiérarchies et évaluations dans l'oeuvre littéraire*. Paris: Presses Universitaires de France, 1984.

HABERMAS, JÜRGEN. *Legitimation Crisis*. Trans. Thomas McCarthy. Boston: Beacon, 1975.

HEGEL, G. W. F. *Vorlesungen über die Aesthetik*. In *Werke*. Vol. 14. Frankfurt: Suhrkamp, 1970.

HGPF. See Bellanger et al.

HJELMSLEV, LOUIS. "Langue et parole." In *Essais linguistiques: travaux du Cercle Linguistique de Copenhague* 12 (1959):80–93.

HOBSBAWM, E. J. *The Age of Capital, 1848–1875.* New York: New American Library-Mentor, 1979.

———. *The Age of Revolution, 1789–1848.* New York: New American Library-Mentor, 1962.

HOLLAND, EUGENE. "Toward a Redefinition of Masochism: A Cultural History of Late Nineteenth Century France." Ph.D. diss., University of California, San Diego, 1981.

HORKHEIMER, MAX. "The End of Reason." *Studies in Philosophy and Social Science* 9 (1941):362–90.

———. "Feudal Lord, Customer, and Specialist" (1964). In *Critique of Instrumental Reason.* Trans. Matthew J. O'Connell et al., pp. 124–35. New York: Seabury, 1974.

ISAAC, BONNIE J. "'M'introduire dans ton histoire': Communication in Mallarmé and his Critics." Ph.D. diss., Johns Hopkins University, 1980.

IVANOV, V. V. "The Science of Semiotics." 1962. Trans. Doris Bradbury. *New Literary History* 9, no. 2 (Winter, 1978):199–204.

JAKOBSON, ROMAN. *Essais de linguistique générale.* Paris: Minuit, 1963.

———. "Linguistics and Poetics." In *Style in Language,* ed. T. A. Sebeok, pp. 350–377. Cambridge: MIT Press, 1960.

JAMES, HENRY. *Daumier, Caricaturist.* London: Rodale Press, 1954.

JAMESON, FREDRIC. *Marxism and Form: Twentieth-Century Dialectical Theories of Literature.* Princeton: Princeton University Press, 1971.

———. "On Aronson's Sartre." *Minnesota Review,* n.s. 18 (Spring 1982):116–27.

———. *The Political Unconscious: Narrative as a Socially Symbolic Act.* Ithaca: Cornell University Press, 1981.

———. *The Prison-House of Language: A Critical Account of Structuralism and Russian Formalism.* Princeton: Princeton University Press, 1972.

JAY, MARTIN. *The Dialectical Imagination.* Boston: Little, Brown, 1973.

JOHNSON, BARBARA. *The Critical Difference: Essays in the Contemporary Rhetoric of Reading.* Baltimore: Johns Hopkins University Press, 1980.

———. *Défigurations du langage poétique: la seconde révolution baudelairienne.* Paris: Flammarion, 1979.

KAHN, COPPÉLIA. "Excavating Literature." *Diacritics* 12, no. 2 (Summer 1982):32–41.

KANES, MARTIN. *Balzac's Comedy of Words*. Princeton: Princeton University Press, 1975.

KRAVIS, JUDY. *The Prose of Mallarmé: The Evolution of a Literary Language*. Cambridge: Cambridge University Press, 1976.

KRISTEVA, JULIA. *La révolution du langage poétique: l'avant-garde à la fin du 19e siècle: Lautréamont et Mallarmé*. Paris: Seuil, 1974.

——. "Le sujet en procès." In *Polylogue*. Paris: Seuil, 1977.

L. D. *See* Delteil.

LACAPRA, DOMINICK. *"Madame Bovary" on Trial*. Ithaca: Cornell University Press, 1982.

LACLAU, ERNESTO, AND CHANTAL MOUFFE. "Recasting Marxism: Hegemony and New Political Movements (Interview)." *Socialist Review* 12:6, no. 66 (Nov.-Dec. 1982):91–113.

LEFEBVRE, HENRI. *Everyday Life in the Modern World* (1968). Trans. Sacha Rabinovitch. New York: Harper & Row, 1971.

LE GOFF, JACQUES. "Au Moyen-Age: temps de l'église et temps du marchand." *Annales E.S.C.* 15 (1960):417–33.

LENIN, VLADIMIR ILYICH. *Lenin on Literature and Art*. Moscow: Progress, 1970.

LENTRICCHIA, FRANK. *After the New Criticism*. Chicago: University of Chicago Press, 1980.

LETHÈVE, JACQUES. *La caricature et la presse sous la IIIe République*. Paris: Armand Colin (Coll. "Kiosque"), 1961.

LEWIS, DAVID K. *Convention: A Philosophical Study*. Cambridge: Harvard University Press, 1969.

LEWIS, PAULA GILBERT. *The Aesthetics of Stéphane Mallarmé in Relation to His Public*. Madison, N.J.: Fairleigh Dickinson Unversity Press, 1976.

LOTMAN, YURI M., AND A. M. PIATIGORSKY. "Text and Function" (1968). Trans. Ann Shukman. *New Literary History* 9, no. 2 (Winter 1978):233–44.

LOTMAN, YURI, M., AND B. A. USPENSKY. "On the Semiotic Mechanism of Culture." 1971. Trans. George Mihaychuk. *New Literary History* 9, no. 2 (Winter 1978):211–32.

LOWE, DONALD M. *History of Bourgeois Perception*. Chicago: University of Chicago Press, 1982.

LUKÁCS, GEORG. *History and Class Consciousness*. Cambridge: MIT Press, 1971.

——. *Studies in European Realism*. New York: Grosset & Dunlap. 1964.

LYON, JOHN. *Introduction to Theoretical Linguistics*. Cambridge: Cambridge University Press, 1968.

MACHEREY, PIERRE. *Theory of Literary Production* (1966). Trans. Geoffrey Wall. London: Routledge & Kegan Paul, 1978.

Manuel. See Barbéris and Duchet, eds., and Duchet, ed.

MARCUSE, HERBERT. *Counter-Revolution and Revolt*. Boston: Beacon, 1972.

——. *One-Dimensional Man: Studies in the Ideology of Advanced Industrial Society*. Boston: Beacon, 1964.

MARX, KARL. *Capital: A Critique of Political Economy, Volume One*. Trans. Ben Fowkes. Harmondsworth: Penguin; London: New Left Review, 1976.

——. *Class Struggles in France, 1848–1850*. New York: International Publishers, 1964.

——. *A Contribution to the Critique of Political Economy*. Ed. Maurice Dobb. New York: International Publishers, 1970.

——. *Grundrisse: Foundations of the Critique of Political Economy*. Trans. Martin Nicolaus. New York: Vintage, 1973.

——. *Theories of Surplus Value* (Volume 4 of *Capital*). 3 vols. Moscow: Progress, 1969.

——. "Toward the Critique of Hegel's Philosophy of Law." In *Writings of the Young Marx on Philosophy and Society,* ed. Lloyd D. Easton and Kurt H. Guddat, pp. 249–64. New York: Doubleday-Anchor, 1967.

MARX, KARL, AND FREDERICK ENGELS. *The German Ideology*. 3d ed. Moscow: Progress, 1976.

Marx/Engels on Literature and Art. Moscow: Progress, 1976.

MAST, GERALD. *A Short History of the Movies*. Indianapolis: Bobbs-Merrill, 1976.

McKENDRICK, NEIL, JOHN BREWER, AND J. H. PLUMB. *The Birth of a Consumer Society: The Commercialization of Eighteenth-Century England*. Bloomington: Indiana University Press, 1983.

MEDVEDEV, P. N., AND MIKHAIL M. BAKHTIN. *The Formal Method in Literary Scholarship: A Critical Introduction to Sociological Poetics*. Trans. Albert J. Wehrle. Baltimore: Johns Hopkins University Press, 1978.

MEHLMAN, JEFFREY. "Baudelaire with Freud/Theory and Pain." *Diacritics* 4, no. 1 (1974):7–13.

MELCHER, EDITH. *The Life and Times of Henry Monnier, 1799–1877*. Cambridge: Harvard University Press, 1950.

MEPHAM, JOHN, AND DAVID-HILLEL RUBIN, EDS. *Issues in Marxist Philoso-*

phy. Vol. 3: *Epistemology, Science, Ideology*. Atlantic Highlands, N.J.: Humanities Press, 1979.

MILLER, MICHAEL B. *The Bon Marché: Bourgeois Culture and the Department Store, 1869–1920*. Princeton: Princeton University Press, 1981.

MONGAN, ELIZABETH, ed. *Daumier in Retrospect*. Los Angeles: Armand Hammer Foundation–Los Angeles County Museum, 1979.

MOUFFE, CHANTAL. "Hegemony and Ideology in Gramsci." In Chantal Mouffe, ed. *Gramsci and Marxist Theory*. London: Routledge & Kegan Paul, 1979.

——. "Recasting Marxism." See Laclau, Ernesto, and Chantal Mouffe.

MOUFFE, CHANTAL, ed. *Gramsci and Marxist Theory*. London: Routledge & Kegan Paul, 1979.

MUKAŘOVSKÝ, JAN. "Art as a Semiotic Fact" (1934). In *Structure, Sign, and Function: Selected Essays by Jan Mukařovský*, trans. John Burbank and Peter Steiner, pp. 82–88. New Haven: Yale University Press, 1978.

MUSSET, ALFRED DE. "Le poète et le prosateur" (1839). In *Oeuvres posthumes*, vol. 10. Paris: A. Lemerre, 1876.

NAAMAN, ANTOINE-YOUSSEF. *Les débuts de Gustave Flaubert et sa technique de la description*. Paris: Nizet, 1962.

——. *Les lettres d'Egypte de Gustave Flaubert*. Paris: Nizet, 1965.

NORRIS, CHRISTOPHER. *Deconstruction: Theory and Practice*. London: Methuen, 1982.

PASSERON, ROGER. *Daumier: témoin de son temps*. Paris: Bibliothèque des Arts and Fribourg: Office du Livre, 1979.

PAXTON, NORMA. *The Development of Mallarmé's Prose Style*. Geneva: Droz, 1968.

PEIRCE, CHARLES SANDERS. *Elements of Logic*. In *Collected Papers*, vol. 2, ed. C. Hartshorne and P. Weiss. Cambridge: Harvard University Press, 1960.

POULET, GEORGES. *La poésie éclatée: Baudelaire, Rimbaud*. Paris: Presses Universitaires de France, 1980.

PRATT, MARY LOUISE. *Toward a Speech Act Theory of Literary Discourse*. Bloomington: Indiana University Press, 1977.

PRINCE, GERALD. "Introduction à l'étude du narrataire." *Poétique*, no. 14 (1973):178–196.

RANUM, OREST. *Paris in the Age of Absolutism*. Bloomington: Indiana University Press, 1979.

REITLINGER, GERALD. *The Economics of Taste: The Rise and Fall of Picture Prices 1760–1960*. London: Barrie and Rockliff, 1961.

RICOEUR, PAUL. *Le conflit des interprétations: essai d'herméneutique.* Paris: Seuil, 1969.

RIFFATERRE, MICHAEL. *Semiotics of Poetry.* Bloomington: Indiana University Press, 1978.

ROSSEL, ANDRÉ, ed. *Un journal révolutionnaire: Le Charivari.* Paris: La Courtille, 1971.

ROSSI-LANDI, FERRUCCIO. *Linguistics and Economics.* The Hague: Mouton, 1975.

RYAN, MARIE-LAURE. "Is There Life for Saussure after Structuralism?" *Diacritics* 9, no. 4 (Winter 1979):28–44.

RYAN, MICHAEL. *Marxism and Deconstruction.* Baltimore: Johns Hopkins University Press, 1983.

——. "New French Theory in New German Critique." *New German Critique* no. 22 (Winter 1981):145–61.

SAHLINS, MARSHALL. *Stone Age Economics.* Chicago: Aldine, 1972.

SAID, EDWARD W. *Orientalism.* New York: Random House, 1978.

SARTRE, JEAN-PAUL. *Critique de la raison dialectique.* Paris: Gallimard, 1960.

——. "L'engagement de Mallarmé." *Obliques,* no. 18–19 (1979):169–94.

——. *L'idiot de la famille: Gustave Flaubert de 1821 à 1857.* 3 vols. Paris: Gallimard, 1971–72.

——. "Mallarmé." In *Situations IX, Mélanges,* pp. 191–201. Paris: Gallimard, 1972.

——. *Saint-Genet.* Trans. Bernard Frechtman. New York: New American Library, 1963.

——. *What Is Literature?* Trans. Bernard Frechtman. Harper & Row, 1965.

SAUSSURE, FERDINAND DE. *Cours de linguistique générale.* Ed. Charles Bally and Albert Sechehaye. 3d ed. Paris: Payot, 1964.

SCHUDSON, MICHAEL. *Discovering the News: A Social History of American Newspapers.* New York: Basic Books, 1978.

SLOTT, KATHRYN ELEANOR. "Poetics of the Nineteenth-Century French Prose Poem." Ph.D. diss., University of Pennsylvania, 1980.

SPIVAK, GAYATRI CHAKRAVORTY. Preface to Jacques Derrida, *Of Grammatology.* Baltimore: Johns Hopkins University Press, 1976.

STIERLE, KARLHEINZ. "Baudelaire and the Tradition of the *Tableau de Paris.*" *New Literary History* 9, no. 2 (Winter 1980):345–61.

TERDIMAN, RICHARD. "Deconstruction/Mediation: A Dialectical Critique of Derrideanism." *Minnesota Review*, n.s. 19 (Fall 1982):103–11.

——. *The Dialectics of Isolation: Self and Society in the French Novel from the Realists to Proust.* New Haven: Yale University Press, 1976.

——. "Flaubert formaliste." *Revue des sciences humaines,* 35 (1970):541–58.

——. "Materialist Imagination: Notes toward a Theory of Literary Strategies." *Helios* 7, no. 2 (Spring, 1980):27–49.

THOMPSON, E. P. "Time, Work-Discipline, and Industrial Capitalism." *Past and Present* 38 (1967):56–97.

TODOROV, TZVETAN. *Introduction à la littérature fantastique.* Paris: Seuil, 1970.

VANNIER, BERNARD. *L'inscription du corps: pour une sémiotique du portrait balzacien.* Paris: Klincksieck, 1972.

VANNIER, HENRIETTE. *La mode et ses métiers: frivolités et luttes de classes, 1830–1870.* Paris: Armand Colin (Coll. "Kiosque"), 1960.

VINCENT, HOWARD P. *Daumier and His World.* Evanston: Northwestern University Press, 1968.

VOLOŠINOV, V. N. [M. M. BAKHTIN]. *Freudianism: A Marxist Critique.* New York: Academic Press, 1976.

——. *Marxism and the Philosophy of Language.* Trans. Ladislav Matejka and I. R. Titunik. New York: Seminar Press, 1973.

WARNING, RAINER. "Irony and the 'Order of Discourse' in Flaubert." Trans. Michael Morton. *New Literary History* 13, no. 2 (Winter 1982):253–86.

WEBER, MAX. *Economy and Society: An Outline of Interpretive Sociology.* 2 vols. Ed. Guenther Roth and Claus Wittich. Berkeley: University of California Press, 1978.

WECHSLER, JUDITH. *A Human Comedy: Physiognomy and Caricature in 19th Century Paris.* Chicago: University of Chicago Press, 1982.

WHITE, HAYDEN. "Getting Out of History." *Diacritics* 12, no. 3 (Fall 1982):2–13.

——. *Metahistory: The Historical Imagination in 19th Century Europe.* Baltimore: Johns Hopkins University Press, 1973.

WILLIAMS, RAYMOND. "Advertising: The Magic System" (1960). In *Problems in Materialism and Culture: Selected Essays.* London: NLB-Verso, 1980.

——. *Marxism and Literature.* Oxford: Oxford University Press, 1977.

WILLIAMS, ROSALIND. *Dream Worlds: Mass Consumption in Late Nineteenth-Century France.* Berkeley: University of California Press, 1982.

WURMSER, ANDRÉ. *La comédie inhumaine*. Paris: Gallimard, 1970.

ZELDIN, THEODORE. *France 1848–1945*. 2 vols. Oxford: Oxford University Press, 1973–77.

ZIMA, PETER V., ed. *Semiotics and Dialectics: Ideology and the Text*. Amsterdam: John Benjamins, 1981.

Index

357

Mukařovský, Jan, 37 n. 16
Musset, Alfred de, 88 n. 1, 266

Napoléon (emperor), 246
Napoléon III (emperor), 45, 165
Nerval, Gérard de, 231, 236
Newspapers, 47, 93, 302–3, 314
  censorship, 160–62
  as dominant discourse, 117–22
  and ideology, 125–27
  organization of, 122–25, 128–35
  proliferation of, 118–21, 128–33
  and readership, 128–35
  resistance to, 141–46. *See also*
    Mallarmé
Nodier, Charles, 230
Norris, Christopher, 33 n. 9

Organicism, 269–70
Orient, 70
  "absorption" of, 233
  obliteration within, 237–38
  and Occidental discourse, 234–39, 253–
    55
  and romantic imagination, 230
  sex and prostitution, 249–51
  and sociopolitical reality, 231, 238, 246
  See also "Appropriation";
    "Penetration"

Paris. *See* France, nineteenth-century
Parody, 76, 202. *See also* Satire
Peirce, Charles Sanders, 29–30
Pelletan, Eugène, 266
"Penetration" (rhetorical strategy), 239–
  45, 253. *See also* "Appropriation"
Petit Journal, Le. See Millaud
Philipon, Charles, 52, 151–54. *See also* Le
  Charivari; Daumier
Physiologies, 94, 96, 164–65
Piatigorsky, A. M., 90–91
Poème en prose. See Prose poem
Poète maudit, 267–68, 299
Poetry, and economy, 321–23, 329, 331,
  336–39. *See also* Writing, and
  commercialism
Poire (caricature of Louis-Philippe), 159
  n. 17, 188–89
Pound, Ezra, 251
Power, 13, 19, 38–40, 308

and knowledge, 103–4
and language, 107
Pratt, Mary Louise, 60
Presse, La. See Girardin
Prince, Gerald, 62 n. 59
Prose, as apparatus, 261, 264–65, 274–75,
  279, 296–98, 302, 310–11, 329
Prose poem, Chaps. 6 and 7 passim
  as genre, 264–69, 279, 295–99, 304–5,
    307, 311, 313
  as intervention, 261, 265, 270, 273, 279,
    300, 312
Proudhon, Pierre-Joseph, 71, 79, 316–17
Proust, Marcel, 102
Prudhomme, Monsieur. *See* Monnier

Ranum, Orest, 95
Ratapoil (Daumier character), 165
Realism, 88–91, 195 n. 51
Re/citation, 68–70, 279–80, 294
  defined, 210
  See also De/citation
Referentiality problem, 306–13, 320–21
Renan, Ernst, 75
Revolutions, and discourse, 80
Riffaterre, Michael, 143
Rimbaud, Arthur, 51, 252, 278, 334 n. 38
Roman d'éducation, Chap. 1 passim, 210
  and criticism, 87–88
  defined, 88 n. 1
  project of, 85–87
  and signs, 96–97
Romanticism, and bourgeois writers, 92
Rossi-Landi, Ferruccio, 114 n. 53
Rubin, David-Hillel, 108 n. 44
Ryan, Michael, 41 n. 23

Sade, Marquis de, 224
Said, Edward, 231, 234, 246
Sainte-Beuve, Charles-Augustin, 134
Saint-Simon, Claude-Henri de, 50 n.
  42, 71
Sartre, Jean-Paul, 38, 48, 74, 216, 219,
  223, 264
  on Flaubert, 229, 232 n. 11, 244 n. 25
  on Mallarmé, 313, 332
Satire, 142–43, 202. *See also* Parody
Saussure, Ferdinand de, 15, 26–29, 217,
  274, 296 n. 50
  and Bakhtin, 34–36

Library of Congress Cataloging in Publication Data

Terdiman, Richard
    Discourse/counter-discourse

    Bibliography: p.
    Includes index.
    1. French literature—19th century—History and
criticism. 2. Semiotics and literature. 3. Marxist
criticism. 4. Prose poems, French—History and criticism. I. Title.
PQ283.T47 1985   840'.9'15   84–17666
ISBN 0–8014–1750–3